SEP 0 5 2002
W9-AXK-936

THE MAKING OF REVOLUTIONARY PARIS

The publisher gratefully acknowledges the generous contribution to this book provided by the General Endowment Fund of the University of California Press Associates.

DAVID GARRIOCH

THE MAKING OF REVOLUTIONARY PARIS

University of California Press
Berkeley
Los Angeles
London

University of California Press
Berkeley and Los Angeles, California

University of California Press, Ltd.
London, England

© 2002 by the Regents of the University of California

Library of Congress Cataloging-in-Publication Data

Garrioch, David.
The making of revolutionary Paris / David Garrioch.
p. cm.
Includes bibliographical references and index.
ISBN 0-520-23253-4.
1. Paris (France)—History—1715–1789.
2. Paris (France)—Social life and customs—18th century. I. Title.
DC729 .G33 2002
944'.36—dc21 2001008255
CIP

Manufactured in the United States of America

11 10 09 08 07 06 05 04 03 02
10 9 8 7 6 5 4 3 2 1

3 1984 00195 6133

The paper used in this publication meets the minimum requirements of ANSI/NISO Z39.48–1992 (R 1997) (*Permanence of Paper*).⊗

For Colin, with thanks

CONTENTS

ILLUSTRATIONS

FIGURES

MAPS

ACKNOWLEDGMENTS

I became aware of the need for a general history of eighteenth-century Paris when I taught a course on the making of modern Paris, jointly with my colleague Wallace Kirsop. He originally proposed that course and over the years has helped me understand aspects of the history of Paris that were quite new to me. The students who took our course, from both the French and History Departments at Monash University, also contributed much to the form this book has taken. Guy Lobrichon's suggestion that I should write such a book gave me the incentive to set aside other projects, and my sincere thanks go to him. Other people will perhaps recognize ideas born of conversations with them, especially Michael Sonenscher, Colin Lucas, Alain Faure, Robert Descimon, Daniel Roche, Bill Kent, Jan Pinder, Andrew Brown-May, Alexandra Michell, and Julie Burbidge. Julie Burbidge also gave me invaluable research and editorial assistance. Jan Pinder, Barbara Caine, Fiona Graham, Tim Tackett, Sheila Levine, Juliane Brand, and the anonymous readers at the University of California Press read and commented on the manuscript; their suggestions have made this a far better book. Rachel Berchten helped me through the production process, and Edith Gladstone's superb copyediting has saved me from many errors and infelicities of style.

The academic and administrative staff in the History Department have provided a friendly and well organized work environment, and I would especially like to thank Val Campbell and Rosemary Johnson. I also owe a huge debt to my colleagues in the department, for their friendship, guidance, intellectual stimulation, and practical support.

Gary Swinton in the School of Geography did an excellent job on the maps. The Monash University Library has provided most of the secondary material I needed, despite struggling to maintain collections in the face of deep budget cuts. This feat was achieved, I know, through the sacrifices and hard work of staff, and my particular thanks go to Robert Stafford and Grace Giannini. The Monash Rare Book Room possesses a valuable collection of eighteenth-century material and reflects the wisdom of a policy of targeting a number of areas of strength. I have benefited greatly from the help of the staff there, especially Richard Overell. Thanks also to the extraordinarily efficient staff of the Document Delivery Service, who found me many items that an Australian university library cannot hope to have on its shelves.

The Australian Research Council provided the funding for several visits to Paris, for microfilm, and for my release from teaching for a semester. Without this I would never have been able to complete either the research or the writing. The Arts Faculty has also accorded me important financial assistance.

I and my family have always enjoyed extraordinarily generous hospitality in France. I would particularly like to thank Marie Delavesne, Lucien Eymard, Alain Faure, Danielle Duclos-Faure, Guy Lobrichon, and Geneviève Brunel. And of course my thanks go to the helpful staff in a wide range of archives and libraries, mostly in Paris but also in Grenoble, Orléans, and Lyon.

Any synthesis is impossible without the wealth of work done by other scholars, past and present, as my bibliography and notes amply testify. In the last few years Daniel Roche and Steven Kaplan, in particular, have revolutionized our knowledge and understanding of eighteenth-century Paris: a glance at the notes will indicate the extent of my debt to their research. There are many others, of course, who have contributed new understandings, not only scholars working on Paris or on French history, but also a great many writers on urban and family history, historical anthropology, French literature, and politics. Any work of history is in this sense a collective enterprise.

INTRODUCTION

For hundreds of thousands of weary eighteenth-century travelers, the first glimpse of Paris came from one of the low hills on the city's perimeter. In still, cold weather, a gray haze masked the city, mixing wood smoke and mist—a contemporary likened it to the city's breath in the cool air.[1] In summer the whitewashed walls and pale stone reflected the light back into the sky. Some found Paris beautiful, exceeding their expectations; others were disappointed. But almost all were struck by its sheer size: 810 streets (not including 88 culs-de-sac) and 23,019 houses, according to one popular description.[2] Unless the traveler was a blasé Londoner, accustomed to the bustle of an even larger metropolis, the scale of Paris came as a shock even to those who had read about it. From the North Sea to the Mediterranean, there was no human settlement so large, although no one knew exactly how large. Guesses at the number of inhabitants ranged from 500,000 to over a million.[3]

Threading their way through the ribbon of suburbs and into the maze of the center, newcomers lost all sense of direction. Most came from small towns and villages, and they searched in vain for landmarks amid the profusion of spires, the long lines of tall whitewashed houses, and the stone-faced public buildings. The average traveler was overwhelmed—many of them recorded these first impressions—by the din, the confusion of traffic, animals, cries, the crowds of people, the labyrinth of streets winding interminably in every direction. In provincial cities, even during Carnival, there was nothing to compare with this.

Figure 1. Paris and the Seine: the city viewed from the quai in front of the Louvre. Jean-Baptiste François Genillion, *Vue générale du Pont Neuf,* ca. 1780, in *Voyage pittoresque de la France* (Paris, 1781–84), vol. 7. Bibliothèque historique de la ville de Paris, photo Jean-Christophe Doerr.

But that was merely the beginning of the city's wonders. At night the streets were lit by thousands of tallow candles, later by oil lamps, a wonder to eighteenth-century eyes accustomed to the pitch-darkness of overcast nights. By the end of the century the luxury shops for which Paris was famous boasted painted decors, mirrors, and elaborate window displays to delight the eye and—in the case of food shops—make the mouth water. Inside the great noble houses were riches untold, burnished interiors that shone in the living light of a hundred pure wax candles. Silk and satin, velvet, gilt, and silver were the stuff of life for the wealthy. The huge central market was another amazement, street after street of stalls laden with every kind of produce, even if a significant part of the population could not afford to buy it. Magnificent public buildings lined the bustling riverbank.

Even the longtime Paris resident was hard-put to encapsulate this reality. Eighteenth-century writers strained for the right metaphors. Instinctively, many reached for organic ones: Paris was the swollen head on the body of France; it was the heart of the kingdom; a mouth that devoured innumerable immigrants; a stomach consuming the wealth and the products of the provinces. Increasingly, commentators drew on contrasts as a way of describing the city. In Jean-Jacques Rousseau's best-selling novel *La nouvelle Héloïse,* written in the late 1750s, the hero, Saint-Preux, spoke of Paris as a place "dominated simultaneously by the most sumptuous opulence and the most deplorable misery."[4] Twenty-five years later Louis-Sébastien Mercier, who loved his native city, nevertheless painted his vast *Tableau de Paris* in similarly contrasting colors, luxury and plenty juxtaposed with poverty and dearth. The same theme was taken up by many lesser figures: the now-forgotten novelist Contant d'Orville had his heroine exclaim, "What a contrast between these immense and magnificent residences, which reflect the greatness, luxury, and corruption of their masters, and those humble forests inhabited by misery, and sometimes despair!"[5] This was also how many visitors saw Paris. "I doubt," wrote a Sicilian visitor to Paris in 1749, "that there can exist anywhere on earth a hell more terrible than to be poor in Paris." For a German tourist, "Here was certainly not the new Jerusalem I had finally arrived in, but rather had I fallen into hell." In 1759 Louis-Charles Fougeret de Montbron published a biting critique of Paris and subtitled it "the new Babylon." Images of hell and of heaven, of Eden, Babylon, and the new Jerusalem sprang more readily to the early modern mind than to ours and had far more concrete meaning.[6]

Literary contrasts provided a convenient way of summing up a labyrinthine reality. Yet too often they have been taken at face value and endowed with a kind of explanatory force: excessive luxury and extremes of wealth and poverty inevitably produced bitterness, social tension, and revolt, turning the City of Light into the City of Revolution. This is the Dickensian picture, one influenced by nineteenth-century fears of a bitterly divided society, and it retains a superficial appeal to a post–Cold War world. The real Paris, like today's Rio or Bombay, was indeed a place of contrasts; but there is more to the story. As in some of today's megalopoli the city's extremes and contradictions were crucial to its economy. The flourishing industries that made Paris the capital of eighteenth-century European fashion, luxury, and culture reposed on a large informal sector, on the immense unpaid labor of women, children, and the elderly. The Parisian economy depended on the conspicuous consumption of the nobility and on the city's status as the capital of an absolutist state. So too did the Enlightenment. Around the royal court, government ministries, and the attendant cluster of religious institutions and law courts, lived a large, educated, and affluent population that provided the critical mass indispensable for a brilliant intellectual and cultural life.

Eighteenth-century Paris was the home, usually physically but always intellectually, of most of the philosophes: Montesquieu, Voltaire, Diderot, Rousseau, Holbach, d'Alembert, Helvétius, Condorcet, and many others, most of them dependent—directly or indirectly—on the very disparities of wealth and political practices that some of their work brought into question.

Yet the existence of extremes and paradoxes did not make Paris a jungle or create a society perpetually on the brink of disintegration. Life may have been fragile, but most Parisians were bound to their city by powerful affective ties and by bonds of community and moral obligation. The city created its own networks, to some degree reproducing those of the villages and small towns from which two-thirds of the population came, yet imposing distinctive patterns of its own.

Recent research has placed far less emphasis on the extremes in Parisian society. It has revealed the existence of a large and growing consumer market. Despite widespread poverty, eighteenth-century Paris was a dynamic and expanding society built on thriving trade and industry. Even servants and other working people were beginning to buy consumer items in the second half of the eighteenth century, and many of them were materially better off than the previous generation. The gap between rich and poor was widening, yet the "middling sort" were growing in numbers and prosperity.[7] Their expansion and wealth helped make Paris unique in France, and as the work of two generations of historians has shown, these were the very people who led the Parisian Revolution after 1789.

Thus an old paradox remains. How could Paris have produced the revolution that took place there? (I refer to the revolution in this city, not the French Revolution as a whole.) How could a metropolis with low rates of violence and apparent political passivity have led an upheaval that would transform Europe? Where did the energy come from, the motivation for enormous sacrifices of time, effort, and money by thousands of people—even of their lives, in the case of thousands of Parisian men who volunteered to serve in the revolutionary armies? Where did they draw the inspiration, the heroism, the faith? If some of it came from the Enlightenment, then how could the city of Enlightenment, with its growing material prosperity, growing religious toleration and humanitarianism, its exceptionally high rates of literacy and education, and its extraordinary confidence in the perfectibility of humanity, have become the scene of revolutionary violence, of extremism, persecution, and bloodshed? These questions haunt all writing on eighteenth-century Paris and they are one of the central preoccupations of this book.

To address them we need to go back at least to the beginning of the century and to strive for a long-term view of the city's development. Too much writing on the French Revolution, even on its causes, begins with the 1770s or at best the 1750s. The "Old Regime" becomes simply the status quo ante: the political and social system that existed before 1789, static, "traditional," and unchanging.[8] It is true that the revolutionaries, who first used the term *ancien régime,* portrayed it this way. It was in their interest to do so, since the idea of a new departure, a regeneration of debased and corrupt Babylon, was the whole justification for their enterprise. The prerevolutionary monarchy also portrayed itself as static: again it had to, because tradition, precedent, and stability were its sources of legitimacy. Yet Old Regime Parisian society was far from static. It was changing rapidly, and particularly after the middle of the eighteenth century, when demographic and economic expansion and the Enlightenment began to have a major impact.

A great many books have been written about Paris. Yet a few years ago when I taught a course on the history of Paris I was astonished to find that there was no readily available general history of the city in the eighteenth century. Certainly, some aspects of Parisian life have been exhaustively researched, and much of that work is available to English readers. Students of literature have pursued novelists and philosophes into the salons and the libraries of the city. Robert Darnton and others have written wonderful accounts of some of the journalists, printers, and booksellers for whom the Enlightenment was a means of livelihood.[9] Architectural historians have traced ideas about building styles from blueprint to completed edifice.[10] Higher education and the medical world have been comprehensively explored by Lawrence Brockliss and Colin Jones.[11] A number of studies focus on politics in Paris, and much work about France as a whole inevitably contains much on the capital.[12] There are also a great many books and articles dealing with particular institutions and those who peopled them: hospitals, theaters, the courts.[13] Our understanding of the Paris trades has recently been revolutionized by Steven Kaplan and Michael Sonenscher.[14] There are some partial social histories available in English, such as Arlette Farge's *Fragile Lives* and my own work on neighborhood communities and on the Paris middle classes. Other books deal in an anecdotal way with daily life in the city, usually primarily with the social elites, and some of them make good reading. Several new studies appear every year; Clare Crowston's *Fabricating Women* came out after this book was written and adds significantly to our knowledge of the role of women in the city.[15]

Yet in the last thirty years, only two works available in English can claim to be general introductions to the social and economic history of eighteenth-century Paris. Jeffry Kaplow's marvelously evocative work *The Names of Kings,* although focusing on the laboring poor, is a rich source for the social and economic geography of the city, and for elite as well as popular ideas and attitudes. Kaplow drew attention to the importance of the dissident religious movement known as Jansenism, to the significance of the city's floating population, and to the relevance of medical thought to the program of late-eighteenth-century urban reformers. He found and used sources hitherto neglected. But *The Names of Kings* came out in 1972 and has been superseded by a large quantity of new work. We now know far more about the economy and politics of the city, and about both the popular and the middle classes. Furthermore, the conceptual and historiographical framework of Kaplow's book is now dated—its quest for an eighteenth-century Marxist-style proletariat and its organizing notion of a "culture of poverty." Since the 1970s, too, feminist history and the "new cultural history" have transformed our approaches to social relationships and to social change.

The second general introductory work on eighteenth-century Paris, available in an excellent English translation, is Daniel Roche's enormously rich *People of Paris,* first published in 1981. It is informed by an innovative approach to material culture that Roche has subsequently developed in other work and that has inspired many other historians. *The People of Paris* focuses on wage earners but sheds some light on other social groups. It too contains a superb survey of the social and economic geography of Paris and more thoroughly explores the social composition of the popular classes. It employs new sources and methods and, unlike Kaplow's book, has much to say about changes across the century, in living conditions, patterns of consumption, and manners.

Yet both of these books deal primarily with the popular classes and therefore offer only hints of some of the wider changes that were taking place in the city. Neither has much to say about politics or gender. Both are organized thematically, and it is not easy to get a sense of how the city operated at any one moment. Nor does either author take the story into the revolutionary years or explore the ways in which changes during the eighteenth century help us understand the Parisian experience of revolution. Kaplow, in the end, finds little evidence of change in the politics of the laboring poor, and Roche does not attempt to link the evolution of material culture to the mentality and politics of revolution.

My purpose is to explore how the city and the lives of its people changed between 1700 and 1800. My primary focus has been on social relationships, not institutions or occupations. I have tried to show how the transformation of material life, the appearance of new ideas and social practices, demographic shifts, and far-reaching religious, political, and institutional change all had a profound long-term effect on Parisian society and on the ways of thinking of the population. Obviously, not every aspect of life or every social group can be included. There are some we as yet know only a little about: Jews and Protestants, much of the foreign-born population, the ordinary clergy of the parishes, homosexuals.[16] Some of the key sources—the parish registers, the tax records, and the archives of the trades corporations—have disappeared. These misfortunes leave the economic and demographic history of Paris little known, while huge areas of religious and lay sociability remain mysterious to us.

This also is a local history, not a national or even a regional one. Paris cannot be separated from the rest of France, of course, and some of what I say about Parisian society is true of other parts of eighteenth-century France, particularly the cities. Yet Paris is not France. The social changes I am describing often happened differently, or at different times, in other places. The Parisian urban environment itself was hugely important, the city far more than a backdrop against which events took place. The size and topography of Paris not only created practical problems for administration and economic life but promoted ways of thinking and social practices that were at odds with the "official" social order. Parisians' relationship to space, whether they saw it as sacred or secular, as belonging to them or to someone else, as friendly or hostile, had a big impact on their thinking and their behavior. Interpretations of the urban environment as pestilential, or unnatural, or ugly, were influential components of the social and gender ideologies of the late eighteenth century. In all of these ways the city was a player in its own history.

Through the first half of the eighteenth century Paris remained overwhelmingly a "corporate" and "customary" society characterized by a powerful sense of hierarchy. It is a world very foreign to us today. The whole political and social structure of eighteenth-century France was based on the idea of "corporations," in which the original organic sense of "body" remained strong. "All of your subjects, Sire," the Parlement of Paris reminded Louis XV in 1776,

> are divided into as many different bodies as there are different groups (*états*) in the kingdom. The clergy, the nobility, the sovereign courts [of

> law], the lower courts, the officials attached to these tribunals, the universities, the academies, the financial companies, all represent, throughout every part of the state, bodies that one can consider as the links of a great chain, the first of which lies in the hands of Your Majesty as the head and sovereign administrator of the whole body of the nation.[17]

The Parlement might have added to its list every town and village council in France, the forty thousand or so parish councils, and hundreds of thousands of other bodies. In Paris alone there were around fifty parish vestries, hundreds of religious confraternities, over 120 trade guilds, and many other professional groupings. Even the soldiers of the city watch, the fishermen on the River Seine, and the town criers had a corporate identity. Every one of these bodies was legally constituted, with its own statutes, approved by the Crown and legally registered. Each one ran its own affairs, held meetings, elected its own officials. Membership of a corporation bestowed legal rights, privileges, and indeed obligations. This was where local political life took place in Old Regime France.

It was possible to belong to more than one corporation. But those who belonged to none—many unskilled laborers, the homeless, beggars, some of the peasantry, more women than men—had no legally enforceable rights. Even so, the corporate mentality was so powerful that some of these people were part of neighborhood or trade communities that, while lacking any legal existence, offered them customary rights and gave them a place in a hierarchically ordered society.

Custom and hierarchy were the organizing principles of this corporate society. Within every community, however humble, innumerable unwritten conventions and usages governed the relationships between people. Poor, rich, female, male, young or old, all were subject to the dictates of custom. It determined the calendar, the rituals of state and Church, the rights and privileges enjoyed by families, individuals, and groups. Each person, according to his or her rank and station, had customary rights and obligations, determined (in theory at least) by long practice. The early chapters of this book explore how the corporate city functioned; how it was governed; and how it was held together by relationships—often tense and conflictual ones—that nevertheless bound not only people of similar rank but also rich and poor, the powerful and the powerless.

By the 1750s and 1760s, though, the customary, corporate, and hierarchical social organization of Paris was being seriously challenged—though not eliminated—by changes in the city's economy and demography, by new ideologies and new social practices. Attempts to reform and "civilize" the city, often initiated by the royal authorities and spurred by changes in religious thinking and by new medical theories, were beginning to affect people's everyday lives. From midcentury on, educated Parisians were increasingly influenced by enlightened ideas and by economic and material changes that were widening the gulf between rich and poor. They were more anxious about the physical and moral consequences of city life, and about rising crime rates. They were adopting patterns of cultural and material consumption that combined to broaden their horizons not only beyond their quarter or parish, but beyond the city and even outside France. In response to all these things, many began to abandon their commitment to collective values and sanctions, and to place more stress on individual religious belief and on individual rights.

Both the "middling sort" and the noble and wealthy elite of Paris began to aspire to a broader "metropolitan" culture, a shared culture yet one that each group lived and interpreted in different ways.[18] The old hierarchies certainly did not disappear, but they became blurred. A "confusion of ranks"—something the upper classes often complained about—was facilitated by the growing wealth and consumer practices of part of the population, by greater movement around the city, and by the impossibility of enforcing either sumptuary laws or deference. The rule of law was actively promoted by magistrates, lawyers, and by servants of the state and was gradually accepted by the nobility. In a large and increasingly anonymous city the rule of law was in almost everyone's interest, yet it supplanted older codes of civility and of custom. In tandem with all of these developments, the philosophers and novelists of the Enlightenment disseminated new ideologies of "equality." So too did new social practices. The Société philanthropique founded in Paris in 1780 not only proclaimed the equality of all its members, whatever their rank, but constituted a new form of lay organization with no statutes and hence no legal existence. It is one of the best examples of "private people come together as a public," creating new forums for social and political action.[19] These were all steps, as we can see with hindsight, toward a class society, although the completion of that process would take decades longer.

The social and cultural transformations of the eighteenth-century city did not in themselves cause the Parisian Revolution of the 1790s. But they do explain a great deal about the form that it took. I say "Parisian Revolution" deliberately. The revolution that took place in the capital was in many respects different from the one that convulsed rural areas and small towns. It was in general more radical and less easily controlled (by either local or national elites), thanks in part to the size and economic dynamism of the city, in part to the strange mix of subjection and independence specific to the prerevolutionary urban environment. The culture of Paris was more egalitarian and more secular, strongly influenced by Jansenism but also by the particular relationship between state, monarchy, Church and city. The character of the Parisian Revolution was influenced by the monarchy's attempt to reform and control urban life. Arising in part from Enlightenment thought, in some measure from state building, and partly from social change, the action of the Old Regime authorities helped broaden political awareness and encouraged the growth of a participatory political culture. Another significant factor was the way emerging uses of urban space by all groups in Paris helped create new alliances alongside new social and political ideologies that were also stronger in the capital than elsewhere. The burgeoning consumer culture, in its origins an urban phenomenon, was one of the bases of significant social tensions both during the Old Regime and in the revolutionary years. Alongside all these changes, the continuing importance of a customary culture among certain elements of the Paris population helped create expectations of what the Revolution would bring and prompted disappointment and sometimes direct action when it fell short. While many of these characteristics applied to other urban centers, notably Marseille and Lyon, and indeed to cities outside France, they were more marked in Paris.

Nevertheless, I am not suggesting that the evolution of eighteenth-century Paris predetermined the shape of revolutionary events. Decades of historical research have demonstrated that it is impossible to predict, from the prerevolutionary career or socioeconomic position of most individuals, precisely how they would react when confronted with an entirely unforeseen situation. It is not as if the teams were already lined up in 1789, waiting only for the signal to begin. Certain events of the 1790s—the persecution of nobles and of the clergy, even the overthrow of the monarchy—were produced by developments during the Revolution itself and were not inevitable in 1789 or even in 1790. Yet to suggest that changes in thinking during the preceding decades opened the way for these developments and helped shape the way they happened involves no contradiction. The Parisian Revolution did not spring from nowhere. Changes in the city and its society during the eighteenth-century made certain events possible and sometimes even likely. They helped shape the reactions of Parisians to new situations and provided the physical, social, and cultural context for revolution.

The events of the 1790s in turn did much to shape the nineteenth-century history of Paris. Conservatives have seen in the French Revolution a great disaster, a bloody spectacle that hindered economic growth and fostered irreligion. Left-wing and liberal historians, until recently, have portrayed the Revolution as a victory for the bourgeoisie, opening its way to political power and greater economic control. Both representations are oversimplifications. The Parisian Revolution brought tragedy, misery, and disillusionment yet fostered new ideologies of hope. It reinforced trends that were already present before 1789—the social and cultural continuities are very important—but at the same time transformed the earlier period's political and social ideologies, including those of gender. It was both destructive and enormously creative. Whether interpreted positively or negatively, the revolution penetrated every cul-de-sac and attic room. It changed the city's social organization, urban environment, and the way people thought about the world around them. It was, to use a favorite eighteenth-century metaphor, the phoenix's pyre: both a culmination and the beginning of a new world.

PART I

THE SOCIAL ORDER OF CUSTOMARY PARIS

CHAPTER ONE

THE PATTERNS OF URBAN LIFE

Urban life has its rhythms, as regular as those of the village. At the same hour of every working day, a little stream of men and women emerges through the archway into the rue St-Honoré, which even in the early morning is filled with wagons. They are wearing long robes and carry a satchel over one shoulder, while prominently displayed on each one's breast is a copper badge in the shape of a fleur-de-lys. Some are carrying musical instruments, violins or hurdy-gurdies. They pause in the doorway, alert to the traffic noises: the rumbling of a heavy wagon laden with barrels of salt fish or wine, the lighter clatter of a handcart, the hollow tapping of horses' hooves on the large cobblestones. If the way seems clear they step out into the street, most of them turning right toward the city center, some left toward the city gate where on market days long lines of vehicles form outside the customs post to declare what produce they are bringing into Paris. Most members of the ragged procession carry sticks held out protectively in front of them, and some walk with a strange gait, heads turned toward the wall or into the street. They are the blind inmates of the Quinze-Vingts hospital, turned out each day to beg a living from more fortunate fellow citizens.

They cannot see and do not heed the summer sun shining on the tall whitewashed houses that makes the eastbound coachmen squint under their broad-brimmed hats. Nor do they see the flowers in pots on upper-story window ledges, the washing hanging on long rods projecting from the upper windows, or the colors of the cloth displayed for sale outside the innumerable drapers' shops in the rue St-Honoré. But they are sensitive, more than other city dwellers, to the fragrance of apples and pears of many varieties (many that the twentieth century does not know), of apricots and peaches in season; to the reek of freshwater fish that has been too long out of the water; to the odor of the different cheeses—Brie and fresh or dried goat cheese. The street sellers display these and other produce on tables wherever there is space to set up a portable stall. For the blind the smells are signposts, markers not only of the seasons but also of the urban landscape. They recognize the pervasive sweetness of cherries on the summer air or the garden smell of fresh cabbages in winter, marking the stall of a woman who sells fruits or vegetables at the gateway of the Feuillants monastery in the rue St-Honoré near the Place Vendôme. The aroma of roasting meat from a *rôtisseur* in a familiar street, the smell of stale beer at the door of a tavern, the sudden stench of urine at the entrance of certain narrow alleyways: these are landmarks by which the sightless navigate.

In the early eighteenth century there was no escape anywhere in Paris from the pungency of horse droppings or from the foulness of canine and human excrement. Like human body odor, it was ever-present but normally unremarked. Some quarters, though, were distinguished by other, more particular smells. The central market—les Halles—was unmistakable, with its olfactory cocktails of fruit, vegetables, grain, cheese, and bread. "It is common knowledge," wrote an eighteenth-century critic, that "the whole quarter of the Halles is inconvenienced by the fetid odor of the herb market and the fish market; add to that the excrement, and the steaming sweat of an infinite number of beasts of burden."[1] Even when the market was over the odors lingered. The stink of fish bathed the arc of streets from the rue de la Cossonnerie to the rue Montorgueil and St-Eustache. To the south, rotting herbs and vegetables polluted the rue de la Lingerie, the rue St-Honoré, the rue aux Fers. Worse exhalations rose from the neighboring Cimetière des Innocents, from the huge pits where only a sprinkling of lime covered a top layer of bodies already beginning to decompose. In summer only the hardiest inhabitants of the houses overlooking the cemetery dared open their windows.[2]

Other neighborhoods had different smells to contend with. Around the river end of the rue St-Denis were streets where passers-by were overwhelmed by the smell of drying blood: "it cakes under your feet, and your shoes are red."[3] The beasts once killed, the tallow-melting houses near the slaughterhouses produced an even fouler and more pervasive odor. Through the archway under the Grand Châtelet prison and along

Map 1. Paris in 1740. From Jean-Baptiste Michel Renou de Chauvigné, dit Jaillot. Bibliothèque historique de la ville de Paris, photo Jean-Christophe Doerr.

the quais of the city center the air was heavy (especially in summer) from the effluent of the great sewers that oozed into the Seine between the Pont Notre-Dame and the Pont-au-Change. Even in the otherwise pleasant gardens of the Tuileries, a witness tells us, "the terraces . . . became unapproachable because of the stink that came from them. . . . All the city's defecators lined up beneath a yew hedge and there relieved themselves."[4]

Not all the smells were bad, though. Perfumes greeted visitors to the flower market on the riverbank, and in autumn migrants nostalgic for their villages could inhale the odor of hay brought by long lines of wagons to sell near the southern gate of the city. Except in Lent, mouth-watering aromas wafted along the quais from the Left-Bank market known as la Vallée, where shoppers could find fresh or cooked poultry and game. Other city locations were equally distinguishable: the veal market further east; and Paris's second-largest fruit and vegetable market in the Place Maubert.

More distant still, up and over the steep Montagne Ste-Geneviève, the valley of the tiny Bièvre River was awash with industrial exhalations: the strong but not unpleasant aroma of processed hops from the breweries; the far less agreeable smell from the starch factories; and, hanging over everything, the suffocating stench of drying hides from the tanneries that lined the stream. When the wind blew from the southeast these smells reached the whole city.[5]

The city odors had a timetable and a calendar as well as a geography. In the early hours of the morning the whiff of baking bread was on the air as the bakers prepared the heavy 4-, 6-, or 8-lb loaves for which working women and the servants of richer people began to line up before the morning mass at five o'clock. The aroma of hot, sweet coffee rising from the large canisters and pewter cups carried by the coffee sellers was another matitudinal pleasure, from the mid eighteenth century onward. By late morning delicious smells wafted from shops selling cooked food, a little later from the kitchens of monasteries and of middle- and upper-class homes where the early afternoon meal, the main one of the day, was being prepared. In the depths of winter some of these smells, along with less pleasant ones, were deadened by the cold. But summer heat heightened putrefaction, and its breezes wafted scents and odors through open windows.

The blind from the Quinze-Vingts also had sounds to guide them around the city. Most resonant were the church bells: fifty-odd parish churches and over one hundred monasteries all had their bells, each peal with a distinctive timbre and pitch that the local people recognized. At

St-André-des-Arts the four main bells sounded F, E, D, C. Those of the Carthusian monastery, on the southern fringe of the city, played liturgical tunes in the early morning hours.[6] The proximity of churches and chapels was also signaled by the chanting of priests, monks, or choirboys.

Certain sounds were even more local. Particular houses, for those who knew, were marked by the crow of a rooster, the bark of a dog, or the creaking of a house sign swinging in the wind. Snatches of conversation and song and the clunk of pewter pots on wooden tables drifted through the open doors of wineshops. The hammering of cobblers and the grinding of wood turners' lathes marked their workshops, while shopkeepers at their doors, skilled at identifying prospective customers, went through their patter in cadences familiar to all the locals. Every neighborhood had its street sellers, too, with their distinctive calls. Many of them, in defiance of police regulations, set up small tables on busy corners to sell fruit, left-over food from the tables of the rich, tobacco, ribbons, baubles of every kind. The novelist Nicolas-Edme Restif de la Bretonne reflected somberly on the distraction the street cries afforded sick people during the daylight hours, whereas "in the silence of the night [they] . . . hear only the succession of long painful hours that pass without sleep."[7]

Every quarter had its bottlenecks, the intersections and narrow streets where wagons locked wheels and stalls were toppled regularly, where tempers frayed and angry exchanges punctuated the busy times of the day. The town criers beat their drums along the major thoroughfares and paused at crossroads to announce an order of the king's council or of the municipality, less frequently a death sentence. Every quarter had its prostitutes, soliciting from curbsides or windows as the evening approached.

There were parts of the city that even a visitor could at once identify by ear. Loud, irregular thuds echoed along the quais near the laundry boats where as many as two thousand washerwomen hammered the linen with their wooden batons.[8] The central market rang with the cries of vendors advertising the week's best buys. Occasionally their sharp tongues cut too deeply and good humor turned to anger. Sometimes the target of their scorn was a customer who rejected a price reached after much haggling, or a passer-by overdressed in ribbons and lace. Around the market pillory, where convicted offenders spent two hours a day in the stocks, ballad singers and street musicians hawked the latest broadsheets. They also congregated on the Quai de la Ferraille where their songs competed with those of the caged birds on sale outside the shops. They were even more numerous on the Pont Neuf,

> . . . the customary theater
> For sellers of ointments and poultices;
> Dwelling place of tooth pullers,
> Of secondhand dealers, booksellers, and pedants,
> Of balladeers with the latest songs.[9]

Especially on Sundays and feast days, people flocked to see the burlesque and bawdy *parades* put on by itinerant actors on makeshift platforms. Competing with them were puppet shows, magicians, acrobats and harlequins, sellers of miracle cures. At intervals between 1711 and the early 1750s the crowds gathered to watch Grand Thomas pull teeth. A giant of a man, he could extract a stubborn molar in seconds.[10] Even the sightless could appreciate the screams of his patients and the gasps of the crowd.

Many of these sights and sounds drew comment from foreign visitors. For them, though, the city's geography had a different focus. Typically, they stayed in a hotel in one of the affluent areas on the city's western side. Some chose the aristocratic faubourg St-Germain, "reckoned the politest Part of the Town, . . . where all the Foreigners of any Distinction are lodged." Others preferred the faubourg St-Honoré near the Palais-Royal and the Tuileries palace, the king's home when he stayed in Paris and, according to the Reverend William Cole in 1765, "the noblest Pile of Building I ever saw."[11] In either case they were well placed to attend the opera and the principal theaters, located on that side of town, and to visit the nobles, scientists, or intellectuals to whom they invariably bore letters of introduction. They strolled in the gardens of the Palais-Royal, "extremely full of well-dressed people," and thus a good place for well-to-do Germans, English, Italians, and others to observe the behavior and costumes of rich Parisians.[12] Later in the century, when the Champs-Elysées and the northern boulevards also became favorite promenading areas, the St-Honoré area was even more popular with visitors. It also lay a little closer to the extensive Tuileries gardens where respectable people took the air. Those interested in shopping could stroll to the nearby rue St-Honoré with its displays of luxury furnishings and clothes, while a short carriage-ride away lay the rue St-Denis where beautiful cloth and lacework were sold.

For most visitors a high priority was the cathedral of Notre-Dame, on the central island, the Ile-de-la-Cité, though their view of its crumbling statues was limited by the cloister on one side and by houses crowded close on others. Its towers afforded almost the only elevated view of the city accessible to the public. Some tourists, while in that vicinity, seized

Figure 2. The ballad singer. Note the women chatting in left foreground and the presence of children. Antoine Borel, *Le charlatan* (1774), Musée Carnavalet, © Photothèque des musées de la ville de Paris, photo Briant.

the opportunity to visit the huge central hospital—the Hôtel-Dieu. Also on the island lay the rambling ensemble of law courts called the Palais de Justice. The Palais housed the most important judicial body in the city, the Parlement, whose members assembled in the ancient hall behind the two medieval towers that still dominate the river at the end of the main road from the north, the rue St-Denis. Serving as chapel to the Palais de Justice was another tourist attraction, the Ste-Chapelle with its magnificent stained-glass windows, gothic vaulting, and its precious relic, a fragment of the Crown of Thorns.

Directly opposite the Cité, on the Left Bank, lay the Montagne Ste-Geneviève, the only hill within the eighteenth-century city limits. It was named for Saint Genevieve, the patron saint of Paris, whose tomb lay in the abbey church on its summit. This shrine was particularly important to Parisians, a place of pilgrimage, and in times of drought, flood, or famine crowds flocked to beseech the good saint to come to the aid of her people.[13]

On the slopes of the Montagne Ste-Geneviève lay most of the thirty-eight colleges that made up the University of Paris, the Sorbonne only one among them, although as the theology faculty, it was very important.[14] Here, too, a visitor could find bookshops aplenty, and a large number of convents and monasteries where people with time to spare could admire paintings, tombs, and elaborate altarpieces.

But there were other parts of Paris where foreign visitors rarely went. They generally spent little time on the quais, a haunt of the common people, although most did take a carriage to view the Hôtel de Ville (the city hall) and the central Place de Grève on which it lay. Few tourists, unless they had a particular interest in manufacturing, ventured to the east, past the huge Bastille fortress into the faubourg St-Antoine. There, thousands of artisans produced many of the furnishings for which Paris was famous, but their dingy, dusty workshops were not tourist destinations. Nor was the extensive faubourg St-Marcel, although the Jardin des Plantes—the royal botanical garden on the city side of the faubourg—did attract many visitors.

The Paris that visitors saw, therefore, overlapped only in part with the city that most Parisians knew. People who spent only a brief time there remained insensitive to the regular rhythms and meanings that structured the lives of most of the city's inhabitants, blind and sighted alike. Familiar sounds marked the hours, from the first angelus that roused the weary workers through to the compline bells of the convents and monasteries. At dawn, or even before, the hooves of horses and the rumble of wagon wheels echoed between the tall houses along with the tapping of wooden clogs on the paving stones. The *sonneurs* also passed early, ringing their handbells to warn the shopkeepers to sweep the rubbish away from their doors and into the central gutter of the street. Their rounds coincided with the rattle of shop shutters and the grinding of hinges, the first conversations exchanged across courtyards and from windows to the street below. Work noises, too, began at first light, hammering and dragging, swearing, shouted instructions. A Parisian (like other eighteenth-century city dwellers) did not need a timepiece.

For the locals, the street cries also marked the hours, since many itinerant vendors followed a regular route and passed at roughly the same time each day. Every shop had its busy times: the bakers early, the wineshops at nine or ten when many workers broke their fast after some hours' labor and again in the evenings when they paused for a drink on their way home. The traffic-noises often had local rhythms, too. Six days a week the slumber of residents of the rue St-Honoré, the rue Montmartre, and the rue St-Denis was disturbed at one or two in the morning by the first farmers' carts going to the central market. Along all the main streets the more rapid passage of carriages and the coachmen's cries of "Gare, gare" (look out), were on the whole early afternoon and early evening sounds.

Some visitors noted religious festivals with interest, but few had any real sense of the cycle the city followed from week to week and year to year. Sundays punctuated the workday routine and major feast days dotted the annual one. Christmas and New Year, Easter, All Saints (1 November), Saint John the Baptist (24 June), the Assumption (15 August) were key occasions, and "from time immemorial Saint Martin's Day, the Feast of Kings, and several other saints' days are celebrated." On these occasions, and at Mardi Gras, according to the same author, "Parisians would sell their shirts the day before rather than not buy a turkey or a goose at the Vallée market." In 1775 the police rosters allowed for thirty-five holy days, and earlier in the century there had been more.[15] Interspersed through the citywide calendar were particular saints' days observed by every parish and each trade. In addition, many religious occasions had secular significance: the days of Saint Remy (1 October) and Saint John the Baptist, along with Easter and Christmas, were particularly important because they marked the terms when rents were due. The feast of Saint Charlemagne (28 January) was the day the judges of the commercial court were chosen.[16]

Purely secular festivals also punctuated the calendar. Carnival with its feasting, dancing, and ribaldry celebrated both the end of winter and the beginning of Lent, usually in February. Other annual ceremonies, such as the procession of officers attached to the Châtelet courts on the day after the feast of the Trinity, often attracted large crowds.[17] Even the sporadic royal ceremonies obeyed a pattern: the birth of a prince, the death of a queen, a royal marriage, all these followed the life cycle of France's rulers and provided external markers for people whose lives were charted more by personal, family, and community happenings than by calendar dates or distant world events.

Celebrations, like many other aspects of life in eighteenth-century Paris, followed familiar, time-honored rituals. Yet they were not static, and the evolution of rituals like royal entries to the city and *lits de justice* (when the king came to impose his will on the powerful judges of the Parlement) reveals a great deal about changing political and social realities. Even minor changes in costume or the arrangement of individuals on the dais reflected the rise and fall of dynasties and the shifting fortunes of particular social and occupational groups. Experienced procession watchers, like the lawyer Edmond Jean François Barbier or the bookseller Siméon-Prosper Hardy, were able to "read" and interpret every such detail and sometimes included a full description in their respective journals. The order in which the participants marched, whether or not they wore hats, the length of their robes, and the colors they bore were all social and political signifiers.[18] The presidents of the different chambers of the Parlement were readily identifiable by their scarlet robes trimmed with ermine and a black velvet mortarboard with gold lace. Being seated on the right or the left, at the front or the back, had do-or-die significance for officers of the Crown, the courts, or the city.[19] Paintings and engravings (see Figure 3) recorded the position of each group.

Even the choice of route and destination formed part of an elaborate semiotic system. Processions generally followed one of a number of set itineraries, depending on the purpose of the event. They normally included the main squares and ceremonial sites of the city: the Place de Grève in front of the Hôtel de Ville; the Place des Victoires and the Place Louis-le-Grand (today's Place Vendôme) with their statues of Louis XIV; the Pont Neuf and its statue of Henri IV; the open spaces in front of the Palais de Justice and Notre-Dame. Each key location had its own significance: an association with a particular monarch, a saint, or a key institution of government. In 1763 the addition of the Place Louis XV to the usual itinerary linked the reigning king symbolically with his ancestors: it was an innovation, but one consistent with and justified by custom.[20]

This, and more, the blind of the Quinze-Vingts—like every Parisian—understood. Themselves part of the city's daily and weekly cycles, they were known to the shopkeepers who watched from their doorsteps at quiet moments, ever ready for a chat. They were recognized by the women who leaned on their windowsills during breaks from sewing. Some of the blind beggars stopped in fixed places in the market, by a church door, or outside the gate of one of the great private houses that dotted the city.

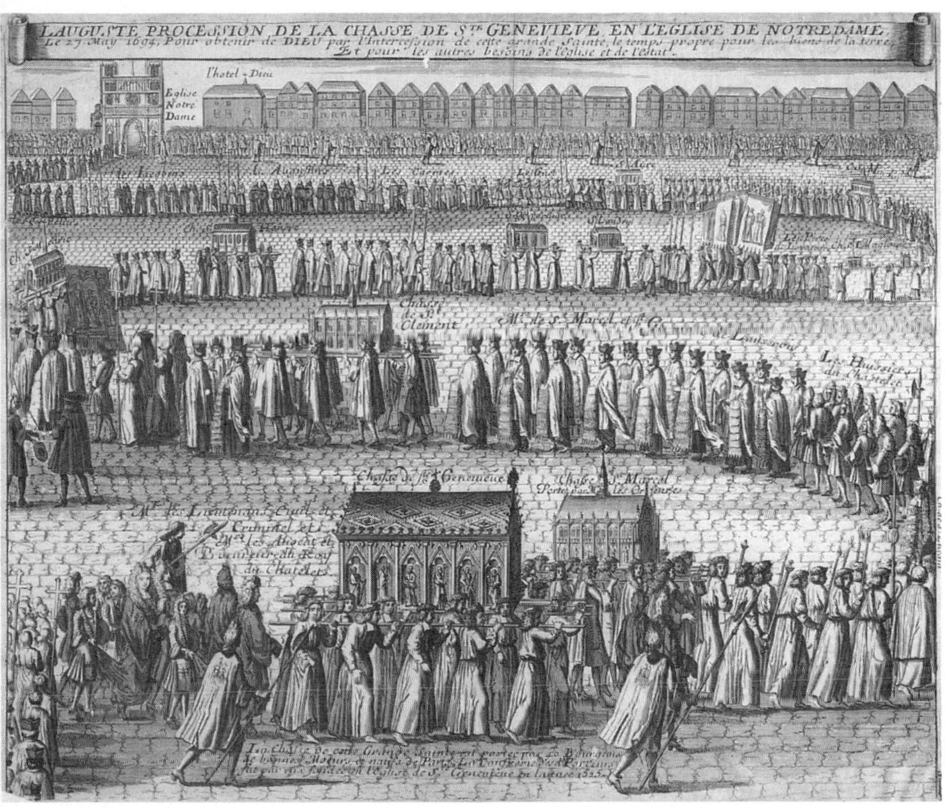

Figure 3. Procession of the relics of Saint Genevieve, patron saint of Paris, 1694. The procession went from the abbey of Ste-Geneviève to Notre-Dame cathedral and on this occasion was undertaken to obtain good weather for the harvest. This anonymous engraving illustrates the order of the procession, led by representatives of the principal religious orders with the relics of their saints. The reliquary of Saint Genevieve is in the foreground, and in the place of honour behind it are the leading magistrates of the Châtelet court. Musée Carnavalet, © Photothèque des musées de la ville de Paris, photo Degraces.

Others went from door to door to beg alms. Many were greedy for conversation and gossip, the currency of social exchange.

Like the other neighborhood beggars, like the hawkers and the street traders, the blind were part of the informal news network of a city without newspapers. It was from two blind beggars that a wine merchant learned of an attempt to break into his cellar several blocks away from his home.[21] Other news was delivered by the water carriers who came each day to noble houses, exchanged for tidbits from the doormen's lodges, the story of a court case or a fire, perhaps an echo of happenings at court that had already been passed from chambermaids to cooks and from kitchen hands to the loiterers in the courtyard.

NEIGHBORS AND KIN

Thus news traveled between the overlapping neighborhoods that made up the city. Neighbors were, after all, the ones with whom most people passed most of their time. Housewives, servants, masters, and employees chatted while waiting in line at fountains in the streets, since only a third of Paris houses had their own wells and only the affluent had their water delivered. Women sat shelling peas on straw-bottomed chairs outside the doors of their houses, one eye on the children playing in the street, and told of a domestic quarrel, a nasty work injury, a suspected pregnancy. Master craftsmen returning from the hairdresser, hair trimmed or wig powdered, brought salacious tales to share with their workers, who would later pass on the choicest ones, suitably embroidered, to drinking partners at the Lion d'or or the Armes de Beauvais. The women met again at the baker's, at the grocer's where they bought candles, and at fruiterers' stalls in the street. They talked in the pastry shops, where for a couple of sous they could have a meal cooked and save on firewood. Everyone stopped to chat on the stairs and in the street: not to do so would have been the height of rudeness. Working hours were long, but social interaction was part of the daily routine.[22]

Limited leisure time, as often as not, was also spent with neighbors. The men were likely to be found playing board and card games in one of the local wineshops, or bowls in summer. On winter evenings they sometimes went with their wives to sit by the fire. Or else the whole family might visit neighbors or relatives to dine, play cards, or just to chat. On holy days people promenaded in groups along the newly built quais. Courting couples, on summer Sundays, preferred the fields and vineyards around the city, often going with neighborhood groups to the villages of Gentilly, Vaugirard, or Belleville beyond the customs posts where the taverns were cheaper and the air cleaner. When there was an execution at the Place de Grève the men often went with fellow workers, the women with others from the same house. Ordinarily, women did not venture outside the quarter alone unless their work took them to clients or employers further afield. Given the choice, it was with neighbors that they went to the market, to watch fireworks on the river, or down to the laundry boats to do their washing.

For much of the century the narrow streets were shared spaces where,

Figure 4. Street sociability. Anonymous engraving, 1783. BN Coll. Hennin 9983. Photo Bibliothèque nationale de France.

if there were not too many wagons passing, groups of men played bowls and skittles and women sat with their sewing. The children ran free, climbing the dung heaps and the woodpiles, conducting mock religious processions, letting off firecrackers. Handcarts were parked outside doorways, building materials stacked against the walls, and in fine weather workbenches were brought out for cumbersome jobs. The glazier Jacques-Louis Ménétra recalled his father laying out sheets of glass that he was working on, and his fury when a bitch in heat ran across the middle of them followed by all the male dogs and a number of boys of the neighborhood![23] On clear Sundays and feast days and on summer evenings the houses emptied as couples and families strolled the streets of their quarter, greeting neighbors and acquaintances as they passed. Celebrations and festivities, too, often took place in the street. The most spectacular was Carnival, when the streets were full of masks and costumes, the children beating drums and going wild. Occasionally there were neighborhood bonfires: a distiller and his wife lit one to celebrate the queen's processional entry into Paris in 1722, though the police frowned on such festivities because of the risk of fire.[24]

Grievances, too, were aired in the street, sometimes family quarrels but more often gripes between neighbors over an unpaid debt, something borrowed and never returned, an imagined slight. In 1698 a gauze maker removed a line that his neighbor used for hanging washing from her window—or so she claimed: they were still arguing about it two years later! When such tensions erupted the neighbors gathered round to watch and evaluate the exchanges: "she had been a whore in her home village . . . bugger of a scoundrel, I'll give you twenty blows of my stick . . . thief, bandit"; "whore, slut, witch . . . she carried on with soldiers, she had the pox."[25] The onlookers enjoyed the clash of wits but remained ready to intervene if things came to blows.

Each neighborhood was a little like a village. Its residents—those who had been there for some time, or whose work brought them into contact with the locals—knew what job each had and what province each person hailed from (no more than a third were born in Paris). They were familiar with everyone's habits, moods, and daily movements. They knew who was courting whom, whether a person's business was flourishing or stagnating. Thin walls and narrow streets allowed the neighbors a more intimate knowledge than it would have been polite to admit: whether a couple lived in harmony; whether they were energetic in bed; whether either partner drank to excess. In the court case that Jeanne Bricard brought against her husband, a master gilder, to win legal separation and so protect her property from his creditors, like many women in a similar position she was able to call on neighbors to testify to his neglect of their business.[26]

Neighborhood familiarity was intrusive but could also provide assistance and protection. The children could roam safely within a block or two of home because everyone knew them and kept an eye on them. If an old man or woman on the top floor did not labor down the stairs as usual someone would check that they were all right. A woman beaten by her husband could usually count on the neighbors for help: they might even break down the door if she seemed in real danger. A stranger on the stairs aroused suspicion: when fifteen-year-old Madeleine Resnoire heard someone at her neighbor's door she went out and asked what he wanted, then watched to make sure he left the building.[27] The arrival of bailiffs to confiscate goods or to arrest someone who had not been able to pay a debt always aroused the indignation of the neighborhood. On occasion, if the victim resisted or the action seemed particularly unjust, their anger would explode and they would drive out the intruders. Similarly, an attempt by the police to arrest a journeyman locksmith who had helped organize a strike provoked a riot in the rue St-Honoré in 1746. A police witness testified that "the wife of the said Fontaine and another young woman who was in the shop cried out 'Help, help, we're being attacked,' and as the witness saw an open rebellion about to take place, since several individuals were trying to enter the said shop and others were crying out 'why don't we take some iron bars and break the arms of those scoundrels,' he drew his pistol."[28] Neighborhood solidarity was a reality that the authorities ignored at their peril.

It was a neighborhood obligation to exchange greetings each day, to observe rules of politeness that made the promiscuity bearable and that created a pretence of equality between people of very different conditions and levels of affluence. The poor widow living in a fifth or sixth floor attic room, wretchedly paid for ruining her eyes over the buttonholes of a shirt that might be sold at a price exceeding her annual income; the journeyman and his seamstress wife relaxing on their Sunday promenade after a week of fourteen- or sixteen hour days; the servant-shop girl who rose at four in the morning to do her household chores before spending a day in the shop, returning at seven to prepare an evening meal that she would not share: all of them merited the polite greeting of "Monsieur" or "Madame" when they went into the mercer's shop around the corner. While the rich could use the familiar "tu" when addressing their social inferiors, ordinary people employed the polite "vous" to their neighbors and to strangers. A medical doctor, trained in Montpellier and now practicing in Paris, was not above conversation with a seller of herbs.[29] Any inhabitant of the quarter, a laborer or even a prostitute, could complain to the police if someone impugned his or her reputation, no matter if the someone concerned was a master guildsman or a professional with ten times the status and income. Such a complaint might cost anything up to a week's wages but it would be made because eighteenth-century Parisians valued their local reputation as people of integrity and respectability.[30] That reputation was often their only real asset: an economic one in part, because no one would deal with a dishonest trader. But above all local reputation and honor was a source of self-esteem. The respect of the neighborhood made life tolerable, despite its uncertainties, despite abject dependence and often grinding poverty.

The bonds and obligations of neighborhood were reinforced by the fact that very often some neighbors were also kin. A document from 1752 enables us to locate the heirs of an egg-and-butter merchant living next to the central market. He had a relative in the same street, probably a daughter. Another lived in the adjoining rue de la Cossonnerie. She was married to a pork butcher named Marin. A third kinswoman had also married a Marin, again a pork butcher, and lived barely 200 meters distant in the rue St-Jacques-de-la-Boucherie. Another example is Madeleine Farcy, who lived in the rue de la Vannerie, near the Hôtel de Ville. Her parents, who were corset makers, lived just around the corner at the foot of the rue St-Denis, and her husband's shop boy was also a relative.[31]

Kinship networks were for many people the primary means of integration into the great metropolis and a defense against its potential anonymity. A joiner, newly arrived from Normandy, went to live with "a distant relative," the widow of a master cutler. Marie Voisin came to Paris in 1748 and lodged with her brother-in-law near the river end of the rue St-Denis. She soon found work as a domestic servant and moved out, but kept some of her belongings there. Each time she left an employer she returned to her brother-in-law's house: not to have done so, she admitted, would have raised suspicions about her conduct, since a young unmarried woman could not live alone in eighteenth-century Paris.[32]

It was not always possible to live where one wanted. Servants, apprentices, and many journeymen had to live with their employers. People took work wherever they could find it. But it was often through family networks, and in the same neighborhood, that they made their way in the great city. A shoemaker in the rue Mouffetard engaged his nephew, living in the same street, as his apprentice. It was common for brothers to run a small business jointly and to live nearby. Their children, first cousins, grew up together and often formed strong bonds, later reinforced when they took on nephews and nieces as apprentices.[33]

In certain areas of the city marriages took place not only within the quarter but within the same trade. Along the Bièvre River leather workers were bound by complex kinship networks. Butchers congregated at the river end of the rue St-Denis and on the Left Bank around the Vieille Place aux Veaux. In the faubourg St-Antoine lived dynasties of furniture makers and upholsterers, while families of joiners congregated in the rue de Cléry near the Porte St-Denis. Intermarriages were common among the grain merchants along the rue de la Mortellerie, and family networks riddled the mercers' and drapers' corporations that concentrated in the

St-Eustache and St-Roch parishes. The women of the markets—les Halles in particular—"are linked by kinship or friendship to all the gentlemen of Paris who shine shoes, carry coal, clean the sewers, build or demolish walls," observed a German visitor.[34] On the fringes of the central market clustered families of secondhand clothes dealers and oyster sellers. Complex family ties united the Seine fishermen and the other river trades were little different. The booksellers and printers who congregated around the university, and especially on the rue St-Jacques, also intermarried: the Lottin, d'Houry, Didot, and other famous names. So too the bookbinders, three-quarters of whom lived in five adjoining streets in the parish of St-Hilaire. Even bakers, who needed to be close to their clients rather than to one another, were often related to others of their calling in the same quarter.[35]

All round the fringes of the city the market gardens were worked by men and women whose family ties would take months to disentangle. Indeed many of the old villages on the fringes of the swollen city still retained something of their cohesion and separate identity: Clamart, at the end of the rue du faubourg St-Victor, which kept its market cross and its cemetery until at least the 1740s; Ville-l'Evêque, where the market gardens were slowly displaced by taverns and semisuburban residences; La Rapée, home to dynasties of laborers on the port; Gros Caillou, near the Invalides, where the same names recurred again and again; or Le Roule, swallowed up by the fashionable faubourg St-Honoré. Long after their physical identity was gone these villages retained their dense fabric of kin and occupational ties.

There were sound economic reasons for families to concentrate in particular trades and in specific areas. Apprenticeship was expensive and much of the cost could be defrayed if masters and mistresses trained their own sons and daughters or those of brothers, sisters, and cousins. They continued to help once the apprenticeship was over, finding suitable premises, building up the initial stock, providing contacts with suppliers and clients. Virtually all of the 120 or more Paris trades corporations of the early eighteenth century openly favored the sons of masters and daughters of mistresses. Like many others, the linen weavers entirely exempted the daughters of mistresses from the apprenticeship and from the crafting of a chef d'oeuvre—the test of expertise required of anyone else wishing to join the corporation. The goldsmiths did require sons of masters to complete the chef d'oeuvre but not to undertake a formal apprenticeship. The tanners retained their five-year apprenticeship for sons of masters but charged them 200 livres instead of the usual 600.[36] These concessions protected families already in the trade from outside competition but also encouraged parents to train their children in their own occupation.

The uncertainties of the commercial world were yet another strong reason for the dense networks of family ties within many trades. The bankruptcy or dishonesty of a shopkeeper could spell ruin for merchants who had supplied goods on trust. Yet credit was indispensable. The tanning of a large hide took up to three years so the butchers who provided the raw hides often had to wait for payment. A joiner might not be able to pay for the high-quality timbers and exotic veneers required to make a chest of drawers and therefore needed to find a wood merchant who was content to be reimbursed after the customer had paid for the completed piece. The nobility were notoriously bad payers, and merchants often had to wait a long time for their money. Families coped with these uncertainties through economic cooperation. Merchants frequently lent funds and materials to relatives, secure in the knowledge that kin could be relied upon to repay the debt. Kinsmen collaborated on big jobs that required an investment beyond the resources of an individual: the brothers Guillaume and Etienne-Simon Martin, famous in the mid eighteenth century for the *vernis Martin,* a lacquer applied to furniture, screens, snuffboxes, and even coaches, formed a partnership in 1727. The pair periodically employed two of their other brothers on a subcontracting basis.[37] In such ways families shared risks and costs, where a man or woman alone might go under. Suppliers were more likely to offer credit if they knew the family, and customers preferred the son of a recognized merchant rather than a stranger.

There were often geographical reasons for concentrations of trades, too. Because wood was brought down the Seine it made sense for the furniture trades to be on the upstream side of Paris. For tanners, dyers, and launderers ample supplies of running water were essential, so they worked along the Bièvre and the Seine (although after 1673 the tanners were exiled, along with other noxious occupations, from the city center). The grain merchants clustered around the central market. Sometimes there were other factors. The concentration of artisans in the faubourg St-Antoine reflected the area's exemption from taxes and corporate regulation and its status as a sort of early modern free trade zone designed to stimulate industry in the city.[38]

A further reason for occupational clusters was the sheer difficulty of moving around what was for the time a huge city—approaching half a million people in 1700. The streets of Paris were not designed for rapid

Figure 5. Wagons near the central market. Rue de la Grande Truanderie, ca. 1865, from an original photo by Charles Marville. The wagons and water-delivery barrel (*left foreground*) are of the same form as those used a century earlier. Note the butcher's shop (*right foreground*) open to the street. Bibliothèque historique de la ville de Paris, photo Jean-Christophe Doerr.

transit. They were narrow and winding, particularly in the center, and clogged with stalls, carts, piles of produce, and refuse. There were often cattle, flocks of sheep, always horses—ten to fifteen thousand of them in 1700—and slow, heavy wagons that blocked the whole thoroughfare.

By 1720 there were perhaps fifteen thousand carriages, a permanent hazard to pedestrians.[39] The bridges were hopeless bottlenecks, inadequate for the amount of traffic crossing the river. Early-eighteenth-century Paris remained a walking city but even on foot, a journey to the opposite side of the city was slow. It was preferable to live near one's place of work, near suppliers and customers, near family members.

These crisscrossing bonds of kinship, work, and neighborhood gave each locality a powerful affective hold, particularly for the Paris-born—a third of the population—whose ancestors lay in the local parish cemetery. Some merchant, artisan, and professional families remained for generations in the same trade and the same quarter. The lawyer Barbier, whose detailed diary is much used by historians, spent his life in the same house that his parents had occupied and was buried near them in the family chapel. Like him, roughly half of the Parisians who left wills in the second half of the seventeenth century, and nearly a third in the first half of the eighteenth, specifically requested burial in their parishes. The grave brought separation enough, yet there was comfort in the thought of passing eternity in a familiar place close to family, friends, and neighbors.[40] Whatever myth later chroniclers wove of a secular eighteenth century, it was an age when the dead still watched over the affairs of the living. At the insistence of a great many families, masses continued to be said daily for the souls of ancestors who had been dead for two hundred years.

For immigrants—overwhelmingly from the Ile-de-France region, with substantial contingents from Picardy, Normandy, Champagne, and Burgundy—the bonds were not of this kind. Yet for them too the neighborhood was the central focus of daily life and an important means of integration. Although migrants from the same area sometimes lived near one another, the difficulties of finding work and accommodation generally forced them to spread out.[41] And because the population was so mixed people had to accept each other. The idea that high rates of immigration produced conflict and damaged local solidarity is another urban myth. On the contrary, the neighborhood provided migrants with a scaffolding of economic and emotional support without which the great city would have destroyed them. It was a place where they could quickly become known and find assistance and reassuring familiarity, in an environment whose pace and diversity were very different from the small towns and villages from which most came. But outside the quarter, the faces were strange and one never knew with whom one was dealing.

LOCAL HIERARCHIES

Yet the family ties, the solidarities, and the urbane civility of eighteenth-century Paris should not mislead us into thinking that this was a cozy, egalitarian, or conflict-free society. Neighbors spied on each other as much as they offered assistance, and each neighborhood was riddled with quarrels, grievances, and sometimes long-running feuds. Both locally and across the city there were yawning discrepancies of wealth and status. At one extreme were the nobles, upper churchmen, and magistrates, the 3 or 4 percent of the population who monopolized the royal administration, the courts, the municipality, and the cultural institutions of the city.[42] When they came to the parish church the local notables fawned on them. If they spoke to a poor craftsman he doffed his hat awkwardly and fumbled for words.

But in everyday life the big fish were the lawyers and the officeholders who peopled the lower ranks of the administration, and the prosperous merchants and well-educated tradespeople: grocers, mercers, drapers, apothecaries, booksellers, goldsmiths, and their wives. Where an ordinary male wage earner early in the century might have total assets of between 200 and 300 livres, a female wage earner less, prosperous merchants and their widows sometimes left estates of well over 100,000 livres and gave their children dowries of anywhere between 5,000 and 30,000 livres.[43]

Between these dignitaries and the common people stretched a gulf that was far more than economic. The lawyers and merchants sat at the front of the church and the poor stood at the back. The affluent spoke with respect yet as equals with Monsieur le curé, the parish priest, who blessed their unions and buried their dead, whereas ordinary folk rarely approached him, even hat in hand. The children of the common people were baptized by a humble hired priest, with no frills. Messengers and porters, laundresses and dairymaids, each time they were employed by a prominent local notable, paid the tribute of deference in exchange for a meager payment. Even at the end of the century a bourgeois like the wood merchant and building contractor Gentil expected respect: "one could only approach him cap in hand."[44]

In between the *gros* (big shots) and the *petits* (little people) were many finer gradations. There were innumerable minor officeholders, from the ushers in the courts to the grain measurers and inspectors of pigs in the central market. Each group of officeholders formed a corporation with its own statutes and conventions, written or unwritten, its own elected officials, its feast day and its celebrations. Each one had a title and a collective identity that set them apart from the common herd. Even the *forts de la Halle*—the porters of the central market—had a distinctive costume and felt themselves a cut above ordinary laborers. Like skilled artisans, they looked down on the shoeshine boys and the lantern bearers, although this did not prevent them from passing the time of day or sharing a joke.

One of the key determinants of status was the degree of independence a person enjoyed. This was why Parisians looked down on domestic service, although it was one of the few plebeian occupations that—given the right employer—might permit economic success and even relative prosperity in old age. Barely 5 percent of the 40,000 or so servants in the city were Paris-born, because Parisians refused the total loss of independence that the job involved. "Lackey" was a term of abuse, and early in the century the numerous liveried male servants of great noble houses were feared for their aggressive behavior and violent group solidarity. But mockery of servants who assumed airs and aped their masters was a common theme in eighteenth-century social commentary.[45]

Yet servants were never a single group. There was a world of difference between the well-educated, well-paid stewards and house managers, at one end of the scale, and the cooks' assistants and stable boys at the other. In between came secretaries, personal valets, doormen and coachmen, cooks, and others. Yet even many of these were career servants, far higher in status than the majority of Paris domestics. Over a third of Paris families had at least one servant, and those in shopkeeper and artisan households were invariably poor young women from the provinces struggling to save a dowry. While the conditions of domestic service varied wildly and the relationship between servant and mistress followed no set pattern, it was always unequal, and the servant had little chance of redress if she were poorly treated. Blows and abuse (verbal and sexual), long hours of back-breaking work, and irregular payment were so common as to arouse little notice. Some servants became almost companions for their mistresses, but they were always dispensable. Not surprisingly, many went from one employer to another.[46]

Even among artisans, who prided themselves on their independence, there was a complex hierarchy that was reflected in subtle ways in daily interaction. Ménétra the glazier was contemptuous of the men with whom he did service as a voluntary fireman: "they were only cobblers and saddlers good for sewing up the hoses or pumping water or working the

Figure 6. The dismissed servant. Engraving by Etienne Jeaurat, *La servante congédiée*. Photo Bibliothèque nationale de France.

nozzles." Sometimes the hierarchy was very different from the modern one. Ménétra also knew a surgeon who lived in the same house: "his profession aside, he was a gentle friendly kindly man." On one occasion this surgeon met a chief clerk (*chef de bureau*), who found him charming and invited him to share a glass. Afterwards, "when I asked if he knew what kind of man he'd been drinking with, when I told him I saw him change color and say 'Is it possible?' "[47] In neighborhood relations everyone did know whom they were dealing with and the way people spoke and behaved reflected the subtlest distinctions of rank.

Local hierarchies were further complicated by gender, because the pecking order was often different in male and female occupations. The tripe seller with her tiny shop on the ground floor might be married to an artisan. Françoise Moreau, who sold fish in the Place Maubert, was the wife of a master tanner and displayed a certain proficiency with a quill.[48] Yet in most manufacturing trades, the hierarchy was reversed. The women almost invariably did the least independent, least skilled, and most poorly paid tasks: polishing wood and metal objects that the men had made; weaving the straw bottoms of chairs. They were far from being the equals of the men who worked almost alongside them.[49]

Male-female relationships were fundamentally unequal, though like other relationships they observed outward forms of respect. Men frequently had no scruples about seducing women of equal or lower rank, and female servants and shop girls were the most common targets of masters, journeymen, shop boys, and male domestics. These women were highly vulnerable because of their physical proximity, the fact that they were usually young, often without family in the city, and with no secure position within the household. There were no social or legal sanctions against single men who were sexually promiscuous, and this encouraged a predatory male culture. Given the association of masculinity with sexual prowess, some families were happy for sons to sow their wild oats and thus testify to their virility.[50]

For women, in contrast, there were strong community sanctions for transgressing conventional moral codes, unless a firm promise of marriage had been recognized by the whole neighborhood. It was considered quite acceptable that Léger Letourneau and his girlfriend Anne Claude "often went off alone together and often did not come back until eleven o'clock or midnight." "They loved each other a lot," observed a neighbor and friend, "always calling each other 'tu,' often kissing and behaving in a familiar fashion that indicated they were lover and mistress, and the witness was told by the said Claude girl that she was going to marry the said Letourneau."[51] But it was quite a different matter if no promise of marriage had been made or if a married woman was suspected of infidelity. A sexually promiscuous woman was the butt of jokes directed not only against her but against her whole family. A woman's reputation, in fact, was largely constructed on sexual "purity," whereas a man's depended on his skill in trade, his straight dealing in commercial and neighborly transactions, and on his reliability as a breadwinner. Ultimately, for a woman, there was the biological sanction of unwanted pregnancy. An unmarried mother had no standing in law and might find herself in the situation of Marie Catherine La Boissière, rejected by her lover when pregnant with their seventh child. "In the most extreme poverty," she pursued him across the city until he had her arrested. The police officer ordered her locked up, "on account of her libertine habits."[52] A woman in her position faced rejection by the local community and without strong family support would soon find herself in dire poverty.

Yet despite women's inferior economic and legal position, they exerted considerable power through their role as neighborhood opinion makers and commentators. The streets, and particularly the markets, were in a sense female territory: at the St-Germain market forty-eight of the fifty-seven places were held by women.[53] Most stallkeepers were women and they knew more about neighborhood affairs than anyone else. The women in the street—including those who brought their work downstairs to sit with neighbors outside the house—kept an eye on what was going on and were often the first to intervene in quarrels, even plunging in to separate men who were fighting. Their commentary on the dress and behavior of the passers-by was itself a form of social control. Ménétra recalled as a boy being pursued down the street by his father, brandishing a rope to beat him with, but the jeers of the women at their stalls allowed the child to escape with a scolding.[54]

Collectively, women had authority even over men, particularly the matrons whose judgment on people helped determine the opinion of the whole neighborhood. Considerable social power of a different sort was also exerted by the widows and wives of master craftsmen and merchants, who often gave orders to male employees and ran their own businesses. When Marie Anne Roussel and her brother Charles together took over their father's foundry it was only natural that their mother would keep the accounts, as she presumably always had.[55] There was an ambiguity about real male-female relations that tempered contemporary assertions of male superiority.

The same ambiguity permeated relationships between husband and wife. In law the male was the head of the household and without his permission his wife could not enter a contract or even dispose of her own property. It was also generally acceptable for a husband to chastise his wife, as long as he did not overdo it: the market women told the police in September 1752 that no one had intervened to stop a man punching a woman because everyone thought he was her husband. Yet in shopkeeper, artisan, and sometimes merchant families, the wife usually kept the accounts and often made business decisions. She might also decide on the children's education and line up eligible marriage partners, perhaps—like Ménétra's wife—without even consulting her husband: "for the sake of peace and quiet," he confessed, "I made no objection."[56]

The independence that Parisian women enjoyed—by comparison with their provincial sisters—was a product of the urban environment. Most worked, either with their husbands (usually handling the income of both) or alone, making money for themselves. In the course of their work they moved freely around the city and dealt alike with male and female customers. A Chinese visitor to Paris in 1723 was shocked at the way women walked boldly around the streets. The Auvergnat Pierre Prion was surprised when, in a crowd of onlookers at a fireworks display on the Quai du Louvre in 1739, several ladies whom he did not know struck up a conversation with him and offered him snuff.[57]

In male-female relationships, as in other neighborhood interaction, there was a mixture of dependence and independence, of exploitation and respect. There were unwritten rules of behavior that were peculiarly urban, and indeed primarily Parisian: a formal politeness that belied the very real inequalities between male and female, between employer and servant, between trades of quite different status. Yet habits of deference betrayed the enormous social gulf even between people who lived side by side. A doffed hat, a respectful silence, stepping aside to let another pass: this was the tribute of esteem offered to those with influence by others who had none. It was proffered without premeditation, without artificiality. It was accepted in the same way, as the birthright of men and women whose ancestry, family connections, and weight in local affairs gave them power and responsibility within the quarter.

CUSTOMARY CULTURE

The rules and hierarchies of neighborhood interaction were part of a broader pattern of unwritten conventions and obligations. Nearly every aspect of life in Paris was conducted according to what one historian has called the "everyday order," something "not codified or formalized in a legal grammar but allowed to evolve constantly in the vernacular of custom."[58] Where no rule was written down (and even sometimes even when it was), custom and usage determined what should be done. Providing accommodation for the leading journeyman was "based on custom," affirmed a wagon maker in Paris in 1773. It was customary for a worker to give prior warning before leaving an employer, claimed a master wood carver.[59] Wages, conditions, and perquisites were determined by established practice, and many industrial conflicts were over such "usages." Failure to respect them led to complaints: an apprentice's work had not been inspected by all the officials, "as is the usage"; the men attending a meeting of the rope makers' corporation had not been given their tokens in cash, as "has always been the practice." Occasionally, even a technical breach of guild statutes might be justified: "If he lent his share [of barley] to his brothers," said a brewer, "it was because he regarded this to be permitted by custom and daily practice."[60]

Religious affairs were another area in which custom was particularly important. Many Paris parishes had their own order of service and observed their own holy days: workers on one side of the rue St-Denis did not work on Saint Nicolas's Day though those on the other side of the street did—they were in the next parish.[61] Even the absolute monarchy knew that it had to observe custom, since its own legitimacy depended in part on the observance of ritual and long-standing practice. As every administrator, magistrate, and lawyer knew, the best guide in most circumstances was precedent. A dispute in 1661 over parish boundaries between four Paris parishes was resolved by requiring each parish to name twelve of the oldest parishioners to testify where the boundary lay. When, a century later, the churchwardens of St-Médard claimed the right to hold a requiem service for a dissident priest, they got several elderly members of the parish to attest that such services had always been the local custom—the service was permitted.[62]

Law was often simply the codification of custom. This was explicit in the "customary law" that governed inheritance practices and many other aspects of civil law. It was recognized by tribunals like the commercial court of Paris, which made its judgments (a guide of 1789 tells us), according to "the laws and the usages of commerce."[63] Although commercial law was by then well established, things like property rental, credit arrangements, the settlement of debts, and the sharing of profits and risk continued to be governed very largely by custom.

For much of the eighteenth century, to call something an "innovation" was to condemn it. A midcentury refutation of the religious reform movement known as Jansenism, for example, asserted that a feature of its "pernicious doctrines" was the attempt to *innovate.*[64] The Jansenists, for their part, took care to present their reforms as a return to practices followed "from time immemorial" but that had become lost or corrupted. They appealed to what was also a classic device of Old Regime political debate. The older a practice was, the more authentic and legitimate it was deemed to be. On the very eve of the Revolution there were vigorous arguments about the "ancient constitution of France": how had Charlemagne treated the Estates General? Had the monarchy usurped the "ancient liberties" of the French people? Only in 1789 did the new National Assembly decisively reject historical arguments in favor of "natural rights."[65]

For most of the eighteenth century, therefore, custom was a key ingredient in the cement that held the political and social edifice together. It was part of a whole way of looking at the world, as the historian E. P. Thompson pointed out in the context of eighteenth-century England, that drew on a cyclical conception of time very different from the dominant Western one today. Each generation expected to live in much the same way as the previous one, and the proper way to do things was passed on through apprenticeship and oral communication. In Restif de la Bretonne's autobiographical novel *Monsieur Nicolas,* the hero, about to be apprenticed to a printer, is reassured that "Everything you have to do will not be too wearisome, because it will only last a certain time, and you will have the prospect of being obeyed in your turn. It will therefore be in your interest . . . to maintain the rights of [the journeymen] over you." Individual and collective survival depended on maintaining the cycle. Inherited wisdom was preserved through apprenticeship, through ritual, in custom and proverb, and taught people how to deal with situations that recurred endlessly.[66]

Underlying the customs that people observed was a powerful sense of the rights and obligations that went with belonging to a community. It parallels the "moral economy" first described by Thompson. He defined it as a notion of "social norms and obligations, of the proper economic functions of several parties within the community." These norms were expressed, enforced, and passed on through ritual and stylized performance—none of which excluded violence.[67] This moral economy is very clear in eighteenth-century Paris.[68] Parisians believed they had a right to abundant white bread at low prices. Price rises during a shortage not only caused hardship but were considered morally wrong and provoked attacks on bakers and sometimes on the authorities held responsible. In all these conflicts there was a strong element of symbolic action and ritual that everyone understood.

But this sense of customary rights and obligations was not confined to bread riots, and even everyday neighborhood and work disputes observed a stylized (though endlessly inventive) ritual.[69] Failure to do what was deemed customary, in any area of life, was morally repugnant and provoked indignation. In 1783, when the curé of St-Merri ordered the annual Corpus Christi procession to return to the church because of rain, "there was immediately such murmuring, and popular anger was so pronounced, that . . . the said curé found himself forced to go out and to continue his procession, and thus to bow to the law imposed by the common people of his parish who cried out aloud *that the clergy was not too much to be pitied, since they had a whole year to dry out.*"[70]

In this instance, Parisians were enforcing customary norms even when hierarchy and authority were on the other side. Customary culture was both conservative and potentially rebellious.[71] Admittedly, the ability to define what was "customary" was not given to all to women less often than men, to unskilled workers less than to those with qualifications. But it did provide some leverage for people who otherwise had little power.

Yet it operated effectively only within communities where people were familiar with one another and with the usages followed, since these might vary from place to place (even within Paris), and from one trade to another. It was the community that enforced customary rights and obligations, initially through formal or informal sanctions, through ridicule and laughter, and ultimately by rejecting people who refused to conform. Riots, attacks on bailiffs, and resistance to soldiers arresting beggars, by men and women alike, show us the neighborhood uniting to protect its members. In the corporate trades, which had statutes and a legal existence, many such rights were defended through court action. But sometimes court action was not an option, for example when labor was brought in from the provinces at lower wages. Then Paris workers often united to ostracize them.[72] Here too solidarity was the best guarantee of survival. Even though the neighborhoods and trades of Paris were by rural standards relatively open to outsiders, they continued to function as communities because most Parisians remained deeply dependent on their fellow citizens for material assistance, human contact, and recognition.

Nevertheless, community and customary culture did not imply equality. On the contrary, custom and ritual helped entrench the principle of hierarchy. They granted fewer rights to women, to children, to outsiders. People knew their own place and that of others, and while minor distinctions were constantly being challenged the principle itself rarely was. Yet the more powerful members of the community were expected to deal fairly with the poorer and less privileged ones, and to contribute to the general welfare. The "notables" should provide references, contribute to poor funds, and help a local person in trouble—as in 1742 at St-Médard when a pastry cook was wrongly accused (in the eyes of the locals) of murdering his mother.[73] Within the household a husband and father should provide for his family and servants and not treat them harshly. In the trades corporations the richer members were expected to contribute proportionately more to assist others who were sick or in difficulties, and to observe restrictions designed to keep all members of the trade in business. Guild statutes outlawed price-cutting and advertising as unfair competition. They usually forbade members to have two shops, or to poach another's employees with promises of better wages. And when raw materials arrived in the market—a consignment of rope, of tanned hides, or of barley for brewing—they were shared out in lots so that the poorer masters did not receive goods of inferior quality.[74]

The officially established guilds were not the only occupational bodies to operate in this way. In 1752 one of the market porters was accused of stealing a small sum from their common purse: each man deposited part of his earnings into a collective fund that was then divided between them all. This evened out income, guaranteeing that men past their prime, for example, would not be disadvantaged. It also imposed an obligation on each member of the group to earn his share but not to undercut the others.[75] Given the difficulties of surviving in a society with very low wages and a hopelessly inadequate welfare system, such cooperation was in the interests of all. Nor was it confined to the poor. A very similar system operated even among the *commissaires de police;* these well-paid officials also had a common purse and a strong collective identity. Cooperation and mutualism were part of the early modern Parisian mentality.

Eighteenth-century Paris was a turbulent, noisy, apparently anarchic place that visitors at first found incomprehensible and overwhelming. There was endless variety, continual movement. Yet for the people who lived there, life obeyed familiar rhythms and patterns that most believed to be unvarying. For all its apparent confusion the city was a place of regular itineraries and well-trodden paths. Yet custom did not preclude change. Both geographical and social mobility were greater than in the countryside and there was constant jockeying for position. Custom was a way of defending the status quo but could also be used to formulate new demands, to affirm the rights of the underdog, and ensure that obligations were fulfilled in changing circumstances. Like the city itself, customary culture was a living amalgam of norms, beliefs, and practices, continually readapting to a changing world, certainly not static or "traditional."

CHAPTER TWO

THE POOR YOU HAVE WITH YOU ALWAYS

The winter of 1709, *le grand hiver,* was still remembered at the end of the eighteenth century. In Paris the temperature stayed below -10° Celsius for two entire weeks, and on 13 January it reached -20°. The Seine froze solid and in the surrounding countryside "the trees in the forest exploded like gunshots" as they froze. Fruit orchards were decimated. Wine and oil froze and broke their casks and even inside the houses bread had to be cut with an axe. The contents of chamber pots froze under beds. Pigeons and hens died of cold. A partial thaw on 24 January brought floods, but then the thermometer fell again, once more reaching -15° in February. When spring finally came, in many areas the grain did not sprout. Late frosts in June made the meager harvest even worse. In the normally fertile plains of the Paris region many farms did not produce enough to sow the next year. Widespread starvation was averted only by a superb crop of oats and barley, grains that could be planted in the spring.[1]

The price of food rocketed. Although part of the previous year's crop remained in the warehouses, frozen or dangerous rivers and impassible roads made it almost inaccessible. In January the price of wheat doubled in the wholesale markets. Given that bread was the staple food of most of the population, everyone was fearful of famine so even places that had reserves were reluctant to share them. Farmers and merchants with stocks of the previous year's grain knew that prices would rise sharply, so were inclined to wait to improve their profit. In April 1709 the price of grain at Gonesse, in one of the key supply areas for Paris, reached three and a half times its usual level; a month later it was nearly six times.[2]

The misery was acute, aggravated by an influx of provincials attracted by the remote possibility of finding work or assistance in the city when there was none at home. "Paris is a theater of horrors," wrote one observer. "The poor besiege us on all sides, they disturb the quiet of the night with cries and sobs, stopping only when they expire." "A terrible thing," wrote another well-to-do inhabitant. "I saw two poor errand boys found dead, completely frozen, in a doorway where they had taken refuge and huddled together to warm themselves."[3]

In such conditions disease thrived. Dysentery reached epidemic proportions and scurvy became widespread because of the shortage of fresh food: out of 3,000 people at the central hospital (the Hôtel-Dieu) in April 1709, a third had scurvy. Altogether, 30,000 acutely ill people passed through its doors in 1709, many of whom did not survive. In February 1710, 5,500 inmates still shared its 2,500 beds. Many more unfortunates did not gain admission to the hospitals. The police lit fires in the main squares to warm the homeless, but still people froze to death. The number of abandoned children rose from the normal annual figure of 1,600 to more than 2,500. In the central quarter of St-Jacques-de-la-Boucherie 45 babies, most only a few days old, were picked up alive: most years there were about 15.[4]

There is no way of knowing exactly how many people died of cold in Paris in that terrible winter. The official toll for the year was 29,300, 10,000 to 12,000 more than usual and the highest annual figure recorded before 1794.[5]

But even more terrible than these statistics is the fact that a great many who did not survive the winter of 1709 would in any case have died of fevers and poverty-related diseases in the spring of 1710 or in 1711. The great crisis was only an extreme variant of a recurrent pattern. Other winters were not so bad, the food shortages less severe, the deaths less numerous and less public, but every year there were old people who died of cold, newborn children who were abandoned because their families could not feed them, thousands who were undernourished and vulnerable to fevers and epidemics.

This was true everywhere in eighteenth-century Europe. But Paris amplified problems because it concentrated people. A larger population in one place meant more dramatic consequences when an epidemic struck. It meant a greater likelihood of adulterated food than in the countryside, and higher levels of water pollution, because the drains discharged into the same water courses that provided drinking water. Many diseases were borne by the river water that poor Parisians drew for themselves and that the better-off purchased by the bucket from the water carriers. When Pierre Prion visited Paris in the summer of 1738 he did not have enough money to drink wine or beer, and within days had a fine case of diarrhea: "it rasped all my bowels, boiling oil could not have been worse."[6] But he could easily have contracted typhoid, again carried by the river water—or malaria, known as autumn fever, which annually reaped a macabre harvest. Measles preyed primarily on the very young. All these complaints claimed their victims selectively from those weakened by malnutrition or by other diseases. If smallpox and syphilis were less selective, sparing neither paupers nor kings (Louis XV died of smallpox), the tuberculosis that ravaged the population was directly linked to poor nutrition and cramped and damp living conditions. Parisians lived with all of these afflictions as we live with colds and influenza. To them 1709 was qualitatively different, a crisis year, yet its raging mortality only illuminates more starkly than usual the contours of poverty and desperation.[7]

The poor were always the most vulnerable because they had trouble making ends meet even when food was cheap and the climate kinder. In concrete terms being poor meant having enough to eat only in the good times. It meant dressing in rags, in the cast-offs of others. It meant living in a single room, with inadequate heating. And it implied being at the mercy of other people for credit or for alms, sometimes for shelter, even for tolerance of expedients like begging and gleaning that might inconvenience the better-off and therefore be illegal.

WHO WERE THE POOR?

No one knew how many poor there were in eighteenth-century Paris. The parish priest of St-Médard, in the indigent faubourg St-Marcel, estimated in 1743 that twelve thousand of his fifteen to eighteen thousand parishioners depended on assistance just to survive, even in good times. His colleague at St-Sulpice, a much larger and wealthier parish, claimed in 1708 to have thirteen to fourteen thousand poor.[8] This takes no account of the thousands of temporary migrants who left their homes in the Paris region, in Normandy and Picardy, or even in the Auvergne and the Limousin, "*misérables* who come from all parts of the realm . . . to seek employment, but not all of them can succeed," observed an official report of 1767.[9] On the basis of deaths at the central hospital Daniel

Roche has estimated there may have been between one hundred fifty thousand and two hundred thousand indigents in 1700, roughly a third of the capital's population. This number rose dramatically in bad years, a reminder of the fragility of life for up to another third of Parisians who were vulnerable to any rise in prices or drop in income.[10]

Furthermore, the indications are that it was getting harder to make ends meet. Ernest Labrousse estimated that while wages rose about 17 percent between 1726–41 and 1771–89, the prices of necessities went up 62 percent. Rents in Paris rose by 130 to 140 percent. This translates to an increase from 46 days' wages for a laborer to 75. Not all trades were affected in the same way—the real wages of building workers did keep pace with inflation, and the same probably applied in other rapidly growing sectors of the city's economy. But the percentage of Parisians able to leave something to their children diminished across the century: an increasing proportion left only debts.[11] Both the numbers of poor and of those on the brink were growing.

But the poor did not make up a single, undifferentiated category. Much later, in 1790, an investigation launched by the new revolutionary authorities distinguished "those who, without property and without resources, try to earn their living by working; those whose age does not yet or no longer permits them to work; and finally those who are condemned to long-term inactivity by the character of their infirmities, or to temporary inactivity by short-term maladies."[12] There were also, added the report, the "dishonest poor," those who did not want to work. Eighteenth-century governments did not recognize the existence of structural unemployment and underemployment.

This last category aside, the report was broadly correct in its description of the types of poor, especially in its distinction between temporary and permanent poverty. A great many of the Paris destitute were old people, who in a life of labor had never accumulated enough to provide for their declining years and who—whether at the age of eighty or at fifty—found their earning capacity reduced by illness or frailty. A fairly typical sample of twelve beggars arrested by the police outside the Bon Secours monastery in 1750 included seven over sixty years old (four of those over seventy).[13] Most elderly people continued to do whatever work they could, like the widow Husson, who lived in a tiny room on the top floor of a house in the vieille rue du Temple and who, right up to the time of her final illness—to judge from the objects found in her room—upholstered chairs. When she died in 1709, at the age of sixty, she possessed a shabby bed with some sheets, two blankets, a quilt and several cushions, two small tables, a chair, and three small chests. Her clothes comprised seven skirts, mostly very old, two pairs of stockings, and a supply of shirts, "the most part very worn." Her other possessions, apart from various rags and dirty cloths, consisted of a copper urn holding about three bucketfuls of water, four small tablecloths, a cooking pot and pan, a pothook and trivet, a few pewter plates, and some broken earthenware. She appears to have had no family, and this was all she had to show for a lifetime's work.[14]

Also prominent among the permanent poor were those with physical disabilities, often from birth. The risks of injury in birth were high and midwives often did further damage, either through intervention or through negligence: "How many feeble children, atrophied, hunchbacked, deaf, blind, one-eyed, bloodshot . . . with twisted legs, lame, contorted, hare-lipped—deformed, ill-shaped children, almost useless to society?" asked a critic rhetorically.[15] Fear of deformed children haunted parents, hence the still universal practice of swaddling babies for the first year of their lives—tight wrappings were believed to assist tiny limbs to develop strong and straight. A great many deformities, though, were caused by childhood illnesses or nutritional deficiencies, because a diet consisting mainly of soup and bread was often short on protein and vitamins. Maternal malnourishment produced sickly infants, and in older children rickets was very widespread. The poor were also the most likely victims of contaminated food, such as the cheap wine to which some unscrupulous merchants added lead oxide to take away the sharp taste.[16]

Even the sturdy survivors of birth and infancy were not safe from later accidents: two-year-old François Lebrun had his hand and thigh crushed by a wagon when he wandered out the door of his father's fruit shop in the rue de la Grande Truanderie. Childhood pranks and games could have tragic outcomes: a woodpile falling on children in a yard in the faubourg St-Antoine; a nose blown off by a firecracker. There were dangers, too, from animals. Young Simon Gautier was on an errand to buy some spirits when he was badly bitten on the head and shoulder by a horse. Large dogs sometimes inflicted nasty injuries, and so did the pigs that fed on rubbish in the backstreets, despite bans on allowing them to roam. Another hazard was fire, and serious burns were common when small children, often left alone for an hour or two, fell into the fire. Even adults, exhausted from a long day's toil, sometimes fell asleep too close to the fire.[17]

Many of these dangers were universal, but some were particularly Parisian. The police archives contain innumerable reports of traffic accidents, all recorded in matter-of-fact official prose that masks the individual tragedy but conveys the banality of the event. Work accidents were also very common and people left seriously injured were in a sense worse off than those killed outright. Roofers, carpenters, and other construction workers often fell from buildings—and in Paris that could mean they were six or seven stories high. Market porters and port workers carried huge loads that produced back injuries and hernias. The loss of a limb, a hand, or an eye could leave even a skilled worker in dire poverty. What became of the victims of these accidents? The lame might perhaps find some sort of job but many others were condemned to a life of absolute dependence. Around 15 percent of beggars arrested in Paris across the eighteenth century were invalids, and others were mentally ill.[18]

The very nature of the work in many trades induced maladies sooner or later, and this outcome too was often a big-city phenomenon because of the concentration of manufacturing. Tailors, bent cross-legged over their work in bad light, suffered back injuries, eye strain, and eventual blindness. Lace makers and weavers also often went blind. Papermakers, wool carders and beaters (usually women), flax combers, and a host of other workers in the booming textile industries developed respiratory illnesses from inhaling fibers. Lung and throat diseases also afflicted those who polished metal and glass, who worked in an environment filled with dust. Many trades used poisons without taking adequate precautions. Gilders handled mercury and as a result suffered dizziness and eventually a permanent trembling in hands, feet, and legs. Pewterers and mirror makers used lead every day, as did many printing workers. Dyers and painters used other toxic chemicals.[19]

Accidents and illnesses did not affect the injured worker alone. The death or injury of the principal wage earner could leave a whole family in desperate poverty. There was rarely compensation, either for the injured worker or for the family, no medical insurance, and no unemployment benefits. And few people had resources to fall back on. Daniel Roche has calculated that in 1700 an average male worker could, by selling all his clothes, have raised enough to keep himself (though not his family) supplied with grain for three months.[20] An accident, a prolonged or permanent illness, sudden death—any of these could plunge an entire family into destitution.

Abandoned wives and single mothers found themselves in a position like that of a widow left with children. Women's wages were generally half those of men, and a woman with children could not get work as a servant or shop girl. She might make a living spinning, ironing, or sewing,

Figure 7. The beggar. Engraving from Jean Duplessi-Bertaux, in *Recueil de cent sujets* (Paris, 1814). Bibliothèque historique de la ville de Paris, photo Jean-Christophe Doerr.

or if she were a little more skilled embroidering or making lace. She would earn between 8 and—if talented and lucky—20 sous a day. Restif de la Bretonne's character Babet earned 9 sous a day by sewing and spent 3 on rent, 3 on bread, and 3 on soup. This calculation ignores Sundays or other nonworking days and makes no allowance for sickness or any rise in prices.[21]

But even a couple in full employment might be hard hit by an unlooked-for birth or an awkward pregnancy. High infant mortality made the survival of numerous children unlikely, but life was a lottery and while some couples lost all their babies, others had more than they could feed. As a result thousands of newborn babies were left in church porches and at the doors of the wealthy—once again an urban phenomenon, because in the city no one could trace the mother.

An inexhaustible source of poor people was the thousands of immigrants, especially numerous in bad years. Many were unemployed rural laborers with no special skills, or indebted peasants with insufficient land. The majority were illiterate. Many ended up begging and when arrested would plead that they had been "in Paris only a day, with neither money nor family in this city."[22] Some were little more than children, prematurely orphaned, others single mothers who had come to Paris to give birth anonymously. Some found a niche but many never knew anything better than the wretched lodging houses in the backstreets off the ports where a couple of sous would provide a flea-ridden straw mattress in a crowded room. A frightening number ended their days in prison, or in the Hôtel-Dieu as victims of disease, but all in reality victims of poverty.

These were the permanent poor. But there were many others on the borderline, able in normal years to survive but going hungry as soon as the price of bread rose. A 4-lb loaf of bread usually cost 8 or 9 sous and contemporaries estimated that a family of two adult laborers and two children would consume 8 lbs a day (the hospital ration was 1½ lbs per person). Given that a male laborer earned 20 to 30 sous a day and a female worker half as much, a couple with two young children could expect to spend nearly half their normal income on bread.[23] But they did not earn this much every day. There were between 110 and 150 Sundays and feast days—estimates vary. And there were inevitably days when they could not get work. Nor was food the only expense. In 1700, 30 or 40 livres a year (there were 20 sous to a livre) was the minimum rent for a tiny garret, 60 livres if they aspired to two rooms.[24] They also needed clothes and shoes, vegetables to make soup, firewood, and perhaps candles and wine. A couple with children not only had extra mouths to feed and extra bodies to house and clothe, but their income fell as long as there was a small one to look after—generally the woman's task, because she earned less and because child care was regarded as women's work. When the price of bread rose sharply, perhaps to 12 or 15 sous for a 4-lb loaf, one or more members of the family would go hungry. If one of them fell sick or was unemployed, the whole household would be in trouble.

Skilled workers in good health, the journeymen and their wives who made up perhaps a fifth of the Paris population, were not usually to be found among the poor as long as they were able to work. A mason might earn 40 sous, a more skilled worker 50 sous or more per day. He might also enjoy additional perquisites such as the privilege of keeping offcuts of timber or metal. The memoirs of the glazier Jacques-Louis Ménétra give the impression that for a young man at the height of his skill, money came and went easily. There was always enough for urban pleasures: for a bottle of wine with a friend, a wager, and for the ribbons and other accoutrements that enabled a young man to swagger before his friends.

But skilled workers were in a privileged position. The growth of Paris and its labor market and economic expansion across the eighteenth century meant that in most trades there was fairly steady demand. But bad harvests and high prices hit even skilled workers from time to time. They suffered from the speculation and monetary fluctuations in the early 1720s, following Finance Minister John Law's ill-fated attempt to introduce paper money, and again in the commercial crisis of 1729–31. Overproduction and inflation produced widespread unemployment in the skilled trades immediately after major wars in 1715, 1763, and 1783. Because the luxury trades produced for a relatively small market, a change in fashion could disrupt an entire industry. A royal death would send the court into mourning and abruptly end sales of colored silk. Paris was less vulnerable to such slumps than a city like Lyon, which relied heavily on one major industry, but serious industrial crises of this sort did occur.[25]

Even someone with a relatively well paid job might find it a struggle to bring up a large family. Jacques Rivaud was director of coach services to the lower Seine in the 1780s but paid no tax because he and his wife had seven children.[26] And well-paid workers knew the time would come—if they lived to old age—when they could no longer work and were more than likely to join the ranks of the destitute. Among the common people the only ones who were sometimes better off in old age were servants—an unusually large occupational group in Paris. Although domestic service was generally a temporary and very insecure condition, those who could find a good and well-off employer might be looked after. Louise Michelin, widow of a master tanner, promised her servant a life pension of 30 livres per annum, representing a capital investment of 600 livres.[27] But such good fortune was exceptional. In any case, the security of this woman's declining years was the reward for a lifetime of menial work and dependence.

There were therefore several categories of poor in early-eighteenth-century Paris: the really destitute, who had nothing; the permanent poor, who in good years and sound health had just enough to live on; and the temporary poor who were in trouble when prices rose or when a breadwinner was incapacitated or unemployed. Many found themselves in penury when old age destroyed their independence.

THE KNOWN AND THE UNKNOWN POOR

But eighteenth-century Parisians did not divide up the poor in quite this way. The crucial distinction most of them made, as the parish priest of St-André-des-Arts pointed out in 1789, was "between the poor whose birth and occupation make them resident among us, and the poor who live in our lodging houses."[28] The known poor included most of the old and infirm, people who had once been independent members of the community. Widows or abandoned mothers were often in this category, along with the sick and the victims of personal or family tragedy. The crippled and the mentally ill, particularly if they had lived in the quarter for many years, also had a claim on the charity of neighbors. All of these people had a recognized place, even the beggars.

The neighborhood not only provided assistance but defended their poor against outsiders. In the early years of the eighteenth century employees of the Hôpital général were paid a bounty for each beggar they arrested. They generally neither knew nor cared who belonged and who did not, and their actions therefore provoked many riots. In a typical example from 1725, a highly sensitive time when bread prices were high, a commissaire and the watch on patrol in the faubourg St-Antoine tried to arrest a beggar in the main street. She dived into a mirror maker's shop. Before they could follow her, a local laborer began pelting them with stones. A hatter came to the door of his shop and shouted out that they were thieves and ne'er-do-wells and that they deserved a good beating. A large crowd gathered, assaulting the patrol with stones and sticks, and they were lucky to get away with their lives: if a carriage had not been passing at that precise moment they would have found the city gate at the Porte St-Antoine closed against them, cutting off their escape. There were many such incidents where laborers, hawkers, artisans, and shopkeepers rushed to the defense of the local poor.[29] These were veritable community revolts, acknowledgment that the known poor had a right to beg. Even if they committed small crimes, their sin was only venial.

The "unknown poor" were quite different. In this category were those who had fled to the city in quest of work or alms, the unemployed of the lodging houses, and the homeless of all ages. Such people were never in the same place long enough to get onto the lists of parish poor, and without a fixed address or anyone to speak for them they were feared and condemned as vagabonds. No one knew their names or occupations, or where they came from. They could disappear into the crowd and no one would remember their faces. In a society in which social relationships still, particularly in the early eighteenth century, depended overwhelmingly on familiarity, the usual reaction to such people was mistrust. In times of shortage it was often resentment: they had no right to be there, taking the bread of others.

The ecclesiastical and secular authorities, and even the local elites of Paris, thought of the poor in a slightly different way. They too distinguished the deserving from the undeserving, but for them it was not sufficient to be settled and known locally to be counted deserving. Only the "honest" and godly poor should be helped, proclaimed the Paris Parlement in 1764, not "the drunk, those who swear, the idle, nor those who neglect to send their children to school or to the catechism."[30] Able-bodied beggars, unmarried mothers, and the irreligious were all a threat to the social order, whereas the honest poor were pious and accepted their state without question, displaying a proper humility in their requests for assistance. Poor widows, orphans, and the infirm were the archetypes of the deserving poor and each parish had funds earmarked for them. Some came from donations left in the poor box in the church or from special collections: in 1742 the offerings for the ten to eleven hundred "honest poor" dependent on the parish of St-André-des-Arts amounted to 2,400 livres.[31] Other small sums were bequeathed by God-fearing parishioners to be distributed annually (on a particular feast day or on the day of their death) in the hope that the grateful prayers of the poor would ease the passage of their souls. Occasionally a rich and childless person left a house, the rent to be distributed to the honest and deserving poor by the clergy or by the parish administrators. The permanent presence of the poor was useful to society, according to the contemporary wisdom, because it reminded the wealthy of their Christian duty.

Some of the parish clergy, themselves men of little property, earned the respect of the poor with their concern. François de Pâris, a priest at St-Médard, was acclaimed as a saint by many of the Paris populace because of his charity and his asceticism. He was exceptional but he was not entirely alone. Many of the curés, the priests in charge of the parishes, demonstrated genuine concern for the poor even though many came from wealthy backgrounds and were figures of considerable stature in Paris—Mercier described them as "small bishops." Most were conscientious pastors, particularly in the poor faubourgs. Successive curés at St-Jacques-du-Haut-Pas were highly respected for their care of the poor: one was said to have "lived poorly for himself, richly and lavishly in dealing with the poor."[32]

Most parishes had charity committees of local bourgeois who met regularly to assess requests for assistance from the poor. The ladies were often given particular responsibility "for helping the sick poor, infants fed on milk and flour, and others who according to custom or propriety can be attended to only by them."[33] At St-Séverin they included the wives of prominent local citizens like Madame Lottin of the wealthy printing dynasty, who would go through the clumsy notes that poor women had scribbled: Madeleine Durant, "unmarried, sixty-four years old, living in the parish for sixteen years without ever requesting assistance, with poor eyesight."

Invariably the poor women asked not for money but for thread to help them earn their living—they knew what their betters liked to hear. One of the ladies would comment on each request: "received 6 livres on 8 June 1734"; "Sara Robequin, newly converted . . . got nothing 6 July 1734—evidence that she neglected the education of her only son."[34] The ladies and gentlemen of the committees sometimes visited the poor to distribute alms, but the hard work of preparing food, attending the sick, even getting them ready to receive communion, was done by the "Grey Sisters," the order founded by Louise de Marillac and Saint Vincent de Paul in the early seventeenth century. The charity committee passed on modest sums to provide the poor with bedding, food, and basic medical care. Sometimes they also paid for the free school for poor children of the parish.[35]

In addition to these committees, most parishes had confraternities—pious associations of lay people—that specialized in helping the poor. That of the journeymen hatters at Ste-Marie-Madeleine-en-la-Cité advertised itself as "a society for the relief of those of their brothers who find themselves in need of assistance, and by means of a modest sum which each of them, without distinction, pays every two weeks."[36] Many of these bodies also paid funeral expenses, a less immediate benefit but a psychological comfort to those fearing a pauper's grave. The confraternity of Saint Francis de Sales in the parish of St-Jean-en-Grève had operated at least since 1674 and its administrators were among the principal inhabitants of the parish. But like the parish charity committee it was very selective. Potential recipients were visited to ensure they were of good life and morals, and suitably deferential. They were given food, blankets, or clothes, not cash that might be squandered. Institutions like this were designed to keep the poor in line as much as to assist them.[37]

The good citizens who served on the charity committees felt they were doing something for the poor, but parish charity did little to alleviate the lot even of the lucky few, much less of the enormous mass of the destitute. At St-Médard in 1742 the allocation was 10 sous a week, enough for a 4-lb loaf of bread—barely a day's supply. Not only were the resources grossly inadequate, but they did not always reach the real poor. Often they were diverted to assist former shopkeepers who had fallen on hard times. Occasionally they even ended up in the general parish coffers. In 1763 the administrators of Ste-Marguerite, one of the poorest parishes in the city, decided to invest 1,000 livres of poor funds, "not having been able to find any use for them."[38]

In addition to poor relief from local sources, the parishes controlled access to most of the external services available. They decided who would occupy the beds that the parishes funded at the Incurables, the 300-bed hospital for the terminally ill. They distributed money from the government: in 1724 the curé of Ste-Marguerite received some 6,600 livres for distribution in the faubourg St-Antoine, a third of the parish's poor relief budget that year. All the Paris churches were given small amounts from the annual profits of the royal lottery.[39] Further funds came from a central poor relief agency, the Grand Bureau des pauvres, which levied a tiny annual poor tax on every property. From this money, together with donations, the Grand Bureau des pauvres provided small cash payments to about twelve hundred aged persons, but they had to be born in Paris or have been resident there for three years and to have at least the status of master artisans. The money was handled by the parish administrators and it was from their lists that the beneficiaries were selected. Those assisted were not to leave the parish without permission from the *commissaire des pauvres,* an official elected from among the local bourgeois. The Grand Bureau also ran the Hospice des petites maisons in the rue de Sèvres, which housed three hundred elderly poor, and the Trinité, a home for a hundred orphaned boys and thirty or forty girls who were taught a trade.[40]

Most private institutions also restricted their intake to the "deserving poor" and required a recommendation from the parish. La Miséricorde in the faubourg St-Marcel took in one hundred orphan girls and looked after them until the age of twenty-five, when they were given a dowry. They had to be Paris-born, legitimate, and in good health. The three hundred blind people at the Quinze-Vingts hospital also had to be born in the city. These places were for an elite, even among the "honest" poor.[41]

Much of the poor relief provided by the parishes was symbolic rather than practical, and it exalted the donors as much as it assisted the recipients. Marble plaques on church walls testified publicly to the generosity of local bourgeois. Dowries provided for poor young women were awarded at a special marriage ceremony in the parish church, and if the young women were the center of some attention on these occasions, so too were the notables who handed over the dowries—presumably in the form of trousseaus rather than cash. The same was true of other special ceremonies: in at least one parish it was the custom that the first child born on Christmas morning was baptized by the curé and had as godmother the woman who headed the charity committee—a great honor. The baby received a small gift, the mother some swaddling clothes, and the structure of deference in the parish emerged reinforced.[42]

Nevertheless, deference came at a price. The parish poor were not quite the passive and humbly grateful souls that the local notables wished them to be. While parish charity was in principle conditional on good behavior, it was often perceived by the poor themselves less as a reward than as a customary right that went with membership of the community. The parish priest of St-Médard, desperately short of money because of an expensive court case, repeatedly complained that the poor were "harassing" him for assistance. Some years later a churchwarden received an abusive anonymous letter from one of the local poor who apparently had been unable to obtain a recommendation and had therefore not received anything.[43] One of the functions of the parish was to provide charity to the deserving, and the poor grew resentful if the bargain was not fulfilled.

A few institutions catered both to the "deserving" and to the "undeserving" poor. The main one was the Hôpital général, formed in 1656. No distinction was made between the old, the infirm, and the needy, and some parts of the Hôpital général were used for locking up delinquents as well. The hospital at Bicêtre, outside the city to the south, specialized in the treatment of venereal disease, but was also a prison for hardened male criminals and a hospice for the needy poor. It had 1,313 inmates in 1713, including 486 elderly invalids, 182 mentally ill, 70 blind men, 70 syphilitics, 195 vagrants, and another 150 men confined for various offences. The Salpêtrière, another part of the Hôpital général, took in poor women and their young children. In 1713 it held 1,570 children under fifteen, 1,200 mentally or physically ill women, 260 elderly married couples, 149 pregnant women or nursing mothers, and 900 prisoners incarcerated for vagrancy, prostitution, or libertine behavior: over 4,000 inhabitants in all. Another institution, La Pitié, contained around

3,400 children under seventeen years of age, while the other three houses—Scipion for pregnant women and new mothers, St-Esprit and the Enfants-Trouvés for foundlings—accommodated a further thousand. Allowing for deaths, the total numbers given shelter in each institution were high: at the Enfants-Trouvés well over half the babies died before their first birthday.[44]

A number of religious houses in Paris were also open to all comers. Many new arrivals in the city went immediately to the centrally located Saint Catherine Hospital (for women) or the Saint Gervais Hospital (for men). In principle they received up to three days' accommodation and food, but demand was frequently so great that people were turned out after the second night. Handouts of food, and sometimes accommodation, could also be had at the St-Lazare monastery, at the Franciscan sisters, at the Filles-Dieu monastery, and three days a week at the Célestins. The sick were also received without question at the Hôtel-Dieu, a huge, smelly, rambling collection of buildings described by one writer as "the shame and the ordeal of the poor."[45] They found themselves in one of the twenty-five great wards, often several to a bed, frequently alongside someone with a completely different disease. But at least they were fed and tended day and night—as well as two thousand or three thousand patients could be—by upwards of a hundred Augustinian nuns and a team of orderlies. The nuns displayed a real concern for the souls in their care and were sometimes accused of receiving people who were homeless rather than sick.

They did their best, but the Hôtel-Dieu, despite its nearly thousand-year history and impressive assets, was all but bankrupt by the second half of the eighteenth century.[46] Like other Parisian institutions it was totally incapable of meeting the demands placed upon it. This was not just because of the growing numbers of poor but also because of an increasing reluctance on the part of government and of the well-to-do to take responsibility for them. The authorities had little sympathy for the "undeserving poor" and like most of the Paris population would have liked the unknown poor to go back where they came from. When the numbers of beggars grew noticeably or when there were complaints, the police would round them up or try to drive them from the city, threatening imprisonment, whippings, the pillory, even the galleys, or deportation to Louisiana or Canada. This happened after the bad winter of 1684 and again in 1700. Following a particularly bad period in the early 1720s, a royal edict renewed earlier instructions to lock up all beggars and vagabonds. Those genuinely unable to work would be helped, but the able-bodied were to be set to building roads or drafted into the army. As the funding was inadequate, this plan was ineffective, but it did produce bouts of arrests.[47] Those identified as beggars and "vagabonds" were banished from the city and branded on the right shoulder so they could be identified if they returned. Floggings and confinement in the royal galleys (often in practice a death sentence because of high mortality there) were dispensed liberally to any beggar accused of theft or who had been caught for the second time. But in a city as large as Paris, with the limited resources available to the police, it was impossible to catch and incarcerate all the "undeserving poor" and equally impossible to eliminate begging or homelessness by harsh punishments. Only after about 1750 did the authorities recognize the failure of this strategy and begin opening temporary workshops to provide work for the unemployed.[48]

SURVIVING IN PARIS

If the poor of Paris survived, it was mostly through their own efforts, by what Olwen Hufton has termed "an economy of makeshifts." And the city offered almost limitless possibilities to the inventive. Like many others, the widow of a laborer living near St-Etienne-du-Mont picked up splinters of wood around the woodpiles on the quais. People raised rabbits in upper-floor apartments and fed them on scraps collected in the streets. Washerwomen were reputed to put on their clients' clothes to save wear on their own. There were many ways of surviving in the city for those who knew their way around.[49]

For this very reason, the known poor had a far better chance of surviving without turning to crime. Although anyone could pawn a mattress or a few old clothes, people were more likely to get a fair price if they were known. Credit and neighborhood assistance depended on belonging. An old woman who died in the Hôtel-Dieu in April 1752 collected rags in the street but really survived thanks to a grocer in the rue Jacob, just behind St-Germain-des-Prés, who let his attic to her at well below market prices and did not insist on payment even though she was years in arrears. He and his wife had even lent her the bedding, the chamber pot, and the broken chair that comprised almost the entire furnishings of her room. Another poor woman received scraps of meat and cheese from the hospital where her friends worked, while a coachman's wife asked no payment for looking after a solitary man when he fell sick. If times were simply bad and there was some chance of later improvement, regular customers could borrow a few sous from the local baker or wineshop keeper. Marguerite Loriot "would have nothing to eat if the women in the [Halles] market did not give her credit on a small quantity of fruit and vegetables." The old and the very young might go begging, generally a safe enough occupation if they were known locally.[50]

Most of these options were closed for the unknown poor, so petty crime—usually theft—was a common expedient. After two months' unemployment the building worker Jacques Bazin, 22, stole a wagon driver's lunch from the back of his cart. "It is misery and hunger . . . he and his mother aged seventy-five not having eaten between them a pound of bread for three days." But he had chosen a part of the city where he was not known. Of those arrested for thefts of food in eighteenth-century Paris, 63 percent either had no residence or were living in a lodging house.[51] Smuggling was also an option, since the heavy dues payable on most consumer goods entering Paris made it lucrative, though always risky, for a woman to hide a liter of eau-de-vie under her skirts. Pierre Jeanson, an unemployed rural laborer who had been in Paris for three months "selling and buying different merchandise," was locked up for both smuggling and poaching after being caught at the city gate with several rabbits that he claimed to have bought at Versailles. Unfortunately for him, they were still warm.[52]

The other obvious occupation for the unemployed was begging, but able-bodied beggars were far less likely to provoke sympathy than were helpless babies, the infirm, and the elderly. Other beggars were very likely to find themselves in the damp and dark Châtelet prison just north of the river. Only small children were virtually immune from arrest—though not from police harassment—and it was they who clustered at church doors on Sundays and holy days to seek alms. They were experts at making the most of their youth and helplessness but many were not above picking pockets and filching anything left unattended. The homeless among them huddled on winter nights on top of the lime kilns on the slopes of Montmartre or Belleville or slept where they could. They aroused scant tolerance from Parisians. Sixteen-year-old Jean Jamet and his slightly older companion Michel Berthaud, unemployed and homeless, slept in the shell of a house that was being built in the rue d'Enfer until one of the neighbors had them arrested, fearing they would rob him.[53]

For young women who could not find work, particularly those from the provinces with no family in the capital, prostitution might be the only means of survival. It provided subsistence to somewhere around 10,000 to 15,000 young women, though was by no means the resort solely of poverty-stricken provincials: female wages were so low that a woman alone, worse still with small children, had trouble making ends meet. Every quarter therefore had its *filles du monde,* who despite police bans on renting to prostitutes had little trouble finding suitable rooms overlooking the street. Despite their worldly profession, like the beggars they were often accepted members of the neighborhood community. But here, as in other occupations, the unknown poor were likely to find a niche on the least lucrative and most exploitative fringes of the trade: in the streets adjoining the ports, with their cheap lodging houses and mobile population; around the Pont Neuf, the rue St-Denis, and the markets, and near the barracks of the French Guards. The risks of violence and abuse, of venereal disease, and of arrest were greatest for young women without contacts or protection.[54]

Everything we know about eighteenth-century conditions indicates that the numbers of the poor were growing, despite the fact that 1709 was the last great, kingdomwide subsistence crisis in France and that the following decades saw generally improving economic conditions. Across the century improved roads, faster vehicles, and more navigable rivers and canals reduced the likelihood of famine. Mortality rates gradually fell, the chances of survival improved for children, and life expectancy increased. After the setback of 1709 the population of the kingdom grew, at first slowly and then rapidly. In the Paris basin, the primary catchment for the city, it increased by 32 percent between 1750 and 1790.[55] Yet all this only increased the numbers of poor: as has often been said, in the seventeenth-century people died of hunger whereas in the eighteenth they just suffered from it. Even had the proportion of poor remained constant, there would have been more of them than ever before.

At the same time, the distance between the better-off and the impoverished multitude was widening. Even among wage earners the gap between those with something and those with nothing was greater at the end of the eighteenth century than at the beginning. Measured by the estates they left when they died, better-off workers were a third richer than at the start of the century, but the poorer ones were both more numerous and significantly poorer.[56]

Perhaps in part because of the growing distance between affluence and poverty in eighteenth-century Paris, attitudes toward the poor were gradually changing. Not among the mass of the Paris population: after all, at least a third of them could still say "There but for the grace of God go I." The presence of permanently large numbers of poor gave immediate resonance to biblical injunctions to "help thy neighbor." Yet at the same time it accentuated all-too-real terrors about what the morrow might bring and increased anger at any action by government or by individuals—especially speculation on food—that might upset the fragile household economy. None of this made people better disposed to the unknown poor, however genuine. The social horizons of most eighteenth-century Parisians remained limited and they felt little obligation to support outsiders. In the ordered, hierarchical world that most people held to as an ideal, the mysterious "vagabonds" who appeared, apparently from nowhere, were never welcome.

But the growing problem of poverty in eighteenth-century Paris was also a stimulus to new social and political ideologies that were to gain ground after 1750. Among the propertied classes, an organic conception of society—in which God had given the poor a necessary function—was slowly being abandoned. No longer would the poor be regarded as simply a fact of life: they were to become further evidence of urban corruption, of the sins of Babylon. "How could you expect," asked Louis-Sébastien Mercier rhetorically, "that with so many signal abuses, this city that is called *superb* could fail to be teeming with beggars?"[57] There was therefore to be more emphasis on distinguishing the "deserving" from the "undeserving" poor. Adding force to such sentiments was the fact that the old forms of poor relief were clearly inadequate: from there it was only a step to the conclusion that the system of charity and the urban environment itself were among the causes of the problem. The solution, therefore, was to change the system, to reorganize the city, to assist the honest poor, and to reform the rest—by coercion if necessary.

CHAPTER THREE

NOT SERVANTS BUT WORKERS

The trouble began early in August 1746, when the Parlement approved a decision of the locksmiths' corporation that required every worker to register at their corporation's central office. Furthermore, in future every man looking for work would have to present a certificate of good conduct signed by his previous employer. And he would have to give at least a week's notice before he could leave.[1]

The journeymen—those skilled workers who had completed their apprenticeship and were qualified to work under a master locksmith—reacted angrily. They accused the corporation of trying to take away "the freedom to work . . . for whoever they wished and at the price they wished to agree upon together." A number of the employers agreed: "his journeymen were neither servants nor lackeys, but workers," one asserted angrily.

A couple of weeks went by, and the men's anger grew as they discussed the new rules in workshops and wineshops. A group of them had a poster drawn up by a professional letter writer and pinned copies on the doors of the *jurés*—the officials of the corporation—and on the door of the church of St-Denis-de-la-Chartre (on the central Ile-de-la-Cité) where the masters had their confraternity. Two of the *jurés,* it read, "let themselves be led like asses" and another was a cuckold. The fourth—one Pierre Testard—received special treatment: not only was he too a cuckold, but "he would do better to assist his mother who was at the door of a church with a begging bowl." The insults hit their target: the neighbors gathered round the posters in great amusement and the *jurés* complained bitterly.

On 28 August, bands of locksmiths were seen making their way noisily through the Place des Victoires toward the city gates, decked in their Sunday finery. Some stopped to hear mass on the way; others did not bother. There was nothing unusual about any of this: on fine days in summer, working people often strolled out to the suburban taverns known as *guinguettes,* large rambling establishments with rows of wooden benches, room for dancing, and pleasant gardens with games of bowls. They clustered just outside the gates, where there was no city tax on wine or food, so their prices were lower.[2] But on this particular Sunday the locksmiths' outing had another purpose as well. Over the preceding few days many of them had been notified of a meeting in a particular *guinguette* called Le Roi d'Yvetot, in the part of the northeastern suburbs known as les Porcherons. The meeting was organized by the leaders of the journeyman's confraternity, most of whom were employed in one large workshop in the rue du Temple. Their names reflect the variety of their origins: Pierre Comte, better known as "Toulousain" or "la Balafre" (scarface); Antoine Chamonin, called "Piedmontais"; Royer, nicknamed "Touranjou" (from Touraine); and another man known only as "Avignon." They had decided to raise funds for a court action against the corporation's new ruling.

The meeting was chaotic. The numbers were too large for the one tavern, so they overflowed into an adjoining one. Toulousain la Balafre and eight or nine others sat at one table, some papers and a largish book in front of them. There was no order to the proceedings, and many of the men came and went, so no one could say exactly how many had attended. Nevertheless, there was general agreement that the new rules were unfair and by the end of the day Piedmontais had laboriously noted—mostly under the appropriate letter of the alphabet—the names of 345 journeymen, the majority of whom had handed over 12 sous. The leaders then engaged the services of a legal official, went through the corporation's ruling and the Parlement's ratification with him, and asked him to consult some lawyers on their behalf. This he did, returning with a three-page brief advising, in essence, that "without any masters at their head to undertake the case with them, they would not be listened to."

A number of the masters were sympathetic but none was prepared to be the first to sign. Facing an impasse, many of the journeymen grew impatient. A second meeting was held on 11 September in another *guinguette,* this time on the outskirts of the faubourg St-Antoine. About two hundred men attended and, against the better judgment of the more senior journeymen, decided to stop work. Several men were detailed to go round the more than three hundred locksmiths' shops to notify all the workers, and a number of them warned that anyone found breaking the strike would be beaten up. It seems the work stoppage was widespread. It lasted for three days, until the police arrested the leaders of the confraternity and the rest drifted back to work.

This was only one of dozens of strikes in eighteenth-century Paris. Historians used to see them as evidence of increasing class tension, a response to proletarianization and to the development of capitalist industry that threatened the work of "preindustrial" artisans. Conflict was assumed to be growing across the century, a precursor to revolution. But recent research has made this interpretation difficult to sustain. Steven Kaplan's writing has made baking the best-known trade, and there neither the techniques nor the organization of production changed significantly across the century. Yet the baking trade was as turbulent as any other, with six major industrial disputes between 1700 and 1750 and another five before 1789.[3]

In printing, however, the size of workshops increased significantly, though there was hardly any change in technology. The trade experienced seven major disputes between 1750 and 1789 and four in the first half of the century. The last of these disputes, in 1785–86, was over wage rates that the journeymen deemed inadequate at a time when prices were high. The very same issue had underlain a major dispute that racked the trade from 1720 to 1725. The other significant source of tension, sparking industrial action by printers in 1700, 1723, 1751, 1757, 1761, and 1777, was the employment of "unqualified" workers: those who had not completed a Paris apprenticeship. There is little evidence of growing class tensions here.[4]

Eighteenth-century industrial action was mainly to do with short-term fluctuations in wage rates and with recurrent issues of labor supply. A period of inflation following a financial crisis in 1718 produced a crop of demands for higher wages. Another outbreak occurred between 1746 and 1751, when there were disputes involving twenty-five different trades. There tended to be clusters of disputes associated with economic adjustment just after the end of major wars. They are not evidence of social crisis and have no direct connection with the Revolution.[5]

What they do reflect, though, is the complexity and the size of the urban labor market and of the Parisian economy. They also tell us quite a lot about social relationships and identities: during industrial disputes journeymen and masters put into words many of their ideas about work and about their place in Parisian society. They, and in some cases women in the skilled trades too, emerge as people proud of their independence, with a strong sense of their own rights and a willingness and ability to use a range of devices—including the law—to defend them.

THE CORPORATIONS

The corporate system was central to the Parisian labor market. Anywhere up to two thirds of the adult male population and a smaller proportion of the adult female population were grouped into over 120 officially recognized trades corporations, while another 16 or 17 trades had a guild structure but no legal standing. This number was reduced drastically in 1776 when many corporations were amalgamated to form 50 much larger bodies. Until then the majority of trades were only for men, while a handful—including the bakers, the starch makers, and the grain merchants—admitted women as well. A further half dozen or so were all-female. They included, at different times, the dressmakers, linen weavers, midwives, makers of floral bouquets, flax makers, women's hairdressers, and sellers of women's fashion clothes. Three of the women-only corporations were abolished in 1776 when all of the others were legally opened to both sexes.[6]

Alongside gender, the most crucial distinction within the trades was between those that both produced and sold their wares, and the ones whose members did no manual labor. At the peak of the pyramid were the great merchant guilds known as the Six Corps: the drapers, grocer-apothecaries, furriers, silk merchants, goldsmiths, and mercers. They were joined, through the amalgamations of 1776, by the hatters, wine merchants, gold beaters, ribbon makers, and manufacturers of luxury cloths. The mercers were described in the major business manual of the century, Jacques Savary des Brulons's *Dictionnaire universel de commerce,* as "the noblest and most excellent of all the merchant guilds, since those who belong to it do no manual labor"; and more pithily, as "sellers of everything, makers of nothing"![7] Their headquarters was a magnificent double-fronted stone house in the central rue Quincampoix, its elaborately carved facade dominated by a huge coat of arms: "no less superb," according to one description, "than that of the drapers," which lay a few streets distant.[8] Collectively, the Six Corps provided both the *juges-consuls* (the minor magistrates who heard commercial cases) and two of the *échevins* (aldermen)—the members of the municipality who in theory represented the trades. The latter office bestowed life nobility.

Next came the most educated and skilled craftsmen, the jewelers and clockmakers who clustered in and around the Place Dauphine; and the printers, concentrated near the university and among whom even the ordinary workers needed a smattering of Latin. Among the most prestigious trades too, strangely enough, were the wineshop keepers. Then came literally hundreds of others: saddlers, bakers, linen weavers, locksmiths, founders, painters, corset makers, and many, many more. Even the market gardeners scattered around the urban fringe, the roofers and other building trades who might have no fixed workplace, the Seine fishermen and the night-soil men had their corporations, their statutes, and their pride.

All the corporate trades were organized in roughly the same way. To become a rope maker, for example, Etienne Binet had to complete a four-year apprenticeship with a master, learning to make different types and strengths of rope as well as items like nets for fishing and hunting. At the end of this time he was allowed to work for any of the 130 registered master rope makers in Paris. After a certain time as a journeyman, gaining further experience in Paris or in the provinces and perhaps waiting for a vacancy, because the corporation only admitted a certain number of masters, he applied to become a master himself. He then had to demonstrate his skill by presenting a masterpiece, an often very elaborate and decorative example of his work, which was presented for examination to the *jurés* of the trade. If they were satisfied he was admitted as a master, subject to payment of an entrance fee of 180 livres and various "expenses" (which might include a donation to the hospital, legal fees, and sometimes a dinner for the twenty-four or so members of the corporation's governing body). Only then did he become a full member of the corporation, allowed to open his own shop in Paris and employ journeymen himself. He undertook to pay an annual fee to the corporation, allow its officials to inspect his premises, and abide by its rules, both about the quality of rope and about trade practices: deliberately undercutting other rope makers, for instance, was not allowed. He was expected to attend religious services organized by the corporation and the funerals of fellow masters.[9] The different corporations all operated in more or less this way, despite the disruption to the apprenticeship system created by the 1776 reorganization.

The corporations varied enormously in size. Only 36 printers were allowed to operate at any one time, because the government wanted to control the print media. The goldsmiths had around 300 members at the end of the Old Regime and allowed in newcomers only when there was a vacancy. The mercers were the largest of all, their numbers rising to over 3,000 in the 1770s—though that included both the sellers of objects d'art and the humble retailers of ribbons and baubles who trudged the streets with their wares on a tray suspended in front of them. At the other extreme were the two tiny corporations of dyers (with different specializations) with 9 and 14 members respectively. There were about 1,500 mistress dressmakers, nearly 2,000 tailors, about 300 hatters and 50 furriers in the first half of the century. Altogether Paris then contained around 35,000–40,000 masters and 3,000 mistresses overall, and their number probably grew slowly, with more rapid expansion after 1776.[10]

All the trades gave preference to sons of masters or daughters of mistresses, and many favored those who had trained in the city, sometimes insisting on four, five, or more years of work with Paris employers. The joining fees varied enormously: the more prestigious the trade, the more it cost. Where the rope makers demanded 180 livres and the cobblers 226, the official fee to become a bookseller or a mercer was 600 livres.[11] Apprenticeship costs varied in similar fashion, averaging around 540 livres with a mercer and close to 700 with a clockmaker. Again, less prestigious trades charged lower fees: to become a cabinetmaker required anywhere between 50 and 250 livres. But since the master did not always provide clothing or full board the apprentice needed family support, often for a long period: eight years for goldsmiths, six for engravers, joiners, and saddlers.[12]

It was worth paying, though. Joining a Paris corporation made a man or woman a member of an elite. Not only were there individual privileges, but the humblest trades corporation could petition ministers, undertake legal proceedings, and be represented at the Estates General (though none were allowed there in 1789, to the intense annoyance of the Paris trades). All the corporations had a proud sense of history and of rights, important possessions in a society in which status was linked to antiquity and to symbols. The possession of a corporate coat of arms, prominently displayed on each corporation's city center office, hinted at the nobility of the trade. Jacques-Louis Ménétra bore the arms of the glaziers' guild on his cane and on his watch.[13]

One of the most important features of the corporations, in a world that prized independence highly, was that they ran their own affairs. Although supervised by the police, they remained independent organizations, run by elected officials chosen by the masters from among their

Figure 8. Doorway to the office of the linen weavers' corporation. Original photo by P. Emouts, 1881. Bibliothèque historique de la ville de Paris, photo Jean-Christophe Doerr.

own number. Subject to final approval by the Parlement, their rules were determined by a meeting of all the masters or mistresses, or of their elected representatives if there were too many of them.

Being a master or mistress in a Paris corporation was a source of status and pride, though it carried different significance for men and women. For the mistress linen weavers, the corporation bestowed "a title, a public character." It gave them "their status of public merchant, recognized by the government." The linen weavers did not say so explicitly, but this meant the opportunity to run their own lives free from male control. Single and widowed women, who may have comprised up to 40 percent of mistresses in the female corporations, could make a living without (re-)marrying, while for married women the status of mistress allowed them to take court action, buy and sell property, and borrow money without their husbands' permission or knowledge.[14] These were rights most women did not enjoy.

Widows in other trades also possessed some of these rights, since most allowed them to keep running their former husbands' businesses. In 1764 widows ran a fifth of the tanneries along the greasy Bièvre River, in the faubourg St-Marcel; some of them had been in business alone for years. The starch makers counted a similar proportion of widows, while in printing widows owned between a fifth and a quarter of all print shops and some—like the widow d'Houry who for nearly twenty years printed the prestigious annual *Almanach royal*—ran very big businesses. We find widows running foundries, breweries, bakeries, saltpeter works, jewelers' shops, and wood-turning and barrel-making establishments. Nevertheless, most did not have quite the same rights as the masters—they usually could not take on apprentices or participate in deliberations of the corporation. If a widow remarried outside the trade, in most cases she lost the right to practice it—which may also help explain why so many did not remarry.[15]

For a man, too, corporate membership was very important. "The title of master flatters men more than people realize," the pewterers argued, when the government proposed abolishing the trade organizations in 1775.[16] But for a man it was also linked with family identity and with masculinity, since his responsibilities in the workshop and as head of household were inseparable in the social imagination of the day. Obtaining a master's certificate and setting up an independent business often coincided with marriage and the same word—*s'établir* (to become established)—applied to both. In apprenticeship contracts the role of employer was described as a paternal one, and when the guilds were temporarily abolished in 1776 their defenders warned that their disappearance would threaten the master's authority in the workshop and hence that of the father in his household.[17]

For women there was no such link between marriage and setting up in business, and no similar connection—in the social imagination of the day—between femininity and control of household and workshop. Yet a woman who became a mistress in her own right did acquire household power through having an independent income and a separate identity from her husband. A woman who married a master also changed both her personal and her public status. In day-to-day dealings she often adopted her husband's title, even though she was not legally entitled to it, and to the neighbors she became "la boulangère" or "l'épicière"—the (woman) baker; the (woman) grocer. In most trades she ran the shop and dealt with clients, kept the books, and often paid the journeymen. This role often gave her authority within both the shop and the household, as well as standing in the neighborhood. Such status extended to the children as well. Marie Baremont boasted that "she is the daughter of a master *rôtisseur* (keeper of a grill), whereas the said Usé is only a mere servant." Being the daughter of a master, even in a corporation of middling status like the *rôtisseurs,* was a source of pride and an important part of public and personal identity.[18]

This identity also had a significant religious dimension. In joining a particular trade, an individual became part of a spiritual as well as of an occupational community. Until 1776 every corporation had its own confraternity—the larger trades more than one—to which all the masters and mistresses paid a small annual fee. The trade rules often required members to attend its regular masses. The church in which the confraternity was based became a gathering-point for the trade—for the locksmiths, as we have seen, it was the tiny church of St-Denis-de-la-Chartre near Notre-Dame. It provided a point of contact even for wandering journeymen, implanting them in the urban environment and its community. Each trade, too, had a patron saint—Saint Clair for the lantern makers, Saint Laurent for the sellers of roasted meat (because he was martyred over a fire)—to whom all the members owed a particular devotion and who in return would watch over them. The saint's feast day was a festive occasion for all members of the corporation, marked by a special mass and usually by a banquet: a sharing of both holy and secular bread.

Membership of the confraternity imposed obligations to one's spiritual brothers and sisters. The statutes of the dressmakers' confraternity required all "to pray once each day for each other's needs, so as to be more perfectly united by these bonds of charity." They were also required to attend at the bedside when holy communion was carried to the sick and to go to the funerals of fellow members. These were often paid for by the confraternity, a real boon to poor families. Most confraternities also provided limited alms for sick masters and mistresses.[19]

In the second half of the 1700s the trades corporations came under increasing attack from enlightened thinkers, particularly from economists like Quesnay and Turgot who saw them as impediments to trade. They were accused of being cozy monopolies that prevented competition, wasting their energies in petty demarcation disputes, hindering innovation. There was an element of truth in all this, but the accusations came from a particular ideological viewpoint and should be seen for the political rhetoric they were. Only recently have historians begun to recognize this bias.[20]

In fact the Paris trades corporations were not uniformly hostile to innovation and were sometimes the driving force behind it. The cabinet-makers created new items like bedside tables and reading chairs, introduced new materials like tropical timbers and mother-of-pearl, and created many of the styles that made Paris the center of furniture production in the reign of Louis XV. In the clothing and accessories industries the *marchandes de modes* and the mercers played a key role in creating and disseminating new consumer products like porcelain, the fashions, and the furnishings that made Paris a by-word for luxury and elegance. Many small changes in materials and in ways of working helped increase productivity and were embraced by employers.[21]

In many cases guild officials turned a blind eye to technical breaches of the rules. The Dutch loom was introduced by the ribbon makers, despite official bans, while the glaziers—Jacques-Louis Ménétra among them—used forbidden Baccarat glass. Major button makers freely used cheap labor in the surrounding countryside. Despite the corporate hostility to merchants owning more than one retail outlet, wineshop keepers seem to have had no trouble placing agents (nominally independent masters) in shops they stocked and drew the profits from. And no one stopped Charles Raymond Granchez, the fashionable mercer, from illegally operating a chain of stores.[22]

In any case, the corporations were often helpless to prevent new practices. Many hundreds of artisans evaded their rules by working in one of the "privileged areas" of the city where the corporations' officials could not enter: the Temple in the city's north; the rue de l'Oursine in the faubourg St-Marcel to the southeast; or the entire faubourg St-Antoine. In these areas artisans could set up shop legally without joining the corporation. And although they were forbidden to sell their goods in other parts of Paris, in practice a great many did so: the comb makers complained in 1761 that there were thirty-eight shops in the faubourg St-Antoine that sold their wares all round the city.[23]

Furthermore, the government actively undermined the authority of the corporations when it saw an advantage in doing so. It maintained the privileged areas. After the 1750s, with the arrival in power of officials and ministers imbued with new ideas, government policy increasingly favored innovation and broke its own rules. The cotton industry, though technically illegal because it competed with established French linen and wool, flourished in Paris in the last decades of the century. Exemptions from guild rules and membership became easier to obtain. One way was to seek the title of *manufacture royale*—there were nearly thirty such establishments in Paris by the 1780s. The government also sold masterships to people not ordinarily able to join the guilds, the largest number in 1767 when the king announced that twelve would be made available in each corporation. Large numbers of newcomers entered the corporations after 1776 when the rules were changed.[24] In fact the authorities tried to have it both ways: to encourage innovation, while maintaining the system of privilege that facilitated control and that was in theory the basis for social and legal distinctions.

Yet the corporations were never as closed to outsiders as used to be thought. Only a third of nearly 350 new masters admitted to the locksmiths' corporation and of over 800 admitted to the bakers' guild in the middle decades of the century were sons of masters. Three quarters of new dressmakers and an even higher proportion of seamstresses were not daughters of mistresses.[25] Despite the accusations of nepotism and oligarchy, the system probably favored the Paris-bred rather than simply the sons and daughters of existing guild members. In practice corporate restrictions weighed most heavily on the poor and immigrant outsiders who worked illegally because they could not afford the mastership. They were constantly harassed by guild officials and the confiscation of their merchandise and few tools was a real disaster.[26]

There is probably some truth in the accusation that the innumerable court cases of the corporations took up valuable time and resources. The lieutenant general of police in 1775–76 estimated that legal fees cost over 400,000 livres a year. Yet the trades that used the courts most aggressively—the mercers and comb makers, for example—generally did so in order to open up new areas for their members rather than to restrict trade.[27]

The trades corporations were not declining in the eighteenth century, even in the years immediately before 1789. Most remained lively institutions that fulfilled a range of vitally important functions for their members. Officially they were there to protect standards, in the interest of consumers and of the trade's own reputation. They were also supposed to shield their members from unfair competition, whether from outside cheap labor, sometimes a major threat in bad years, or from powerful masters within the trade itself. And to some degree they did.

Yet there was little substance in the comforting image of apprentices taken under the wing of a fatherly master, graduating to the status of journeymen, then serving time before becoming masters in their turn. Important as this image was in corporate and gender ideologies, in reality the trades—like Parisian society as a whole—were riddled with divisions and tensions.

DIVISIONS WITHIN THE TRADES

Divisions between masters and journeymen were certainly the most obvious, sometimes over wages and conditions but just as often about rights and independence. In fact, the two issues often cannot be separated. When journeymen wheelwrights, carpenters, and furniture makers claimed the right to keep offcuts of wood, and roofers asserted their exclusive right to old slates and lead pipes, it was not just the economic value of the materials that mattered but the fact that only journeymen had a right to them—not casual laborers. These were also issues of status and respect, enshrined in customs that governed each aspect of work. "Only the journeymen," affirmed a plumber, "have the right to carry plumbers' hammers."[28]

Many disputes—like the one this chapter opened with, involving the locksmiths—were over control of labor.[29] Many sectors were seasonal: the building trades are the clearest example, slumping in the winter months and picking up in summer. The small scale of production also made the Paris trades very vulnerable to fluctuations in the economy and even in fashion. In the luxury trades—silver and gold, books, silk, and carriage making, to name just a few—the numbers of clients were small. Even in a major industry such as furnishing, a large order for a noble family's Paris residence might occupy a whole workshop of joiners and wood carvers for several weeks. But once the job was finished, there might be no more work for some time. To guarantee completion in a set time the employer would need to find extra workers but might not have the reserves to keep them on afterwards. Very often, therefore, employment contracts were for the duration of a particular task.

So many journeymen changed their place of work frequently. In furniture making the periods of employment were generally between three and six months; in tailoring from one to two weeks. The glazier Ménétra, before setting up his own business, changed employer six times in under two years. Even in sectors with less dramatic fluctuations many workers did not stay long. The grocers estimated that a third of their 1,500 shop boys changed shops each year, while the journeymen wig makers thought that most of the 18,000 employed in their industry moved three times a year.[30]

Each trade had its own employment networks. Journeymen visited former employers to see whether anything was coming up and asked in wineshops or lodging houses frequented by men in their trade. Les Trois Cuillères at La Courtille was a favorite watering place for journeymen bakers and so was a certain billiard room on the Quai de la Ferraille. In the early 1770s over sixty tailors lived in a lodging house in the rue des Arcis, so someone there always knew which employer had work. There was another inn for tailors toward the western end of the rue St-Honoré; lodging houses for wig makers in the rue St-Denis and the rue de la Vannerie; one for blacksmiths in the rue Jacinthe.[31] A cobbler could often find work through the merchants who sold shoemakers' tools. A few industries had regular places where masters could look for workers. Unemployed stonecutters, roofers, house painters, and masons congregated in the Place de Grève at dawn. Someone wanting a pastry cook could hire one in the rue de la Poterie.[32] Sometimes the journeymen themselves found jobs for newcomers. The officials of the pastry cooks' corporation complained in 1739 that a small number of journeymen spent all their time running an employment service, while the hatters accused the journeymen's confraternity of trying "to reduce the masters of the said trade to the necessity of taking whichever journeymen they chose to provide."[33]

Yet most individual workers looked for work for themselves: that way they could see the premises and negotiate directly with the employer. They particularly resented any centralized system run by the corporation as an infringement of their "liberty," an attempt to dictate to and even "enslave" them: these were the words they used. For Parisian journeymen "tyranny" had a very concrete meaning: it meant treating them like servants, as dependent and subservient beings rather than men.[34]

This sense of independent worth came partly from a pride in craft skills. Most journeymen owned their own tools and often did the same work as the master: both journeymen and master glaziers, for example, glazed windows and made lamps, working independently and seeing the task through from beginning to end. But the pride of journeymen was not just the possession of particular skills. Being an artisan was more than a job: it was an identity.

Work and independence were a vital part of what it was to be a man. Becoming an apprentice and then a journeyman were rites of passage that corresponded to life stages. An apprentice was no longer a child, though not fully adult either. He was (usually) living with the master, physically independent of parents but still in someone else's household.

Apprenticeship brought rights and responsibilities: to work hard and obey, but not to undertake demeaning domestic chores. "They should do nothing that is not of their trade," confirmed a manual of 1700, "such as washing the dishes, taking the children for walks, or caring for them."[35]

Subsequently becoming a journeyman, a qualified worker, meant an end to subservience, the freedom to choose and change employers. Simultaneously it meant being admitted to the fraternity of the workshop and its extension in the wineshop and elsewhere. Neither apprentices nor women were accepted in the drinking circles of journeymen. Sometimes, in fact, apprentices were treated almost as servants: according to the late seventeenth-century moralist Audigier, apprentices "should serve the journeymen well, and hand them what they need for their work, bring them food and drink . . . it is also they who make the beds of the journeymen." In print shops they brought drinks for the journeymen and fetched water to wash the ink off the movable type. Moving on from this stage meant growing up. The few firsthand accounts we have of journeymen's lives—by the glazier Ménétra and the printers Nicolas Contat and Restif de la Bretonne—make much of the carefree companionship of these years, a time of heavy drinking, fighting, whoring, and wandering, but above all of fraternal generosity. Even tinted by nostalgia, they reveal a world of exclusive masculine loyalties, within the workshop and beyond. Acceptance into this world symbolized becoming a man—it was more than a way of earning a living.[36]

As befitted men, with highly developed skills and intense pride in their status, journeymen often behaved as if they were totally independent. In some trades they had their own associations, modeled on those of the masters: though rarely *compagnonnages*—the famous societies of journeymen with their secret rites—that flourished in other parts of France and peaked in the early nineteenth century. These were of little significance in eighteenth-century Paris, and only on the eve of the Revolution did they appear in one or two trades.: "What the journeymen workers call *devoir* is not practiced in Paris," confirmed the city authorities of Bordeaux in the 1720s.[37] On the other hand, there were at least forty-seven journeymen's confraternities in thirty-six different Paris trades, some of them of very long standing: that of the *garçons rôtisseurs* dated from 1634, and the journeymen shoemakers claimed that their confraternity at Notre-Dame went back to 1379.[38] These bodies very often, as in the case of the locksmiths, provided the core organization required for industrial action, but they were above all expressions of independence from the masters.

Such associations had little relevance for women workers. While almost as numerous in the corporate trades as men, women did not usually express the same sense of rights. They often worked at home on piece rates, rather than in workshops: sixty-three of the sixty-six women employed by a major button maker, for example, took their work home.[39] Like many unskilled workers, therefore, they less often formed bonds in the workshop as most male artisans did, and they rarely displayed the commitment to the trade or the strong work identity of their male counterparts.

This distinction seems to have held true even in exclusively female workshops where the work done was highly skilled, perhaps because women who made dresses, linen, lace, and flax, and those who worked for embroiderers or marchandes de modes enjoyed far less freedom than their male peers: in principle to protect their morals. An agreement signed between two women lace makers "to form a partnership both for food and work and for the care and education of apprentices and boarders" provided for their workers to be taken to church and for walks and for one of the two employers to be present at all times.[40] Male workers did not suffer, and would not have tolerated, such restrictions. But for many young women the restrictions coincided with a phase of saving in anticipation of marriage. Once married, the vast majority would either work with their husbands, keep a shop or stall, or do piecework at home. So the discourse of the corporate trades was not theirs. In general, independence was part of the image and rhetoric of masculinity, not of femininity.

But although Paris journeymen spoke of themselves as free agents, they knew they were not. That is another reason why they were so sensitive to any infringement of their independence. Whatever their skills, they lacked the highly prized independence that went with running one's own business. There was always a potential tension in their relations with the masters: "they work for them," admitted the journeymen shoemakers in 1757, "but they are not the masters' valets."[41] Their ambiguous, even marginal status within the corporation sharpened disagreements over wages, over control of the labor market, or over rights. They shared in much of the life and culture of the trade but were not full members. Their work determined their identity but they did not control it or have a voice in the corporation. They were occasionally obliged to contribute to the corporation's confraternity yet were not full participants in what they sometimes called "the masters' confraternity." There was also an issue of masculinity, since full manhood was often equated—however unrealistically—with being head both of a household and a workshop. There were many married journeymen in Paris, but they belonged neither to the idealized fraternities of journeymen nor to the world of married masters.[42]

These ambiguities made journeymen particularly defensive of their rights and especially sensitive to being treated as less than men. However poorly paid a male artisan was, whatever his age or ability, he saw himself as a full member of society. "Is not the virtuous citizen always free, as long as he can dispose of himself and of the fruit of his labor, . . . never a form of slavery but an honest occupation which is the equal of any rank in the sense that he who works at it is dependent on no one but himself?"[43] In this convoluted passage André-Jacob Roubo, the son and grandson of journeymen joiners, was describing an aspiration rather than a reality. But it is how journeymen felt. Their sole desire, the saddlers stated in 1768, was "to avoid the tyranny and the slavery that they are threatened with."[44]

Even before the Enlightenment introduced the language of individual liberty and human rights, artisans spoke of their freedoms and rights and condemned "tyranny." As Michael Sonenscher has insisted, "artisans did not need to read Rousseau or form popular societies to learn about slavery and freedom, dependence and independence, natural rights and legal obligation."[45] Like the locksmiths, journeymen frequently took court action in defense of their rights, and they sometimes won. In 1767 two journeymen joiners successfully sued to recover wages owing to them, then again won their case after their employer and the corporation appealed to the Parlement. Their success produced a rash of similar cases. At least forty groups of journeymen took this sort of legal action between 1650 and 1789.[46]

But the division between masters and journeymen was not the only tension within the trades. It is the one we know most about because historians have seen in it the origins of nineteenth-century class conflict. Yet the masters were often deeply divided among themselves. Sometimes one group of masters took the side of their journeymen, as in the locksmiths' dispute. Corporate officials, anxious to influence the authorities in their favor, always tried to conceal this and to portray disputes as straightforward "insubordination" by their employees. In 1741 the officials of the dyers' corporation complained to the police that journeymen were assembling in the tiny chapel of St-Bon "on the pretext of a confraternity" but really to concert action against their employers. When the police raided the premises, however, they found not only journeymen but also seven masters around a table covered with jugs, wine glasses, and fragments of communion bread. A few years later, in a dispute in the hatmakers' trade, at least a dozen masters took the journeymen's side. Dissident master painters and decorators blocked efforts to establish a central employment register and 150 grocers (out of 1,100) tried to do the same in their corporation.[47] Rarely were the masters unanimous even in disputes over wages.

Naturally, different kinds of employers had divergent interests. In many trades there was a small core of wealthy masters and a larger periphery of small producers. Half of the 546 journeymen hatters in Paris in 1739 were employed by only 10 masters, the rest spread among another 50 masters. This was a larger gap than in most trades but sharp divisions between large and small employers were common. Those with large workshops and a high turnover were more likely to want an employment register to enable them to find workers quickly. They were also more likely to have disputes with their employees because, with large numbers of journeymen, they were often distant and authoritarian. Some employed foremen and had little contact with their workers.[48] But the master of a small workshop usually had only one or two employees. They sometimes lived with his family, worked closely together, and might form close personal ties. Jacques-Louis Ménétra's sister, much to his chagrin, married their father's journeyman. An eighty-year-old hatter whose one employee had been arrested pleaded for his release because the journeyman was "his sole support . . . a very good man . . . , faithful, and the only one who knew all his customers." The industrial disputes that shook the Paris trades frequently had little relevance to small employers.[49]

Although the divisions were not always between large employers and small, these were the most common because the wealthiest masters or mistresses had more influence in the corporation and often tried to operate it in their own interests. In 1775 a group of master papermakers spoke out against a new rule on apprentices that disadvantaged the smaller masters. They attacked the officials of their corporation and the other wealthy masters "who together control most of the production, jealous always to preserve their despotism within the corporation."[50] In the locksmiths' strike the masters who wanted stricter controls on journeymen were primarily the officials of the corporation and the large employers.

But it was not solely wealth that determined a person's place in the trade. It was also family. Sons of masters and daughters of mistresses were favored by corporate statutes: they served a shorter apprenticeship or no formal one at all and usually paid far less for the mastership. This encouraged the formation of trade dynasties, and the system of elections allowed them to consolidate their position. Until 1776 new officials were

Figure 9. Cauldron maker's workshop. Engraving by Jean Duplessi-Bertaux in *Ouvriers et métiers de Paris* (n.p., n.d.). Bibliothèque historique de la ville de Paris, photo Jean-Christophe Doerr.

(in principle) chosen in a meeting of past officials and a selection of well-established and more recent masters. In the huge shoemakers' corporation the statutes required the presence of twenty recently accepted masters and twenty older ones. But the fifty or so former officials, if they united, could combine to elect their own candidates.[51] This gave them a determining role in trade policy and enforcement.

Thus, among the tanners and leather dressers, a few interrelated lineages controlled the corporation. Similarly, the director of the book trade wrote in 1759 that "one cannot aspire to become a bookseller in Paris without belonging to one of the families who control this occupation, or without having married into them." Eleven families accounted for between a quarter and a third of the booksellers' officials between 1745 and 1775.[52] It was a common pattern. Brewers, starch makers, butchers, bakers, and grain merchants, furniture makers, silk merchants, drapers, glaziers, booksellers and printers, the Seine fishermen, and even the market gardeners all had their leading dynasties.

The masters in many corporations were thus divided not only between rich and poor but between entrenched dynasties and outsiders—those who had worked their way up or immigrants from the provinces. The journeymen were divided in similar ways. Sons of masters were often a group apart, virtually guaranteed promotion: among the printers there was often resentment of those "who were masters at the breast and for many even in the womb of their mother." The Paris-bred were also far more likely to become masters.[53]

There was also in many cases a division between settled men and those who moved around, often in practice a distinction between younger and older journeymen. When the locksmiths discussed going on strike in 1746 the *anciens* opposed the motion but the "young ones" retorted "that it was because they were in the best workshops" and outvoted them. Men who had been in the city for some time or who had married and settled down were often able to obtain the small number of permanent jobs, while newcomers moved from shop to shop. The little we know of journeymen's confraternities suggests that their officials were older, settled men.[54] The apparently simple hierarchy of apprentice, journeyman, and master conceals a far more complex structure, concentric circles of status and power in which age, family, and place of birth were just as important as skill and wealth.

All these divisions notwithstanding, the integrating social role of the corporations should not be overlooked. They provided an important mechanism of conciliation: the officials handled a great many conflicts both between masters and between employers and employees.[55] The corporations also accorded limited but valuable assistance to poor members. Above all, they provided a community and a collective identity which gave their members a clearly defined place in the big city.

In this sense trade complemented neighborhood, although in different ways for different groups within the population. A worker from the provinces, moving from shop to shop, had little sense of belonging to any particular neighborhood but might identify strongly with the trade. Widows running businesses had less stake in the corporation than masters or mistresses in their own right. Well-to-do masters who belonged to local dynasties and played a role in parish affairs were likely to identify, in different contexts, with parish, family, and corporation. For many workers, trade and neighborhood were both, in different ways, foundations of a sense of belonging. Yet corporate membership both complemented and transcended neighborhood. Masters and fellow workers owed one another loyalty against outsiders, and their centralized structure and citywide culture created an identity that was genuinely Parisian.

Despite the existence of similar institutions in many other places, the Paris corporations were distinctive in a number of ways. They gave their members significant rights that in most other parts of France were the monopoly of a much smaller elite.[56] In fact they brought over 40,000 Parisian masters and mistresses as close to citizenship as anyone came under the Old Regime. Even for journeymen the corporation provided an ambiguous legal status that enabled them to bring court cases and sometimes win. At the same time corporate government and even the defense of vested interest gave masters and mistresses a civic and political education of sorts, in which journeymen shared to a degree.[57] And—in the boom years of the mid to late eighteenth century—their prosperity made them participants in a burgeoning consumer culture that may have had its origins in noble extravagance but was beginning to change the lives and identities of nearly all Parisians.

CHAPTER FOUR

EACH ACCORDING TO HIS STATION

One of the best-known incidents in early-eighteenth-century Paris is the attack on Voltaire (born François Marie Arouet) by servants of the chevalier de Rohan. The precise details and even the date are not certain, though it was probably in late February 1726. Voltaire was a dinner guest of the duc de Sully. During the evening he was told someone wished to speak with him at the door and, when he went to see who it was, received a thorough beating from Rohan's servants, who set upon Voltaire the moment he appeared.[1]

The attack was retaliation for the response Voltaire had made to Rohan a few days earlier. Rohan had for the second time made a disparaging comment, in the young poet's hearing, about the name he had adopted: "Monsieur de Voltaire, Monsieur Arouet, what's your real name?" Rohan's remark was as much directed against the common bourgeois habit of adopting a noble-sounding name containing the particule *de* as it was a personal attack on the young wit who was being feted by the Paris nobility. Voltaire had replied something along the lines of "He did not bear a great name, but he honored the one he had." Rohan belonged to one of the greatest noble families in France and took this as a profound insult.

What initially incensed Voltaire was what he viewed as the cowardly use of servants to punish him. But he was equally annoyed by the refusal of the well-bred people he had begun to consider his friends to back him up when he sought restitution. The duc de Sully would not accompany him to the police to make a formal complaint. Others agreed that Rohan was in the wrong, but none would support any action against him. After all, some pointed out, Voltaire was only a poet, Rohan a nobleman. Many (like the baron de La Brède et de Montesquieu, also himself a philosophe) suggested that even though Rohan had acted badly, Voltaire had been impertinent. "An amusing tragedy" were the words the marquis d'Argenson used in his journal.[2] Voltaire never forgave them. Nor did he ever forget his subsequent stay in the Bastille, brought on by his efforts to force Rohan to a duel.

The episode demonstrates the social distance between noble and bourgeois. It was below Rohan's dignity personally to challenge the son of a notary, and he expressed his contempt by sending servants to do the job. The refusal of the police to take any action against Rohan, the reactions of other high-ranking people in Paris, their solidarity with a fellow nobleman even if he was in the wrong, similarly point to the unbridgeable gap between the two ranks.

THE NOBLE WORLD

We do not know how many nobles lived in Paris. Late-eighteenth-century estimates ranged from two to six thousand families. Modern authors suggest that they made up around 3 percent of the population, perhaps twenty thousand men, women, and children. This total includes a large number of army officers and clergy who were not necessarily living with their families.[3]

Although the Voltaire incident suggests solidarity against other ranks, nobles did not form a single group. Many families were ennobled for their service to the king or simply by the purchase of a position that bestowed hereditary nobility. Even the Paris public executioner Sanson was able to secure noble status for himself and his male descendants by paying out a large sum for the honorific office of *secrétaire du roi*. Beaumarchais, born Pierre-Auguste Caron and the son of a clockmaker, did the same.[4] Many new noble families had appeared in the late seventeenth and early eighteenth centuries, faithful servants of Louis XIV's expanding state apparatus or beneficiaries of the monarchy's financial difficulties and willingness to sell titles. In 1726 just under two-thirds of the *fermiers généraux*—those who ran the indirect tax system and who mostly lived in Paris—were nobles or were in the process of acquiring noble status. Most such families fairly rapidly acquired land, coats of arms, and other noble attributes and sought marriage alliances with older titled lineages. In most parts of France (though not all), nobility was conveyed in the male line, and there was no loss of status for young men who married the daughters of wealthy financiers.[5]

It is conventional to distinguish three main groups among the eighteenth-century French nobility: "sword," "robe," and "finance." The "sword" nobles belonged to ancient titled families with a military tradition. The "robe" nobles were those ennobled as a reward for illustrious administrative or legal service, many with generations of noble rank behind them. The third group comprised families whose noble status resulted from the purchase of an office—often purely ceremonial—that conferred hereditary nobility. There has been a lot of debate among historians about the relationships between these three groups, and sometimes they are depicted as socially distinct. It is certainly possible to find examples of military nobles like the duc de Saint-Simon who disparaged the "robe," and even more criticisms of jumped-up financiers who bought their way in.[6] Yet most families of magistrates in the Paris Parlement and many in the Châtelet courts, who would generally be classified as "robe" nobles, had in fact been ennobled in other ways. There was also a huge amount of social contact and intermarriage between noble families of all sorts, and in any case only a minority could trace their noble ancestry back for centuries. Families of all three types found places for their sons in the army and the Church, and in practice they are hard to tell apart. The three are better thought of as different occupational categories, having much in common but distinguished by aspects of their behavior and culture.

These internal differences extended to their relationships with other Parisians and with the city, particularly in the first half of the century. While military nobles were concentrated in the faubourg St-Germain, on the Left Bank in the area of the city closest to the court at Versailles, those of the robe were more to be found in the Marais and in the old city center. Those with a finance background were more likely to live in the faubourg St-Honoré, on the Right Bank. Robe families had judicial training and culture, and their occupations brought them into frequent contact with a wide range of people right across the city. Those with connections in finance were obviously likely to have extensive business ties. But whereas some families belonged clearly to one group, others crossed the boundaries repeatedly.[7]

In reality, these categories were no more important than certain other divisions within the nobility. A key one was between those who had been presented at court and those who had not: in 1752 the duc de Luynes, a keen observer of court etiquette, estimated that this honor gave exactly

306 ladies the right to offer condolences to the royal family after the death of Princess Henriette. Across the century, a thousand noble families were admitted at court and had the right to attend balls, royal receptions, and other events, a measure of a family's influence and a gateway to royal favor.[8] Yet among the court nobles there were many further distinctions. The dukes and peers of the realm were incontestably the leaders, while behind them came others distinguished by the offices they occupied, by the antiquity of their lineage, by their influence and connections, or by the precarious gift of royal favor. Fine gradations of rank were marked by privileges of all kinds, from tax exemptions to the right to wear a hat when others had to doff theirs.

There were also huge divergences in wealth among nobles living in Paris. First came the dukes and peers, some forty families with huge incomes. The duc d'Orléans enjoyed 2 million livres each year, while the prince de Conti spent nearly double that sum. Behind the dukes and peers came perhaps one hundred families with incomes between 50,000 and 200,000 or 300,000 livres a year.[9] These included many great military lineages, but some financier and magistrate families too.[10] Behind them again came the majority of nobles in Paris—three or four hundred more families with 10,000 to 50,000 livres a year—several hundred times what they would pay one of their servants. A few Parisian nobles were less wealthy still. The Lowendal family, with only 6,000 livres a year, could not afford to buy a house in Paris and instead rented one. Even so, they were richer than most of the wealthy merchants in the city and certainly considered themselves elevated by many degrees above any merchant, however affluent.[11]

The proud ancient families often spoke of their "race," a word carrying none of the negative connotations it has today but rather conveying a sense of inherited distinctiveness. Real nobility could not be bought or learned, they insisted. As in a good horse or hunting dog (both of them *animaux de race*) it was an inherent quality, though had to be cultivated by a noble education. A good upbringing, wrote Henri de Boulainvilliers early in the eighteenth century, could "render certain virtues hereditary."[12] This same discourse was to be found in the mouths of robe nobles like the magistrate Chassepot de Beaumont, who publicly boasted of the ability of his colleagues and of the "honor they have inherited from the nobility and virtue of their ancestors."[13] It was these qualities, nobles of all kinds believed, that justified their privileges, including preference in appointments to public office.

This claim to a monopoly of honor distinguished nobles, as a group, from other Parisians. It had nothing to do with moral behavior or Christian charity. Maintaining honor meant, first, refusing to do anything that might demean the family name: engaging in trade or manual work or accepting a job (like that of lawyer) that was inconsistent with the family's dignity; serving anyone other than the king or a noble of higher standing; allowing the family name to be besmirched. "When it is a question of maintaining your rank, present yourself with dignity, and never back away a single step," the young duc de La Trémoille was advised. Second, noble honor meant keeping one's word and behaving with probity toward one's peers. (Subordinates did not matter: a debt to a shopkeeper was of little consequence, whereas a gambling debt to a fellow officer was of the highest importance.) Noble honor was a guarantee of fidelity—to the king, to the lineage, and to one's calling, be it military or judicial. These were all things that could not automatically be assumed in a commoner.[14]

For males, noble honor remained closely associated with military values. Boys entered the army as officers at fifteen or sixteen, and if they had the right connections often commanded a regiment by their midtwenties. Riding, fencing, weaponry, and the habit of command were indispensable accomplishments. And although by the early eighteenth century those destined for other careers (in the Church or as magistrates and administrators) were receiving a much more intellectual education at one of the prestigious Paris boarding schools like the Collège d'Harcourt, the Collège de Clermont, and above all at the Jesuit-run Collège de Louis-le-Grand, they too learned riding and fencing and defended their honor in duels. In 1739 the young Monsieur d'Aligre, member of one of the leading robe families, fought and defeated d'Argenlieu, a noble lieutenant in the army. For robe and sword alike, both personal honor and that of the lineage (there was little distinction between the two) was a matter of arms.[15]

Noblewomen's accomplishments were of a different sort. "A woman has no personal ambition to satisfy," mused the duc de La Rochefoucauld. While this was certainly not always true, the conventional view was that a noblewoman's duty lay in defending the honor and advancing the interests of her family. When she married, often very early like Henriette de Fitz-James (at the age of thirteen), her duty was to create a suitable alliance. To do otherwise would have been dishonorable.[16] Once married, her task was to look to the suitable upbringing of her children (though not to undertake it herself), and to defend the interests of the lineage by using her influence and social skills in support of her husband, to find suitable positions and promotions for siblings, cousins, and later for her own descendants.[17] If she had a position at court she would be able to pull strings there. As the wife of a prominent nobleman, maintaining a social round that included the "right" people was an important part of her role. Madame Dupin, the wife of a financier with marriage connections to a number of magistrate families, was an active socialite whose midcentury visiting list has survived. It contains 223 names and includes people drawn from all types of Parisian nobles, though the largest number were women of the court nobility.[18] Quite a number of noblewomen—not only well-known figures like Madame de Tencin and Madame du Deffand—maintained regular salons, where invited guests met for conversation, readings of literary works, and sometimes meals. These too were a way of cementing relationships among the Paris elite, establishing them as arbiters of fashionable social interaction, important players in the world of patronage and influence. Such salons formed an important link between the court at Versailles and the city's polite society.[19]

The promotion of the family and its honor not only took different forms for men and women but also for older and younger sons. "The eldest must maintain the family name through his opulence and the younger sons must lend it brilliance through their noble virtues and their achievements," contended four young noblemen, scholars at the Louis-le-Grand school, in a public debate staged in 1722.[20] And that was precisely how a great many nobles behaved. "*Les grands* are so persuaded of the respect that display gives them in the eyes of their equals, that they do everything possible to maintain it," wrote the historiographer royal Charles Duclos in a widely read book published in 1751.[21] Early in the century the great nobles had hordes of servants, sometimes richly dressed, many of whom had little to do other than testify to their masters' rank. Audigier's book on household management, published in 1692, assumed that a great noble household would have between thirty and thirty-six servants. Most magistrates of the Parlement had about eight, and many less wealthy noble families between five and ten. It was rare for a bourgeois family to have more than four servants, and more common for them to have only one or two.[22]

Distinction was expressed through personal appearance, too. Noble men and women dressed differently from commoners, more flamboyantly, colorfully, and fashionably. The chevalier de La Barre, in 1711, owned a green silk waistcoat with purple satin lining, perhaps worn with his purple velvet breeches. He had an underwaistcoat made of green, purple, and white satin with gold trim. Depending on the weather and the occasion, he might don a pink coat or a heavier scarlet or purple cloak trimmed with gold.[23] Such flamboyance was not normally possible for magistrates, constrained by law and custom to wear black or gray when in Paris, but some of them made up for this restriction by choosing sumptuous silk, velvet, and woolen cloth or adding gold and silver trim. Some wore elegant wigs or distinctive perfumes. Their somberness was in any case balanced by the colorful costumes of their wives and daughters, who dressed just as richly as other noble ladies.[24] Notwithstanding the restrictions placed on them, the magistrates believed—wrote the Chancellor d'Aguesseau at the very start of the century—"that a brilliant appearance is the prerogative of public office." Display was one of the key markers of social power in eighteenth-century Paris.[25]

Other forms of ostentation were restricted only by price. Wealthy nobles had elaborately decorated carriages and rich furnishings. In 1709 the marquis de Barbezières had not only silver spoons and forks, but vases, gravy boats, saltshakers, numerous candlesticks, goblets, and even a teapot (a rare luxury item in a society that drank little tea). Expensive jewelry and tapestries were rare outside noble houses in the early part of the century. And unlike other social groups in early-eighteenth-century Paris, some noble families owned harpsichords, whose presence in the salon of their town house testified to the leisured accomplishments of the female members.[26] Indeed, the size and decoration of the entire house was a social statement. Many noble residences had grand sculpted doorways that proclaimed the wealth and power of the occupant to all who passed. Elaborate balconies, once a sign of noble rank, were becoming a bourgeois attribute, and noble houses renovated in the eighteenth century adopted instead a severe classical appearance that proclaimed elegance and taste. But the courtyard inside the carriage entrance continued to present the visitor with an imposing facade.[27] Gardens—an immense luxury in the overcrowded urban environment—became increasingly popular.

The maintenance of distinction through opulence was a responsibility for noble families, but outward concern about money was condemned as a bourgeois trait. Certainly some nobles, like the duc de Saulx-Tavanes, were extremely astute business managers, and many of them invested in industry and various commercial enterprises. Yet publicly they affected a disdain for trade and finance: "a kind of occupation that results in more

Figure 10. *La grande toilette.* Servants assist a nobleman to dress for a major ceremony. Note the luxurious decor. Engraving by Jean Michel Moreau, in *Monuments du costume physique* (Paris, n.d. [1775]). Bibliothèque historique de la ville de Paris, photo Jean-Christophe Doerr.

profit than glory," commented the noble *salonnière* Julie de Lespinasse.[28] The story is told that when Arthur de Dillon, an archbishop and a member of a great noble family, was asked sternly about his debts by the king, he replied that he would have to ask his estate manager. Noble contempt for commerce and industry, the archetypal urban activities, helped distance nobles from the merchants of Paris.[29]

Figure 11. Gateway of a noble house in the Faubourg St-Germain: 67 rue de Lille (author photo).

Figure 12. Garden of the Hôtel de Rohan: private space for the very rich in the heart of the city (author photo).

NOBLES AND THE CITY

Many Paris nobles had an ambiguous relationship with the city. They looked on themselves as quintessentially Parisians, in contrast to ignorant, uncultured provincials. They lived in the city because it was the capital, close to the court, and the place where they met other families of similar rank. Paris was the key social and cultural center and marriage market for nobles whose pretensions extended beyond their province of origin. Through the winter it offered opera and theater and was the center of the social round: the provinces in winter held only boredom. But over the summer months they would flee the city, eager for rural pleasures. The fermier général Claude-Adrien Helvétius, whose name is inseparable from the Parisian Enlightenment, actually spent eight months of the year on his country estate.[30]

Many nobles retained a psychological investment in their country estates that distinguished them from other Parisians. Wet-nursed in the country, they fraternized with the village children in a way they would never have been permitted to do with the city urchins. Like Charles Perrault, a courtier at Louis XIV's Versailles who produced the Mother

Goose stories in 1697, they remembered folk tales told by their peasant nannies. These same nannies accompanied them to their residences in Paris and Versailles, because noble parents generally preferred to entrust their children to servants from their provincial seat, believing them less venal and more reliable than city people.[31] During their stays in Paris, nobles kept a close connection with the countryside. They had their estate managers send produce from their estates. Madame de Bertier de Sauvigny even dispatched the laundry to be done on her country estate.[32]

For nobles of ancient lineage and those who wished to imitate them, land was a crucial element of the family identity. The illustrious ancestry (genuine or not!) that determined their rank was located in the province from which they came. The titles they bore were frequently taken from their estates, where their ancestors were interred. If, for practical reasons, those who died in Paris were buried in city churches, their hearts were sometimes removed and taken back to the estate.[33] For many males, too, hunting and riding were important pastimes. Their first horse and their first stag were key moments in their transition to manhood, and a passion for horses was a hallmark of young noblemen: their insistence on riding through city streets, often at high speed, was a constant source of tension with the people and government of the city alike.

Most noble families appear to have had little attachment to the parish or quarter in which they lived. Many were quite unsentimental about their town houses and changed them frequently: the Scépeaux de Beaupréau family moved six times over a forty-year period, and they were not unusual. Even nobles who owned hôtels in Paris were quite prepared to rent them out and live somewhere else.[34] There were some notable exceptions, particularly but not exclusively among magistrates whose ancestral and occupational base lay in the city: the Lamoignon and Le Peletier families kept up their residences in the Marais for generations. In their case, an important part of the family identity and power base was urban, and real estate in Paris made up a considerable proportion of their wealth.[35] Even for nobles with a provincial seat, though, the Paris residence could be the principal statement of their status, the place where they hosted brilliant soirées and showed off their finery. Once again, their relationship with the city was ambiguous: it was part of who they were, yet they never entirely belonged to it.

Without the nobility, though, Paris could not have functioned. They did much of the key work of government and administration. Most important, in practical terms, was the lieutenant general of police, who throughout the century was either of ancient noble stock (like the two members of the d'Argenson family who between them held the post for a quarter of the century) or a man recently ennobled. Other key figures too—the archbishop, the *prévôt des marchands* (head of the municipality), the governor of Paris (responsible for the military forces stationed in and around the city), and over six hundred magistrates in the Parlement and other leading courts—were all nobles. Many worked extremely hard: the Parlement regularly began sitting at seven or eight in the morning.[36] It was these or other noblemen who were given oversight of the postal services, the book trade, Paris taxes, the sale of offices, ecclesiastical affairs, royal forests and waterways, building permits, and a range of other matters. Not all of these were exclusive to Paris but the capital was a central part of each portfolio.[37] Certainly, most of the day-to-day work was done by subordinates, but policy was largely in the hands of these men. There were many nobles, too, whose private initiatives had a major impact on the lives of Parisians: an example is Claude-Humbert Piarron de Chamousset, founder of the *petite poste* (the city's internal postal service), who also established a small hospital and played a part in the creation of the Mont-de-Piété, the state-run pawnbroker.[38]

A further key role for Parisian nobles was that of patrons and protectors, without whom success in any area of city life was difficult to achieve. But the nature of noble patronage was changing dramatically. There had been a time, even in the second half of the seventeenth century, when a small group of nobles had been able to maintain a power base in Paris that was almost independent of the monarchy. In the late seventeenth century there remained nineteen seigneurial jurisdictions in Paris, mostly ecclesiastical but often in practice overseen by great nobles. The faubourg St-Germain was ruled by the abbey of St-Germain-des-Prés, with Louis de Bourbon-Condé, comte de Clermont, at its head. It passed its own bylaws, had its own court and sheriff, and its own prison. The priory of St-Martin, which had been headed by Cardinal Richelieu in the early seventeenth century and by one of the powerful Breteuil family in the late eighteenth, had a similar role in much of northcentral Paris.[39] These were almost cities within the city. By the eighteenth century they had lost most of their independence, but on occasions their rulers still flexed their muscles. At a stage when cotton was banned because of the competition it provided for the domestic linen industry, one of the first French cotton factories in France was set up in the early 1750s in the Arsenal, a small triangle of territory next to the Bastille controlled first by the duke and duchess of Maine and later by the comte d'Eu.[40] In 1765 the prince de Conti welcomed Jean-Jacques Rousseau to the safety of the

Temple, the largest of the privileged jurisdictions where the police and even the Parlement had no power. The comte de Clermont remained active in the powerful jurisdiction of the abbey of St-Germain-des-Prés.[41] The heads of some of the major religious houses of Paris also continued to play a key role in their locality: the workers of the faubourg St-Antoine repeatedly turned to the abbesses of St-Antoine for protection from guild inspections. The abbess of Montmartre—from 1761 to 1794 a member of the ducal Montmorency-Laval family—was powerful enough to have the legal boundary of Paris redrawn in 1786 in the interests of her abbey and of the inhabitants of Montmartre.[42]

Another older form of noble patronage continued to operate through the parishes. The prior of St-Martin named no fewer than six Paris curés, and the comte de Clermont, as honorary abbot of St-Germain-des-Prés, two. The abbé du Bec named the curé of the rich parish of St-Jean-de-Grève.[43] As the Paris curés were themselves powerful local figures, such an appointment was an important form of influence for noble patrons who cared to use it. So too was the position of first churchwarden, often reserved for a noble. At St-André-des-Arts, St-Séverin, and a number of other churches he was usually a magistrate.[44] At St-Jacques-du-Haut-Pas the first churchwarden for most of the 1730s was Louis François Maboul, marquis de Fort (a former magistrate who was also briefly administrator of the Paris book trade).[45] St-Nicolas-des-Champs succeeded in attracting as honorary churchwardens, along with a sprinkling of first presidents of the Parlement, a couple of counts, a marquis, and a member of the king's council.[46] Usually this was a purely ceremonial role, but a few nobles were very active, using their influence on behalf of the parish.

There were many less formal types of patronage, too. Wealthy nobles were regularly approached by people seeking assistance to obtain a job, a pension, or a contract, sometimes hoping to sell them something or to use their name to help launch a book or a new invention. Many artisans owed at least some of their success to noble patronage, like the future Madame Roland's father, engraver to the comte d'Artois. The government minister Jean-Baptiste Fleuriau d'Armenonville agreed to act as protector to the Magasin général, the first furniture emporium in France established in 1722, and he presumably assisted in getting the royal permission it needed. In 1703 the princesse de Conti insisted that a particular man be appointed organist at St-Merri.[47]

Nobles were major employers of valets, coachmen, stable boys, hairdressers, cooks, porters, secretaries and bookkeepers, musicians, tutors, governesses, and a host of others. They engaged huge numbers of artisans to maintain and refurbish their houses, repair their carriages, tailor their clothes, and make their wigs and ordered vast quantities of food for their households. The five immensely rich noble families whose spending has been analyzed by Natacha Coquery patronized no fewer than 1,116 Paris merchants, from pavers and roofers through to butchers and wood merchants. When the king sacked and exiled the magistrates of the Parlement in 1771 there were an exceptional 2,350 bankruptcies in Paris.[48] The economic weight of the nobility was enormous. Noble families also offered positions to professionals: architects and lawyers, doctors and surgeons, oculists and apothecaries. The philosophe Julien Offroy de La Mettrie was physician to the duc de Gramont, while the duc de Bouillon accommodated in his Paris residence a doctor and a surgeon, along with the secretary, treasurer, and manager (*intendant*) who ran, from a distance, the tiny principality of Bouillon (in present-day Belgium).[49]

New avenues for patronage opened up as social practices began to change. While noble society remained highly exclusive, providing introductions and welcoming newcomers to high society was a way of demonstrating benevolence while at the same time displaying the cosmopolitan taste that was becoming characteristic of sections of the Parisian nobility. The English writer Edward Gibbon, visiting in 1763, compared Paris favorably with London: once the original introduction has been made, "your new friends make it their pleasure to find you friends still newer. . . . In London one must learn to make one's way; houses are very difficult of access; a host thinks of himself as one who gives pleasure to an invited guest. Whereas a Parisian considers that the pleasure is his."[50] This welcome applied not only to foreigners, but to outsiders of other kinds. Celebrated men of letters, even those of humble social origins, were invited to some of the great houses. The presence at Madame de Tencin's salon of Fontenelle, son of a provincial lawyer, of the hatter's son Houdar de La Motte, or of Marivaux, whose father was a minor officeholder, was testimony to the talent and wit of these men but also to noble modishness. The now forgotten playwright Charles Palissot de Montenoy was a protégé of the princesse de Robecq, while the duchesse du Maine provided a venue and an audience for plays by Voltaire and others. Madame d'Epinay acted briefly as patron to Jean-Jacques Rousseau, helping him gain access to the society he yearned for and soon rejected.[51] And because these were powerful and well-connected people, the conversation could touch on topics that landed lesser mortals in the Bastille. The restricted but open sociability of Paris and the patronage of cultivated nobles made it the capital of the Enlightenment.

Nobles now rarely used patronage to build a personal following in the city. In the seventeenth century noble networks had often been a threat to public order, because the great families considered themselves and their servants to be exempt from laws administered by their social inferiors. In 1646 there was a riot by servants and noble friends of the comte de Roquelaure over a court decision that had gone against him, and such events were not uncommon.[52] Liveried servants were difficult to prosecute because their employers protected them. In the late seventeenth century, therefore, the police of Paris gave a very high priority to controlling nobles and their households, partly because of the recent experience of the Fronde, a revolt against the monarchy led by the great nobles.[53] By the eighteenth century, this had all changed. The nobles themselves had become part of the royal government, exercising authority—or intervening in an individual's favor—in the name of the king and not for the benefit of their own household.

The Paris nobility played a huge role as cultural consumers, creating a very significant market for literature, music, and art. Indeed, by the eighteenth century richly bound books were part of the image of power: they began to appear in the background of noble portraits, displacing the military accessories once dominant in such representations. Admittedly, it was mainly the robe and office-holding families who owned large numbers of books, while many of the military and court nobles had none at all. Yet already at the end of the seventeenth there were over a hundred sizeable noble libraries in Paris. Later came the huge library of the marquis de Paulmy d'Argenson—housed in the seventy-two rooms of his Paris residence—the basis of today's Bibliothèque de l'Arsenal. It, like the royal library and those of a number of monasteries, was open to the educated public. Book-owning nobles read above all history and literature, but many owned key works of the Enlightenment.[54] About a third of the members of the scientific and literary academies of the capital were nobles, and as authors they contributed directly to the Enlightenment: among those active in Paris in 1740s and 1750s were Jean Le Rond d'Alembert; Claude-Adrien Helvétius; Paul-Henri-Dietrich d'Holbach; Louis, chevalier de Jaucourt; and the brothers Gabriel Bonnot de Mably and Etienne Bonnot de Condillac—better known as the abbés Mably and Condillac, relatives of the *salonnière* Madame de Tencin.[55]

Yet the huge role that Paris nobles played in the city's administration, economy, and cultural life did not bring them closer to the mass of the population. Nor did the economic dependence of many Parisians on the nobility necessarily imply any particular bond or loyalty—on either side. The relationship between noble employers and servants was becoming less and less a personal relationship of mutual obligation than a commercial contract, service for payment.[56] From a noble's perspective, artisans and suppliers were social inferiors, to be dealt with by servants and house managers; one consulted in person only with the elite of architects, carriage makers, and fashion suppliers. The rapport nobles had with most of the Parisians they encountered was primarily commercial, and perhaps more so as the century went on: in the 1760s some suppliers began to charge interest on the duc de Tavanes's debts, and by the 1780s most were doing so. The sixty or more court cases launched in the later part of the century against the Fitz-James family and the forty or so against the La Trémoille family for nonpayment of debts testify both to the exasperation of their creditors and to the absence of a sense of mutual obligation or forms of reward that were other than pecuniary.[57]

In the eighteenth century, the nobles' way of life separated them from most of the capital's population. Where working people made maximum use of daylight, in high society the day began late. "In Paris," explains a character in an eighteenth-century novel, "ladies cannot be visited before midday, at the earliest." Theater began in the evening, followed by supper at nine or ten, then socializing, gambling, and other pleasures. In another novel a provincial noblewoman, Madame de Colbale, plunges into society, going every day to balls or the theater and not coming home before two or three in the morning.[58] Noble society in Paris kept very late hours, another form of ostentatious consumption, since it meant burning huge numbers of candles in an age where light was a great luxury.[59] Not all nobles gambled or kept such late hours, but the aristocratic taste for theater and opera, and the association of these with actresses and sexual diversions gave Paris much of its reputation as a capital of pleasure and vice.

Nobles used urban space differently than other Parisians. Within the city their palaces, gardens, and town houses were the key meeting places, not only for visiting but for balls, theater, and concert. There was also the opera, in the Palais-Royal, the location not only of theatrical performances but also of notoriously gallant balls, held three times a week in winter. Many nobles had private boxes in both of the official theaters—the Comédie-Française (now the Odéon) and the Comédie-Italienne.[60] The fashionable promenading places varied, but the Tuileries gardens and the Palais-Royal were regular haunts for some, the gates guarded to

Figure 13. Home from the ball. Engraving by Jacques-Firmin Beauvarlet, *Le retour du bal* [ca. 1750], from the painting by Jean-François de Troy. BN, Coll. Hennin 8680. Photo Bibliothèque nationale de France.

exclude the common herd. Nobles rarely went shopping: suppliers came to them. When they had to move around the city they went by carriage or in a litter carried by servants; the men sometimes on horseback.

In the first half of the century, almost the only socially promiscuous places were the annual fairs; in the latter half, the Palais-Royal and the

Figure 14. The Tuileries garden. Well-dressed people were allowed to promenade in the garden of the Tuileries palace. Reinier Vinkelès, *Le suisse du Pont Tournant,* BN, Coll. Destailleur 1306. Photo Bibliothèque nationale de France.

northern boulevards, though historians are divided on how much social mixing there was in these places.[61] Even in the churches, most noble families had their own pews at the front of the church or in a screened side chapel. While there was much contact with employees, artisans, and suppliers, and with various kinds of clients and supplicants, none of this was casual contact on a familiar basis. Indeed, one function of servants, carriages, large houses, and private gardens was to create a distance that helped maintain hierarchy.[62]

This had not always been the case. It had once been perfectly acceptable for senior magistrates, for example, to ride a mule or even to go on foot: Barnabé Brisson, first president of the Parlement in 1591, was in the habit of walking to the court each morning, passing through the busy market called the Marché Neuf. Men like Brisson were well known in their quarter.[63] But by the eighteenth century most nobles were distant

Figure 15. Hôtel of the duc du Châtelet, 127 rue de Grenelle (1770). Built for the son of Voltaire's companion, Mme du Châtelet. Typical of the new noble residences in the faubourg St-Germain, with no shops in the facade, and designed for people who went everywhere by carriage (author photo).

Figure 16. Garden side of the duc du Châtelet's residence (author photo).

figures, glimpsed when their carriage or horse went past, perhaps known by sight to people in their immediate vicinity but with little or no personal following. This distance was accentuated during the century as more noble families moved from the crowded center out toward the west and the north where they could build large hôtels with extensive gardens: at St-Gervais in the 1760s, complained the curé, "you will see neither Prince nor Chancellor, no Dukes or Peers, no Maréchaux de France, Intendants des finances, or Fermiers généraux, such as once were to be seen there."[64]

In a variety of ways, the nobles' relationship to the city was rapidly changing, even while they continued to dominate it socially and economically and to control its administration. Without them, it would not have been Paris: more than any other section of the population, they made it the new Babylon, renowned throughout Europe for fashionable luxury, spendthrift magnificence, and a relaxed moral code. The city in turn set its mark upon them, celebrating wit and elegance, offering an unsurpassed cultural and artistic environment. Yet the Parisian nobility had a more ambiguous relationship with the city and its inhabitants than did the patriciate of other European cities. They were members of a national elite, with family ramifications and networks of influence extending well beyond the city and sometimes beyond the frontiers of the kingdom. Many had courtly, military, and administrative functions that required them to leave the city for long periods. Some were more attached to their provincial estates. And even when they were in Paris, many had little contact and little rapport with the rest of the population: "the people . . . sees them without approaching them," wrote Charles Duclos.[65] Even those with a Paris ancestry played little role in the parishes and quarters, leaving the bourgeois to take their place.

BOURGEOIS DE PARIS

Like nobility, "bourgeois" status was legally defined. According to Paris customary law, to become a *bourgeois de Paris* a man had to have lived there for a year and a day, and to make the city his principal residence. He had to own property there, pay taxes in person, and have no direct involvement in agriculture. As a *bourgeois de Paris* he received exemptions from various taxes and obligations that fell on the rest of the population, could seize the property of people from outside Paris who owed him money, and could insist on trial in the city if he were arrested elsewhere. He enjoyed rights (such as the privilege of a crested escutcheon) that set him and his family apart. In a world in which titles and even small marks of distinction were highly prized, the title of "bourgeois" was borne with pride, even by men like the notary Delarue, who "belonged to one of the first families among the Paris bourgeoisie and was even ennobled."[66]

But by the early eighteenth century the pure legal meaning of the title was slowly fading. In everyday usage, "bourgeois" increasingly referred to someone who was not a noble but who lived from investments or rent rather than trade or manual work. By midcentury all sorts of people were calling themselves "bourgeois de Paris" or simply "bourgeois": retired servants, merchants, and artisans. They chose the title because it implied status without any particular occupational connotation.[67]

In everyday language the term was even vaguer, though it always retained the sense of being established in the city. In 1720, the diary of an employee of the royal library tells us, a squad of soldiers was employed to round up vagabonds but forbidden to arrest any "bourgeois."[68] Journeymen and servants often used the term, in both masculine and feminine forms, to refer to their employer: "mon bourgeois," "ma bourgeoise."

Despite the ambiguity of the word, there were people it clearly excluded. The high nobility were not bourgeois, although it was possible to be a noble and still qualify as a *bourgeois de Paris.* The term also excluded anyone who was not deemed prosperous and educated enough to be independent: journeymen, servants, laborers.[69] In social terms, as opposed to legal definitions, the bourgeois of Paris were those who in England were commonly called "the middling sort." If rents are taken as a guide, by the 1780s there were around 25,000 Parisian households in the middle income range, around 14 percent of the city's population. Earlier in the century the percentage was probably a little lower.[70]

Nevertheless, the bourgeois of Paris should not be seen as a single class. In particular, a distinction must be made between professional and commercial bourgeois. The first group included lawyers, doctors, architects, writers, students, engineers, and a wide variety of administrators and officeholders. In the 1760s the abbé Expilly estimated the number of lawyers, clerks, and officials of various kinds attached to the different legal jurisdictions of Paris at around 3,300. Around 2,000 men served in the central administration at Paris and Versailles, and there were a few hundred professors, doctors, and teachers attached to the university, with perhaps 1,500 students.[71] All these groups were distinguished by their education. Lawyers and doctors took a master of arts degree consisting mainly of the study of Latin authors, followed by a smattering of Greek philosophy.[72] Legal clerks and surgeons, however, had a more ambiguous status, because most of them did an apprenticeship rather than a university degree: the surgeons were therefore looked down on by physicians.

The commercial bourgeois were even more diverse, including merchants and master artisans of many sorts, with a wider range of incomes than the professionals. The assets of merchant and shopkeeper couples who married in 1749 ranged from 1,000 to 100,000 livres. At one extreme was a man like the furrier Pierre Goblet, who lived in almost noble luxury, renting an entire house in which he, his two children, and two servants occupied nine rooms. Yet in the same guild were modest shopkeepers who ran small businesses from rented premises.[73]

The professional and commercial middle classes were also differentiated by dress. Professionals did not spend heavily on clothing and the men wore mainly black. Merchants tended to dress more richly though still conservatively, perhaps because in business a man should appear prosperous but sober. There was possibly a social imperative, too: whereas the professional bourgeois possessed a cultural capital that elevated them above the plebs, the prosperous artisan and shopkeeper were distinguished from their employees by wealth and station. Clothing, jewelry, and other trappings of affluence were thus more important to them. Yet in both groups, the women dressed more richly than the men: what Daniel Roche has called the "shop-window effect"—women showing off family wealth while the men dressed more soberly—was becoming apparent among all types of Paris bourgeois.[74]

The bourgeois families of Paris were scattered across the city and divided by occupation, appearance, and level as well as source of income. Yet several things did unite them. One was the political and social power bestowed by elected office. Within the trades corporations the commercial middle classes reigned uncontested, while lawyers, merchants, and to a lesser extent their wives shared effective power in the parishes. They looked after the finances of the churches, distributed much of the poor relief available, and dispensed patronage within the parish. They were to use this power very effectively in the political struggles of the 1720s–60s, as we shall see later. It was merchants, lawyers, and minor officeholders, too, who controlled most of the parish confraternities. The position of administrator of a confraternity, while a step down from that of churchwarden, was a source of prestige and authority both for the individual (usually a man, but sometimes a woman) and for the family.

The same occupational groups monopolized the few areas of local government that remained open to the citizenry in an increasingly bureaucratized monarchy. They dominated the meetings held to divide up taxes for streetlighting and maintenance; those which oversaw the policing of the Bièvre River (in southeastern Paris)—including the allocation of taxes for river maintenance—and the administration of the annual fairs of St-Germain, St-Laurent, and St-Ovide.[75] The city council, though its role was primarily ceremonial, was largely bourgeois in composition, and so was the administration of the Hôpital général: half of its administrators between 1700 and 1750 were Jansenist barristers![76]

The bourgeois inhabitants of Paris were also united by a distinctive culture that placed considerable emphasis on work and thrift, the bases of bourgeois wealth. The wife of a master wig maker had her son locked up for repeatedly refusing to work, while the two teenage granddaughters of a respectable manufacturer suffered a similar fate: theirs was, he asserted, "an age to be feared when one has been set a bad example."[77] Not only was the work ethic strongly implanted in children, but even among prosperous merchants retirement in old age remained unusual.

Another plank of early- to mid-eighteenth-century Parisian bourgeois culture was religion. Theirs was a Jansenist-influenced faith that stressed the universality of human sinfulness, the importance of individual conscience, and hence the need for true repentance, piety, and charity. Believing in the necessity of divine grace, Jansenist theologians argued that external observance was not enough, and that God's Elect would come from the godly of all classes in society. They offered a vision of the universal church in which all were spiritually equal and in which both laity and ordinary clergy should play a key role—not solely the bishops and cardinals. Far stronger in Paris than in many other parts of France, Jansenism took root there in the late seventeenth century largely through the influence of the local parish clergy and of a number of key religious orders, particularly teaching orders like the Oratoriens (who ran the main seminary in the diocese). The Paris middle classes rapidly came into contact with Jansenism through the parish clergy. Their children attended schools run by Jansenist-leaning priests, many of whom were in any case drawn from Paris merchant families: men like Jean Lamoureux, a member of an extensive clan of gold beaters in the parish of St-Nicolas-des-Champs.[78]

But the influence may also have worked the other way round. It could be that many priests were predisposed toward Jansenism by their family background and inherited religious culture. There were strong reasons why Jansenism might have appealed to the professional and merchant classes. It offered them salvation on equal terms with their social superiors and stressed values that were consistent with the early-eighteenth-century bourgeois way of life. It condemned the ostentation and impiety of the rich and placed enormous weight on charity: and it was after all the local lawyers and merchants who dispensed parish charity in Paris. In their wills they included donations to the needy and dowries for poor girls, paid for hospital beds for the poor of their parish, and founded free schools. Some Jansenist-leaning clergy deliberately increased the role of the local notables in church affairs, according recognition and honors to those willing to give time to the parish.[79]

Bourgeois women too had a far more significant role in early-eighteenth-century Jansenism than in mainstream Catholicism. The curé of Asnières permitted "a kind of deaconess" to read the gospel at services. But it was particularly in the administration of poor relief that bourgeois women shared power. This was by no means confined to Jansenist parishes, yet one of the first actions of the Jansenist churchwardens of St-Nicolas-des-Champs after their hostile curé was exiled in 1759 was to remove the poor funds from clerical control and share them between the men's and a women's charity committees.[80] At St-André-des-Arts or at St-Gervais a woman (the *trésorière*) was in charge of all the poor relief monies. She therefore had great influence in the parish, working closely with the curé. The *trésorière* at St-Jacques-du-Haut-Pas was also on the board of the parish hospice, later to become the Hôpital Cochin.[81] In all the Paris parishes, men and women of middling rank, hungry for recognition in a world dominated by nobles and magistrates, assumed positions of honor and authority that distinguished them from the common herd, serving as churchwardens, administrators of confraternities, and distributors of poor relief.

Bourgeois circles, like many other groups in customary Paris, were characterized by high levels of intermarriage: there were probably more marriages between bourgeois residents in a single parish or quarter than within any other section of the population. Occupational continuity was also marked. Of Paris barristers admitted to the bar between 1661 and 1715, 66 percent were sons of legal officers, and there were recurrent complaints—as in the trades corporations—that certain families largely controlled the profession.[82] The elite of bourgeois society centered on a small number of wealthy and ancient interconnected lineages concentrated mainly in the central quarters on the Right Bank—the Nau, Brochant, Quatremère, Santeul, Geoffroy families, and a few others, while among the Paris aldermen at least 70 percent of those whose connections can be traced were related to one or more of the others.[83] The elevated status of these families came partly from their wealth and ancestry but was inseparable from their occupations: they were primarily associated with the prestigious merchant guilds, and hence they frequently provided judges of the commercial court and members of the Paris city council.

A particular commitment to the city (and within it to the parish or quarter) distinguished the bourgeois from most nobles. They involved themselves in local administration, through the now largely ceremonial offices of *quartinier* and *dizainier* and within the parishes. And they invested in real estate: while only around 14 percent of Parisians owned the houses they lived in, 43 percent of those were professionals or merchants; and another 30 percent were master artisans and shopkeepers.[84] This was more than a commercial investment. Close ties to the soil are often regarded as a peasant characteristic, yet many bourgeois in early modern Paris demonstrated a strong emotional attachment to family real estate—their patrimony. Houses were passed down, sometimes for generations, and were given names that had family significance. Some time before 1638, Joseph Prévost and his wife built themselves a house in the rue du Fer-à-Moulin and gave it the name of his patron saint, "Saint-Joseph." In the 1790s it was owned by a female descendant and still kept its original name. By contrast, the "St-Louis" house in the neighboring rue Censier retained its name only until it left the Michelin family in 1759: it was then rebaptized by its new owners.[85] The Paris-born children of house owners and even of shopkeepers grew up in a world in which the very walls of the city bore reminders of their ancestry and bourgeois status.

Even great bourgeois families who could aspire to noble status displayed a marked preference for urban real estate. After 1706 the position of alderman conferred nobility, opening a ready path to social promotion for the city elite. Yet only a tiny proportion of aldermen bought noble estates, although most could have afforded to do so. Instead they, like other bourgeois, invested primarily in houses within the city.[86]

HIERARCHY AND MOBILITY

Throughout the first half of the eighteenth century, Paris was a society in which people knew their place. Hierarchy remained strong and most individuals expected to remain in the social group into which they had been born. While young men and women came in large numbers to make their fortune in the big city, few people really anticipated rapid social promotion. Their ambition was usually to maintain the rank they had inherited, and at all levels of society people took pride in their respectability and their trade skills. They expected, furthermore, that others would recognize their standing and accord them the rights and privileges that matched their social position: "Man is always desirous of signs of honor, and it is fair to accord to each, according to his station, some small prerogatives," wrote two master artisans in the late 1720s.[87] The nobility, while they would have scoffed at the idea of artisans having any claim to honor, wholeheartedly agreed that birth should determine rights. They rejected utterly the notion of equality before the law. "The first rule of justice," asserted one noble magistrate early in the eighteenth century, was "to render to his client the preference and the honor to which the virtue of his ancestors, the rank he holds in the world, or his personal merit entitle him."[88] Such views remained widespread in some circles throughout the century, and everyone agreed on the necessity of hierarchy. The abbé Grivel, who ran a boarding school in the faubourg St-Antoine, was expressing the dominant attitude when he wrote around 1780 that "the letters one addresses to one's superiors must always be very respectful; those one addresses to one's equals should be *honnête* and always convey marks of consideration and respect. As for those one writes to one's inferiors, one should always give them evidence of affection and kindness."[89]

This view of society was reflected in what Daniel Roche has termed the "hierarchy of appearances." Most people, in the Paris of 1700, dressed according to their station: nobles richly, ostentatiously, colorfully, while the middling sort were identifiable by their choice of quality cloth and discreet ornamentation. Occupation also determined appearance: the clergy wore robes that reflected their status in the Church; magistrates and lawyers chose somber clothes, and artisans, shop assistants, and fishwives wore aprons appropriate to their work. The hierarchy of appearances was a complex semiotic code in which external display matched rank rather than simply wealth.[90]

Public behavior, furthermore, was heavily determined by this code. In Paris, where it was common to meet individuals whose identity and position were unknown, people of all ranks judged by appearance. This situation provoked a fierce debate on luxury. Still in the late 1770s, the writers of a popular dictionary condemned "the ridiculous desire to appear more than one is, by making oneself equal, in external appearance, to those who are of a condition superior to our own."[91]

But already by 1700 the old hierarchy of appearances was beginning to fray. In a city with a population of several hundred thousand, outside one's own quarter or occupation it was relatively easy to put on airs, to dress and behave above one's station. Certain social groups were particularly tempted by the lures of elegance—servants, journeymen, some merchants, and women more than men. What constrained them was the social commentary of those who did know them, because dressing above one's station attracted both envy and mockery. It might even provoke arrest: the police frequently arrested non-nobles who wore swords and were highly suspicious of anyone who appeared to be what they were not (they used a particularly heavy hand against any gender cross-dressing). But an appearance below one's station was equally unwise: it would attract contempt and might be taken as an indication of imminent bankruptcy. Despite contemporary anxiety about "the confusion of ranks," for most of the century Parisians were what they wore.[92]

Paradoxically, despite this observance of custom in dress, social mobility was high. Yet it occurred in ways that made possible the maintenance of myths about social stability. Individual ascent from poverty to riches was extremely rare, and such individuals were generally regarded as upstarts. Beaumarchais, who went from clockmaker to noble in only a few years, was feted for his wit and his plays but never fully accepted in noble society. Most upward mobility took place more slowly, over two or more generations, at the blurred edges of established status groups. Thus the sons and daughters of financiers bought ennobling offices and estates and brought their children up in noble style. Historians have focused most on the noble-bourgeois divide, which has been seen as central to understanding social change before the French Revolution, and their work has revealed that across the century several thousand French families at least made the jump to noble status. There were probably more after 1760 than before, but even in the early eighteenth century the most exclusive caste in the kingdom was absorbing large numbers of newcomers.[93] Similar movement was taking place at all levels of society. Provincials were buying Parisian masterships and offices and making their way slowly into the bourgeoisie. Lesser families married into greater ones and gradually, over two or three generations, won acceptance in their own right. Others, of course, died out or went bankrupt and lost their standing, particularly in the aftermath of the crisis in the early 1720s when thousands lost everything and others got rich overnight as a result of John Law's investment schemes.[94]

But another type of mobility was taking place at the same time, as not just individual families but entire groups underwent social promotion. A well-documented example is the Paris surgeons, who struggled for decades to distinguish themselves from the barbers' corporation (both being experts with a razor!). In 1731 they founded their own society, which in 1748 became the Académie de chirurgie (academy of surgery). After 1743 a university degree was required for all master surgeons.[95]

They were not alone. The status of others who were becoming "professionals" was also rising. The Paris barristers worked hard to win public respect, creating their own association that set standards, and already by the early 1730s the Paris law faculty was attracting a provincial elite who might once have studied locally. Similar developments took place, a little later, in the training and standing of engineers, pharmacists, dentists, and veterinarians.[96] Writers had no formal structure, but by the second half of the century their standing was certainly higher than their incomes. Some, even those of plebeian birth, would be accepted into high society: the tailor's son Marmontel would rub elbows with the rich and powerful in Madame Geoffrin's salon. The cutler's son Denis Diderot, the printing worker Edme Restif de la Bretonne, and Louis-Sébastien Mercier, born into a swordsmith's family in central Paris, became household names. The growing incomes and prestige of notaries, auctioneers, stockbrokers, and legal officers of all kinds are suggested by dramatic rises in the value of their offices.[97]

Customary Paris was far from static. A huge amount of internal movement was taking place, for families and for particular occupational groups. Still, most people continued to speak as if there should be none. In social and political discourse, birth and lineage remained the basis of rank, and subordination and hierarchy won lip-service as the key principles of social order. Only later in the century would overt challenges disturb them, and only a revolution would eventually sweep them away altogether.

PART II

CITY GOVERNMENT AND POPULAR DISCONTENT

CHAPTER FIVE

BREAD, POLICE, AND PROTEST

At around midday on 23 June 1725, the commissaire Labbé was informed that a crowd was pillaging the shop of the baker Charier in the faubourg St-Antoine. On arrival at the scene he found the baker's wife standing amid the ruins of her shop, her hair disheveled and her clothing torn. The shop boy, who had tried to hold off the rioters, was bloody and dazed. An angry mob was still in the street outside, threatening to attack other bakers and accusing them of lifting the price of bread and making excessive profits. The 4-lb loaf had risen overnight from 12 to 14 sous (the usual price was 8). Labbé immediately sent for the soldiers of the watch and together with several of the shopkeepers in the street tried to calm the people, keeping them talking until eighteen or twenty soldiers arrived. The crowd then dispersed sullenly and, after making a short promenade through the neighborhood to ensure that all was calm, the commissaire and the watch went back to their usual duties.[1]

But this was not the end. Two weeks later, at two in the afternoon, Labbé was summoned to another bakery in the main street of the faubourg. This time he took six guardsmen with him and was in time to see the crowd still milling around the shop, carrying away pieces of wood from what had been the counter. The widow Chaudron, who owned the shop, was away but her shop boy was bleeding from a head wound, all the bread from the three or four bakings of the morning had been taken, and the windows and furniture had been deliberately smashed. The plates, cooking pots, and about four dozen napkins had disappeared from the kitchen and even the scales had been stolen from the shop. The commissaire and his men managed to arrest two looters and took them off to his residence some distance away. Having hastily scribbled a note requesting reinforcements, he returned to the faubourg St-Antoine where the enraged crowd was now attacking other bakers' shops. All the shopkeepers were closing their shutters as fast as they could. The parish priest of Ste-Marguerite, a man much respected in the area, emerged from the side street leading to the church and tried to pacify the people, but they went on shouting that the bakers were all villains, preying on those with no work and no money to buy bread. When the commissaire reappeared with his little troop of soldiers he was at first ignored. But he had not gone far along the street before he was surrounded by a hostile crowd demanding the release of those arrested earlier. Shaking their fists in his face and seizing his arm, angry people warned that his last hour had come if he did not let his captives go. At that moment several local merchants or shopkeepers intervened, pushing through the crowd and escorting the commissaire and his little band of men into a nearby house. Almost immediately the crowd returned to the attack, threatening to burn the house down. The soldiers fired several shots over their heads but were eventually forced to release a third young man they had arrested. At last mounted soldiers arrived at a gallop and the crowd fled before the approaching horses.

The accounts of the various witnesses whom the police subsequently interviewed reveal a great deal about social relations within the city. The first riot on 23 June had begun, the witnesses agreed, when the wife of a journeyman cabinetmaker named Desjardins, herself a hawker of newspapers, stormed into the baker's shop. The street being narrow, the day no doubt warm and all the doors open, the neighbors could hear clearly as she argued with the shop assistant. Twelve sous for a loaf was as much as she would pay, not the 14 he demanded. "Dirty bugger of a dog, give me bread for my money." When he pushed her out of the shop, she picked up one of the loaves on display at the front and began to walk off, saying that if he would not give her bread at the price she was prepared to pay then she would take it for nothing. He then ran after her, grabbed her hair, and pulled her to the ground to recover the bread. The baker's wife then appeared and tried to reason with the woman, offering to let her pay later if she did not have the 14 sous. But this was not the point. Blows were exchanged, though the witnesses differed on who struck the first one. Someone ran to tell Desjardins, the woman's husband, who arrived a few minutes later and told her not to make a scene. But a group of women—some witnesses say "several," others a hundred—assured him "that it was not his wife who was in the wrong, but the baker who was overcharging for his bread." At this he too became angry and began throwing stones into the shop. Some children copied him, then other people began to do the same. The "populace"—"a large number of people" said other witnesses—then invaded the shop, smashed it up, and took the bread. What had begun as an individual dispute had become a riot.

The events of 9 July had followed an almost identical pattern. A female customer had argued with the baker about the price; the dispute had escalated; the woman's son had joined her and the two had thrown rocks into the shop. Finally the crowd joined them in the attack and pillaged the premises.

Why did this happen? There was obviously already bad feeling between the bakers and many of their clients. The "populace," to use the same term as the witnesses did, believed that bakers were deliberately and unnecessarily raising the price of bread, the staple food for most of the population. Many of the rioters were regular clients and lived locally but this did not hold them back: they clearly felt that the bakers had broken the unwritten rules of civilized behavior and deserved punishment. This was perhaps why there was no trace of the practice common in food riots, where the pillagers left what they considered to be the fair price of the produce instead of the higher price that was being asked. The crowd simply took the bread and some of them, to punish the bakers further, broke the furniture and removed other items as well.

The bakers, for their part, felt they had been unreasonably treated. Even though the penalty for riot and pillage was in all likelihood hanging, they were angry enough to name quite a number of the culprits. The solidarity that usually marked the neighborhood community in its dealings with the authorities was conspicuously missing. The hard times and price increases had opened one of the major fault lines within eighteenth-century urban society, that between suppliers and consumers. It was not a permanent gulf but was ever latent, and it was to be reopened many times during the eighteenth century.

But this was not the sole division revealed by the events of 1725. The rioters were not representative of the whole local population. The witnesses (mostly the bakers themselves) spoke of a lot of women among them and mentioned by name the wives of a joiner and a soldier and the daughters of a matchseller and of two laborers. The men recognized by the witnesses were a tinker, a beggar, a stonecutter, two inlayers, two journeymen joiners, three shoemakers, a stable boy, a laborer, two weavers, an agent for the horse merchants, a glass worker, and the son of a nail maker. This list suggests that the crowd was composed largely of unskilled or semiskilled workers, with some journeymen and sons of master artisans: mostly people with little property. The bakers, on the other hand, were master craftsmen and shopkeepers with a substantial investment in their trade, and the widow Chaudron seems to have been one of the most affluent and influential.[2] The other witnesses (if we exclude the soldiers) were all artisans, most with their own businesses. The fact that they testified suggests that they did not condone the rioters' actions. Several claimed to have tried to prevent the baker's house from being ransacked along with the shop. There is also the evidence of the commissaire Labbé himself: he was rescued by "several of the most charitable bourgeois of the said faubourg."

Here then was another division within the neighborhood, broadly along socioeconomic lines. On the bakers' side were a number of the highly skilled and better off local inhabitants—who could after all afford a loaf even at 14 sous. They had assets, a substantial investment in skill and property. On the other side were the poorer and less skilled people, without assets.

This division was neither as deep nor as momentarily bitter as that between the bakers and their erstwhile clients. Only one of the nonbaker witnesses was prepared to name anyone clearly enough to put them at risk of punishment, though as neighbors they must have known who they were. Desjardins and his wife were mentioned by name, but only in the context of a neighborhood dispute, and none of the witnesses accused them of playing any role in the pillaging of the shop. The woman involved in the initial dispute on 9 July was described only as "a local woman" and the other rioters were similarly anonymous: "several women"; "a large number of people"; "the populace." Thus neighborhood solidarity held. The respectable members of the local community were not prepared to betray—and see hanged—their poorer and less qualified neighbors.

The way the riots took place also provides eloquent testimony to the roles of men and women of the Paris lower classes both in movements of protest and in everyday life. Since the women were normally the ones who did the shopping, they were more aware of the prices than the men. When the price rose suddenly, they gathered outside the shop, muttering and massaging their anger. The dispute involving the wife of Desjardins (we never learn her name), bolder or more hot-headed than the others, provided a bridge from verbal to physical violence. When she seized a loaf, she crossed the invisible line between an ordinary neighborhood quarrel and a true breach of order. Her theft provoked the baker's assault on her. But in seizing her by the hair rather than by snatching the loaf back or grabbing her arm, he too escalated the exchange, and she responded with blows. At this point in any ordinary quarrel the onlookers would have intervened, but this time the women were angry and thought the baker was in the wrong. When Desjardins appeared, ready to punish his wife for causing a quarrel, the neighborhood women could have allowed matters to rest but instead inflamed the incident by telling him the baker was to blame. It then became his affair, a defense of his honor since his wife had been assaulted.

Yet the husband was also acting on behalf of the local poor against the maneuvers of the bakers. With a substantial section of the neighborhood exasperated beyond all limits, the riot—in their eyes—became legitimate. Once stones had broken the shop windows and the bakers were on the run, the bread was there for the taking. The majority opinion within the neighborhood was now (at least momentarily) in favor of violent action, and the usual figures of authority—the priest and the commissaire—were powerless.

Both Desjardins's wife and the anonymous woman in the second dispute also acted as spokeswomen for the poor of the neighborhood, and in each case the dispute with the baker was a litmus test of local opinion. For these same neighborhood women—perhaps together with others—acted as a kind of tribunal, judging the rights and wrongs of the dispute. They could have prevented the riot but chose instead to prosecute it. The incident reveals the opinion-making role that even poor women played—collectively—within the neighborhood, a role that could on occasion give them considerable power.

This all shows how tensions built up and how riot could arise, in a moment of crisis, out of ordinary neighborhood conflict. The first outbreak, on 23 June, did not lead to anything more serious because of the timely arrival of the soldiers. But on 9 July the violence had already spread by the time they got there. The earlier action against the baker Charier, widely discussed across the faubourg and followed by two more weeks of high prices, had electrified the whole area. Another individual dispute was enough to set up the new explosion that everyone half expected, and this time a chain reaction down the whole length of the main street.

Yet—and this too is revealing—at the end of the street it stopped. No spark crossed the open Place St-Antoine or flashed through the arched gateway through the old city walls that divided the city from the faubourg. The faubourg St-Antoine was both physically and socially distinct, even though there was continuous traffic through the gate. Because the police knew this well, it was there that another two commissaires and a relieving squad of the Paris guard stopped, waiting for further reinforcements. They could hold the gateway but they could not advance.

The riots of 1725 tell us a great deal about the relationship between the urban community and the central authorities. The riots were not directed against the police or the government. Food supply was a government responsibility but the overnight price rise was interpreted as profiteering by the bakers. It was therefore a local matter: a certain section of the local community was punishing a number of individuals who had in their view acted improperly. The efforts of the police to prevent pillage were viewed simply as meddling. The commissaire tried to appease them by promising to take action himself, but "they all cried that it was impossible to make the bakers see reason except by pillaging their shops . . . that they were determined to pillage everything and to take the law into their own hands and told us that we would be doing worse than wasting our time if we wanted to prevent them and that we should go away."

The moral authority of the police and of the parish priest of Ste-Marguerite did not extend to community self-regulation of this kind. They might simply have been ignored, as was the priest, if a number of local people had not been arrested. The arrests were what put the commissaire Labbé and his men in physical danger.

The riots very clearly underline not only the limits to the moral authority of the police and the clergy but also their physical and organizational weakness. Because moral authority normally sufficed, it took the police nearly five hours to muster sufficient force to quash the riots. By then the violence had achieved its goal. They were able to arrest only three people. It is a reminder that even a great city like Paris, in the early eighteenth century, was essentially self-regulating. If the police were able to "control" the city it was only so long as their moral authority was recognized, and because they were able to claim the support of a substantial section of the local population. They had no other effective means of crowd control except the army, which took a long time to mobilize.

Although the police and the government were not directly challenged in these riots, implicitly the whole of the government's food supply policy was at issue. Feeding the people was considered one of the principal functions of the monarchy, and it had failed both to provide adequate supplies and to control the activities of the bakers. Although the immediate concern of the rioters was with those members of the local community who had "misbehaved," there were hints that the police were not considered blameless. Informers reported hearing people say that "the good commissaire Labbé . . . has raised the price on several market days, either to have his cut from the bakers or to hurt the people by stirring them to rebel against the government."[3] Similar accusations were made against other police officers and even against the lieutenant general of police himself.

In the months after the riots, the belief that some officials were conspiring to drive up the price of grain is well documented. "There are secret orders emanating from the court that enjoin all grain merchants and farmers as far away as 20, 30, and 50 leagues not to ship any grain to Paris until further notice," assured one rumor. There were reports that the government had sent buyers to purchase the remaining stores and even the incoming crop. The diarist-lawyers Mathieu Marais and Edmond Jean François Barbier firmly believed that the court was involved, and in the markets of Paris even bakers and grain measurers were discussing the government's profiteering.[4]

FOOD SUPPLY AND ITS PROBLEMS

Such accusations arose partly because of the way the food industry was organized. It was no easy task to provide for a population of nearly half a million. According to a visitor to Paris in 1738, the city then consumed annually "150,000 *muids* of wheat, not including the bread that is brought from all the environs to the different markets twice a week; 60,000 cattle, 400,000 sheep, 125,000 calves, 40,000 pigs and about 340,000 *muids* of wine, not counting the extraordinary quantity of spirits, beer, cider, and other drinks that are consumed there."[5] There is no way of knowing whether these figures are correct, but certainly the quantities of bread, meat, and drink required were immense. In addition, vast amounts of vegetables, milk, cheese, and eggs were consumed.

A small amount of this produce came from within the walls. Carp and pike caught in the Seine were regularly on sale, and most convents and monasteries had their own gardens. In all the peripheral quarters farms and orchards were common and gardeners made up a significant proportion of the population. No space was wasted and even private gardens, except those of the very rich, had to pay their way. Sheep, pigs, rabbits, and hens were kept in courtyards.

But the bulk of the food consumed in Paris had to be brought from outside. Fresh fruit, the ubiquitous lettuces, turnips, carrots and cabbages, peas and beans, apples and apricots, cherries and raspberries were grown in the rich market gardens at Aubervilliers, Passy, Belleville, Montreuil, and other nearby villages. Increasingly these received in return the sweepings of the streets, rich in horse manure and human excrement. Mushrooms were grown in artificial beds at Vaugirard. Eggs too came from the surrounding villages or from Brie, pork from Nanterre.[6] The most common cheese in Paris was Brie from around Meaux. Goat cheese was readily available, while Dutch cheeses had been imported since at least the sixteenth century. Gruyère, Parmesan, and—most expensive of all—Roquefort were all to be had in the Paris markets.[7] Veal, beef, and mutton came partly on the hoof from various parts of the Ile-de-France and from Normandy and Picardy, but a great deal of livestock was also brought down the rivers from Champagne or by a tortuous route from the Auvergne. Saltwater fish came from the Norman ports, and much of the butter that was widely used for frying also came from Normandy or Brittany.[8]

Much of the wine consumed in Paris came overland from Orléans and Blois, while more took the river route from Burgundy and from the Beaujolais and Rhone valley. It was illegal for Paris merchants to import wine from the areas adjoining the city, for fear of driving up the prices and depriving the local people of wine. But the many Parisians who owned property in the region were allowed to import their own produce. Nor were the winegrowers of Argenteuil prevented from selling their *piquet* to the owners of the taverns just outside the city boundaries.[9]

Many new products arrived in the course of the eighteenth century: oranges, cauliflower, new varieties of apricots, tomatoes. Coffee, at first a luxury, became a popular drink sold by street vendors, consumed with milk and large quantities of sugar. This democratization of coffee and sugar testify to the vast growth in transatlantic trade and to the development, thanks to slave labor, of plantations in the West Indies.[10]

But the most important product of all was grain. For human consumption Parisians scorned anything but wheat. Most was grown in the Beauce and Hurepoix regions to the southwest, in the Vexin and Picardy to the northwest, in the Soissonnais to the northeast. Huge barges towed by teams of twenty horses made their slow way upstream from as far as Normandy, while both unmilled grain and flour came downstream to the Port de Grève. On occasion grain came even from the Mediterranean provinces.[11]

Figure 17. Barrière d'enfer. Most produce arriving at the gates was subject to a tax. From J. L. G. B. Palaiseau, *La ceinture de Paris, ou recueil des barrières* (Paris, 1819–20). Bibliothèque historique de la ville de Paris, photo Jean-Christophe Doerr.

The nightmare for the people of Paris and for the authorities was a bad harvest, or worse still a series of bad harvests. When this happened, once or twice a decade throughout the century, there might be a gap of two or three months when the previous year's supply was running low before the new harvest was ripe. Then prices rose sharply. This situation was aggravated by profiteering. Everyone knew that prices would reach their peak just before the new crop arrived, and the big farmers and merchants could afford to hold onto their stocks until this happened. If enough of them did so, they created an artificial dearth and prices rose ahead of the real shortage. The Paris population was well aware of this practice and was liable to become murderous when it scented speculation.

But the trauma of supplying Paris was not over even when a good harvest was reported. Shortages arose just as often from poor transport. For several weeks a year the smaller watercourses froze and several times in the century even the larger rivers froze over. A sudden thaw brought new problems, melting the ice unevenly so that large blocks would float downstream, endangering boats and bridges. Flooded rivers were perilous to navigate, and when the Seine was high there was a danger of boats smashing into the quais and bridges. And dry weather was just as bad. The upper reaches of the Seine often became inaccessible and the Briare and Orléans canals that linked the Loire and the Seine—of central importance in supplying the capital—were closed between August and late October.[12]

The road system was also very vulnerable to bad weather. Heavy snow hindered wheeled vehicles, and since even the major highways were not all paved, a thaw or heavy rain turned the roads to quagmires and brought wagons to a standstill. As the mud dried, the wheels left it corrugated and rutted, further slowing traffic.

Even when grain arrived safely the problems were not over. It still had to be milled into flour. Steven Kaplan has estimated that there were some 2,000 water or windmills supplying Paris. When the streams froze or water levels dropped, the water mills could not turn. Ice in the streams could smash the wheels and flash floods could damage them or simply turn them too fast: to grind grain finely and evenly the millstones had to turn at a steady pace. A sudden storm could wreck half the windmills around the city. On at least ten occasions across the eighteenth century grain rotted before it could be milled.[13]

Storage was a further major problem. A portion of each year's harvest got damp in poorly ventilated granaries and fermented. Grain was transported in open boats, and there was no cover either at the Port de Grève or at the Halles. The tenants of the houses overlooking the grain market were known to empty their chamber pots onto the roofs of the shops and the piles of grain below, while hens and rodents broke open the sacks and left to spoil what they did not devour.[14] Even when flour was available, a shortage of wood for the ovens could still hinder bread production. Since most of the wood was floated or brought by boat down the Seine, very dry weather, ice or floods prevented it too from arriving.[15]

The problems of supplying Paris were horrendous and they lay as much in the methods of supply and production as in inclement weather. The government responded by imposing controls that reveal much about the eighteenth-century attitude to the market. Both in government circles and in the population at large there was a strong sense that the interests of merchant and consumer were fundamentally opposed: the merchant made money at the expense of the customer and would go to great lengths to conceal the means and extent of this profit. "Ill-intentioned merchants, always greedy for profit, will seize upon any pretext," read the standard manual used by the eighteenth-century police.[16]

To combat these evil practices the police devised detailed rules. Merchants supplying Paris had to be registered and had to be people of sound reputation. Farmers, bakers, and millers were not allowed to trade in grain as well. To prevent prices soaring in markets close to the capital, and to expand the supply zone, merchants were forbidden to purchase grain within ten leagues of Paris (approximately 45 kilometers). Every shipment of grain had to be accompanied by a certificate so that its route could be traced. Supplies brought into the city could not be reexported even if they were not sold: this too was designed to keep prices down, though it might also make suppliers hesitant to bring too much.[17]

Even with all these precautions, the dangers were multiple. There was a well-founded fear of poor-quality ingredients. In times of shortage rumors abounded that spoiled grain was being used for bread, and indeed the bad taste of some of the bread on sale in 1725 led the police to remove it. False weights were another preoccupation, both of the public and of the authorities. Loaves had to be marked with their weight and anyone caught selling even an ounce or so below weight was fined heavily.[18]

Because of the public's conviction that merchants would combine to fix prices if left to themselves, eighteenth-century officialdom had none of the modern economist's confidence in competition. Hence great emphasis was placed on openness. This did not apply only to food. It was illegal for a shoemaker or saddler to buy directly from the tanners. All rope offered for sale had to be brought to the central market, and only on official market days. All goods had to be sold in the open market, in full view of the public and of the authorities—private deals could only lead to profiteering.[19]

The conviction that commerce needed to be open helps explain the requirement that traders and shopkeepers be members of a recognized trade corporation and operate when and where the corporation specified. This was a guarantee, if not of their honesty, at least that they could be traced, inspected, and kept to the rules. Those who betrayed public trust could be caught and punished: a number of bakers were sentenced to have their shops walled up after being caught selling loaves well under weight.[20] Since only members of the corporation could practice the trade, they could not set up shop elsewhere in Paris or in any other town. Such punishments were designed to reassure the public, yet they could equally be taken as confirmation that fears of sharp practices by merchants were well founded.

In times of plenty the rules were relaxed, but in a crisis the authorities implemented them strictly. They would also introduce emergency measures, buying grain abroad and imposing extra controls. Ironically, these well-meaning efforts proved politically dangerous for an unpopular government with financial problems. The imports of grain financed by the Crown—"the king's grain," as they became known in 1725—were often of poor quality after a long sea voyage. Yet the authorities were unwilling to lose what they had paid and there were instances when they refused to allow other supplies onto the Paris market until the royal grain was sold, which provoked accusations of profiteering. But the spoiled grain could hardly be destroyed either, for tipping it into the river would be seen as another way of driving up the price. Suspicion was further fueled by the special privileges accorded to entrepreneurs and financiers commissioned to act as intermediaries. In 1725 the chief minister and member of the royal family, the duc de Bourbon, was singled out in public rumor as the chief profiteer.[21]

The government again commissioned massive purchases of foreign grain in 1738–40, and when the daughter of Lieutenant General Hérault married in 1738 there were rumors that he had increased the price of bread to provide her with a rich dowry. This time accusations were also leveled against the finance minister, the chief minister Cardinal Fleury, and even against the king himself. Similar rumors in 1752, in the mid-1760s, and in the early 1770s again targeted the finance minister and the king. In each case the government was clumsy in its handling of the issue and the rumors were encouraged by the political enemies of those in power.

The royal government took some steps to reduce the risk of harvest failures. The bread shortages of 1725 were probably behind the establishment of a permanent police council composed of the lieutenant general of police, the principal magistrates of the city, and the head of the municipality. They discussed not only food supply but also poor relief, sanitation, the rules of the corporations, and indeed any matter concerning the administration of Paris. With their support the police chief, Hérault, pressured convents and monasteries to store a year or more's grain that would be available in case of famine, and these stores provided limited relief during shortages in 1738, 1740, 1751, and 1768. In 1736 a royal declaration ordered the building of a huge granary, but it never materialized.[22]

Surprisingly, the riots of 1725 led to very little change in security arrangements. Almost the only response, and a belated one, was the permanent positioning of a commissaire in the faubourg St-Antoine in 1730. Before this the closest officer was several blocks away near St-Paul in the rue St-Antoine.[23] It is remarkable that the government ordered no increase in the numbers of soldiers in the capital, and not until 1750 was a detachment of the watch stationed in the main street of the faubourg. The authorities clearly felt that the forces available were adequate, provided they were mobilized in time. The commissaire's moral authority was deemed sufficient—further confirmation of the self-policing nature of the urban community. The police felt secure against mob action, and their attitude would change only after 1750.

THE IDEAL OF THE URBAN COMMUNITY

On the whole the authorities seem to have felt that the food supply system and its safeguards worked well enough. In the 1720s their main effort went not into improving the provisioning of Paris but rather into trying to keep the population of the city stable. Because we have lost the parish registers for Paris we cannot be sure what the population was, but most historians agree that between 1600 and 1700 it had grown from around 200,000 to between 400,000 and 500,000 and was continuing to expand.[24] Growth of this order alarmed the government. On 18 July 1724 the king decreed that the continued spread of the city could not be allowed "without endangering its survival; the number of inhabitants, which is already so great and which would increase in proportion to the new constructions, would further augment the price of food and the difficulties of provisioning." But fear of famine was not the only motive.

> Public order would suffer because of the impossibility of policing every part of such a great body; the distance of the quarters would destroy the ease of communication that should exist between the inhabitants of a single city with regard to the different matters that summon them often in a single day to different and very distant quarters; and it must be feared further that the buildings in the center of the city would become dilapidated, while new ones went up beyond its boundaries.

The monarchy was defending a certain conception of the city. Paris should form a single, hierarchically organized community. "We wish," the declaration of 1724 continued,

> to reserve important buildings for the interior of the city which they ornament . . . And, if the principal inhabitants were to take up residence at the extremities of the faubourgs, we wish furthermore to prevent their attracting by their example and in their train a great number of people . . . While the center of the city became eventually deserted and abandoned.[25]

The upper classes were imagined as the heart of urban society, their location at the center symbolic of this role. The faubourgs should be reserved for industry and for the common people. The government wished to maintain both the magnificence of central Paris and an ideal social hierarchy mirrored in its geography.

Accordingly, nearly 300 boundary markers were erected and one and a half thousand maps and plans drawn up to record the existing limits of the city, beyond which no new building would henceforth be allowed.[26] Yet any attempt to limit the growth of Paris and to maintain an ideal urban geography was doomed. The population grew because the city offered services, employment, and sometimes relief that was missing in distant, isolated provinces. It grew because a move to the capital often represented upward social mobility. Provincial nobles and officeholders sought places around the court or in the administration. Affluent provincial merchants bought their sons admission to the high-status Paris guilds. Peasants' sons could sometimes get apprenticeships, while their daughters sought places as lace makers or domestic servants. The city also expanded physically because of the aristocracy's growing taste for extensive gardens and new kinds of accommodation. No eighteenth-century Canute could turn back the tide.

The ideal of the urban community expressed in the 1724 and 1726 declarations was equally unrealistic. Many of the court aristocracy had already deserted the crowded central districts for the more distant faubourgs St-Germain and St-Honoré. Their social leadership was much reduced since the sixteenth or early seventeenth centuries when the great noble families had extensive patronage networks that infiltrated the urban community and bound it to them. Early-eighteenth-century Paris was controlled by the police and the Parlement at the center and by the wealthy middle classes at the local level. Yet those middle classes were themselves highly fragmented, divided among the quarters and parishes, with no common identity. It was a long time since the city had formed a single community in the sense imagined by the 1724 declaration.

There were nevertheless many others who shared a yearning for a hierarchically organized urban community. Many of the magistrates and bourgeois who comprised the social elite looked back to an older model of oligarchical city government similar to that which still existed in many other French and European cities. In the sixteenth and for much of the seventeenth century Paris had been run primarily by representatives of each quarter meeting at the Hôtel de Ville—the city hall. There were sixteen quarters, each headed by a *quartinier.* They were in turn divided into four *cinquantaines* with a prominent local citizen—the *cinquantenier*—responsible for each one. The smallest division was the *dizaine*, each with its *dizainier*. All of these men were in principle elected by the local bourgeois. At any one time, therefore, 336 men had shared administrative responsibility for street cleaning and maintenance, for public health, law, and order. The *quartiniers* maintained the official lists of *bourgeois de Paris*, ran local elections, could impose fines for breaches of the bylaws, and had a role in tax assessment. They met at the Hôtel de Ville to confer on matters of citywide importance and each year selected eight of "the most notable inhabitants of the quarter," who together with other local officials would elect the city council.[27] Sometimes they were given further duties: a sixteenth-century order of the Parlement instructed them "to find out in each individual house in this city and its faubourgs what people are living there, in what number, their quality, rank, and means of support."[28] In addition, the *quartiniers* usually commanded the sixteen regiments of the citizen militia. These were further divided into 133 companies, each based in a particular neighborhood and commanded by a prominent bourgeois, often a merchant. They were called out frequently, whenever the moral authority of the police proved insufficient. Officer rank in the militia was an important source of status and power for the local notables.[29]

The local notables worked closely with representatives of the royal government: in 1635 an "assembly of police" brought together the principal figures in the Châtelet, the senior commissaire of each quarter, two members of the municipality, and thirty-two "bourgeois."[30] Although there were—inevitably—tensions between the various institutions responsible for governing Paris, this participatory model of city government, under the overall authority of the Parlement, remained the norm until the 1670s.

But following the creation of the position of lieutenant general in 1667, the participatory model was slowly abandoned. Administrative tasks were gradually transferred to the police. The militia was called out less and less often and eventually dismantled. The last elections of local representatives were held in 1681.[31] The lieutenant general reported directly to the king, although the Parlement kept nominal authority over him, and in practice the Paris Parlement found its oversight of the administration substantially undermined. Historians have generally ascribed this change to royal mistrust of Parisian autonomy after the troubles of the League in the sixteenth century and the Fronde in the mid seventeenth, but the explanation may equally well be that the royal government had found magistrates and professional police officers to be much more supple and reliable administrators than elected notables.[32]

The municipal government retained some of its functions, though in practice it too was run more by professional administrators than by elected representatives. The river, along with the quais and bridges, remained under its control, and so did the city gates and ramparts (progressively transformed into boulevards). In principle any offence committed in these areas was judged in the city court. The municipality also made rules governing river traffic, which included the immense number of boats supplying the city. The Seine fishermen, the owners of the laundry boats, the public baths, the water pumps, and the boats that used the river current to grind grain all had to deal with the Hôtel de Ville.[33]

More important still was the financial role of the municipality. It received the huge income from the tax levied on all goods entering Paris, fixed in 1721 at 20 percent. Admittedly, it did not get to keep all this money. A good deal was used to pay interest on government bonds: those issued by the City of Paris were favored by Parisians, who believed them more secure than many other sources of investment. But the municipality did spend a great deal, across the century, building fine stone quais and new bridges, the most visible urban developments of the century. Altogether the different activities of the Hôtel de Ville employed nearly 1,000 officials in the middle years of the century.[34]

The ceremonial role of the municipality also kept it very much in the public eye. It provided the annual midsummer celebration in the Place de Grève as well as many of the fireworks displays to celebrate royal births and military victories, some of them so spectacular that young Parisians remembered them years later. Officials of the city had a role in most official celebrations, for example in the big procession on the feast of the Assumption (15 August). And when members of the royal family visited Paris they were received with great pomp by the municipality.[35]

Enough of the form and functions of the municipal government therefore remained for it to continue to provide an alternative model for the administration of Paris. Although the head of the municipality and the aldermen were now in reality named by the government, an "election" was still held each August. Each of the sixteen *quartiniers* summoned the lesser officials of his quarter and selected eight voters from among the "most notable persons of the said quarter": thirty-two of them would eventually solemnly cast their vote for the candidates whom the government had already chosen![36] There was an elaborate public ceremony, including a procession through the center of the city, to which the rep-

Figure 18. The Hôtel de Ville and the Place de Grève. Jean-Baptiste Lallemand, "Vue de l'hôtel de Ville de Paris" (ca. 1780), in *Voyage pittoresque de la France*, vol. 9. Bibliothèque historique de la ville de Paris, photo Jean-Christophe Doerr.

resentatives of the bourgeoisie were taken by carriages bearing the city arms. A magnificent dinner was given, then the newly elected officials processed to Versailles to swear an oath of loyalty to the king. It was an unforgettable occasion—"magnificent and august," wrote one of the notables.[37] Everything was calculated to make it memorable for the bourgeois who were invited, to make them feel like important members of a proud urban community centered on the Hôtel de Ville. There seems to have been a convention that as many different individuals as possible should be involved. Between 1776 and 1788, for example, some 400 men were called to elections at the Hôtel de Ville, and they included a wide cross section of the wealthy Paris middle classes. The legal professions represented nearly half of the sixty-nine whose occupations are given (eleven notaries, ten barristers, seven magistrates, three police commissaires), but there were also four clergymen, three mercers, two silk merchants, a doctor, a university professor, a draper, a spicer, a printer, two pharmacists, and a number of unspecified merchants.[38]

The collective memory of municipal independence and of local autonomy, "under the authority of the bourgeois of each quarter" as the police put it in 1737, therefore remained strong. Still in the early decades of the century the property owners in each street had met annually to elect the lamplighters. The local offices remained in existence, and just occasionally they were still given jobs to do: in 1744 assemblies of bourgeois were convened by the *quartiniers* to advise on "the most rapid and equitable manner" of levying the new streetlighting and cleaning tax. Even in 1789 a number of the *quartiniers* were named to preside over elections to the Estates General.[39]

The Hôtel de Ville continued to bulk large in the awareness of bourgeois Parisians, its importance extending far beyond its real role in city government. Most maps and guidebooks continued to divide Paris according to the sixteen quarters used by the Hôtel de Ville, in preference to the twenty police quarters. And the idea of the municipality served to unify a large and very diverse metropolis. Civic ceremonies created the illusion of an urban community to which prominent Parisians, despite their disenfranchisement, still wished to belong.

THE POLICING OF CUSTOMARY PARIS

The police too shared this ideal of the city as a community, though their interpretation of it was different again. Until the late seventeenth century their primary concern had been the political stability of the city, above all the activities of dissident noble families and their lackeys and those of Protestants and Jansenists. But by 1700 the focus had shifted. Like most early-eighteenth-century Parisians, the police imagined society as a body in which different organs had different functions. Their own task was twofold: to keep the city orderly and to keep the social body healthy by removing elements that might harm it, physically or morally: the undeserving poor, able-bodied beggars, vagabonds, thieves and criminals, prostitutes. The first lieutenant general of police, Nicolas La Reynie, had cleaned out the notorious Cour des Miracles, so called because in popular mythology crippled beggars who returned home there could suddenly walk again, and the blind see. Subsequently the big criminal gangs that periodically terrorized propertied citizens were hunted down: that of Cartouche in the early 1720s, that of Raffia in the 1730s.[40] But after the appointment of Marc René de Voyer, marquis de Paulmy d'Argenson, as lieutenant general in 1697 a sustained effort went into "moralizing" and disciplining Paris in many other ways: clamping down on work done on holy days, on "insubordination" among journeymen, on prostitution, on "libertinage," and on "vagabonds." D'Argenson wanted to impose a new order on the city, and this meant changing the day-to-day behavior of Parisians. During his years in the job the number of police ordinances issued annually more than doubled, and their character changed. People were repeatedly enjoined to stop emptying chamber pots out the windows and not to answer the call of nature in whichever alleyway they happened to be. The saddlers of the rue St-Antoine were told to work inside rather than spreading their leather in the middle of the street. Building materials, flocks of sheep, packhorses, handcarts, and artisans' benches were to be removed from the main streets so that wagons and carriages could pass. The massive *Traité de police* produced by Nicolas Delamare in the early eighteenth century, often quoted to illustrate the activities of the Parisian police, was in reality a statement of intent, a blueprint for a Parisian version of the "civilizing process."[41]

The key instruments of this effort were the police inspectors and their employees, who answered directly to Lieutenant General d'Argenson. They kept registers of innkeepers, goldsmiths, and secondhand dealers, watching for known criminals and for stolen goods. They regularly patrolled the city's trouble spots, recruited informers among domestic servants and brothel keepers, and specialized in dawn raids and arbitrary arrests. Inspectors Marais and Dumont, in midcentury, were forerunners of the vice squad, and another inspector oversaw gambling establishments. As police concern about "vagabonds" grew, inspectors arrested the prostitutes and beggars who had formerly been the concern of the hospital guards.[42]

These attempts to purge and reform the city were motivated by fear of its rapid growth, and perhaps too by a sense that older forms of hierarchy and control were no longer working. Such concerns were shared by many Parisians. Yet the police were now intruding—often violently—on many aspects of life that had previously been unregulated or had been the province of the clergy and of other urban authorities. The methods the inspectors used, furthermore, often provoked hostility. Parisians were particularly offended by what they saw as the illegality of many actions: arrests without due process before a commissaire, the charging of fees and "commissions," arbitrary fines. Furthermore, the inspectors were widely accused of extorting protection money from the keepers of lodging houses, brothels, and gaming rooms. The magistrates of the Parlement and the commissaires, who felt their responsibilities for local policing were being usurped, were hostile to d'Argenson's men. The Parlement first rebuked the lieutenant general, then in 1719 prosecuted several inspectors. Further accusations led to a reorganization in 1740 when the number of inspectors was reduced from forty to twenty. The prerequisites for holding the office were tightened up and they were made subordinate to the commissaires.[43]

But in 1743 the inspectors again came to prominence through an operation to enforce militia service. The government had decided to raise an extra regiment in Paris and all young men of military age were required to register with their local commissaire, who would draw lots to decide who would go. The whole exercise was bitterly unpopular with the ordinary people, all the more so since the sons—or even in some cases the servants as well—of officeholders, magistrates, lawyers, doctors, and police officials were all exempt. The drawing of the ballot was followed by a police round-up of all those who had not registered and a bounty was offered for each man captured. This encouraged some of the inspectors and their employees not to be too fussy when making their arrests, which reinforced public prejudice against them: "people continue to say that the police officers are profiting from the drawing of the militia to make something on the side."[44] Memories of this remained fresh when, in 1750, they once again began arresting young men.

THE RIOTS OF 1750

One of the glazier Jacques-Louis Ménétra's boyhood memories was of his father, accompanied by seven stout barrel makers, coming to collect him from school because "it was rumored that they were taking young boys."[45] He did not give the date but we know this was in May 1750, when Paris witnessed an extraordinary series of riots provoked by police arrests. In the worst incident a spy—or, in official terminology a police "observer"—named Labbé (a man unrelated to the commissaire Labbé introduced earlier) was recognized in the rue St-Honoré. He was attacked, tried to take refuge in several different buildings, but each time was turned out. An effort to save him was made by a member of the mounted police, who placed him under arrest and escorted him to the nearest commissaire. But the crowd thought he was going to be released and attacked the house, throwing stones through the windows and threatening to kill all the occupants. The commissaire Delavergée took fright and after a brief resistance the city guard pushed the unfortunate Labbé back into the street, where he was again assaulted with sticks and stones. Badly injured, no longer with any hope of escape and begging for a confessor, he stumbled as far as the church of St-Roch before finally expiring. The crowd then dragged his body to the house of the lieutenant general where they broke the windows and threatened to kill everyone inside. The police chief made an undignified escape through the gardens at the rear.[46]

This was the most serious of the attacks on police spies (and on several innocents unfortunate enough to look like known police employees). The subsequent enquiry by the Parlement revealed that in March 1750 the lieutenant general had given orders to a number of his subordinates to arrest young "vagabonds and libertines," especially those who gathered near the river. They were to be paid for each arrest they made and had clearly exceeded their orders. Thirteen-year-old Nicolas Savoye was picked up with two friends while watching a game of chance in the fairground at St-Germain-des-Prés. Others, according to their families, were on their way to school or even returning from catechism classes.[47]

In making their arrests the police were committing a profound miscalculation. Knowingly or not, they were confusing two sorts of young men who loitered around street corners and played card games along the river: the homeless who lived by their wits, and the sons of established citizens. No one protested when the authorities arrested the "unknown poor," whom most Parisians found undesirable. But in 1750 the lads arrested were more often of the other sort. Admittedly it was almost impossible for the police to tell the difference, for the boys might be some distance from their own quarter. This was, in a way, the point of the arrests: the lieutenant general had reportedly said it would be a good lesson if a few sons of "bourgeois" (in this context meaning master artisans and shopkeepers) were taken into custody.[48] From the police point of view the boys should not be allowed to roam in this fashion, precisely because they were then indistinguishable from the young "vagabonds." In short, they made policing difficult.

What the authorities were overlooking was the fact that this wandering and loitering was an important stage in the male life cycle, even for the sons of master craftsmen and shopkeepers. Right from the time they were old enough to run, most Parisian girls and boys spent a good deal of their lives in the streets and courtyards. While they were young—up to five or six—they stayed under the eye of parents and neighbors. But surveillance was difficult for working parents. There were of course schools, over 166 officially recognized elementary schools and many more unofficial ones by the late seventeenth century. By the mid eighteenth almost every parish had at least one free school for boys, though there were only half as many for girls.[49] Most Parisian children attended long enough to learn to read and write, though according to one lawyer "the common people . . . send their children to school not to educate them but to be rid of them." Not all attended school, and even those who did still had ample time to play in the streets. That too was part of their education. As Louis-Sébastien Mercier pointed out, "at a young age they develop an assured air . . . they are not much surprised by the things of life nor by the problems of city living."[50]

As soon as children were old enough they began to contribute in small ways to the family income. The ten-year-old son of a laundryman carried loads of washing for his father. A baker's niece, aged eight, delivered small quantities of bread to the neighbors. Another ten year old, a goldsmith's son, was sent out before seven one morning to get spirits for the journeymen. There were close to 100,000 children between seven and fourteen in mid-eighteenth-century Paris (perhaps a sixth of the population), a permanent juvenile presence in the streets.[51] Very often they tarried on their return from an errand to exchange greetings with a small friend, to gaze at the laundrywomen and the boats on the river, or to play a quick game of quoits in a courtyard.

The city elites were beginning to perceive street children as a problem, particularly where girls were concerned. The curé and wealthy parishioners who founded the free school of St-Agnès in the parish of St-Eustache in 1729 hoped to save the bodies and the souls of girls whose working parents left them alone all day: "left to themselves at the most dangerous age . . . one sees them run and go everywhere in the streets, squares, and public markets where they are corrupted by bad examples and by the fatal force of habit that familiarizes them with the language typical of these places of perdition."[52]

But the ranks of the street children soon thinned. The offspring of wealthy noble and bourgeois families had never been among them: they were brought up by servants in the safety and isolation of a hôtel or large apartment. The daughters of professionals and better-off merchants likewise rarely appeared in the streets. "They are locked up in convents until the day of their marriage," observed Mercier.[53] But many sons of the professional and better-off shopkeeper classes did spend their early childhood in the streets, until at the age of eight or nine they found themselves plucked away from their playmates and sent to a small boarding school to learn Latin, rhetoric, and the manners considered appropriate to the century of *les lumières*.

By then the girls of shopkeeper families—"those of the second floor" in Mercier's phrase—had already disappeared: for them the teenage years

Figure 19. Children's games: the top. Boys playing on a building site. Engraving by Augustin de Saint-Aubin, in *C'est ici les différens jeux des petits polissons de Paris* (Paris, n.d.). Bibliothèque historique de la ville de Paris, photo Jean-Christophe Doerr.

brought reduced freedom. Many worked under the maternal eye in their parents' workshop or stall. They were less likely than the boys to be formally apprenticed and more commonly stayed at home learning to spin cotton or wool, to do embroidery and sew on buttons.[54] Those who were apprenticed, frequently to a seamstress or an embroiderer, often remained under surveillance even during their leisure hours. In chapter 3 I mentioned an agreement between two lace makers to supervise their apprentices' outings and never to leave them on their own. Male apprentices suffered no such restrictions, and indeed their contracts sometimes expressly required that on Sundays the boy would be free "to go wherever he wished." Their different relationship to urban space emerges clearly if we look at where male and female apprentices worked: between half and three quarters of the girls apprenticed to dressmakers lived in the same parish as their new employer, but only around one tenth of the male apprentices did.[55]

So by the teenage years it was mainly boys of the laboring and artisan classes who remained in the streets, and at this point they began to leave their own quarter and move farther afield. Jacques-Louis Ménétra's childhood years were spent in the compact maze of small streets between St-Germain-l'Auxerrois and the Seine, but as an adolescent he roamed far more widely.[56] These were years of independent apprenticeship in urban life. Boys wandered along the quais to see the marionettes and listen to the ballad singers. They watched executions on the Place de Grève and threw stones or rotten fruit at the unfortunates in the pillory at the central market. In warm weather they plunged into the Seine with blissful disregard for police bans, effluent in the water, and the fact that most could barely swim. They explored the isolated urban periphery, the fields and disused quarries where soldiers fought duels, the woods and vineyards where lovers went. Frequently they got into mischief. They threw stones at street lamps and over the walls of monasteries; slipped firecrackers under the chairs of women selling apples in the street; climbed down into the open drains that fed the river: "youths and others gather there and primarily on Sundays and feast days damage the banks . . . by pulling out stones and lumps of earth that they throw at each other and even with insolence at the workers who maintain the drains."[57]

This was an intermediate stage of male life in which a degree of riotous misbehavior was considered normal. Right up to the age of twenty young men were still frequently referred to as "children" (*les enfants*), adult yet not fully responsible: for example Toussain, described as "un enfant" when arrested in 1750, was aged nineteen. Most Parisians looked tolerantly on these lads provided they did not go too far. The police, on the other hand, found them a nuisance and readily sent to prison any miscreant over about twelve who was not immediately claimed by a parent or employer.[58]

In 1750, therefore, different conceptions of policing were colliding, and the result was an explosion of popular anger against the inspectors, their spies, and the lieutenant general. But only this one section of the police was indicted by Parisian opinion. Other branches were much better regarded: the guard, for instance, which since 1720 had been doing most of the daily work of sorting out traffic accidents and breaking up brawls. The guardsmen were often underemployed shopkeepers or craftsmen, not professional soldiers, and they were close to the ordinary population. Since their patrols were small in number—six men officially but in practice often four or five—they could not overcome determined resistance and relied heavily on the public for help. Usually they simply took into custody an offender who had already been caught by the crowd. Hence their intense discomfiture whenever they were called on, as in 1725, to use force against a crowd.[59]

The commissaires too generally enjoyed the confidence of the people. In 1750 the mob was initially quite happy to accompany the unfortunate Labbé to the nearest commissaire in the expectation that he would be punished. As one historian has put it, the commissaires represented the same legitimacy that the crowd was itself defending when it attacked police officers who abused their authority.[60]

This trust in the commissaires—forty-eight in number—is easy to understand if we look at their everyday role. Each of them was based in one limited area of the city. They were well educated, usually with legal training, and their job was not only to keep order but also to protect public health and safety. They were supposed to keep an eye on the state of the streets and of the buildings; to enforce quarantine regulations in case of an epidemic; to take charge if there were a flood or a fire. They policed weights and measures and—most important of all—the price and quality of bread. Thieves and suspected criminals were taken to the nearest commissaire for interrogation and imprisonment—just as with the spy Labbé. The commissaires also played an important role as local notables. They convened meetings of inhabitants to elect people to look after the streetlights. They responded to public complaints about antisocial behavior: it was the local commissaire who in 1698 moved against the scavengers and ragpickers of the rue Neuve-St-Martin, "who inconvenience the whole neighborhood with the number of dogs they keep, up to the number of 300, which they commonly let loose day and night, so that the sleep of the citizens is broken by their barking, and several passers-by have been bitten and gravely injured." It was the commissaire who returned to their owners goods that had been pawned at usurious rates of interest.[61]

Another vital service the commissaires provided was the witnessing of statements and complaints. Thefts from poorly secured rooms and disagreements between neighbors were the most common matters, but there were also objects found in the street, work and traffic accidents, babies abandoned on doorsteps, and complaints by people drenched by the contents of chamber pots emptied from upper-story windows. There were declarations like that by twenty-year-old Jeanne Durozay, four months pregnant by her father's journeyman, who hoped that by naming him officially as the father she could persuade him to marry her.[62] The conciliation of disputes was a more delicate matter, a schoolmasterly role in which the commissaire sometimes rebuked, sometimes threatened, sometimes listened and advised. In 1752 the commissaire Rémy intervened following a complaint by a seller of secondhand stockings and her husband, telling a cobbler "to leave the plaintiffs in peace, as for their part they had promised to do."[63]

All of these matters gave the commissaire a very particular relationship with the public. He was, in a sense, at their service. When he witnessed a statement or when a sum of money was left with him for safekeeping, he was a public trustee. The conciliation of disputes gave him a paternalistic and pastoral role very similar to that of the parish clergy.[64]

The riots of 1750 did teach the police a lesson. The inspectors were reigned in again, better controls put in place. But like the bread riots of 1725, they demonstrate that notwithstanding the far-reaching changes in the city since the late seventeenth century, and the decline of the participatory system of administration, customary Paris continued to function. Essentially two things kept the city stable, despite rapid urban growth, dearth, and poverty. The first was the strength of its neighborhood communities, which embraced people of a wide range of ranks and conditions. The neighborhood was not free of internal conflict, but it gave people a station and a role—poor and rich, female and male, young and old. But in return they had to conform to its unwritten laws and customs: otherwise, like the bakers in 1725 or the police in 1750, they were punished. Throughout the first half of the eighteenth century Paris remained very much a self-regulating society. The police were expected to assist in keeping order, in maintaining food supply, and in protecting the city, but their interference in local affairs was not welcome.

The second great force of stability was deference and hierarchy. But deference too was subject to a social contract. The king and his government had a responsibility to rule justly and to feed the people, and in return they were owed obedience, respect, and taxes.[65] In Paris the key intermediaries between the government and the people were the local notables: the police commissaires, some of the parish clergy, and the occasional noble, above all prominent merchants and officeholders. They too enjoyed deference and obedience but were likewise governed by a contract: they could not with impunity override the conventions that governed the community, and their continued influence depended on their fulfilling the role expected of them.

CHAPTER SIX

WOLVES IN SHEEP'S CLOTHING

Religion and Politics

Before dawn on a midwinter morning in 1732, hundreds of soldiers invaded the quiet streets near the church of St-Médard in the faubourg St-Marcel, in the southeastern corner of the city. Meeting no resistance, they watched while the masons who had come with them walled up the entrance to the small cemetery behind the church. Henceforth no one could gain access to the tomb of François de Pâris unless they first came through the house of the parish priest.

Pâris had been the son of a wealthy Parisian family, several of whose members had been magistrates in the Parlement. Initially destined for a legal career, he instead chose the Church. To the further dismay of his family, instead of accepting an illustrious clerical position he gave his possessions to the poor and lived an austere life in a run-down house in a narrow backstreet. He bought a handloom and made rough clothes, winning the respect and affection of the local poor with his charity and practical help. Modeling himself on Saint Francis of Assisi, his name-saint, he took to self-flagellation and to fasting for long periods. In 1727 when he died, at the age of thirty-six, he was already considered a saint by many of the local people.[1]

When miraculous cures began taking place on Pâris's tomb, therefore—a dozen or so between 1727 and 1730 but then some seventy in 1731—they were widely seen as divine confirmation of his holiness. Crowds flocked to the cemetery seeking cures. They scraped up samples of soil, and at the humble house where he had lived people fought each other

Figure 20. François de Pâris. The inscription underneath makes the point that he rejected the bull *Unigenitus*. From *La vie de M. François de Pâris, diacre* (n.p., 1731). Bibliothèque historique de la ville de Paris, photo Jean-Christophe Doerr.

for water from the well and for any object that he might have possessed. In the sacristy of St-Médard they lined up for splinters of wood from his bed and for fragments of clothing. Suddenly hawkers were selling his portraits everywhere, even inside the church. The archdiocesan authorities, impressed by the reports from St-Médard, began an inquiry into the miracles, the first step in the long process of canonization.[2]

At first there was nothing particularly unusual about the case. Miracles were an accepted part of life, even if by definition they did not happen every day. In May 1725 the wife of a wood carver in the faubourg St-Antoine had been cured of paralysis during the annual Corpus Christi procession. In the same year there were miraculous cures in the church of Ste-Geneviève.[3] Admittedly some of the cures at St-Médard were a little unusual, being accompanied by extraordinary convulsions. But what eventually led the authorities to close the cemetery was the association of the miracles with Jansenism.

Jansenism had begun as a reform movement among a tiny number of theologians, disciples of the Dutchman Cornelius Jansen in the mid seventeenth century. They believed that salvation could come only through divine grace and that God would accord it only to a predestined few. They sought reforms in religious practice, stressing true penitence rather than automatic absolution, a more austere way of life, and greater charity. They wanted more people to read and understand scripture for themselves. In France these views were endorsed by men like Blaise Pascal and Pierre Nicole (who was also buried at St-Médard), and the movement was associated particularly with the monastery at Port-Royal, not far from Versailles.[4]

But by the end of the seventeenth century Jansenist influence had broadened. Persecuted by Louis XIV, who looked on the movement as a potential threat to his control of the French church, the Jansenists responded by proselytizing both among the clergy and the laity. They were spectacularly successful, especially in Paris. The examples of faith and charity that many Jansenist priests provided were themselves influential, but many people also responded to their vision of the Church as a community of souls. It led them to offer a far greater role to the lower clergy and to the laity: more than two hundred years before Vatican II at least one Jansenist curé said mass in French (not Latin) and encouraged the congregation to participate more fully.[5] Furthermore, some of the Jansenists whose lives were held up as examples were not the great of this world but ordinary priests and nuns, merchants, even working women distinguished by their piety and charity. Their beliefs implicitly challenged the monopoly of honor claimed by the nobility and the unquestioning obedience upon which Louis XIV's absolutist system was built.

Neither Versailles nor the Vatican looked favorably upon such doctrines. Louis XIV persuaded the pope to issue a special bull condemning Jansenism and in particular the work of that "wolf in sheep's clothing," the exiled French theologian Pasquier Quesnel. This bull, known from its opening words as *Unigenitus*, provoked enormous controversy from the very moment it was issued in 1713. It singled out ideas supposedly advanced by Quesnel, but many of the condemned passages were almost direct quotations from Saint Paul and other biblical authorities. Thirty French bishops and three thousand priests publicly opposed the bull, most important the archbishop of Paris, Cardinal de Noailles. He was joined by nearly two thirds of the curés of the diocese.[6]

Unigenitus made Jansenism into a far more serious issue than it might otherwise have become. The monarchy's subsequent actions further aggravated the dispute. Immense pressure was placed on the Jansenist bishops and on the Paris theological faculty to make them accept the bull. In 1728, twelve months after the death of Pâris and fifteen years after *Unigenitus* was issued, Louis XV's first minister Cardinal Fleury won a major victory when the seventy-seven-year-old archbishop of Paris publicly accepted it. A year later the archbishop died, giving Fleury the opportunity to replace him with a man hostile to Jansenism: Charles-Gaspard-Guillaume de Vintimille.[7]

Vintimille immediately set about cleansing the Paris diocese of Jansenism. In 1730 he dismissed the curés of three parishes: St-Etienne-du-Mont, St-Médard, and La Villette just outside the city. When these dismissals were challenged in the courts, the king's council stepped in, overrode the local courts and the Parlement, and ruled in favor of the archbishop.

It was just at this moment, when the Jansenists appeared to be losing, that the miracles began on the tomb at St-Médard. François de Pâris had trained at the Jansenist dominated seminary of St-Magloire and his own theology was strongly Jansenist. He had been supported by the dismissed curé of St-Médard and had signed the appeal against *Unigenitus*. Those who flocked to the tomb to acclaim him as a new saint included many of the most prominent Paris Jansenists, and the miracles gave apparent divine approval to their cause. Not surprisingly, Archbishop Vintimille and Cardinal Fleury discouraged the growing cult of Pâris. St-Médard was purged of Jansenist priests and placed under permanent police surveillance. None of this was effective. The numbers of pilgrims grew and the Jansenists exulted.

The closure of the cemetery was an escalation of the official campaign against a dissident movement that was getting out of control. But like the other arbitrary acts of the government, it only aggravated the situation, swinging public sympathy behind the Jansenists. Official persecution brought together a powerful coalition in Paris, bitterly opposed to the religious policy of Cardinal Fleury, that was to determine the shape of politics in the city for the next thirty years.

THE JANSENIST COALITION

Leading the pro-Jansenist forces were a significant minority of the lawyers and magistrates of the powerful Paris Parlement. The Parlement was not only the highest court of law in the Paris region—in fact its jurisdiction covered a third of the kingdom—but it also issued decrees that had the force of law. For example it repeatedly banned begging in the streets of Paris. It ratified the rules of the Paris trades corporations on working hours and wage rates and oversaw public morality, condemning works like Voltaire's *Lettres philosophiques* of 1734. The Parlement also registered royal decrees, entering them on its books so they became part of the corpus of French law. In the process it could suggest amendments and point to any contradictions between the new decree and earlier laws. This power of "remonstrance," as it was called, was regularly used to protest against royal edicts of which its members disapproved.

Jansenist magistrates were only a minority in the Parlement, but even the non-Jansenists were infuriated by the government's attempts to impose the bull *Unigenitus,* arguing that in French law the Church was independent of Rome. They also objected when the Crown denied them the right to hear appeals from Jansenist clergy who had been dismissed.[8]

The Parlement's stance was important because of its enormous influence in Paris. Its role as the preeminent court not only for civil suits but also on matters of commercial, administrative, and industrial law made it hugely important to ordinary city dwellers, even to workers who occasionally took cases to the Parlement.[9] A surprising number of the city's inhabitants, at one time or another, had direct contact with the courts. The individual magistrates of the Parlement, furthermore, were very powerful figures. They moved easily in court circles and a number were intimate friends of some of the most powerful houses in France, like the Rohan, the La Rochefoucauld, and the Gouffier families.[10]

The readiness of the police to jump at complaints from members of the Parlement gives us some idea of their influence. In 1769 an actor in Nicolet's street theater made fun of a black-coated spectator whom he clearly took for a lawyer: in fact the man was a magistrate of the Parlement and the theater was closed shortly after. In 1764 the police themselves were the subject of complaints, prompting the leading commissaires

Figure 21. The Parlement of Paris in session, 1754. The first president is in the chair. Anonymous engraving celebrating the Parlement's return from exile, from the frontispiece of an almanac. Musée Carnavalet, © Photothèque des musées de la ville de Paris, photo Ladet.

to address a circular to their colleagues: "You will realize . . . of what consequence these [complaints] will be for each of us individually and for all of us collectively if they reach the magistrates of the Parlement."[11]

Of all the magistrates two figures wielded exceptional power. The first president, effectively the leader of the Paris Parlement, presided even when the princes of the royal family attended sessions. He did not doff his hat when he addressed them, as anyone else had to. Close behind him in prestige and authority came the *procureur général,* the king's representative. In 1733 procureur général Joly de Fleury even rejected a "request" from one of the royal family, saying that "he [took] orders only from the King." He and the first president together guided the deliberations of the court and in consultation with royal ministers drew up the text of many of the laws that the Parlement would register and enforce. They sat together in the *assemblée de police* of Paris and on the board of administrators of the central hospital. The procureur général was also the man with ultimate responsibility for the administration of the Paris churches and so had much contact with churchwardens and curés.[12]

Parisians with a keen sense of their own interests took care not to offend the members of the Parlement. Even nobles had to tread warily: Dupin, the former governor of Coulommiers and a man of wealth and influence, politely declined to assist his anti-Jansenist parish priest because he was afraid of jeopardizing a case before the court.[13] Justice in eighteenth-century Paris was neither blind nor impartial, and even the wealthy took care to maintain good relations with the Parlement. Indeed, ready access to the magistrates and to the influence they could exert on one's behalf was one of the factors that distinguished the powerful in Paris society from the powerless.

The lawyers of the Parlement were a far less distinguished group, but nevertheless quite influential. Most people involved in a case before the court engaged a barrister, who customarily prepared a brief. Increasingly, in controversial cases, these briefs were published, in a sort of public relations campaign designed to influence both the magistrates and a wider public. Some lawyers became well known public figures who attracted crowds when they pleaded.[14]

Another significant group antagonized by the government's stance on the Jansenist issue was a substantial proportion of the Paris clergy. Initially, forty-four of the fifty-odd curés of Paris publicly opposed the bull *Unigenitus* and they were followed by a great many ordinary priests: fifty-six of them at St-Etienne-du-Mont, thirty-seven at St-Jacques-du-Haut-Pas, thirty at St-André-des-Arts, thirty-eight at St-Séverin, forty-three at

St-Jacques-de-la-Boucherie. Several colleges of the University of Paris were strongly Jansenist, and so were the Oratorien fathers, the Pères de la doctrine chrétienne, and a number of other religious orders.[15]

But for them Jansenism was not the only issue. The attempts by the government and the archbishop to impose *Unigenitus* raised serious questions about the independence of the French Church. Since 1516 the right of the kings of France to appoint bishops and many abbots had been virtually uncontested, while a national body called the Assemblée du clergé, composed half of bishops and half of other churchmen, had determined the policy of the French Church. In the 1680s the position of the Gallican Church had been spelled out explicitly: the pope's authority was spiritual, not temporal, and could not override the customs of the French Church. While acknowledging the pope as ultimate leader of the universal church, many of the French clergy were sympathetic to the Jansenist argument that neither the pope nor the government had the power to dictate its theology. They agreed with the former archbishop of Paris, de Noailles, that "it is permissible and canonically correct to appeal to the supreme tribunal of the Church against a constitution [*Unigenitus*] that the Church universal has not agreed to."[16]

Also at issue was the authority of the bishops and archbishops over the lower clergy. Eighteenth-century Jansenism had a particular appeal to many humble priests because it imagined the Church as a community of the elect. "In the final analysis," wrote the abbé Etemare, "belief is a matter for *the elect,* which means that the most elevated man in the Church might be the least of all."[17] This was an extreme view, but many came to agree, as events unfolded, that an archbishop might be wrong and might even be an instrument in the persecution of true believers.

But the Jansenist clergy were not the only ones disturbed by Archbishop Vintimille's removal of the three curés. It was not clear that he had the legal right to do it. The abbey of Ste-Geneviève named the curés of St-Médard and St-Etienne-du-Mont. In fact other authorities—not the archbishop—named most of the curés: abbeys and chapters, the university, religious orders, even noblemen.[18] The archbishop therefore seemed to be attempting to extend his authority, overturning custom and tradition and threatening the independence of the lower clergy. The fifty-odd Paris curés were a proud group and suspicious of outside interference. Most were highly educated churchmen of good family who believed they should be masters of their own parishes. They met regularly to discuss parish affairs (and no doubt Church politics as well) and although they were by no means all Jansenist sympathizers they protested vigorously to Archbishop Vintimille against the dismissal of their colleagues, refusing to recognize either of the replacements he had appointed.[19]

Alienating the curés was a bad move because they were influential figures. It was they, not the archbishop, who appointed most of the other clergy in each parish and who could promote or dismiss them. Where the curé of a parish gave a strong lead it was a courageous priest—or one with influential protectors—who dared to oppose him. If he chose to permit the cult of Pâris, to allow or even foster Jansenism within the parish, the other priests generally seconded his efforts in their sermons, in their advice to parishioners, in the confessional. For the laity too the curé was a figure of great importance. His spiritual functions alone gave him enormous authority: if an ordinary priest had privileged access to the Lord, how much more credence would the spiritual leader of the parish community possess? This authority was given symbolic form in church ritual. He officiated at only the most important religious services. On such occasions he occupied the central place: unless there were a special visitor he was normally the only priest allowed to mount the high pulpit for the oration. In processions he led the way, in full regalia, at the head of anywhere between ten and eighty magnificently robed priests and thirty or forty lay administrators in robes and bands. Rich and influential men and women knelt to receive the sacraments from his hands and to accept the penance he gave after hearing their confession.[20]

If spiritual authority was one source of prestige, privileged access to the secular authorities was another. A curé often assisted parishioners with recommendations and letters. At St-Médard the curé wrote to the lieutenant general of police on behalf of local shopkeepers seeking a reduction in their tax on compassionate grounds; to get confiscated property returned; to help obtain positions for their children.[21] The curé was an immensely influential person, and his lead in a matter such as the *Unigenitus* controversy could be crucial in swinging parish opinion. Furthermore, in the two parishes directly involved—St-Médard and St-Etienne-du-Mont—there was, it seems, considerable affection for the two former curés. "We have no need of a curé or priests in our parish," a master founder told the new priest at St-Médard. "We will send our confession to M. Pommart our [true] curé." As late as 1744 the schoolmaster at St-Etienne told a new parish priest that Blondel, the man dismissed in 1730, was still the real curé.[22]

Opposition by a high proportion of the parish clergy, if not to *Unigenitus* itself, at least to the way the archbishop and the government were handling the issue, was no doubt important in determining the position of many lay people. The ordinary priests were often very close to the ordinary population. Particularly in the early years of the century, many came from local families and lived little differently from the people around them. In 1744 a priest at St-Gervais left "to my brother priests, who are needy, the clothes and linen that I have lent them."[23] Jansenist priests, in particular, made a virtue of their poverty. But the influence of the clergy could work both for and against Jansenism. At St-Nicolas-des-Champs two Jansenist priests were victims of harassment both by the other clergy of the parish and by a number of parishioners.[24]

Attachment to the clergy may have helped determine the attitude of some people, but not of all. Jansenist or not, most people who came to the tomb of Pâris in hope of a miraculous cure or seeking his intercession clearly believed that he was a saint. They had no time for priests or even bishops who said he was not. When the clergy of St-Médard tried to prevent people from saying prayers to Pâris in the chapel nearest the cemetery, they were ignored. When they removed the candles and scraps of paper with scribbled prayers to Pâris (some of which are preserved in the police archives), they were threatened. The new curé had to employ a doorman to prevent people from insulting him in the church. There were limits to the people's respect and many saw the clergy as having no monopoly on God. From the point of view of the ordinary Parisian the priests had a job to do and if they failed to do it properly they would be neither obeyed nor respected.

Jansenist theology in fact encouraged a strong independence of mind in the laity, for it placed a heavy emphasis on individual conscience. The faithful should not go to communion automatically, every week, but only when they were in a state of true penitence. They were encouraged to examine their consciences, to decide for themselves when they were ready to approach the Lord's table. This was a two-edged sword because it left the clergy a far less significant role as intercessors and advisors than in the mainstream Catholic practice encouraged by the Jesuits and others. In fact the Jansenists reproached the Jesuits for leading people to believe that regular attendance at confession and at mass was enough: "one can damn oneself by following the advice of a confessor," warned the Jansenist *Catéchisme historique et dogmatique* of 1729.[25] People needed to listen to the voice within.

And this was precisely what many educated lay people did. In November 1754 one Marie-Gabrielle Lallemant, a linen weaver's shop assistant in the Place Maubert, was refused the last sacraments because of her Jansenist beliefs. She resisted all the efforts of both secular and clerical authority. When the Grand Pénitencier de Notre-Dame (a formidable clerical official close to the archbishop) forced his way in, she "told him that she did not recognize lettres de cachet [royal arrest warrants], that she had made her confession to an approved priest and that she had no need to reconcile herself [with the Church]. The Grand Pénitencier tried to get her to tell him the name of her confessor, but she replied that she was not obliged to give it."[26]

It was quite a performance for a woman of the people. And she was not alone. A few years later, in a dispute at St-Nicolas-des-Champs, forty-three women and men stepped forward to testify, some of them against their anti-Jansenist confessors. The domestic servant Marie Vilmondel, who was also refused the sacraments because of her Jansenism, accused the pope, the bishops, and all the priests who thought as they did of being "so many wolves wearing the skins of ewes," and that was all, she added, predicted in the Scriptures. "Ah well, they deprive me of the body of Jesus Christ, they cannot deprive me of His Spirit."[27]

Jansenist ideas were spread not only by the clergy, therefore, but through other networks as well. Children in the parish school at St-Etienne-du-Mont were taught "that there is no middle way between charity and greed."[28] Those at the St-Médard school were taught prayers to Pâris and after the purges of 1730 were told "that there is no longer a good confessor at St-Médard" and that they should go somewhere else. The parish clergy were slow to realize the importance of these schools as a pro-Jansenist force, but in any case could do little about them since the schoolmasters were mostly appointed by the churchwardens. Even where the schools did not directly inculcate a Jansenist theology, of course, they equipped people to read about it, particularly in the enormously successful Jansenist *Nouvelles ecclésiastiques*. When a brush maker mentioned her prolapsed uterus to her neighbor Louise Grasset, who had a job pasting fans, Louise remembered "having seen in a page of the *Nouvelles ecclésiastiques* the story of a miracle." She took the neighbor to St-Médard, where after completing a novena the woman was cured. In the middle decades of the eighteenth century the marquis d'Argenson could write that "the whole of Paris is Jansenist," and plebeian networks were crucial in this success.[29]

If the "common people," as they were often called, had strong Jansenist sympathies and were prepared to confront the parish clergy, the same was true of many of the local elite. A significant proportion of Parisian bourgeois were genuinely Jansenist, lawyers conspicuous among them. The best-known is Louis Adrien Le Paige, an advisor to the prince de Conti. Le Paige's writing was enormously influential. There were also humbler men like the notary's clerk Elie Radet, who acted as "agent" for the Jansenist-leaning churchwardens of St-Etienne-du-Mont.[30]

Many merchants had similar sympathies. The pro-Jansenist churchwardens of St-Nicolas-des-Champs in 1760 included two grocers, one mercer, a wine merchant, a goldsmith, and an apothecary—all from the prestigious merchant corporations.[31] Jeanne Tavignot, who was denied Easter communion in 1733 because she refused to accept the bull *Unigenitus,* was the daughter of a silk merchant and cousin to one of the pro-Jansenist churchwardens of St-Médard. Jansenism was passed on in families and particularly within the proud dynasties of merchants and master craftsmen who played a key role in many quarters of the city. In 1740 the entire *assemblée de charité* at St-Médard, composed of daughters and wives of local merchants, was accused by a woman of the parish of being "infected with Jansenism."[32]

The adherence to Jansenist principles by lawyers, officeholders, merchants and their families had particular weight because they formed the local elite of Paris and they controlled the parishes. There were admittedly variations according to quarter. In the tiny inner-city parishes and those with few nobles or lawyers, merchants ruled the roost: in 1761 the men in charge at St-Germain-le-Vieux, on the Ile-de-la-Cité, were two mercers and a silk merchant, while at St-Laurent on the northern fringe the parish finances were managed in 1756 by two grocers. In the poorer parishes of the faubourgs, master artisans often dominated: St-Hippolyte was governed by dyers and by furniture makers and painters from the Gobelins manufactory. The richer and more prestigious churches, on the other hand, could attract churchwardens of higher status, so that at St-Gervais or St-André-des-Arts, along with the magistrates who occupied honorary positions, the churchwardens were in roughly equal numbers minor officials of the courts (*procureurs*) and members of the prestigious merchant corps.[33]

These churchwardens were influential local figures. They were responsible for the financial affairs of the parish. They appointed (and could dismiss) the church servants: the doorman and the beadles, the organist and other musicians, the grave diggers and the bell ringer, even the sacristan. They awarded church contracts, sometimes worth a great deal: the mason who maintained the buildings belonging to St-Laurent was paid around 1,800 livres a year. Then there was the laundering and mending of vestments and altar cloths, the maintenance of the buildings, not to mention the major annual expense of candles and communion bread.

On top of all this there were occasional major works: a new roof, a bell, refurbishment of a chapel. The churchwardens had ample opportunities for patronage of local artisans and shopkeepers and for assistance to the honest poor.[34] They even decided which priests would say the masses of remembrance that wealthy parishioners hoped would ease their way through purgatory. These masses sometimes made up a large part of an ordinary priest's income, so the churchwardens had a considerable hold over the parish clergy.[35]

Simply being a churchwarden gave prestige, both to the individual and to his family. It gave immediate access to the curé and other parish notables and brought contact with influential people inside and outside the parish. The local population turned to them for petitions for letters of recommendation and assistance, even in matters unconnected with church business. Marie Elizabeth Colet and her husband Pierre Lenoble, newly arrived in Paris and looking for work, were directed to the iron merchant Charles Hébert, "a very charitable person and first churchwarden of Ste-Marguerite." He found Lenoble a job in a local pottery. A year earlier Hébert had assisted another poor woman by putting her in touch with the then first churchwarden, whom he asked "to make sure her petition was accepted."[36]

Two new churchwardens were elected each year, in theory by all the notables of the parish but in practice usually by the former churchwardens, the *anciens*. They also had the task of checking the annual accounts, of making investment decisions, and of authorizing all major expenses. Although the curé had a voice in such matters, it was the past and present churchwardens—a tiny corporation—who were the legal representatives of the parish. They defended it in disputes over boundaries or processional rights and decided whether to go to court if the heirs of a benefactor challenged a bequest. And they could not be dismissed except for malpractice or by a special order of the king's council. Once the two-year term of new churchwardens expired they joined the *anciens*, retaining a place of honor and an active role in the management of the church for the rest of their lives or until they left the parish. While curés and even archbishops came and went, the assembly of churchwardens was eternal.[37] In this sense they were the real rulers of the parish.

They were therefore formidable opponents for a curé who clashed with them. It was they who, at St-Médard and at St-Etienne-du-Mont, organized opposition to the archbishop and to the new curés he had installed. They passed resolutions condemning the government's action and mounted a legal challenge to the dismissal of their curés. At St-Médard they took the new priest to court over several of his actions, organized a petition against him, and vigorously encouraged the cult of Pâris.[38]

These two were by no means the only churches where the leading parishioners were strongly Jansenist. At St-Hippolyte too the appointment of an anti-Jansenist curé aroused strong opposition, while at both St-Jacques-du-Haut-Pas and St-Landry almost the entire congregation got up and left when the priest read out the archbishop's order banning the Jansenist *Nouvelles ecclésiastiques*. After the curé of St-Nicolas-des-Champs was exiled by the Parlement, the churchwardens imposed a Jansenist regime on the parish and distributed 1,000 livres' worth of Jansenist books as prizes to children in the parish school.[39]

In each of these churches, the role of the local bourgeois notables as administrators complemented their standing as local opinion makers, patrons, and employers. The churchwardens in many cases constituted a self-perpetuating local oligarchy, elected by a small group of the richest and best-established parishioners. "Nearly all the masses have been paid for by the grandfathers of the churchwardens living today," the churchwardens of St-Médard pointed out in 1734, and they might have added the pulpit, the parish school, and many of the altar ornaments and vestments.[40] They therefore resisted when the archbishop attempted to impose an authoritarian curé who wished to concentrate power in his own hands.

Disputes over Jansenism in the Paris parishes, therefore, were often as much over who should run the parish as over what kind of liturgy should be used and which saints' days should be observed. The churchwardens looked on the parish almost as their property, certainly as their domain, and clashed with curés who took a similarly proprietorial view. There are hints that across the entire century the clergy were gradually extending their control over the parishes, just as the archbishop was affirming his authority over the diocese. Numerous court cases led to curés being given greater control of poor funds and allowed them a greater say in meetings of the churchwardens.[41] Jansenism, on the other hand, recognized the claim of the local notables to rule. Its theology of the parish as a community of spiritual equals justified their resistance to clerical domination.

THE STRUGGLE FOR CONTROL

The closure of the cemetery at St-Médard in 1732 marked the beginning of a long struggle and not, as the archbishop had hoped, the end of the affair. Instead of giving up the Pâris cult, the most ardent "convulsionaries," those who had been regular visitors and who had undergone strange convulsions on the tomb, now changed tactics. Small groups began holding secret meetings, evading the police and the religious authorities while actively recruiting new adherents, principally among the ordinary people of Paris. Some groups specialized in trances and speaking in tongues, while others went in for spectacular forms of flagellation, including piercing with swords, beating with clubs, even crucifixion.[42] They were not numerous but they attracted a great deal of attention and somewhat embarrassed the more mainstream Jansenists.

Far more important than the convulsionaries, though, was the continued resistance of parish churchwardens. Throughout the 1730s and 1740s they fought the government and the archbishop in the courts and with dogged obstruction. Everywhere Jansenists rejected the archbishop's priests and disseminated the *Nouvelles ecclésiastiques,* the underground newspaper whose authors and printers the Paris police searched for in vain. They received open support from the Parlement and passive assistance even from within the royal administration. "Three quarters of the commissaires and police employees are in favor of this party and it is not surprising that not everything is uncovered that might be," observed the lawyer Barbier in 1731.[43] Even so, as long as the archbishop could count on the support of the king, time was on his side. One by one the Paris parishes were purged of their Jansenist priests. The king's council systematically overruled the Parlement whenever it decided against the archbishop and the orthodox clergy. The rebellious churchwardens were gradually reduced to impotence.

But then in 1750 came a fresh development. The new archbishop of Paris, Christophe de Beaumont, no doubt believing the battle almost won, decreed that no one would receive the sacraments unless they could present a certificate from an approved confessor (who was expected to ensure that they accepted *Unigenitus*). But he was underestimating the strength of feeling in the diocese. Individual Jansenists took up his challenge with alacrity. Nuns, priests, and lay parishioners, sick and often dying, began to defy the parish clergy by calling for the last rites while making it clear that they did not have the required certificate. Although according to orthodox Church teaching it meant putting their souls in mortal danger, in 1752 both the wife of a magistrate in the Châtelet court and the wife of a lawyer attached to the Parlement were refused the sacraments when they refused to renounce their Jansenist beliefs.[44] The mercer Cousin, proprietor of the Aigle d'or in the rue du faubourg St-Antoine, was denied the last rites in 1755. Marie Thérèse Guerrier, the widow of a master baker in the rue Fromenteau, was refused the sacraments by the clergy of St-Germain-l'Auxerrois in 1762 and died without a priest.[45]

Few things could have more effectively swung public opinion against the archbishop. This was a society in which death and preparations for death played a vitally important role. The graveyard was at the center of each parish, and masses were said daily in remembrance of former parishioners. The handbell that preceded the priest on his way to administer the last sacraments was heard daily in the streets: "whenever this bell rings," observed the American John Quincy Adams, "every man, woman and child fall upon their knees. . . . Every carriage that meets it, even the king's, is obliged to stop; and the persons in it bend the knee."[46] Often people followed into the very bedchamber of the dying. After death the body was placed on display at the door of the house until the local parish clergy came, with the appropriate prayers, to guide it first to the church, then to the cemetery.[47] Death was a very public affair, and thoughts of death were never far away.

The idea of dying without the sacraments was a particularly troubling one, and for most of the century the first thought of the passers-by when someone was seriously injured or collapsed in the street was to seek a priest. The fact that so many Jansenists were able to overcome their fear of dying unshriven reveals the intensity of their faith. Over sixty Parisians were refused the sacraments in the middle years of the century, at least fifteen of them lay people. Their actions deeply impressed other Parisians, who at the same time were shocked that the anti-Jansenist clergy were prepared, apparently without remorse, to let people die in this way. In some cases, furthermore, the people concerned were widely known and respected. One was Jacques Villemsens, who had been a senior priest at St-Nicolas-des-Champs for thirty-seven years and had numerous relatives in the parish. Cousin, mentioned above, had been a churchwarden of Ste-Marguerite and a prominent figure in the faubourg St-Antoine. All this in obedience to a papal decree that many saw as inapplicable to France.[48]

The Parlement sprang to the assistance of the excommunicated Jansenists. As soon as the court was notified of a refusal of sacraments (and the Jansenists ensured there was no delay), it ordered the priests concerned to administer the last rites. Those who refused were arrested, and after the first few episodes they generally went into hiding. At first the royal government supported the archbishop. The king ordered the Parlement to stop all proceedings. It declined and went on strike—refused to hear ordinary court cases—and soon found itself exiled from the city.[49] Meanwhile, Parisians reacted violently. In 1753 the marquis d'Argenson noted in his diary that "ministers of religion scarcely dare to show themselves in the streets without being abused, and this all comes from the bull *Unigenitus,* as well as from the measures against the Parlement."[50]

Even the king was sensitive to such widespread public feeling and in particular to the pressure brought by the Parlement. In 1754 royal policy abruptly shifted with Louis XV's "Declaration of Silence," which attempted to put an end to the religious divisions in the country by forbidding further discussion of *Unigenitus.* This proved unsuccessful since neither side was prepared to cooperate. Having failed to enforce the Declaration of Silence, after 1757 the government tried to steer a more neutral path but largely let the Parlement have its way. The magistrates went on prosecuting priests who refused the sacraments to dying Jansenists, with the result that several parishes lost their curés and at least three ended up with too few priests to guarantee regular services. Where the curé went into hiding, the churchwardens were left in control, and at St-Nicolas-des-Champs they immediately drafted new rules removing his control over poor relief and got the Parlement to approve them before the archbishop found out what was happening.[51] The final victory of the Parlement, in 1762, was the suppression of the Jesuits, the principal opponents of Jansenism.

The hesitations of Louis XV and his ministers eventually allowed the Jansenists to triumph. Yet they would have been defeated easily without support from the Parlement and the lower courts, from the Parisian bourgeois, and from workers faithful to the memory of François de Pâris. But it was not the same Jansenism in all social groups. Between the Jansenist principles of the professional and commercial middle classes and those of the laundrymaid kneeling before the tomb of Pâris stretched a gap just as wide as the social one that separated them. Nor was it just a difference of theological understanding. The magistrates of the Parlement had national interests: the defense of Gallicanism and of their own power in the face of Church and king. The local elites of Paris were concerned with leadership of the parish as well as liturgy and belief. The laundrymaid and others like her held onto a faith that offered the poor full membership of the spiritual community and tried to alleviate their lot in the here-and-now. The irony of political accident made all of them allies against some of the clergy, the archbishop, and for a time the royal government.

There were particular characteristics of Paris life, though, that made it more than an accident. For the environment of the big city in itself encouraged an independence of action and of mind. Despite the presence of great nobles and the proximity of the royal family, the inhabitants of Paris were not subject to the seigneurial controls that weighed heavily upon much of the peasantry. They were only infrequently subject to the humiliating manifestations of deference that even the wealthy peasantry—the *coqs de village*—were required to display each time their lord approached. They were also less subject to the clergy, who were too few to control the enormous population in some parishes, especially those on the rapidly expanding periphery. The church of Ste-Marguerite could hold 3,000 people but in 1766 the parish population was estimated at 42,000. In 1725 the curé complained that former Protestants—many of them converted more or less by force—came to the main services but stayed outside the church on the pretext that there was no room for them within. "It is always impossible to make the new converts conform," he added, "unless one knows them."[52] Herein lay the problem. In such circumstances, the clergy could not know, minister to, or control the population. The city was too large, and parts of its population were highly mobile. These circumstances did not make religious (or political) dissent inevitable, but they did enable dissent to survive and flourish.

As the disputes over Jansenism show, neither the Parlement nor the clergy, despite their considerable power, determined opinions in the streets and markets. To a high degree, moral leadership had become the domain of the legal and commercial middle classes. Through their role as churchwardens, benefactors, and directors of parish charity they knew a significant proportion of the population and were able to exercise direct patronage. They had daily contact with the people, and although unable to appease popular anger they did retain a significant moral influence unmatched by the clergy, the nobility, or the police. Just as local merchants had rescued the commissaire Labbé from a hostile crowd in 1725, it was they, along with lawyers and minor officeholders, who led the local resistance to the anti-Jansenist clergy. From the 1730s to the early 1760s, elements of these middle classes—though divided among the parishes and quarters of the city, with no central organizations through which to coordinate their action, and no class consciousness to unify them—were able to mount an effective rearguard action against the combined forces of the monarchy and the Church hierarchy. If in the end the Parlement won the battle, the parishes had provided many of the activists and the "public opinion" that lawyers and magistrates increasingly referred to in their declarations and that even Louis XV's supposedly "absolute" monarchy could not ignore in the later years of his reign.

The Jansenist controversy reveals the key political forces in early- and mid-eighteenth-century Paris, and the complex networks of patronage and authority through which they operated. But it also reveals their limits. On the one hand, it demonstrates that when the influential groups and institutions who ruled the city—the clergy, the police, the courts, and the local middle classes—were at odds with one another they risked losing control. On the other, it reveals yet again the strong sense among Parisians—shared by working people and the middle ranks alike—that the clergy, the government, and the powerful in society had an obligation to serve the community. If they did not, then ordinary people had a right to protest and even resist.

Jansenism also brought important and permanent changes to the Parisian political and social landscape. It made politics immediately relevant to ordinary people's lives in an unprecedented way. It temporarily poisoned relations between much of the clergy and some of the population, and the refusals of sacraments, in particular, had a huge impact that may have promoted the spread of anticlericalism. Furthermore, Jansenism almost certainly encouraged the independence of mind that was a product of the urban environment itself. Taken together, the religious struggles from the 1720s to the 1750s were one of the most important political events in Paris before the Revolution of 1789.

PART III

MAKING A NEW ROME

CHAPTER SEVEN

AFFAIRES DU TEMPS

The workbook of the Parisian tailor Jean Thomas Terrier, held in the Archives nationales, makes fascinating reading.[1] It began as a record of work he did for different clients between 1758 and 1775, but he used the spare pages at the back to note other things. There are recipes for blackcurrant liqueur, for a tisane, and for a patent cure for corns. There are two drafts of a speech. And inside the back cover is a list of events, without commentary:

The King's accident on 5 January 1757

The Parlement returned 2 September 1757

Monsieur the Archbishop of Paris returned 1 October 1757

Monsieur the Archbishop of Paris departed 5 January 1758

The square in front of the church of Ste-Geneviève was consecrated 1 August 1758

The 2 October 1759 the King orders silverware to be taken to the Mint

The final stone of the lower church of Ste-Geneviève was laid on 9 June 1763

On 20 June 1763 the Place Louis XV was officially opened

On 21 June 1763 peace was proclaimed

On 22 June fireworks display on the water opposite the Place Louis XV

Monsieur the Archbishop of Paris departed 20 January 1764

6 September 1764 the King came to lay the first stone of the church of Ste-Geneviève accompanied by Monseigneur the Dauphin

On 13 November 1765 the shrine of Saint Genevieve was uncovered because of the illness of Monseigneur the Dauphin and was lowered on 16 December and was raised again on the 20th at 6 in the evening and Monseigneur the Dauphin died the said day 20 December

On 17 February Monsieur la Chaussée was received as a master in the year 1763

On 23 August 1774 the King exiled the Chancellor and the Controller General.

There is no way of telling exactly when this list of *affaires du temps* was drawn up. The later events could have been noted as they occurred—the workbook was only begun in 1758, so at least the first three entries were made with hindsight. Perhaps the concentration of dates in the mid-1760s indicates a time of writing around then: the last two entries do look like later additions. The dates are precise, so perhaps they were copied from another record, possibly from collected news circulars.

What seems certain is that these were events that Jean Thomas Terrier felt to be specially significant. Though he gives no hint of what they meant to him, we can make some guesses because there is a certain logic to the selection. They fall easily into several categories. One entry—out of order in the list—appears purely personal: his acquaintance La Chaussée becoming a master. Several record local happenings. Terrier lived five minutes' walk from where the giant new church of Ste-Geneviève (now the Panthéon) was being built, and the stages in its construction were of particular interest to people in this area. So was everything to do with the shrine of Saint Genevieve in the nearby church of St-Etienne-du-Mont, another local landmark. But Saint Genevieve was also of much wider relevance because she was the patron saint of Paris and her shrine was regularly uncovered in times of famine, drought, or national emergency. Through her, local, Parisian, and national events were linked.[2]

Terrier's list included other happenings that many Parisians would remember but that had little importance to people living outside the city. The official opening of the Place Louis XV and the fireworks for the peace of 1763 fall into this category, and perhaps also the successive periods of exile of the archbishop of Paris.

Finally, there were events of national significance. The list begins with the attack on Louis XV by the domestic servant Robert-François Damiens. It records the return of the Parlement and of the archbishop from exile after Louis XV made yet another attempt to settle the refusals of sacraments crisis. The archbishop's continued intransigence soon saw him in exile once more, and in 1764, as Terrier notes, he was to be sent packing yet again after publicly condemning the dissolution of the Jesuits. The melting down of gold and silver ornaments in 1759, to help pay for the Seven Years' War, was a sacrifice not forgotten.

The death of the dauphin, heir to the throne, profoundly affected the king and perhaps marked the imaginations of Parisians more than has been recognized. It disappointed those who had hoped for better things if he became king, though given his pro-Jesuit sympathies, others may have heard the news with relief. Yet it could equally have been remembered as simply one more reversal in a reign marked by disaster after disaster.[3]

Terrier's final entry refers to the sacking by Louis XVI of his predecessor's ministers Maupeou and Terray, hated in Paris for their coup against the Parlement and for the new tax measures they had introduced.

If the tailor meant his list to be a record of the principal events of the last twenty years of Louis XV's reign, it has some conspicuous omissions. There is no mention of the royal coup of 1771, when most of the magistrates of the Parlement of Paris were removed and replaced with men more subservient to the royal will. Nor is the death of Louis himself noted. These absences may be explicable if the list was compiled in the mid-1760s and the final couple of entries added as an afterthought. But there are other major omissions: the brutal execution of Damiens, the suppression of the Jesuit order, the death of the king's influential mistress Madame de Pompadour, and the liberalization of the grain trade in 1763. Were these of less relevance to a Paris tailor?

Whatever interpretation we place upon Terrier's list, it remains interesting because of who he was. Of humble stock, the grandson of a master glazier in Montdidier, near Amiens, he was firmly among the ranks of the skilled workforce. He was a tailor, his wife a mistress seamstress, and his uncle a journeyman goldsmith. Terrier was a little unusual in that he also worked for the Order of St-Jean-de-Latran (Saint John Lateran) and proudly bore the title of *greffier* of the order's estate at Fontenay-aux-Roses just south of Paris. But his duties apparently consisted mainly of recording rental payments and he did not live at Fontenay. He continued his tailoring and the office clearly did not earn him much, though it apparently did provide the substantial bonus of a three-room apartment. After his death in 1778, at the age of sixty-one, Terrier left his two children just over 1,000 livres—an extremely modest estate for a master craftsman.[4]

POPULAR INTEREST IN POLITICS

It is perhaps surprising to find someone of his rank showing interest in issues of "high" politics, well beyond the purely local and personal. Yet there is growing evidence that Terrier was not unusual. In recent years historians have unearthed a lot of evidence of popular interest in politics. There were deep political traditions in Paris, not only within the professional classes but also among merchants, shopkeepers, and artisans, male and female. Some of these people played a significant role in their parishes and in the trades corporations. While their field of vision was primarily local, they were aware of events in the world outside and interpreted them according to their own lights. They were quite familiar, furthermore, with the complex political and administrative system of Old Regime Paris and were well able to interpret the subtle signs of shifting royal policy and favor. Even before the 1750s there existed a "public" sphere of widely recognized political symbols and language.

Some members of the laboring classes also shared these understandings. They were particularly sensitive to religious politics, especially to the conflicts over Jansenism. Arlette Farge has traced in police reports the explosion of discussion about religious affairs around 1730 and the surprise of police observers at hearing "the simplest folk" expressing strong opinions on the subject. In October 1729 "one hears nothing but comments by the least educated people against [*Unigenitus*]; water carriers and porters from the ports speak openly and use most unseemly language against the court of Rome." In 1733 a woman who hawked secondhand clothes was accused of criticizing the archbishop for his persecution of Jansenists.[5]

There is ample other evidence to suggest that awareness of high politics was widespread in Paris. The market women were notorious: their low opinion of the peace treaty of 1749 was widely reported in Paris, and in 1752 they were prominent among crowds who jeered the archbishop of Paris and tore down copies of his decrees.[6] The refusals of sacraments crisis in the 1750s produced an explosion of popular commentary and further evidence of political awareness among people of quite humble status and limited education. The domestic servant Robert-François Damiens himself is an example. The motive for his attack on the king, he confessed under interrogation and torture, was "to prompt [the king] to restore all things to order and tranquility in his states," "to render [His Majesty] more disposed to hear [his Parlement's] remonstrances, to dispense justice, and cease heeding the pernicious advice of his ministers." He returned to this theme in evoking the misery of so many French people and in condemning the archbishop of Paris and other high-ranking churchmen: "If the King had only lopped off the heads of three or four Bishops this would not have happened," he insisted. Or at least Louis should have listened to his Parlements.[7]

The authorities refused to believe that a man of Damiens's station could think in this way or could have acted independently, and they searched unsuccessfully for his accomplices. Instead they uncovered abundant evidence of popular interest in politics. In December 1756 a blacksmith reportedly opined that in the recent royal declaration the king "had done well to say that *Unigenitus* was not a rule of faith"; but he disapproved of the king's treatment of the Parlement. A letter from an apprentice jeweler informed his cousin in the provinces of an imminent "revolution in the state resulting from the suppression of the Parlement." A servant admitted discussing the confrontation between the king and the Paris Parlement with some stocking merchants, with a number of women including "several fishwives," and with two other servants. The illiterate wife of a shoemaker predicted the reinstatement of the Parlement and the exile of the archbishop, though she was wrong on both counts.[8] Such comments reveal a range of ordinary individuals discussing public affairs in the most everyday contexts: among neighbors and fellow workers in wineshops, markets, and at the doors of houses.

These outbreaks of commentary do not in themselves indicate any transformation in popular political awareness across the century. For most people, interest in politics was probably episodic, linked to particular issues. In 1719–20 the attempt by John Law to introduce a paper currency and establish a French central bank had produced immense discussion in Paris, as hopes of overnight wealth rapidly gave way—when Law's scheme collapsed—to fears of bankruptcy.[9] Yet except where high politics impinged directly on their everyday lives, there is no evidence that most Parisians thought it was a domain in which they should have a say. There are nevertheless strong reasons to suspect that the 1750s and 1760s did mark a sea change in Parisian political life. It is likely—

though there is no way of measuring the phenomenon—that more people became interested in politics. Jean Thomas Terrier's list is circumstantial evidence: he was forty in 1757, old enough to remember earlier events clearly, yet he begins with Damiens's attack on the king, as if it were some kind of starting point.

This change, if there was one, did not happen overnight. Already in the 1730s purges of the clergy had angered many people who were normally indifferent to power struggles at the center. The dismissals of the curés of St-Médard and of St-Etienne-du-Mont and the appointment of anti-Jansenist priests in many other churches provoked bitter conflicts between the clergy and the local elite. The high reputation of many Jansenist priests mobilized the ordinary population of their parishes: "The coal heavers on the port . . . have held a meeting and gone to the archbishop's house, they left word for Monsieur the Archbishop that if he tried to do any harm to their curé he would have to deal with them."[10]

Across the 1730s and 1740s the growing involvement of the Parlement brought these multiple local struggles together into a citywide and indeed national cause. The amazingly successful Jansenist newspaper *Nouvelles ecclésiastiques*, reportedly running to 6,000 copies each week, encouraged Parisians of all ranks to connect events in their own parishes with those all over France. Local and national politics were linked in an almost unprecedented way.

Then in the 1750s the actions of Archbishop Christophe de Beaumont outraged a great many people who until then had remained uncommitted. In 1749 his purge of the Hôpital général, not just of clergy suspected of Jansenist sympathies but also of lay volunteers who regularly visited the sick, apparently provoked widespread disgust. But even worse were the refusals of sacraments to individuals like Marie-Gabrielle Lallemant, "known in her parish for her piety." In March 1752 more than ten thousand people (surely an exaggeration) were said to have attended the funeral of the Jansenist priest Ignace Le Mère, who had been refused the last rites. In mid-1754, according to the lawyer Barbier, one reason the Parlement was not recalled earlier was that "there would have been too great a gathering of people, [and] it was even to be feared that the people would commit some indecency toward the Archbishop of Paris."[11] Because the requirement of certificates of confession in principle applied to everyone, it forced people to declare either for or against the bull *Unigenitus*. No other issue could have aroused the same interest or passion. "How can one be a Christian and a citizen," a pamphleteer asked rhetorically, "without taking an interest in the disturbances troubling the Church and the state."[12]

But whether or not *more* people took an interest, the 1750s and 1760s do seem to have brought a qualitative change, and in two ways: in public attitudes toward the monarchy; and in the appearance of what both contemporaries and historians have called "public opinion." These developments need to be examined in turn.

ATTITUDES TOWARD THE MONARCHY

Damiens's attack on Louis XV in January 1757 illustrated how far the king's aura of majesty, a surer protection than any bodyguard, had faded. The fact that religious issues were at stake had serious consequences for a monarchy that claimed to be divinely ordained. The king, at his coronation, was anointed with holy oil and crowned by the archbishop of Rheims in the cathedral. Since medieval times, too, the French kings claimed the power to cure scrofula and on major feast days, five times a year, would duly touch a number of carefully selected sufferers. Louis was described as "king by the grace of God" and any attack on him, or even disobedience, was assimilated to revolt against the divine order and against God Himself. The Bourbon kings deliberately identified themselves with Saint Louis (Louis IX), in whose person kingship and holiness were combined: they gave his name to their sons and observed his feast day as their own. In the seventeenth century the theory of divine right—that the king held his crown from God alone—was used to raise him above the pope and the bishops and hence justify his control of the French Church. The theory reached its peak at the end of the seventeenth century and in the early eighteenth. "You are beholding the image of God in kings," declared Bishop Bossuet, tutor to Louis XIV's son, in 1699. Even in 1730 several Paris lawyers who had questioned the divine basis of royal authority were required to acknowledge that the king "holds in his kingdom the place of God Himself, of whom he is the living image."[13]

Yet in the mid eighteenth century this view of monarchy was coming under attack. It was undermined implicitly by Jansenist theology, which stressed that only God was sacred: hence even kings could not be. And Jansenism was exceptionally strong in Paris. But for practical purposes it was the magistrates of the Paris Parlement and their pro-Jansenist supporters who, particularly in the 1750s and 1760s, constructed a rival theory that the monarch was bound by certain "fundamental laws" of the kingdom and was not accountable solely to God. They were ably assisted by other political writers who, like Diderot in the *Encyclopédie,* held that "the prince derives from his subjects the authority he holds over them; and this authority is limited by the laws of nature and of the state . . . the prince therefore cannot use his power and dispose of his subjects without the consent of the nation." Even some churchmen, like the archbishop of Aix in his sermon for Louis XVI's coronation, argued that the king was bound by the laws of the nation. In educated circles, too, growing skepticism about divine intervention in the physical world, through miracles for example, also weakened belief in the literal sacredness of the royal person.[14]

There is evidence from the streets of Paris as well that belief in the sacredness of monarchy was under challenge. In September 1758 a man named Moriceau de La Motte was hanged for writing "seditious" posters attacking the king. As he was taken to the Place de Grève to be executed, people were heard to say, "people should not be put to death for words and mere writings." In the eyes of the Paris public, such attacks on the king were no longer blasphemous even if they remained so in law.[15] Well before this, in 1739, Louis XV had abstained from the ritual touching of scrofulous poor because—having publicly taken a mistress—he had scrupulously not taken Easter communion. "This caused a great scandal in Versailles and caused much comment in Paris." Yet a year later, when it happened again, Parisians made jokes about it. According to police reports some people were scandalized that he did not take communion, but little was said about the suspension of the touching ceremony. It had, it seems, ceased to be a significant element of educated Parisians' image of royalty.[16]

None of this made opposition, revolt, or revolution more likely. Nor does it indicate either hostility or indifference to the king. In August 1744, when he fell seriously ill, there were 6,000 requests for masses to be said at Notre-Dame for his recovery.[17] But the public idea of the monarch was changing, and even the defenders of absolutism felt they had to find other sources of legitimacy besides divine right. Increasingly, official images represented the king not as the earthly embodiment of divine might but as a generous and humanitarian protector. Jeffrey Merrick has traced this change through the statues erected to successive French kings. The military representations typical of Louis XIV gave way, by the 1750s and 1760s, to images of Louis XV as a peace-loving benefactor seeking the happiness of his people. When the Paris municipality decided in 1748 to erect a monument "to the glory of the King" they commissioned a statue

Figure 22. Edme Bouchardon's statue of Louis XV, erected 1763. Note the panel on the pedestal depicting Louis as peacemaker, with an olive branch. In Pierre Patte, *Monuments érigés en France à la gloire de Louis XV* (Paris, 1767). Bibliothèque historique de la ville de Paris, photo Jean-Christophe Doerr.

of Louis on horseback "as pacifier rather than as conqueror." The monument was eventually unveiled in 1763 (Figure 22), and some observers criticized it for not going far enough. "Why always equestrian statues? Why not a statue of the King standing calmly or seated in the middle of his palace and capital city? A calm King, pacifying and securing about him peace, abundance, the sciences, the fine arts."[18]

Other representations of the king followed the same itinerary. Although a wide range of media continued to glorify the monarch, neither Louis XV nor Louis XVI had a triumphal arch built in Paris. Louis XV did have a magnificent square named after him, but unlike older royal squares this one was designed for urban needs more than royal ones. It was neither a processional avenue nor a space in front of a palace: it was designed for traffic and for festivities, not specifically royal ceremonies. The alternative locations proposed for the statue illustrate the same purpose. Some proposed the marketplace, "in the midst of his people"; others an amphitheater for public festivities where the king would be surrounded by his joyful subjects. Louis himself, when a statue of him was erected in Rheims, chose the inscription "To Louis XV, the best of Kings, who by the benevolence (*douceur*) of his government creates the happiness of [his] people."[19]

In statues and portraits and on medallions Louis was most often portrayed as a human figure, dignified rather than majestic. This image persisted under Louis XVI. He was rarely depicted on horseback, more often as a man of the Enlightenment. A porcelain statue showed him with Benjamin Franklin, dignified but simply dressed and gracious (Figure 23). In a painting of 1785 designed to emphasize his benevolence, Debucourt displays Louis XVI dressed in modest costume, giving alms to a peasant boy.[20] This was a new image of kingship, and it was stressed in the monarchy's own propaganda, alert to the growth of public opinion.

The same evolution took place in the most banal of royal representations, that of the king as father of his people. Louis XIV was regularly described this way in the seventeenth century, yet by the mid eighteenth the connotations of the term were not the same because images of fatherhood were changing. In the 1750s and 1760s the paintings of Greuze, displayed in the biennial salons of the Académie royale de peinture et sculpture in the Louvre, frequently dealt with the conflict between paternal authority and filial waywardness. They bear witness to the tension over traditional images of fatherhood, which was also reflected in many novels of the period. In the late eighteenth century the ideal father remained a figure of authority but less stern, kinder, and more affectionate. Children (like subjects) had a duty to respect and to love their father, but the good father (or king) earned this love and respect by his devotion, kindness, and virtuous example.[21]

The other ideal father, and the other main point of reference for the French monarchy, was God. And there a similar evolution was taking place. God was increasingly represented as a loving father, less often as stern and punishing. And if the ruler "holds in his kingdom the place of God Himself," then a change in understandings of God produced a corresponding change in ideas about the monarch.[22] There was a complex three-way relationship between images of fatherhood, of kingship, and of God, and all three were moving in a similar direction.

The *cahiers* of 1789 showed how the new religious and family sentiments

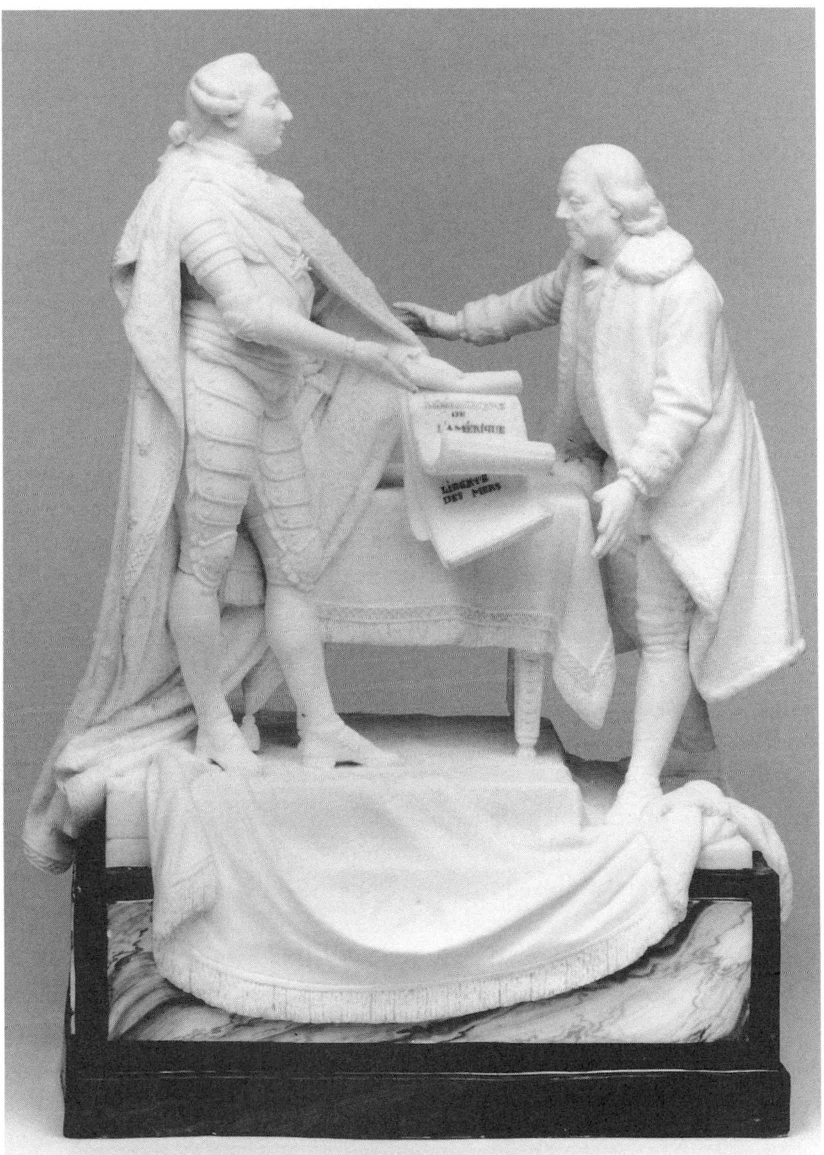

Figure 23. Louis XVI and Benjamin Franklin, Niderwiller Ceramic: Louis is portrayed as benefactor, presenting Franklin with various treaties. Musée Carnavalet, © Photothèque des musées de la ville de Paris. Photographer unknown.

were being carried over into the image of the king. The Paris *cahiers* referred to his "sacred person" but in the same breath spoke of the nation and of individual rights as sacred—the monarch no longer had the monopoly. They also referred frequently to the "fatherly love" of the king for his subjects and expressed their expectation that because of this he would take their views into account in the forthcoming Estates General and in future meetings of the same body.[23]

These new representations of monarchy helped to impose a subtly new role on the king. When monarchical propagandists wrapped him in the mantle of the good father they required him to behave not as an arbitrary ruler concerned with his own glory, but as a benefactor. The monarch had to earn the love and respect of his people through good and wise government and by his embodiment of paternal virtue. "People must love their sovereigns," asserted a minor official of the courts in an eating-place in the rue St-Germain-l'Auxerrois in 1758, "but only when they deserved it." He was arrested for this bold language, yet such views came to be shared by many Parisians.[24]

Despite their own acceptance of some of the new images of kingship, Louis XV and Louis XVI did not conform to them. Both clung to the authority of absolute monarchy and to certain of its symbols. In Louis XV's case the proclaimed *douceur* of his government was hard for many Parisians to reconcile with the early-morning visits by soldiers to 155 magistrates of the Parlement on 20 January 1771, or with the subsequent confiscation of most of their valuable offices. The image of the king as loving father was equally hard to reconcile with his public support for an archbishop who refused many people the sacraments, even on their deathbeds. His honor was undermined, in the opinion of many, by the arrest in the Paris opera itself of Prince Charles Edward Stuart, claimant to the throne of Scotland, who had sought asylum in France. And royal virtue was even less in evidence when the king gave his mistresses an open role at court and voluntarily abstained from Easter communion because of his state of sin: in 1740 some Parisians were reported as saying that "such conduct is scandalous, especially in the person of the King, who owes an example to his subjects."[25]

Parisian discontent with Louis XV was accentuated by a growing sense that he disliked and distrusted the city and its people. It was his great-grandfather Louis XIV who had begun the process of isolating the monarch from his capital. He had constructed the palace at Versailles and, having moved the court there, rarely visited Paris. Many Parisians were pleased when after his death the regent moved the court back to the capital and brought the young Louis XV back to live in the Tuileries palace.

But it did not last. After Louis was crowned in 1722 the court returned to Versailles. The new king had little taste for city pleasures, preferring hunting, and he came to Paris less and less often as his battles with the Parlements became increasingly bitter and his popularity faltered. After 1750 he abandoned the royal *entrées* that had been a royal tradition for centuries. He ceased attending mass at Notre-Dame or the Ste-Chapelle, and no longer came to the Grand Gallery in the Louvre for the touching ceremony. As Robert Darnton puts it, "the king had lost the royal touch, and with it he lost contact with the common people of Paris."[26]

Most damaging of all was the widespread belief that far from looking after his people as a good father should, Louis XV was in fact exploiting their misery. In the mid-1760s an anonymous poster asserted

> That under Henri IV Bread was dear because of the Wars, but in those times we had a King, that under Louis XIV there were again Occasions when Bread was dear, sometimes because of Wars, sometimes because of a real Shortage brought on by unseasonable Weather, but still we had a King; At the present Time the Dearness of Bread could be attributed not to Wars, nor to a real Shortage of Wheat; but that we had no King, because the King was a Grain Merchant.[27]

This accusation had a long history. Already in the 1720s strict government restrictions on the grain trade contrasted with generous concessions accorded to certain merchants, most notoriously the Pâris brothers, one of whose buyers was the father of the future Madame de Pompadour. The government's intention was to stockpile grain when a shortage was feared, but to a skeptical public it looked as if the authorities were actually engineering the dearth so that "government" grain could be sold at advantageous prices.

At first, because the king was a child, the rumors targeted only his ministers. But later they indicted members of his family. Then in 1740 and more assertively in 1747 and in 1752—coinciding with the political crisis over the refusals of sacraments—they accused Louis himself. The monarchy's financial problems provided further circumstantial evidence for the "famine plot" theory. Belief in royal profiteering seems to have peaked when the almost total removal of restrictions on the grain trade in 1763–64 precipitated serious shortages. Even critics of these policies who did not directly indict the king, like the abbé Galiani, nevertheless felt that "all the children of this good father have an equal right to be assured of their sustenance, this is the first duty of a father."[28]

The standing of Louis XV was also damaged by his favors to his mistresses. That the king should have mistresses probably did not upset many people: his decade-long fidelity to the queen, until 1733, seems to have caused some surprise. What attracted criticism was the women he chose, the public role he allowed them, and his subsequent poor treatment of the queen. His first four mistresses were sisters, though all of good noble birth. But Madame de Pompadour was a bourgeoise, Jeanne-Antoinette Poisson, the daughter of a financier, and she succeeded in winning a great many favors for her family and friends, though not as many as public rumor suggested. Then, while she was still the "official" mistress, she apparently assisted the king to obtain the favors of a whole series of young women, one of them the daughter of a Paris shoemaker. Rumors spread with astonishing rapidity, from servants and nobles at court to the houses and shops of the capital. Devout and Jansenist opinion alike were offended by (unfounded) rumors of royal orgies and large numbers of mistresses. Poems circulated both in written form and—more memorably—in song.[29]

Then Jeanne Bécu, who had at one point worked as a shop assistant but was soon to be made comtesse du Barry, became the new royal mistress. Fueled by opponents at court and by the political crisis of 1770, a flood of scurrilous pamphlets depicted her as a common prostitute, and the police were unable to suppress them. All of this inevitably affected the king's personal standing with the Paris public. Even the not particularly religious Paris bookseller Nicolas Ruault commented in 1772 that "the court of France is most attractive: debauchery, impotence, discord, weakness, extravagance, unconcern have united to rule it. We need a modern Suetonius to depict the debauched pleasures of the monarch."[30] Here again Louis was partly the victim of changing ideas. Few had been shocked when Louis XIV openly took mistresses or raised his illegitimate children publicly: it was if anything a sign of his virility. That his great-grandson should be criticized for his sexual liaisons shows how notions of public morality had changed and with them the public image of the monarch.

Despite all this it is misleading to link the unpopularity of Louis XV directly with the crisis and overthrow of the monarchy. By the time of his death in 1715 Louis XIV had been equally hated. There is also ample evidence of the renewed hope aroused by Louis XVI's accession in 1774 and of his popularity in 1789.[31] It is true that a king who inspired hate and—what is far worse—disrespect, did not do the institution of monarchy any good: the stories about Louis XV's immoral life became best-sellers in the 1770s and 1780s, helping to create and perpetuate highly negative public attitudes toward both the king and the court. But the specific accusations leveled against Louis XV did not directly affect his successor, whereas the change in public expectations did.

Yet Louis XVI did not do very much better in meeting them. He was politically clumsy: there is no better example than his monumental gaffe in November 1787 when he told the Parlement that his forcing them to accept new loans "is legal because it is my will." His standing as father of his people was undoubtedly damaged by widespread reports that he was both impotent and unable to control the queen. This was not the popular image of a "good father." The unfavorable comparison made between the last two Louis and their ancestors Henry IV and Louis XIV resulted partly from the excessive influence that women were now believed to exercise at court: Madame de Pompadour and Marie-Antoinette alike had a reputation for political intervention deemed improper in a woman, and for siphoning money from a depleted royal treasury to pay for clothes and other extravagances. Marie-Antoinette was further discredited by the diamond necklace affair, in which she was the innocent victim of an attempt to extort a huge sum of money to purchase a fabulous necklace supposedly destined for her.[32] There was also a growing output of books, pamphlets, and engravings depicting her sexual misconduct and accusing her not only of infidelity but even of incest. Provoked by political enemies who feared her influence on royal policy, the literature may have done considerable damage to the monarchy—though we do not know how widely it circulated. Even so, the queen was cheered at the end of June 1789 when the political crisis seemed briefly to have been resolved. Yet the persistent attacks probably eroded public respect both for her and for the husband who was depicted as a witless cuckold—perhaps the worst accusation that could be leveled against a man in eighteenth-century public life. The merciless accusations were to culminate during Marie-Antoinette's trial in 1793.[33]

Louis XVI appeared briefly to redeem himself in the eyes of Parisians when he appointed (and later reappointed) the popular minister Jacques Necker, and again when he called the Estates General. Perhaps he could have saved the monarchy if he had been able to satisfy the new expectations that the French people—and above all the Parisians—had of their king. Yet perhaps not. For those expectations, like the late-eighteenth-century image of the good father, were in some senses contradictory. He was expected to be at once judge and counselor. As an enlightened monarch he should use his power to reform abuses and better the lives of his people, yet he should not use it arbitrarily. Parisian husbands and parents expected to be able to call on royal authority to discipline disobedient wives or children, yet lettres de cachet were widely condemned as an abuse of power. The contradiction was writ large in the approach taken by Anne-Robert-Jacques Turgot, a well-known reformer, friend of Voltaire, and Louis XVI's minister in 1775. He was genuinely concerned to improve the lot of the people, yet when his abolition of controls on grain pushed up prices and provoked widespread discontent and riots, he repressed opposition severely. Louis XVI himself embodied the contradictions of the monarchy. He wished to be loved by his people and obeyed as an absolute monarch. He wanted to appeal to traditional royal prerogatives, even to divine right, yet also to be a kingly good father. In the 1780s he could not do both.

THE GROWTH OF "PUBLIC OPINION"

It was not simply the image of monarchy that had been transformed—images should not be divorced from their context. Both the nature of government and of politics, in Paris in particular, had changed so much that divine right monarchy of the early-eighteenth-century sort was quite simply no longer possible. And once again it was during the long years of Louis XV's reign that these changes had become apparent.

The years since 1750 had seen the growing influence of what came to be called "public opinion." In practice this meant three things. First, a widening circle of people developed a *continuous* interest in politics and were more informed. Second, they formed strong opinions about national events. And third, an increasing number of them came to believe that their political opinions were not only legitimate but should be taken into account by government. Gradually these views of public opinion came to be shared by royal ministers, and even by Louis XVI himself, although in theory they were incompatible with absolute monarchy.

The idea of public opinion was already around in the 1730s when the *Nouvelles ecclésiastiques* repeatedly called on "the public" to judge the rightness of their cause, "all the other tribunals having been closed to them." In the many court cases brought by or against Jansenists during these years lawyers appealed to "the public" in the same way, both in their speeches (sometimes heard by hundreds of spectators) and in published statements.[34] But it was primarily between the 1750s and the early 1770s that the term public opinion gained currency and that its real influence began to be acknowledged. The refusals of sacraments, then the liberalization of the grain trade in the 1760s, and issues of financial reform after that, all became subjects of widespread public debate that the government was unable to contain. The Seven Years' War of 1756–63 was an event of major importance, and French losses made the government extremely unpopular. The war gave rise to a new language of patriotism that anticipates the terminology of 1789: the words *patrie, patriote, nation,* and *citoyen* (citizen), all rare in book and pamphlet titles before 1750, suddenly became widespread after 1756.[35] Recent writing has also insisted on the importance of the Maupeou coup of 1771, which not only unleashed political passions and unprecedented numbers of pamphlets in Paris but also saw public opinion elevated to the status of a national institution. Even the magistrates of the higher courts now suggested—if more hesitantly—that the Crown had no right to "smother the public voice." Pamphleteers and lawyers on both sides of every argument now appealed to "public opinion," which they described as the true, enlightened arbiter in politics, morality, and in matters of taste.[36]

Over the last four decades of the Old Regime therefore, a new idea appeared in Paris and later in other parts of France: that public intervention in the affairs of the realm was legitimate and that the royal government had a duty to listen to the opinions of those it ruled. This was a revolutionary idea, turning the French people from subjects into citizens with an active voice in their own destiny. In absolutist theory there was no such right, for government remained the property and the concern of the monarch alone.[37]

But who was the new "public"? There are two answers to this question. There was a real flesh-and-blood "public" in Paris and recurrent commentary on current affairs throughout the century. Yet in another sense magistrates, lawyers, and writers created "the public" by asserting that their readers had a right to form and express their own opinions.

Those who bothered to define this public were in no doubt that it included only the educated and enlightened, not "the people." To them it did not include Paris tailors—even one who claimed the title of *greffier.* Yet in 1763 the lawyer Barbier recorded the enthusiastic reception of a free pamphlet proposing a fairer tax system: "All the public are reading it. As a result even the people are discussing it and would welcome its application."[38] A great many Parisians clearly did include themselves in "the public," in the sense of having a right to hold opinions and to have them heard. The diary of the bookseller Siméon-Prosper Hardy is interesting in this respect. Starting in 1764, it is full of reports and speculation about key appointments, likely changes at court, events at the Parlement and at the regular assemblies of the clergy. It is clear that some of the information is taken from newspapers and pamphlets, but often he relies on friends and relatives, or relates "public rumor." He sometimes quotes the key protagonists, for example informing his diary of the conversation between one of the royal princesses and her ladies-in-waiting while in their coach on the outskirts of Paris![39] He also often provides a commentary on events, interpreting the signs of royal favor and disfavor, guessing at the motives of ministers. In April 1771 he concludes that the royal family "were trying harder than ever to convey the truth to the King"—presumably about the reforms being pursued by Chancellor Maupeou—by nearly all leaving the court over Easter. This may have been his individual reflection, but may equally have emerged from discussion with others. He was only one of many Parisians who took an active interest in political matters and discussed them widely.

People of all ranks were able to join in these kinds of discussions, and there are hints that they were doing so. Again, Jean Thomas Terrier's workbook is revealing. His list of political events points to a continuity of political interest. Unlike many of the comments recorded in Hardy's journal or in police reports, it is not an immediate response to a particular situation but a later, reflective compilation. It may even be that for Terrier the various dates were somehow linked: was he in some sense recording milestones in the changing relationship between king and people? Whatever his interpretation of events, his simple list illustrates his membership of the interested public.

This new public extended well beyond the readership of the periodical press, though even that had grown very significantly during the century. The official *Gazette de France* grew from a circulation under 5,000 in the 1670s to over 15,000 in the 1750s, and a few other papers topped 10,000 for the first time in the 1780s. In France as a whole the number of periodicals available expanded from fifteen in 1745 to eighty-two in 1785—and more could be bought in Paris than in most provincial centers. The exclusively Parisian *Journal de Paris* was selling 5,000 copies a day by 1782 and more than double that number in 1789.[40] Jean Thomas Terrier, like the majority of artisans, had no books, newspapers, or pamphlets in his estate, but that did not prevent his taking an interest in politics: he was part of the real public.

The gap between the real and the imagined public came to be of some significance as the authorities slowly began to take notice of public opinion. A new type of politics developed in Paris, a form of lobbying through appeals to the new public. Sarah Maza has shown how judicial *mémoires,* issued to support individuals in cases before the courts, put wider issues on the public agenda, and Jeremy Popkin has looked at the way some of the rich and powerful employed journalists to discredit their political opponents.[41] Other types of pamphlet literature await study. But one example, which also illustrates the range of people becoming involved, is the campaign by the tanner Jean Antoine Derubigny against the *régie des cuirs*. The *régie* was an authority established in 1759 to supervise the leather industry. All leather sold had to be checked and stamped by its officials, who also conducted inspections of tanneries. The tanners complained bitterly that all this was costly and unnecessary: they were perhaps right, but they had no reason to like an outside authority that replaced their own corporation as the controlling body of the industry.

From at least the mid-1770s Derubigny, one of the principal tanners in Paris, waged a tireless campaign against the *régie*. Perhaps Turgot's appointment started him off. In 1775 he received a sympathetic response from the new minister and through him obtained a personal interview with Louis XVI. But after Turgot's dismissal he had to start again from scratch. Over a twelve-year period he bombarded ministers and royal officials with long petitions in execrable handwriting. He also published several pamphlets on the subject, one of which earned him a short spell in the Bastille in 1777. He wrote to tanners all over France to gather data on production and to mobilize their support. In 1787 he attended the Assemblée des notables in Versailles.[42]

Although Derubigny's campaign was unsuccessful, it illustrates perfectly the new brand of politics. He not only sought to influence ministers in a conventional way, with petitions and letters, but also appealed to public opinion through his pamphlet campaign. His case also demonstrates the type of person who could manipulate the new methods. He wrote easily and at length. He had the money to mount an appeal to public opinion: his pamphlets, some of them quite long, were published at his own expense. He enjoyed a certain status—another prerequisite for being heard—both as a man of property (he owned several houses and ran a large business) and as an expert and innovator in his industry. He was mentioned in De la Lande's *Art of tanning*, one of the series of works on the French trades published by the Académie des sciences, and he claimed to have advised Diderot about tanning techniques.[43]

The sound of scribbling was everywhere in these years. Thousands of people like Derubigny jostled one another to bring their claims to a wider public. There were pamphlets—some sold and others free—discussing tax reform, the education of girls, ways to encourage population growth, stimulate industry, eliminate usury, prevent traffic accidents, and improve the capital's water supply. The daily *Journal de Paris* offered thoughts on improving hospitals, while the *Annonces, affiches, et avis divers* reported innovations in medicine and reviewed the reform literature for those who had missed it. The physiocratic *Journal économique* published proposals for reorganizing the grain market and the *Journal des dames* suggested a new education system. Erudite schemes padded the publications of the Société royale d'agriculture, the Académie royale de chirurgie, the Académie des sciences, the Société royale de médecine and many other organizations. Some proposals were self-interested, some funded by government ministers or their opponents, others public-spirited, many utopian. Their authors were booksellers and nobles, fermiers généraux and abbés, lawyers, schoolteachers, and doctors, and a small but growing number of professional writers. They included both respected scientists and marginal figures like the future revolutionaries Jean-Paul Marat and Jacques Pierre Brissot.[44]

"Every citizen," suggested the director of book trade, Chrétien-Guillaume de Lamoignon de Malesherbes in 1775, "can speak to the whole nation by the medium of print."[45] Yes, but only the educated and the reasonably well-off were "active" citizens in this new nation. The division between those able to appeal to public opinion and those who could not became a difference in access to power. The new politics offered little advantage to the illiterate, to the laboring poor, or even to men and women of the artisan class who like Jean Thomas Terrier were interested in what was going on but were in no position to influence it. Some of them nevertheless felt themselves to belong to the public, and to what was with increasing frequency called "the nation." It included many of the men who during the Revolution would provide the leadership of the Paris sections, along with women who even during the 1790s would continue to be excluded from formal politics. It was here, in the last two or three decades of the Old Regime, that many Parisians began their political apprenticeship.

A remarkable change had taken place in Paris politics over the century. Some groups had lost political leverage: the local notables no longer had their former predominant role in the government of the city. Even in the trades corporations, now fewer and much larger, the number of leadership positions was smaller, those elected were probably less representative of the membership, and they had less leverage with the government. Yet by the 1780s the numbers of Parisians who felt that they should have a say in what was going on had increased exponentially. New types of voices were being raised: those of lawyers, most stridently, but also of architects, agricultural experts, reformers of various sorts, and tanners. And although it did not like much of what it heard, the royal government was attentive as never before, no longer just to those who had access via the old patronage networks of nobles and notables but to opinions expressed in petitions and pamphlets.

The political reforms of the late 1780s, and above all the summoning of the Estates General to advise the king on the affairs of his realm, stimulated an unprecedented outpouring of opinion. The lifting of press censorship in 1788 opened the floodgates, at least 1,500 pamphlets appearing between May and December that year and over 2,600 in the first four months of 1789.[46] Among their readers were thousands of Parisians who now believed in their right, not only to be well governed, but to have some sort of say in how government took place.

CHAPTER EIGHT

SECULARIZATION

One of the major events of 1752, now forgotten, was the miracle of the rue Ste-Marguerite. It happened in the faubourg St-Antoine, during the procession on the Sunday after Corpus Christi, not far from the spot where in 1725 Anne Lafosse had been miraculously healed of paralysis. Overlooking the corner of the rue Ste-Marguerite, where it joined the rue du faubourg St-Antoine, was a statue of the Virgin (Figure 24). Just after the procession had passed, someone looked up and cried out that the head of the statue had turned to look the other way, toward the main street instead of away. Word of the miracle spread rapidly, and over the following few days crowds flocked to pray at the feet of the statue. Among them was young Jacques-Louis Ménétra, whose grandmother took him along, and who spent (as he later recalled) "two hours on my knees listening to people murmur between their teeth and each one burned a small candle." There was a grocer's shop on the corner, and skeptics suggested that he had made up the story of the miracle in order to sell more candles and liquor. Ménétra thought he had, and so—thirty years later—did Louis-Sébastien Mercier. But the grocer denied the accusation and threatened to sue the ironmonger on the other corner for spreading such a malicious rumor. He may have been right: when the ironmonger heard of the miracle he retorted that it was the witnesses' heads that had turned, and he had words with the people blocking the entrance to his premises. His disbelief made him the target of angry abuse from the crowd.[1]

This incident points to a significant cultural gap that was opening up

Figure 24. The miraculous statue of the rue Ste-Marguerite. From Balthazar Anton Dunker, *Tableau de Paris* (n.p., 1787). Bibliothèque historique de la ville de Paris, photo Jean-Christophe Doerr.

within the Paris population. By midcentury significant numbers of Parisians, like this ironmonger, were becoming skeptical about miracles. He was clearly among the commercial middle classes: he claimed the title of *bourgeois de Paris,* and his elegant signature testified to schooling well beyond basic literacy. His skepticism marked him off from the people who came to pray, those whom Ménétra later called "the vulgar who love novelties . . . particularly the good wives and all the pious women."[2]

But growing skepticism was only part of the change. Not only did the ironmonger refuse to accept the "miracle," but he was not afraid to express his view. While this earned him some verbal abuse, no lynch mobs gathered outside his door, and he was not ostracized by his neighbors. Furthermore, neither the Church nor the police showed the slightest sign of interest in what might in earlier times have been construed as unbelief. The religious climate of Paris was undergoing a vast and silent transformation that was to accelerate in the second half of the century.

It was not, in fact, a matter of belief or unbelief, but a change in the nature both of faith and of religious observance. For most of the century, the mass of the faithful adhered to a tradition sponsored by the Counter-Reformation clergy: divine (and satanic) intervention occurred often, and the dead remained present among the living and could influence their affairs directly. Custom—both the official ceremonies of the religious calendar and of the life cycle, and the many folk rites that also accompanied them—remained an important way of dealing with the supernatural. While the seventeenth-century clergy and their heirs in the eighteenth tried to purge French culture of its less orthodox elements, they actively encouraged this view of the world. They believed that a constant awareness of the supernatural was the best guarantee of faith and of obedience to Church teaching, both of which were needed to keep simple folk on the narrow path to salvation.

But during the eighteenth century, and particularly after the 1750s, we see clear signs of a decline in religious observance and in the authority of the clergy. We can perceive a widespread and increasingly outspoken anticlericalism. And we can even guess at changes in religious belief that show up in a widespread abandonment of customary practices and of older forms of religious behavior. Although such changes did not occur exclusively or rigidly along socioeconomic or gender lines, the behavior of rich and poor, educated and uneducated, men and women reflects a clear general pattern of long-term change that occurred throughout the Western world, at different rates in different places. It is sometimes called "dechristianization," but a better term is "secularization."

THE LIVING AND THE DEAD

One of the areas in which the change is most conspicuous and has been most studied is that of attitudes toward death and the afterlife.[3] Seventeenth-century reformers had urged reflection on death and—as a corrective to Protestantism and an incentive to moral living—had promoted the cults of the saints, of the sacraments, and of the Virgin. Counter-Reformation preachers constantly referred to hell and purgatory: "Conversion begins with fright," advised a preaching manual of 1712. Their admonitions made the intercession of the saints all the more important and strengthened a cult of the dead that was already strong in popular religion.[4]

But there are clear signs that many Parisians, particularly well-to-do ones, were beginning to think less about their own deaths. We know this from their wills, which dwelt less and less on hopes of resurrection and increasingly concentrated on the disposal of property. Around 15 percent of the population left wills, mainly the wealthier social groups but almost equal numbers of men and women. These Parisians did not worry nearly so much about where they would be buried. Since the 1720s, too, fewer and fewer of them requested masses to be said for the repose of their souls. Even the archbishop of Paris, Monseigneur de Vintimille, who died in 1746, included no religious references in his will and donated his body for medical dissection.[5] Books on preparing for death, having peaked at around 5 percent of all editions published in the last quarter of the seventeenth century, fell to 0.5 percent in the 1780s.[6]

The Parisians who left wills represented an elite. But there is evidence of changing religious attitudes among a much wider section of the population: those who participated in the many religious confraternities. These associations, dedicated to a particular saint or cult, had been founded in large numbers in the boom years of Counter-Reformation piety from the late sixteenth to the late seventeenth century. Each of the larger Paris parishes had a dozen or more confraternities, and while those for men were most numerous, the less prestigious and less public female ones often played an important charitable role and offered a prominent administrative and social position to women from local middle-class families.[7] Male or female, most confraternities had their own chapel in one of the churches and dedicated it to one of the most popular saints and cults. The privileges they provided for their members were highly sought after. At St-Sauveur each man had the special honor of carrying a candle in the public procession held on the first Sunday of each month. The confraternity of the St-Sacrement often organized the important Corpus Christi procession and had the privilege of taking up the collection. Its officials sat in a special pew, usually near the front of the church, and their names were printed on widely distributed posters. In some parishes new churchwardens were chosen from among the administrators of the St-Sacrement.[8]

Yet the number of confraternities in Paris dropped sharply across the eighteenth century. At St-Laurent the number fell from twelve or more in 1700 to only three, and at St-Gervais from ten to six. In 1760 four were suppressed at Ste-Marguerite. While some were abolished in the clampdown on Jesuit associations in the early 1760s and more with the abolition of the guilds in 1776, others died of financial failure linked to declining membership.[9] In 1743 the churchwardens of St-Jacques-de-la-Boucherie complained of "the impossibility of finding notables who will take on the administration of the confraternity [of Saint Charles Borromeo]."[10] This was a gradual process and by no means universal: finding men to run the prestigious confraternities of the St-Sacrement was a good deal easier. Yet even these were losing their gloss. By the 1780s the richly decorated pew in the church and the honor of marching immediately behind the churchwardens in processions were not enough to attract the notables of the wealthy parishes of St-Etienne-du-Mont, St-Sulpice, and St-Roch. In 1786 the men elected to the position refused to take office and it took a special decree of the Parlement to change their minds.[11]

The reason for their reluctance was probably simply that the public honor was no longer adequate compensation for the time and expense involved. The earlier taste for baroque pomp, for processions, candles, special robes, and public display was no longer so strong. The local bourgeoisie of lawyers, officeholders, and merchants, soberly clad in black and brown—a symbol of their sobriety—increasingly deserted gaudy and socially promiscuous religious celebrations. They turned instead to more private devotions.

As far as the bulk of the Paris population is concerned we have mainly anecdotal evidence of declining religious practice. Whereas in 1706 an English visitor could assert "I never saw people more devout," by the early 1780s the Parisian Mercier could write that "the common people still go to Mass, but are beginning to skip Vespers." Elsewhere he wrote that whereas in London all the shops and theaters were closed on the Sabbath, "Sunday in Paris is more a day for pleasure, for promenades, for meals, than of sanctification and rest."[12]

Other evidence supports contemporary statements. Religious bequests declined sharply: in the Latin quarter 70 percent of the small number of wills left by shopkeepers and manual workers in midcentury left nothing to the Church. In a sample of inventories drawn up by notaries in the rue St-Honoré, 63.3 percent of households owned religious objects in the early years of the century but only 50.5 percent in the 1770s and 1780s. There is also clear evidence of the adoption of birth control, in direct defiance of Church teaching. "Well-off people . . . have hardly any children," observed Mercier. "In a well-to-do family, it would be odious to have more than one heir," agreed the author of a book of social commentary in the 1770s. At all levels of Parisian society the age at which women stopped having children was slowly getting earlier, even though they were probably marrying slightly older. In 1700 the average couple who survived the childbearing years were having around seven children (of whom fewer than half would survive): by the 1780s they were having about five. In the wealthier social groups the fall in birthrates was greater. The mean number of children born to the *fermiers généraux* of 1726 was 3.5; to those of 1786 it was 2.6. Among the well-to-do merchant families of the faubourg St-Marcel most mid-seventeenth-century couples had four or five children but by the mid eighteenth century they were down to two or three.[13] Alongside these data we can set the increase in illegitimacy that characterized all French cities in the second half of the century, again in direct contravention of Church teaching. It went from just over 1 percent in the early eighteenth century to between 10 and 20 percent by the 1780s. In Paris it rose to 30 percent of births registered, though that included many babies born to young women who had fled to the big city to avoid shame in their hometowns and villages.[14]

All this is difficult evidence to interpret: does it indicate growing disaffection with the Church, mere indifference, or does it point to a new freedom from traditional religious and social constraints? I would guess it was all three. There certainly was growing religious freedom in Paris in the second half of the eighteenth century, in the sense that people could neglect their religious duties and get away with it. The "respectable" middle classes observed outward appearances. Charles-Alexis Alexandre, from a family of comfortably off cabinetmakers, was baptized, made his first confession at the proper age, and took his first communion. "They viewed it as a duty to be undertaken, and I submitted to it less from zeal than from docility." Later, when his mother was dying in 1790, she requested the last sacraments, confiding to him that it was "because she did not want me to pass for the son of an excommunicated woman."[15] Manon Phlipon, from a similar social milieu, continued to attend mass well after she had ceased to share the faith it celebrated. But others—more determined or less constrained by family pressures—did not conform. Ménétra stopped going to church altogether, probably in the late 1750s. Some of the urban elite openly flouted conventional religious practice, and according to Mercier the upper classes no longer went to confession. Even death, the most solemn mystery of all, became for a tiny minority the subject of widely reported jest. The permanent secretary of the Académie française, Charles Duclos, who died in 1772, reportedly made a pun on the name of his parish priest, René Chapeau: "I came into the world with no trousers, and I will leave it without a hat (*sans chapeau*)." "People are beginning," the lawyer Barbier had written in the early 1750s, "to make fun of spiritual things and of the most holy mysteries of religion."[16] There is no way of telling how widespread this attitude was, but Alexandre recalled that despite the outward conformity of most of his family, when his grandmother died in 1764, at the age of ninety, "it was only with great difficulty that she was persuaded to receive the Sacraments." As she was known as a free-thinker, he added, the priest boasted of having converted her![17] Some Parisians, and in a range of social groups, were now expressing heterodox views without fear of being locked up in the Bastille or of having social opprobrium fall on themselves or their families.

ANTICLERICALISM AND DEISM

The memoirs of Jacques-Louis Ménétra and Charles-Alexis Alexandre suggest the existence of both deism and anticlericalism among the artisan and shopkeeping population. The glazier Ménétra wrote scathingly of priests and summarized his religious views in a remarkable piece—devoid of punctuation—headed "My reflections on truth," probably written in the 1780s:

> Men who try to make people believe in all this jumbled nonsense and in all these dreams and lies must be full of vices all these inventions of religion have produced millions of martyrs who have plunged into fanaticism and superstition, and these men have made simple folk believe in a happy reward
>
> Such are the excesses to which the Roman Religion has led men by degrees by persuading them of all sorts of horrors and all sorts of absurdities

> In the dominant religion that is professed today we find only people full of ambition and avarice who feed us enigmas and say to us that they are holy mysteries I would say to them that all you pronounce are lies[18]

Ménétra rejected belief in miracles, including that of the Eucharist: "I . . . never (believed) and will never believe that any being on earth is capable of calling a God down to an altar at will and swallowing it."[19] He believed in toleration for Jews and Protestants. Yet despite his contempt for the clergy and their teachings, he had his children baptized. He continued to believe in "the Eternal" and "the Supreme Being," and worked out for himself a broadly humanist Christian view.

> For myself I adore a God who sets all things in motion. . . . For me we should live and die happy Yes that is the idea and the love that a virtuous man should have to love everything that the earth has created by the Will of the Supreme Being to try to help all those who are like us not to hurt anyone to do no harm to love a single, unique God
>
> That is the true religion that arises naturally in a man's heart and not all these fables. . . . We will be happy and we will show how in our hearts to lift up our hopes to the eternal and reflect that when our existence comes to an end our soul will go to enjoy the happiness that awaits it and our body will return to the earth which has produced us without going through a thousand debates which in the end are nothing and without moving and tormenting us as our end approaches.[20]

Daniel Roche has identified some of the sources of Ménétra's thought. To some extent this Paris glazier records his own reflections on the catechism and on the reading that he refers to abundantly in his writing. His memoirs reveal that he read almost indiscriminately whatever books came to hand, including a number of anticlerical works that circulated in Paris in a limited number of printed editions, but probably also in manuscript versions. He managed to borrow banned books from various acquaintances and almost certainly read some of Rousseau's work.[21] But he may also be drawing on an oral tradition, communicated in innumerable discussions in wineshops and on the roads that he tramped on his travels around France and across Paris itself.

A lower-middle-class oral tradition of anticlericalism, passed on above all through satirical songs, surfaces in Alexandre's memoirs. He recalled going with his cabinetmaker parents in the mid-1760s to gatherings of clerks and master artisans, men and women, where they sang political and anticlerical songs. "We mocked Jansenism and the bull [Unigenitus], monism, the Parlement, the clergy, the Archbishop of Paris, the priests, whom we did not confuse with religion, their airs, their exaggerations . . .

their fraudulence and the means they employed to extort money from those wanting [religious services]."[22]

Both Ménétra and Alexandre were highly unusual figures: Ménétra's are the only memoirs we possess that were written by a Paris artisan, and Alexandre experienced unusual though not unprecedented upward social mobility. Yet their writings point to an intriguing hybrid of popular anticlericalism and "enlightened" religious thinking that was taking root and spreading among the middling ranks of the Paris population in the fertile political climate of the 1750s and 1760s.[23]

SECULARIZATION

Other evidence of changing religious attitudes, taken from various sources, confirms the picture of an increasingly secular society. Older descriptions of Paris had devoted many pages to churches and convents and the treasures they contained but in the late eighteenth century focused instead on administrative and commercial buildings and leisure activities. In certain respects religious mysteries occasioned less awe than in the past, for example in the shop signs that hung outside most houses. In the late seventeenth century the clergy forced the removal of the sign La Tête-Dieu (God's head) from a wineshop in the rue Montmartre. In the eighteenth, by contrast, no one seems to have worried about the Brewery of the Word Incarnate in the rue Mouffetard![24]

Nor were people so concerned about blasphemy. In the early part of the century it was an accusation commonly leveled at people in complaints made to the police: three journeymen bakers were heard "swearing by the holy name of God"; two journeymen silk workers fought in the street, "denying the holy name of God"; a woman fruiterer complained of being called a "denier of God"; the wife of a port worker accused her neighbor of "swearing and blaspheming against her." In the 1750s, though, such accusations were rare and by the 1770s the boot was on the other foot: among the "frightful insults" directed at the wife of a doorman was that "she was a bigot who went every day to confession at the Carmelites."[25] A more secular, even unreligious outlook had penetrated the most banal aspects of everyday life.

Yet we should not automatically conclude that there was a massive decline in religious belief. Nor should we imagine late-eighteenth-century Paris as a secular society. "Go to the churches: every one is packed," wrote an Italian visitor in 1761 and this was probably still true in the 1780s.[26] Many religious practices, such as the last rites for the dead, remained of enormous importance. Although conventional Christian observance was slowly declining, in the eighteenth century religious belief among the educated classes was modified, not abandoned. "Even the Christian," complained a preacher in 1787, "while he still believes in Hell, only believes in it a little; and when he casts a glance at religion it is to see only its consoling truths, to perceive a merciful God."[27] Indeed, here was a new attitude.

There was also, among both the clergy and the educated laity, a growing emphasis on understanding and on individual reflection. It was already apparent in the translation of the Paris Missal into French in 1701. But it was particularly prevalent in Jansenist parishes where, spies reported, "the Gospels are read entirely in French before being explained to the people."[28] Understanding was important, because for educated Parisians, and for less educated but reflective individuals like Ménétra, religion was more and more an individual affair, a contract between each human being and a personal God.[29]

This changed emphasis had far-reaching implications. It was directly linked with the growing spirit of tolerance of the late eighteenth century. For if belief was a matter for individual conscience and not one of public concern, then why should the state enforce particular forms of religious observance? Hints of tolerance and flexibility in turn, as we have seen, had major repercussions for a monarchy whose power was based in part on divine right.

Secularization was thus, in part, a logical consequence of a new religious sensibility among the elites. In 1777 the Paris municipality decided that in elections of new city councilors the voters would no longer swear on the crucifix. "This is a religious act that contains a reference to one of our greatest mysteries, one that can hardly, without profanation, be confused with simple ceremonies."[30] Even though the motive was respect for religion, the proposed removal of religious elements from a major public ceremony reveals a significant move away from baroque ritual, with its association of the civic and the sacred.

The new religious sensibility is also apparent in the official suppression of feast days and of confraternities in the second half of the century. "Most of the abuses that had accumulated in the confraternities," wrote Lieutenant General of Police Lenoir, "were not to be attributed to their original creation, but to the multitude of members who . . . gathered in tumultuous assemblies on the pretext of superstitious practices, so as to give themselves over to idleness and drunkenness."[31] The archbishop was thinking the same way when he suppressed thirteen feast days in 1778, in the hope of preventing their profanation by revelers. Yet neither popular behavior nor the confraternities had changed, just official perceptions of the forms of sociability they entailed. The Parisian elites were rejecting communitarian forms of religious practice in which drinking and feasting were an integral part of the celebration, a continuation of the shared liturgy of the Eucharist that affirmed the harmony of the ideal urban community.[32]

Other aspects of religious culture that once had been encouraged by the authorities, or at least seen as harmless, were now also drawing criticism. The *Dictionnaire historique de Paris* of 1779, for example, argued that "it would be desirable also to suppress the custom that still continues, of parading . . . in the streets of Paris a gigantic and ridiculous figure, fit only to frighten children."[33] The custom at issue was the annual procession and burning, on 3 July, of a straw mannequin, an effigy of a Swiss Protestant who in the sixteenth century had supposedly struck a statue of the Virgin. The statue had bled and the heretic had been apprehended and executed. This celebration, once approved by the city elite as a pious and Catholic commemoration, was now perceived as disorderly and superstitious. The lieutenant general of police "consulted the bourgeois of the quarter, who approved of my plan to ban the custom of parading and burning the mannequin, but they insisted that the religious principle be maintained."[34] The irony is that these religiously motivated acts hastened the secularization of Parisian society.

The abolition of the confraternities of the trades corporations in 1776 was another major move in the same direction. The physiocrats whose theories underlay the attack on the guilds did not endorse the compulsory Catholicism that the trades confraternities implied, and they and others condemned the constant interruptions that religious festivities and customs entailed. The suppression of twenty-four feast days would greatly improve productivity, suggested *Le Réformateur* in 1762.[35] And indeed, in new statutes issued between 1779 and 1785 the wine merchants, butchers, bakers, pork butchers, carpenters, seamstresses, printers, linen weavers, tailors, and others quietly dropped the requirement that new members be Catholic.[36] Religious practice had ceased to be a necessary part of the corporate identity. Like the sacred and the civic, religion and work—indissociable in the older, customary worldview—were now to be unlinked.

The reasons for changing religious sentiments among important sections of Parisian society are complex. Religious historians have tended to blame the philosophes, the Jansenists, or both. Voltaire's campaigns against many Church practices certainly influenced educated opinion, particularly on the issue of religious toleration of Protestants. Books like La Mettrie's *Homme machine* of 1747 and Helvétius's treatise *De l'esprit* of 1758 and the explicitly atheistic works of Holbach were among the best-sellers of the illegal book trade, circulating very widely, even though they were banned in France.[37] Religious mysteries were discussed skeptically and semipublicly in Paris homes. The very fact that these things were possible in the second half of the eighteenth century indicates that attitudes were changing. Even then, many people were shocked by the ideas expressed in these works and rejected them indignantly. But for others they perhaps made thinkable ideas that even early in the century were too extreme to contemplate.

The religious questioning of the philosophes was directly accessible only to a small proportion of the Paris population. Even though basic literacy was high, books were expensive, time limited, and such works were too challenging for most working people. The indirect influence of Voltaire and Rousseau, particularly through plays and novels, was far more extensive, though mainly later in the century. Jansenism, on the other hand, had an earlier and much more immediate impact on a broad cross section of Parisians. It encouraged a new and more democratic religious sensibility, a reliance on the dictates of individual conscience and on direct communication with God through prayer. Nothing demonstrates its power more clearly than the refusals-of-sacraments crisis, when so many Paris Jansenists would not bow to clerical pressure even on their deathbeds. The Jansenist newspaper *Nouvelles ecclésiastiques* made heroes of these men and women, justifying disobedience to Church and state in the name of individual conscience and legitimizing in print—for a very wide audience—the normally disregarded views of ordinary people.[38] The adoption of birth control measures by many Parisians, including the strongly Jansenist merchants of the faubourg St-Marcel, suggests another possible outcome of growing independence of mind. Although Jansenist writers were among the loudest opponents of the philosophes they were probably more influential than Voltaire in fostering a critical approach to Church teaching among the mass of the Paris population.

The way the Jansenists were treated by their opponents had a huge impact. The spectacle of virtuous, God-fearing Christians being refused the sacraments aroused disgust and perhaps even skepticism among the uncommitted. The marquis d'Argenson was disturbed to learn, in the middle of the refusal of sacraments crisis, that "at St-Eustache, my parish, half as many as last year have consumed the Host at Easter, even though over the past few years this consumption had already diminished by more than half." The same thing, he was informed, had happened at St-Côme and at St-Sulpice. For him "the loss of religion in France [was caused by] the hatred conceived against the clergy, which today runs to excess. These ministers of religion hardly dare show themselves in the streets without being jeered at, and it all comes from the bull *Unigenitus,* as well as the exile of the Parlement." There were renewed attacks on priests in the Paris streets in 1757 and 1758, when two were even stabbed, and in 1765 Horace Walpole told an acquaintance that the regular clergy of Paris "had Orders from their Superiors to keep more within their Cloisters, not to give Offence to their Enemies, by their too open Appearance in the World." These were all moments of tension, but the authority of the clergy was certainly undermined and so perhaps for some people was belief in the mysteries they proclaimed.[39]

The disputes over Jansenism may also have encouraged the spirit of toleration preached by the philosophes. Already in the 1740s and 1750s we find a significant middle group of the Paris clergy who, while accepting *Unigenitus* and the authority of the archbishop, were disinclined to question people too closely about their beliefs. And by the 1750s and 1760s, astonishingly, leading Jansenists had become active proponents of civil toleration for Protestants.[40]

But there were other factors of equal if not greater importance in changing religious beliefs. For educated people the scientific discoveries of the seventeenth century created a new confidence in human ability to control nature. Newton's revelations of the basic laws of physics, finally accepted and taught at the University of Paris in the 1740s, had a revolutionary impact. No longer was repeated divine intervention necessary to keep the universe going. Newton himself thought, since the movement of the planets did not quite match his mathematical predictions, that God must intervene from time to time to make minor corrections. But subsequent work showed such fine tuning to be unnecessary. It therefore became possible for an increasing number of educated people to imagine God as a divine architect-builder, designing, creating, and setting the Universe in motion, then withdrawing from the natural and human world for the rest of Eternity.[41] The writers of the Enlightenment played a key role in disseminating such ideas, but if readers came to share these views it was because they seemed to make sense in the changing world of the "modern" eighteenth century.

Equally dramatic was the effect of medical discoveries and of an increase in life expectancy that most people were only confusedly aware of but nevertheless affected their view of the world. On average, as the new science of statistics was beginning to reveal, French people lived ten years longer at the end of the century than at the beginning. And although most medical intervention was ineffective or even harmful, growing numbers of people were convinced that it was simply a matter of time before many cures were possible. The extraordinary success of inoculation against smallpox, one of the most dangerous diseases of the century, was almost universally recognized by the end of the 1760s, and people's faith in the ability of doctors to defeat disease was transformed. Medicine became, in Colin Jones's words, "one of the buzzwords of Enlightenment optimism." Claims of new cures were widely reported, and the columns of the Paris and provincial *Affiches* and even of the more solemn *Mercure de France* were flooded with advertisements for health-giving foods, for spas and treatments that restored health, for cosmetics and accessories to keep people young. Maille, who is still a household name in France, claimed in the mid-1750s that his *vinaigres* not only cured toothache and combated bad breath but also whitened the skin and got rid of acne. In 1787 twenty-two types of bottled water could be purchased in Paris, preserving people from the asperities of Seine water.[42] Medical books flooded from the presses and a new journal appeared that was entirely devoted to health issues: the *Gazette de santé*. Doctors like the Swiss physician André Tissot and Voltaire's doctor Théodore Tronchin became household names among educated Parisians. By the 1780s, when someone collapsed in the street the passers-by were as likely to call a doctor as a priest.[43]

In the twenty years after 1760 public attitudes to medicine moved from cynicism to extraordinary confidence. "It is impossible to imagine the height to which may be carried, in a thousand years, the power of man over matter," wrote Benjamin Franklin from Paris in 1780. "All diseases may by sure means be prevented or cured, not excepting even that of old age and our lives lengthened at pleasure even beyond the antediluvian standard." Once the laws of nature were understood the sudden appearance of fevers, apoplexies, and cancers became less mysterious. No longer did they seem to be God-sent trials to be endured with the faith of Job. The new approach led to bitter conflict at the Hôtel-Dieu, where the nuns' stress on spiritual exercises was challenged—successfully in 1787—by doctors who insisted on a secular medical regime. They saw disease as a natural phenomenon to be fought and controlled.[44]

The eighteenth century saw the slow dissemination of a "scientific" worldview that sought explanations in natural rather than divine law.

Few people went as far as Voltaire and other philosophes, who condemned many Church doctrines as little better than superstition, but by midcentury many quite ordinary Parisians were beginning to agree with Holbach that "these principles, judged incontestable, are only hazardous suppositions . . . adopted by timid credulity and preserved by custom, which never reasons."[45] A growing spirit of skepticism was abroad, not only in intellectual circles but increasingly among a broad spectrum of the Parisian middle classes.

THE DECLINING HOLD OF THE CHURCH

Changes in religious belief were facilitated by the growing inability of the clergy to enforce orthodox religious practice. By 1789 Paris had some 750 people for every member of the parish clergy. In a poor parish like St-Médard there were more than a thousand communicants (let alone inhabitants) to each priest. (Eighteenth-century Milan, by contrast, had one priest for around 85 inhabitants).[46] In most parishes the clergy could not even identify all their flock, much less enforce attendance at the sacraments. When a priest stepped into the noisy street outside his parish church he was lost in the press of porters, stallkeepers, carters, animals, building workers, servant girls, and idlers. He almost certainly recognized the shopkeepers on their doorsteps, and he knew the people who lived in the immediate vicinity of his house. He could identify the local beggars and some of the children running between the carts, as well as the regular churchgoers who came several times a week. But the rest were strangers.

It was partly that the population of Paris had grown—it may even have doubled in the course of the century. But there was also a problem with the supply of clergy. The religious disputes had worsened the situation since—as one parish priest complained in 1743—many of the local nuns and canons who formerly helped out with the poor school and hearing confessions were Jansenist sympathizers and were barred by the archbishop.[47] Subsequently the expulsion of the Jesuits in 1763 removed still more priests. But the principal problem was the dramatic decline in the numbers choosing a religious life. The number of clergy in France fell by almost half across the eighteenth century, especially after 1750. Government intervention played some role in this: a royal edict of 1768 raised the minimum age for permanent entry to a convent or monastery from sixteen to eighteen for women and to twenty-one for men. In this measure it is hard to separate the influence of the Enlightenment critique

Figure 25. A crowded Paris street. From Balthazar Anton Dunker, *Tableau de Paris* (n.p., 1787). Bibliothèque historique de la ville de Paris, photo Jean-Christophe Doerr.

of teenage entry into religious life from reform efforts within the French Church itself: the architect of this edict was the archbishop of Toulouse, Loménie de Brienne, a close friend of the philosophes Morellet and Turgot, with whom he had studied theology at the Sorbonne.[48] Whatever the reason, in the 1770s and 1780s alone the Benedictines lost a third of their members, the Franciscans more. And the sharpest losses took place in the Paris region, although the ordinary parish clergy and female religious orders engaged in social work or education held up better. The Filles de la charité actually increased their numbers, testimony to the growing interest of young middle-class women in active social engagement.[49] Nevertheless, the general picture was one of decline, and this meant fewer priests, monks, and nuns to assist with pastoral care, instruction, and enforcement of religious observance. As a result, the Englishman John Andrews observed, "one meets with fewer [clergy] in the streets and places of public resort than formerly; one hears less about them; people also seem to think less of them."[50] A striking example of the effect of falling numbers was the situation in the central hospital, where by 1787 the sixty-nine nuns who ran it had an average age of fifty-three and some were in their seventies. Even with a team of lay helpers they must have found it hard to cope.[51]

Yet it was not just a problem of numbers. The mobility of much of the population made the job of the parish clergy next to impossible. Immigration rates were high and almost certainly rose after 1740, but more important still was movement within the city. Journeymen and servants moved from employer to employer. Poor families were forced to move if they could not pay their rent. For whatever reason, in 1793 half the population of one section in the Marais had previously lived in another part of the city, though most had not come far. Some belonged to the huge floating population of seasonal and unemployed workers, anywhere up to 100,000-strong when the economic climate was bad.[52] Enforcement of religious observance was thus extremely difficult. It was, furthermore, a simple matter for people who wished to escape surveillance simply to move outside their quarter, like the couple who on 29 June 1754 brought their illegitimate child to be baptized in the church of St-Nicolas-des-Champs. Both were from other parishes.[53] As the archbishop of Paris discovered in the 1750s, it was no easy matter to guarantee that people had been confessed by an approved priest because there were so many religious communities and unattached priests in the city over whom the archbishop had very limited control. Wanting to get married, Ménétra was refused a certificate of confession by his local priest but through a friend obtained one from a complaisant Franciscan, "in return for a few bottles and 3 livres," or so he claimed. In any case, many people routinely went to mass at a nearby convent or monastery instead of in their parish church.[54]

The campaign against the Jesuits, far from strengthening the hand of the parish clergy, dealt a further massive blow to the Paris Church's ability to encourage orthodox religious observance. For the working population it meant the loss of the lay religious associations that the Jesuits had assiduously fostered to encourage regular communion and confession. In 1760 the Parlement of Paris, in a barely disguised attack on Jesuit influence, required all confraternities to present documents attesting their legality. Robert de Lamennais, the early-nineteenth-century liberal Catholic, suggested that "when in 1762 most of the lay religious associations were destroyed along with the Jesuits . . . in less than eighteen years there was a diminution by half in the number of people in the capital who fulfilled their paschal duty."[55] Lamennais was hardly an unbiased commentator but he may not have been far wide of the mark.

The second half of the century witnessed a new relationship between the Church and the monarchy, as the state moved more and more areas of life into secular control. The expulsion of the Jesuits, who had run a large number of colleges, provided the occasion for a reform of education that removed the power of bishops over secondary schools and placed them instead largely under lay control. A couple of years later sixty new posts in the Paris Faculté des arts were opened to all comers by way of competitive examination.[56] The Paris hospitals were removed from Church control in 1781, and in 1789 the Société philanthropique, a totally independent and secular organization, actually provided more money for home relief than the official poor relief agency operating through the parishes.[57]

In the course of the century, furthermore, the clergy found themselves receiving less and less support from the secular authorities. While the police were concerned about "the spirit of irreligion" that conservatives observed in Paris, they proved less and less willing to prosecute sacrilege, heresy, and blasphemy, or even adultery, bigamy, and sodomy. The army apparently considered it a trifling matter when a soldier was caught impersonating a priest and saying masses to raise some money.[58] The courts stopped prosecuting suicides. The statutory punishment was for the body to be dragged through the streets, hung upside down on public display, and finally burned or buried in unsanctified ground. The suicide's property was then confiscated. But in practice only a handful were punished in this way and most—ten or twelve known cases a year—were quietly buried in the parish cemeteries.[59]

The secular authorities also retreated from certain religious practices they had once sponsored with enthusiasm. They less and less frequently appealed to Saint Genevieve when disaster seemed imminent. They ordered fewer of the Te Deum thanksgiving services that had been an integral part of monarchical propaganda under Louis XIV. More than 200 Te Deums were held between 1643 and 1715 but only 24 between 1750 and 1790.[60] Changing religious sentiments within the government itself, including growing de facto tolerance of Protestants, Jews, and of religious dissent, further undermined the efforts of clerical hard-liners.

THE DECLINE OF THE PARISH

All of these changes had a dramatic impact at the local level. The parish played a less and less important role in the lives of Parisians, particularly in the second half of the century. As a result, it lost much of its importance as a unit of social organization and as a source of identity. Church attendance fell, and people had fewer contacts with the local clergy. The parish played a less significant role in regulating local society, even in matters of morality. "If it was true that he had whores in his house," an innkeeper told a local priest who had come to complain, "it concerned only the police and not priests." The widow of Philippe Gouet, *bourgeois de Paris,* was offended by the "scandal" of an unmarried flower seller sharing a room with a soldier in the house of which she was principal tenant. She went first to her parish but when a visit from the clergy had no effect she too turned to the police. Many Parisians no longer took their quarrels and their domestic problems to a priest but instead approached the secular authorities.[61]

The local elites also took less interest in the parish. They came to see religious belief as a more private matter, gradually lost their taste for the public piety of processions and religious ceremony. Occupying a family pew at the front of the church, marching immediately behind the clergy in processions, or having the right to a longer candle than one's neighbors no longer had the same attraction. Here too, the middle years of the century mark a turning point. After 1750 family pews gradually disappeared from the churches, mainly because the churches could make more money from renting chairs than pews, but it meant that prominent local lineages were no longer associated with a particular space in the church where no one else was allowed to sit.[62] The religious confraternities, whose governing bodies had been an important form of local sociability and honor, now declined, and it became harder to recruit churchwardens to undertake parish administration. Bequests declined, both gifts to the churches themselves—of ornaments, vestments, and the like—and donations to the local poor. The wealthy families of Paris no longer, with some notable exceptions, felt the same sense of responsibility to the poor of their own parish. There was also a dramatic fall in the numbers seeking burial in their parish: around 46 percent in the second half of the seventeenth century, 29 percent in the first half of the eighteenth century, and 8 percent in the second half. The elites also abandoned the longstanding practice of displaying the body of the deceased at the door of their house, a neighborhood ritual that enabled all the local people to pray for the repose of their soul. The presence at the funeral of a certain number of the parish poor was no longer requested.[63]

This growing abandonment of the parish was both psychological and demographic. Whereas in the past many wealthy middle-class dynasties had been firmly centered in a single parish, in the second half of the eighteenth century they were beginning to spread more widely. A good example is the Lepy family, blanket makers in the rue St-Victor on the Left Bank. For at least a century sons succeeded fathers and married the daughters of other blanket makers. But some time around the 1740s or 1750s the pattern began to change: two sons (out of three) did become blanket makers in their turn, but one of them moved to Fontainebleau. The third son went to university, trained as a lawyer, then he too left the city. One of the three daughters married a printer, another a mercer, and all three moved away from the parish. Their two female cousins married a tanner and a wood merchant and also went to other parishes. By the 1780s all the family property in the St-Victor quarter had been sold and the children and grandchildren were scattered across seven parishes and two provinces. They had abandoned the family trade and moved into a wide range of middle-class occupations.[64]

Other wealthy merchant families behaved in a similar manner. The Cochin family, mercers from father to son, for a hundred years married into other families along the rue St-Jacques, usually printers or other mercers. But in the second half of the eighteenth century they too began to spread, marrying both outside the quarter and into other occupational groups. One became a priest, another an officeholder (*payeur des rentes*), while a third qualified as a lawyer before founding a private bank. One of the girls married a notary, another an officeholder. Not all wealthy merchant families behaved this way, but enough were doing so to form the basis of a citywide rather than a parish-based bourgeoisie, linked by complex ties of kinship and acquaintanceship.[65] Their attachment to the locality could not be of the same kind when most of their families lived in other parts of the city and when deceased parents and siblings reposed in other churches.

A CULTURAL DIVIDE

Despite the secularization of almost every aspect of Parisian life across the eighteenth century, not all the city's inhabitants were marked by the change to the same degree. Those with ready access to enlightened literature—not just the works of the philosophes but the growing numbers of plays, novels, histories, travel books, social commentaries, and many of the new periodicals—were potential participants in a new culture. Whereas ordinary Parisians who possessed one or more books—around 13 percent of wage earners in 1750 and close to 35 percent in 1780—owned overwhelmingly religious titles, better-off people were buying secular literature, and in larger quantities. More books were being published and a higher percentage of them were secular: in the quarter century after 1750 the production of religious books went into free fall while scientific titles multiplied. The numbers of travel books more than doubled in the eighteenth century.[66] Mercier's *Tableau de Paris* was a huge success, nowhere more than in Paris, while his utopian fantasy *L'an 2400,* though banned, was also a best-seller. And the enormously successful new genre of the novel produced some of the best-sellers of the century, notably Jean-Jacques Rousseau's *Nouvelle Héloïse.* There were obvious occupational and social differences in book buying: lawyers and magistrates possessed more law books, financiers preferred literature, while the great nobles were far more interested in history. Yet the trend among better-off book purchasers was everywhere the same, away from religious books and toward other genres.[67]

At the same time, the number and social range of book owners was widening, extending further and further into the middling ranks of Paris society. By the end of the century we find collections like that of the master tanner Jean Auffray: fifty pamphlets and five hundred books, including classics of French and Latin literature, history books, and an English dictionary. He also owned two thermometers and a barometer, further testimony to his wide interests and scientific culture. There was no comparable collection in this occupational group before 1750: one of the wealthiest tanners in Paris in the first half of the century, Nicolas Bouillerot, died in 1734 leaving only seventy-three books, all of them religious.[68]

This was an enormous cultural shift and it had far-reaching religious implications—more or less profound according to the mind-set of the individual reader. Jacques-Louis Ménétra, who was given to metaphysical reflection, thought about the fate of the heathen in distant lands whom official theology doomed to eternal damnation. For Manon Phlipon the same idea was prompted by history:

> The first thing that revolted me in the religion I professed . . . was the universal damnation of all those who were not acquainted with it. When, brought up on history, I reflected on the extent of the world, the succession of the centuries, the march of empires, on public virtue, the errors of so many nations, I found small-minded, ridiculous, appalling, the idea of a Creator who condemns these innumerable individuals to eternal torment.[69]

Not all readers of Rousseau (who expressed similar ideas) thought like this and very few followed Ménétra and Phlipon down the road to deism. The effect of scientific and enlightened literature was not the same for all. Yet these examples suggest how the growing awareness of other places and cultures could—given a favorable social and political climate—undermine received certainties.

The gradual secularization of the city and the changes in religious belief affected all Parisians, but the educated classes most of all. Even the local elites, the merchants, lawyers, and master artisans who had once ruled the parish churches, were now looking outwards. More of them were marrying across the city; more were reading the new scientific and enlightened literature. They increasingly adopted a more scientific worldview, defining themselves as "enlightened," in opposition to "the people." A new and widening cultural division now separated the upper and middle classes from the mass of the population, and the new religious sensibility of the elites was central to this development.

The extent of the gulf was exemplified by the response of Lieutenant General of Police Lenoir when in 1780 the wife of a master saddler complained to the police that her step-daughter had had a spell put on her, making her cough up lizards and frogs. Such stories "can have no existence outside the puerile imagination of the witnesses you have spoken to." "Nevertheless," he added, "such miracles can provoke the populace to riot."[70] Neither side in this stand-off had any sympathy for the other: not the "enlightened," who were scornful of popular credulity, nor the many Parisians who still believed in miracles, in witches, and in manifestations of the devil, and who feared the consequences of what they saw as irreligious and even sacrilegious acts.

Yet the division was not absolute. There were educated people who believed firmly in miracles. There were still many middle-class men and women who belonged to confraternities, like the wineshop keeper Clemandot who was both a freemason—which suggests a more secular outlook—and an active member of a religious association devoted to maintaining the statue of Our Lady on the corner of his street.[71] Individual personality could play a role, but so too could social milieu: retail shopkeepers like bakers and wineshop keepers remained close to their local clientele, and many master craftsmen were able to move easily between elite circles and the workshop. But for lawyers and officeholders, who had little unavoidable contact with their plebeian neighbors, the distance was likely to be greater.

It was also a generational difference: older people were more likely to adhere to the older religious outlook. Even so, popular religious sentiment was not unaffected. Following years of often acrimonious debate—the next chapter will look more closely at this struggle—the huge Innocents cemetery next to the central market was finally closed in 1780, on health grounds. Fearful of popular reactions, the authorities left it untouched for five years after burials stopped. Finally, a doctor was placed in charge of exhuming the thousands of bones. He proceeded cautiously, reflecting that "it was an ancient and revered place that a religious sentiment seemed to have made sacred in the eyes of the people and that we had in a sense to violate and destroy." But, he added, "this sentiment had greatly diminished with the passing of time."[72] He was right. There was no resistance, and in 1789 a new market was opened on the site of the old cemetery.

Thus the scientific, "enlightened" spirit had triumphed, and with it a new political and social alliance that rejected not only older religious sentiments but, as we shall see, much of the ordinary sociability and habits of mind of the Parisian population.

CHAPTER NINE

URBANISM OR DESPOTISM?

In June 1787 Louis XVI decreed that the Hôtel-Dieu, the huge central hospital on the Ile-de-la-Cité, would be replaced by four new institutions on the outskirts of the city. This decision was the culmination of fifteen years of public debate, of conflict between the hospital and the government, and of discussion involving doctors, clergy and nuns, architects, the Académie des sciences, and government ministers.[1] The issues went far beyond the institution itself. They included the philosophy of institutional care, urban sanitary reform, and the entire future shape of central Paris.

The Hôtel-Dieu had long had its critics. But the event that provoked real public debate was its destruction by fire, for the second time in sixty years, in the early hours of 30 December 1772. The flames had lit up the night sky for hours and no one could say how many of the 2,000 inmates had perished: the figure of 130 was mentioned, and at least 2 firefighters. Fortunately none of the surrounding houses caught fire, but the risk was high that the whole city center would be consumed. The fire had gone on burning in the foundations for an entire week.[2]

The embers had scarcely been extinguished before fundamental questions were raised about the hospital's future. Should it be rebuilt on the same site? Would it be better to construct several smaller institutions in its place? At first the governing body of the hospital—comprising the archbishop, the principal magistrates of the city, and the lieutenant general of police—seemed unanimous: it should be moved. "The lack of space, the pollution of the air and of the water, the damage that this institution causes by infecting everything around it, the danger of fire, and a thousand other disadvantages seem to have united every voice on this score."[3]

Public opinion, according to the administrators, had even settled on the ideal new site: on the river downstream from the city. "This would purge the water of the Seine of all the waste with which the Hôtel-Dieu infects it; it would provide the patients with clean air, an extensive site, open courtyards and gardens that are essential in their convalescence, would enable their beds to be better arranged and even increased in number, so that each patient could have his own, if at all possible."[4]

But they soon began to change their minds. Perhaps the hospital staff's hostility to any move influenced them, but the decisive factor was certainly the response of the royal treasury. It was not prepared to finance a new hospital, instead proposing to sell the valuable land in the city center and divide the patients and staff among several existing hospitals that would be expanded. The administrators protested. Selling the central site would not bring in as much as the treasury believed, while breaking up the Hôtel-Dieu would increase running costs. Income was already inadequate, with costs over the previous six years exceeding revenue by nearly 1.5 million livres. It was therefore impossible to finance any of the reconstruction from the hospital's own funds, as the treasury wanted.[5]

In any case it was essential, the administrators now argued, to keep some sort of hospital in the city center. Women in childbirth and injured workers needed immediate medical assistance and could not go all the way to the proposed sites on the fringes of the city. Medical students who willingly came to a central location might not be prepared to travel further. And if the site was out of the public eye it would not attract so many donations. The best solution, after all, would be to rebuild the hospital on the old site.[6]

And that was where, in the end, the Hôtel-Dieu remained. But the prospect of reform having been raised, there was an outburst of public criticism when it was dropped again. Louis-Sébastien Mercier informed his huge reading public that the failure to relocate the hospital was yet further evidence of "the vices of an administration that is—to say the least—incompetent": yet another sign of abuses in government, to the detriment of suffering humanity. There was, he asserted, no lack of resources: he was expressing a widespread but revealing misapprehension when he asserted that "the income of the Hôtel-Dieu is so great that it would suffice to feed almost a tenth of the population of the capital."[7]

URBAN REFORM

The fate of the Hôtel-Dieu was tied up with wider discussion of how Paris should be reshaped. This debate went back to the 1750s, a decade in which a remarkable change took place. In the early part of the century representations of Paris, despite comments about its noise and crowds, had been overwhelmingly positive: it remained "the famous city," a place of elegance and sophistication, of attraction for tourists, of opportunity and promise for provincials. But from the late 1750s the images become far more negative. Fougeret de Montbron's *Capitale des gaules, ou la nouvelle Babylone* was one of the earliest of many publications that stressed the corruption of the city. The theme was taken up by Jean-Jacques Rousseau in his best-selling *Nouvelle Héloïse* of 1762, again in his autobiography, and by almost every novelist from then on.[8] "Paris is the center of swindling, of fraud, of theft, of all the vices, of all the crimes."[9] Babylon became a standard metaphor for Paris, in Mirabeau's work *Ma conversion,* in a tongue-in-cheek way in Voltaire's *Princesse de Babylone*, and in any number of now-forgotten novels. This representation was reinforced by a perception that real crime and disorder in the city were growing alarmingly.[10]

Against this background, many educated Parisians dreamed of reforming the city. No longer would it be Babylon, but instead a new Rome (or for the occasional more egalitarian thinker, a new Athens). Mercier published a utopian account of a visit to the Paris of 2440, which he imagined as the most magnificent city in the world: the Louvre completed; a huge city square for public festivities situated on the river and overlooked by a Temple of Justice; clean and orderly streets with a smooth flow of traffic, a place filled with prosperous citizens.[11]

Mercier was expressing the late Enlightenment idea of the city beautiful: open spaces and long vistas, well-ordered streets and "natural" spaces that would, in the words of the eighteenth-century French architect Pierre Charles L'Enfant, designer of Washington, D.C., "afford a great variety of pleasant seats and prospects."[12] The taste for sylvan settings was not confined to nobles or intellectuals, as is clear from the growing appeal of new leisure areas in late-eighteenth-century Paris: the tree-lined boulevards, the Champs-Elysées, and the Palais-Royal with its avenues of lime trees. Even the popular tavern Le Grand Monarque, on the city's northern fringe, had a garden and a cascade called Niagara Falls! But when reformers spoke of "natural" spaces, they meant areas carefully organized in accordance with eighteenth-century concepts of beauty.

Figure 26. The Place Louis XV in 1778. From the drawing by Louis-Nicolas Lespinasse, in *Voyage pittoresque de la France* (Paris, 1781–84), vol. 7. Bibliothèque historique de la ville de Paris, photo Jean-Christophe Doerr.

There were to be no untidy clumps of trees hiding the view. Above all, the real city should not be allowed to intrude: hence (in part) the pressure for the removal of houses on the bridges and overhanging the banks, which hid the Seine from view. The landscape paintings that hung in Paris apartments, even in those of merchants and artisans, were to be reproduced outside the windows. The abbé Laugier, in his best-selling *Essay on Architecture,* challenged architects to think of the town as a forest that it was their task to order and beautify.[13]

The new taste for "natural" spaces had been anticipated by the creation of the huge Place Louis XV—now the Place de la Concorde—on the fringe of the faubourg St-Honoré (Figure 26). It combined wooded surrounds and river views with fountains, statues and an imposing classical facade on the northern side. Close to the upper-class leisure garden of the Tuileries, it was readily accessible by carriage from aristocratic residences in the faubourgs St-Honoré and St-Germain.

What particularly characterized urban reform in the second half of the eighteenth-century was its ambition of rethinking the entire city. "Our towns," wrote Laugier in 1753, "are still . . . a mass of houses crowded together without system, planning, or design. Nowhere is this

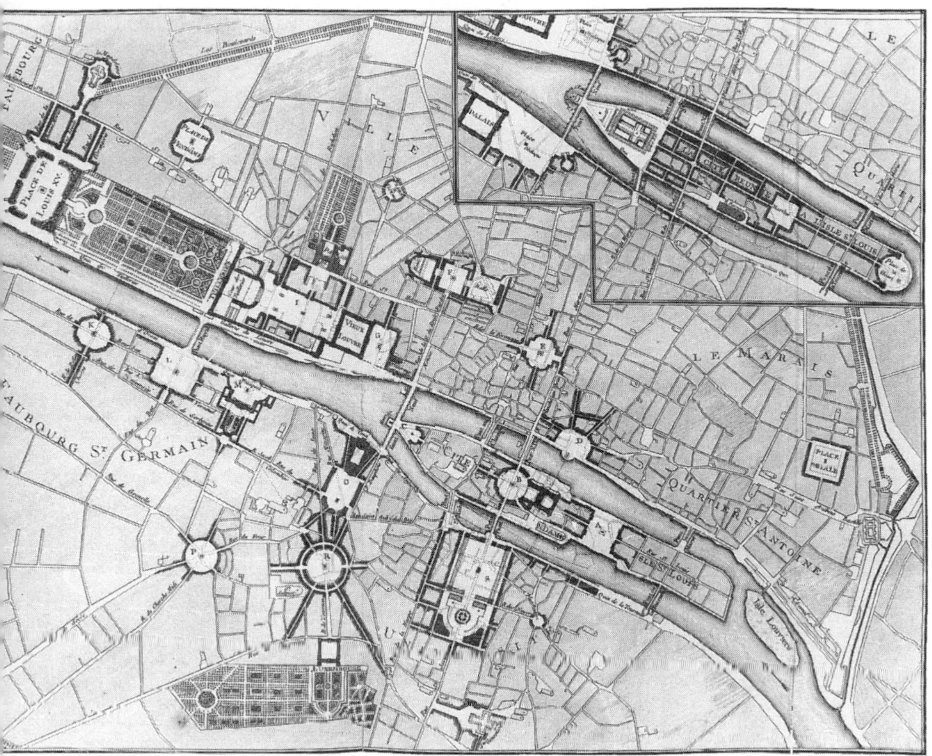

Map 2. Proposed sites for a square dedicated to Louis XV. From Pierre Patte, *Monuments érigés en France à la gloire de Louis XV* (Paris, 1767). Bibliothèque historique de la ville de Paris, photo Jean-Christophe Doerr.

disorder more noticeable and more shocking than in Paris."[14] The first overall plan for the city was put forward by the municipality in 1769, but already in 1748 a competition to design the Place Louis XV—at that stage no site had been decided on—had stimulated architects to reshape the whole city center. Some saw the opportunity to rebuild the Hôtel de Ville, dismissed by Voltaire as "a vulgar building in a small square used for the execution of criminals." Most wanted to enlarge the irregular Place de Grève.[15] Pierre Patte wanted to demolish the church of St-Germain-l'Auxerrois, whose gothic architecture offended neoclassical taste, and create a large square leading down to the river. He would then destroy the houses on the bridges, clear the entire Ile-de-la-Cité, and move Notre-Dame cathedral to provide the necessary focal point for views along the river.[16] There was no room for the Hôtel-Dieu in any of these proposals.

The same ideal of urban beauty led the influential architect Jacques François Blondel to propose squares in front of the churches, "that herald them with dignity," "nothing being so contrary to good taste as to see most of our churches walled in with rented houses, or surrounded by streets so confined, that they obscure the light and destroy the interesting view that a monument of this sort should provide."[17]

Louis-Sébastien Mercier, like other commentators, was offended by the large shop signs—very much a reflection of popular culture—and wrote approvingly of their removal. "The city, which is no longer bristling with these gross appendages offers, so to speak, an urbane visage, smooth and clean-shaven (*poli, net et rasé*)."[18] The class and gender imagery here is not coincidental. A smooth-shaven face was the privilege of men who could afford a barber—the same men whose behavior was characterized by the *politesse* dear to the Enlightenment. The masculine image was also appropriate because the public streets were in Mercier's view properly spaces for men rather than women. His metaphor expresses perfectly the new ideal of the tidy, uniform street, with no unsightly projections or stalls cluttering it, a street refashioned in the image of Enlightened Man. And this was how Paris was portrayed in the engravings sold to tourists. The shop signs were left out; the streets appeared clean, straight, and wider than in real life; the stalls were tidy or not shown; the horses, carriages, and passers-by formed a pleasing composition, graceful and occasionally pastoral (see Figure 27).

Other reformers, applying the principle of overall uniformity, criticized the invisible and irregular division of urban space. A proposal presented to the National Assembly in 1789, signed "a useless citizen who is tired of being so," asked rhetorically,

> Is it not strange that the curé of St-Josse has only twenty-four houses in his entire territory; that the rue Quincampoix should belong to five different parishes; that the curé of St-Laurent should minister to only one house in the rue aux Ours; that the rue des Petits-Champs [near St-Nicolas-des-Champs] should belong to the parish of St-Médéric, and that the rue des Ménétriers which is even closer to the church of St-Médéric should form part of the parish of St-Nicolas?

A more rational division of space would indubitably, this citizen asserted, arrest the erosion of piety by bringing people closer to their parish church.[19]

By a happy coincidence, the aesthetically pleasing vistas and clean-shaven streets of the new Rome were not only more "rational" but also vastly better for public health. With the development of the science of

Figure 27. The ideal streetscape: rue de Grenelle. The engraving shows the street as wider than it actually was, clean, orderly, and clear of obstacles. Anonymous engraving, Musée Carnavalet, © Photothèque des musées de la ville de Paris, photo Ladet.

statistics the authorities were beginning to collate information on urban mortality. The high death rate in Paris provoked concern that the capital was depleting the population of France. The urban environment was obviously unhealthy and medical theorists argued with increasing fervor that the miasmas it produced were potentially fatal.[20]

THE DEBATE OVER THE CEMETERIES

The controversy over the Hôtel-Dieu was not the first one in which public health arguments had been deployed in support of urban reform. A few years earlier, in 1765, widespread debate had taken place over a plan to close the city's graveyards, particularly the central Innocents cemetery. It occupied an extensive site adjoining the central market, and by the 1760s its overburdened soil received the mortal remains of 2,000 or so Parisians every year. Eighteen churches buried their dead there, and more came from the Hôtel-Dieu and the morgue. Most of the bodies were placed in huge pits—up to 50 meters long and nearly as wide—one of which was opened every six months. The open pits were sprinkled with lime but when the weather was warm the smell of decomposition invaded the entire quarter. And increasingly, when new pits were opened, the grave diggers disinterred bodies that had not yet decayed. This was a problem shared by some of the tiny parish cemeteries. The soil, wrote one observer, "is full of grease and decay and . . . has entirely lost its substance." The Innocents, wrote an English visitor, was "of all the Places I ever saw in my Life, the most shocking to mortal Pride and Vanity, the most stinking, loathsome and indecent. . . . It is inconceivable what a Stench issued from such an Aggregation of mortifying and putrifying Carcases: enough to give the Plague to the whole City."[21]

The problem (and the smell) was not new. But complaints began to multiply after midcentury. The government took little notice of the cemetery's neighbors, who were mostly shopkeepers and laborers, but medical opinion was increasingly critical of the practice of burying the city's dead close to its living heart. The smell, more and more doctors agreed, was a serious health risk. With no germ theory to account for infection, they deduced that "some of the diseases that afflict mankind, which corrupt their blood and produce putrid fevers, arise from the fact that the air we breathe is infected with the smell of decaying bodies."[22] Such smells were capable of making meat go bad and if inhaled could even cause death. Those who accepted this miasma theory pushed strenuously for the removal of nuisances and the opening up of confined places to allow fresh air to circulate. There was no more prominent target for their reforming zeal than the putrid Innocents cemetery.

Their voice, growing in strength and public support, did not go unheard. The trigger for action was a report that the parish of St-Sulpice was planning a new cemetery near the residence of the prince de Condé. The Parlement, of which Condé was a member, commissioned a report on the Paris cemeteries, then in May 1765 ordered that after 1 January 1766 no further burials were to take place within the city boundaries. Following the normal funeral service the dead would be taken to special repositories, then collected the following night, and buried in new cemeteries outside the walls.[23]

This order caused a storm. The Parlement received a host of petitions, mostly hostile.[24] The curés of Paris presented a long and closely argued document—which they later published—attacking the whole idea. They claimed that the Parlement's order "has excited a widespread dismay among the two orders who are most numerous . . . , the people and the bourgeoisie (the public cry is: the Parlement is treating us as if we were no better than Protestants)." The Protestants, it was widely believed, did not care for their dead and were prepared to see them taken away with little ceremony (and no one thought of the fact that the French government did not permit them to hold public funerals and obliged them to bury their dead at night). The good Catholics of Paris were revolted by the thought of not being present at the graveside, and by the idea of their loved ones tossed unceremoniously into carts and trundled off to a distant, unknown burial place. It sounded like the collection of nightsoil! "The arrangements for the *dépôts* and for the [new] cemeteries are such," the curés complained melodramatically, "that the son will be deprived of his father's remains before they are really buried and will add to his sorrow that of seeing them torn from him without having paid his final respects. The disgust of the people on this point is well attested." "The very poorest daily do their best," they added, "to have the bodies of their relatives taken from the Hôtel-Dieu to the Innocents [cemetery]." It was important to be there for the burial and to know where loved ones lay. It was equally important to be able to visit the grave later. On All Saints Day the Innocents and Clamart cemeteries were crowded as poor people sought the places where family members were buried.[25]

The Parlement's ruling added insult to injury by allowing the rich to evade the new arrangements. Seeking to defuse potential opposition from powerful interests and perhaps not relishing the idea of members of their own families ending up in the *dépôts,* the magistrates of the Parlement decreed that burials would still be permitted in the churches upon payment of 2,000 livres. It would still be possible to have a tomb in the parish cemetery for 300 livres or to rest in an unmarked grave for a more modest sum, but one equally beyond the means of most of the population. One rule was to apply to the rich, another to the poor.[26]

Other opponents of the new cemeteries had different worries. Parish churchwardens pondered the loss of revenue, since the existing modest payments for burials in the church and cemetery provided significant income. The new, higher tariffs would not make up for this since very few parishioners could afford them.[27]

In the end the Parlement's *arrêt* was to remain a dead letter. Opposition to the closure of the cemeteries was far more vehement than anticipated, and the practical implications and costs of the new arrangements had not been thought through. So the burials went on and the Innocents cemetery remained.

But the campaign continued. As the critique of Paris and of the urban environment became a commonplace of reform literature, growing numbers of Parisians were converted to the view that cemeteries were a danger to health. By the mid-1770s the climate had changed dramatically. In 1775 the Assemblée du clergé urged the closure of the Innocents cemetery for health reasons. And there were few complaints in 1776 when a royal edict banned burials inside the churches.[28]

Nevertheless, no real action came until the next decade. Late in 1779 unpleasant odors began to seep through the walls of cellars under the houses adjoining the Innocents. In February 1780 one of the cellar walls collapsed and the contents of the nearby graves flowed in. Even then action was slow. It was not until November, after a full police investigation, doctors' reports, an inquiry by the Faculté de médecine, and finally agreement from the chapter of Notre-Dame, that the Parlement ordered the cemetery closed.[29]

Further medical reports followed and new knowledge of the composition of air provoked fears that the miasmas still rising from the cemetery would react chemically with the human body to produce deadly fevers. Finally in November 1785 the royal council ordered the remaining bodies and bones to be removed, at night, to the disused limestone quarries at the southern gates of the city—now known as the catacombs. This time there were few protests and some of the Paris curés came out in favor of the move.[30] It was a measure of the medicalization of society and the impact of reform literature that within twenty years many of the most vehement opponents of moving the cemeteries could be converted.

In the meantime the reformers had carried their campaign to other fronts. The cemeteries might be the greatest threat, but the narrow streets and enclosed courtyards were also to blame for the city's bad air. "The opposite wall is so close," wrote the architect Ledoux, "that it compresses the lungs, restricts the senses, and recycles the contagious air currents."[31] Clearly, the solution was to create more open spaces through which the wind could blow. In Paris the obvious conduit for cleansing breezes was the Seine, so here was another argument for the removal of the bridges and the opening of the quais. From there fresh air could penetrate the inner city streets, and there were even proposals for water-powered windmills to assist the process. Allowing air to circulate was also one of the stated aims of a major royal decree of 1783, which required that future streets be wider and the houses on either side lower.[32]

In the late eighteenth century, scientific and medical discoveries inspired a new way of looking at the city. Open spaces were needed, planners suggested, to enable the city to breathe: gardens became the "lungs" of the city. On the model of the circulatory system, streets became "arteries." By an inappropriate but seductive extension of these metaphors it became vital for the health of the metropolis to remove obstructions.[33] Here was scientific confirmation of a necessity that educated Parisians felt urgently for a variety of other reasons.

PROFIT AND GLORY

Despite growing support for urban reform, few large-scale projects were ever realized. Those that were had the additional incentive of political purpose or profit. Paris being the capital, the monarchy stood to gain from its embellishment, and the Place Louis XV was the most obvious attempt to glorify a monarch who was becoming increasingly unpopular. It was commissioned by the municipality but suggested by a royal official—Madame de Pompadour's uncle, in fact—and carried out under government supervision. The royal architect Anges Jacques Gabriel was appointed to design it and the king's statue was to be in the center.[34]

Other urban developments were similarly designed to remind Parisians of the greatness of their kings. The clearing of a square in front of the Louvre was one. Another symbol of royal beneficence was the new grain market with its fine dome (though the treasury eventually went back on its promise of funds). And the church of Ste-Geneviève—now the Panthéon—was undertaken by Louis XV in gratitude for his recovery from serious illness in 1744. Ceremonies were held to mark each stage of construction.[35]

Yet arguably the most successful project, politically and economically, was not a government one at all: the much-praised remodeling of the Palais-Royal by Louis-Philippe-Joseph, duc de Chartres (later duc d'Orléans). Like most great noblemen he was perennially short of money despite his enormous income, and this was the original motive for the astute redevelopment of his huge Paris residence, beginning in 1781. First a long line of stylish houses was constructed around the edge of the garden, with galleries of fashionable shops underneath. The garden itself was then turned into a place of leisure open to the public. The sale of the new buildings brought a handsome return and the amenities in the garden—notably the "circus," a huge building in which races and plays were held and shops were built—guaranteed a regular income.

It also brought the prince a reputation as the benefactor of Parisians, for whom he provided entertainments and a lovely garden—open to everyone—in a city with few such spaces.[36] His popularity at the very beginning of the Revolution resulted not only from his political stance but also from his "generosity" with his Paris estate.

The duc de Chartres was able to exploit changes in the living and leisure patterns of wealthy Parisians. He was fortunate in the location of his palace in the increasingly desirable faubourg St-Honoré, near the northern boulevards that were becoming a mecca for pleasure seekers. But he was not alone. Many owners of property along the boulevards were quick to perceive new opportunities. In the late 1770s and 1780s Charles-Philippe, the comte d'Artois, a younger brother of Louis XVI, created an entire quarter—Le Roule—to the north of the Champs-Elysées, on what were formerly royal orchards. Several fermiers généraux, always alert to profitable schemes, opened new streets adjoining the boulevards. Most successful was the already immensely wealthy Jean-Joseph de Laborde, who constructed luxurious hôtels for sale to court nobles or other fermiers généraux. Over a thirty-year period he made in excess of 2 million livres. Other new streets resulted from the business acumen of Paris convents. In the 1770s and 1780s the Filles-Dieu created a new quarter north of the boulevards, and to the east of Paris the abbey of St-Antoine built the Aligre market and five streets around it.[37]

Some of the new developments were rather different in form from traditional Parisian housing. They incorporated free-standing hôtels for the very rich, designed by some of the leading architects of the period: Ledoux, Soufflot, Boullée, Brongniart. Most had neo-classical facades and carefully landscaped "natural" gardens (see Figure 28). They were far enough outside the city to have the feel of the countryside yet close enough for ready access to the fashionable quarters by carriage.

Other new building took place on more restricted sites within the built-up area, on subdivisions of former noble residences, and provided apartments for a wealthy public seeking exclusive accommodation with modern facilities. Tall, stone-faced houses with identical facades were arranged in graceful curves or squares along broad streets, often around a central monument. One of the earliest such developments was on the site of the hôtel des Soissons near St-Eustache (see Figure 29). Others replaced the hôtel de Condé (around the present Odéon theater) in 1779 and the hôtel de Choiseul (the present Opéra-Comique and the surrounding buildings) in 1780.[38]

The net result of all this new building was a dramatic extension of the

Figure 28. Hôtel of the duc de Montmorency-Laval, in Jean-François Janinet, *Vues de Paris* (Paris, 1792). Bibliothèque historique de la ville de Paris, photo Jean-Christophe Doerr.

city toward the north and west and a slow increase in the density of habitation in the Marais, the faubourg St-Germain, and the faubourg St-Honoré. It also contributed to a growing though still very tentative social homogeneity in the new quarters to the west. By 1789 nine tenths of the fermiers généraux lived in or near the faubourg St-Honoré (compared with four tenths in 1700), and they were imitated by other financiers. Half of the great noble families in Paris in the 1780s resided in the faubourg St-Germain and another third near the Palais-Royal, whereas early in the century they had been more scattered. Among the social elite of Paris, only the members of the Parlement were still spread across almost the whole city.[39]

Figure 29. Rue Sauval. The older section of seventeenth-century houses in the background contrasts with the wider eighteenth-century street in the foreground, part of the speculative housing development around the new grain market. The chemist and fermier général Antoine Lavoisier grew up in the rue Sauval and lived most of his life in the quarter. Original photo by Charles Marville, ca. 1864. Bibliothèque historique de la ville de Paris, photo Jean-Christophe Doerr.

TRAFFIC

There were other more piecemeal changes to the urban landscape that, taken together, had a huge impact on the city. One of the central preoccupations of the authorities, in the second half of the eighteenth century, was congestion in the streets. Traffic had long been a serious problem in Paris. Even in 1719 "[one] was often obliged to stop for some time in the street or to go out of one's way in order to avoid the carriages, and often the people inside them were obliged to alight, if they did not wish to wait for hours."[40]

But the problem was a growing one. Traffic increased faster than population. In the mid seventeenth century there were about 300 carriages in the whole of Paris. Later estimates vary, but by 1765 there were at least 15,000 and by 1789 approximately 22,000. In some neighborhoods, such as the Place Vendôme, even parking became a problem. The number of wagons of all sorts also grew. A reflection of this is the multiplication of houses with entrances for wheeled vehicles: the modest rue des Prouvaires near the central market had only one such entrance in 1650, but thirty-one by the early eighteenth century.[41]

The huge increase in wheeled vehicles, in narrow streets with no sidewalks, caused congestion and endless disputes, since there were no formal traffic rules. If two carriages met in a narrow street one had to back: the one owned by the person of lower rank or more peaceful disposition. If two vehicles tried to pass it was common for the wheels to lock. They also took a heavy toll in human and animal life. "These carriages do not travel slowly," wrote a German visitor. "They move at full gallop. . . . One needs eyes in the back of one's head." The glazier's widow Marie Simon had her leg and torso injured when a carriage ran over her on one of the bridges. She was paid modest compensation, but Catherine Bellusier, a laundrywoman, was not so lucky when she was knocked over near the central market. Perhaps, as the coachman claimed, it was her own fault. Or was it because the carriage belonged to a government minister, the baron de Breteuil?[42]

In the inner city the problems were particularly acute. One of the worst areas was the Halles, the crowded central market where bread and flour were sold on Wednesdays and Saturdays, fruit, cheese, and eggs on the other days. All sorts of goods were sold in the same area, everything from leather, used clothes, and candles to dried peas and fish. The market was too small and the main access roads woefully inadequate.

The authorities responded both by trying to improve access and by decentralizing the market. In 1767 the magnificent new grain market was opened several blocks to the west. The leather market was moved several streets to the north and a new cloth market was constructed. In the late 1780s a new street, the rue Calonne, was cut through to allow access from the west and several of the surrounding roads were widened. A number of constructions in the market square itself were removed, including the large pillory. The fish market was moved in 1789, and part of the old Innocents cemetery became a herb and vegetable market.[43]

Traffic congestion was also acute around the bridges. For most of the century six of the ten bridges (not counting the wooden Pont Rouge between the two main islands) had houses built on them, making them so narrow that carriages could barely pass in the middle. The approaches were equally difficult. Travelers on the rue St-Denis, one of the principal north-south thoroughfares, had to wind through a maze of narrow streets or pass through an arch under the Châtelet prison. Even the Pont Neuf, which had no houses on it, was often so congested that it took some time to get across. As the city expanded, additional traffic from the faubourgs had to come through the center to cross the river.

Primary responsibility for the bridges and their surrounds lay with the municipality, which was very conscious of the problem. There were various projects for new bridges but mainly for financial reasons nothing was done until 1787 when work was begun on the Pont Louis XVI (now the Pont de la Concorde). But in the 1770s the houses were removed from the riverbank along what is now the Quai St-Michel, on the Left Bank, and in 1782 the Petit-Châtelet prison at the end of the rue St-Jacques was demolished. Finally in 1788 and 1789 the houses on all but one of the bridges were removed.[44]

In general the eighteenth-century authorities responded to traffic problems in the same way as most modern governments do: instead of restricting the flow of traffic, they tried to find ways of letting it in and keeping it moving. On the city outskirts the streets were paved to make them accessible to heavy traffic throughout the year: the rue St-Lazare as early as 1729, because it carried market traffic, the northern boulevard in 1772, to "reduce the congestion in the neighboring quarters." By 1780 the ring of wide paved streets went right round the north of Paris.[45] The Porte St-Antoine was demolished at the end of the 1770s so that traffic entering the rue St-Antoine no longer had to squeeze through the arch beside the Bastille.

To ensure that future streets would be less congested, the government

Figure 30. Street clutter: the rue Mondétour. Except for the sidewalks, it might be a typical eighteenth-century street in central Paris: narrow, irregular, and cluttered. In the foreground, the nineteenth-century rue Rambuteau, wider and more evenly paved. Note the pear-shaped shop sign on the corner of the building on the right, under the lamp. Original photo by Charles Marville, ca. 1865. Bibliothèque historique de la ville de Paris, photo Jean-Christophe Doerr.

decreed in 1783 that all new streets must be at least 30 feet (10 meters) wide. Existing streets were to be widened progressively. In fact this had been going on quietly for years. Anyone building a new house had to obtain permission from the Bureau des finances or (on the quais and boulevards) from the municipality, whose inspectors examined the site and issued an alignment, very often back from the street. In 1757 they ordered a residential building in the rue Verderet near St-Eustache to be moved back 5 feet, "to make communication easier from this quarter to the place des Victoires." After about 1780, in the interests of easier traffic flow and a more pleasing uniformity, the Bureau des finances systematically tried to straighten the many dog-legged inner streets where the houses jutted out. For the reconstruction of corner houses the authorities began to insist on the corner being cut away to widen the intersection.[46]

The other front on which the police tried to improve traffic flow was in removing the innumerable "encumbrances" in the streets. Throughout the century bylaws were reissued forbidding building workers from depositing masonry and timber in the streets. Artisans were banned from setting up their workbenches in the street and animals were not to be allowed to roam. As the traffic flow increased most of these activities were driven out of the main streets anyway. But a more difficult target was the innumerable stalls: "it is generally a cobbler, a woman selling tripe or fruit or mending clothes, who always prefer street corners," read a complaint to the police.[47] Even worse were the street hawkers, who in defiance of police regulations set up portable tables to sell fruit or toys or umbrellas in the busiest streets and intersections. These were always being knocked over by vehicles, provoking noisy disputes.

The police tried first to regulate the locations, issuing permits and as early as 1739 banning all unauthorized stalls. Then a series of ordinances from the 1750s through the 1770s suppressed all those around the Porte St-Antoine, the central market, and the 178 stalls on the Pont Neuf. The earlier ordinances were not strictly enforced but in the late 1770s the police began to move on the street traders in earnest. The commissaires drew up lists of all the existing stalls and recommended those that could be retained without hindering traffic. They issued written permission to the remaining ones, giving preference to needy master artisans and noting the exact location and size of each stall: a cobbler in the St-Benoît quarter was allowed a width of no more than 3½ ft. [1 meter].[48]

But the Bureau des finances and the commander of the guard were hostile to all the stalls. Despite the reservations of the lieutenant general a royal edict of May 1784 banned them completely on the grounds that they "block the passage of vehicles, impede that of pedestrians, and each day cause accidents."[49] To enforce the ruling the guard were instructed to undertake special patrols, and across the 1780s they destroyed some 4,000 stalls. This was a key factor underlying popular hatred of them. The guardsmen complained that because of this work they were being insulted daily—they particularly seem to have objected to being called "two-legged miseries" (*tristes-à-pattes*) and "rabbits on horseback" (*lapins ferrés*).[50]

The police were responding to demand from one part of the public—those citizens responsible for "repeated complaints" received by the authorities. They were also sensitive to the arguments of the urban reformers. The cause of easier movement around Paris was taken up particularly avidly by the advocates of political economy and free trade. "Circulation makes for the welfare of states," wrote "a disinterested citizen" in a project for the improvement of Paris presented in 1767, neatly linking the idea of free movement around the city with the development of commerce. Every possible argument was used in favor of "circulation." Medical arguments were advanced: it was suggested that the faster and more frequent movement of carriages would help ventilate the city.[51] The scientific and medical metaphors, discussed earlier, gave the high moral ground to the reformers, and anyone resisting the clearing of the streets for traffic could be portrayed as irrational and unenlightened. By the late eighteenth century a uniform urban environment, a smooth flow of traffic, a clean and healthy city without obstructions, had become important symbols of a well functioning state.

In this way, as in the campaign against the cemeteries, a formidable alliance rallied in favor of reform. Admittedly, property owners sometimes tried to get round the building regulations and were occasionally able to exploit rivalries between administrative bodies: the Parlement regularly overturned rulings of the Bureau des finances, for example. There were also claims for compensation from the owners of houses marked for demolition, while the curé of St-Louis-en-l'Ile requested a tax reduction because the removal of the 54 houses on the Pont Marie had reduced the population of his parish by 1,080 souls, hence its income.[52] But there was no organized opposition, as there had been to the closure of the cemeteries, and no educated advocates like the curés. Those most affected were street vendors and artisans who persisted in leaving their tables and carts in the roadway. The trump cards were held by the reformers, and first the major streets, then in the nineteenth century the secondary ones, were paved, cleaned, and cleared. Traffic reigned supreme.

THE POLICE CAMPAIGN TO IMPROVE THE CITY

The police reform agenda extended well beyond the clearing of the streets. Increasingly influenced by the enlightened critique of the city, but motivated both by conservative concerns about public morality and by a new commitment to public service, the police set out to make the city a better, safer place to live. Their initiative marked a dramatic change in the idea of government, one consistent with changes in thinking about the monarchy. Early in the century the police saw themselves primarily as mechanics greasing the machinery of a "natural" social hierarchy in which children owed respect and obedience to their fathers, journeymen to their masters, and everyone to their social superiors. In return, those with authority guaranteed protection and fair treatment. The police were only required to intervene when the machinery broke down. They had very little armed force.[53] But across the eighteenth century, although the rhetoric of social hierarchy remained the same, true to the spirit of the Enlightenment the police began to try to perfect the machine. With the support of the monarchy they became far more interventionist, and increasingly took on functions that had once been left to the clergy, the courts, or the city notables. They attempted to impose uniform rules and respect for the law on everyone. They were therefore perceived—often with reason—to be trampling underfoot the rights of the common people and of the governing classes alike.

Much of the pressure for change came from successive lieutenants general of police. It had begun with d'Argenson at the turn of the century. By 1750, the first occasion when Parisians responded with widespread violence, the police ordinances and new structures were all in place. But the change in spirit inside the Paris police, particularly among the commissaires, who were part of an older system of governance, took longer. Gradually the lieutenants general tightened their hold. They provided financial incentives to encourage the commissaires and inspectors to do police work thoroughly. They were constantly on the watch for omissions by their subordinates: do not let your clerk make decisions in your place; do not leave the city without permission; notify the lieutenant general immediately of any major crime; make sure that routine reports arrive at police headquarters within twenty-four hours; do not interrogate witnesses but let them testify freely; write names legibly. A system of double reporting by the inspectors and the commissaires was introduced, so that their superiors could cross-check that both groups were doing their jobs properly.[54]

In the 1770s and 1780s the rhetoric of duty, professional integrity, and public service was constantly on the lips of the lieutenants general. They tried to get police officers to see themselves as servants of an abstract state, putting the public good above personal loyalties and even (within limits) above deference to social superiors. An important part of this process was the attempt to apply the same rules to everyone. In his memoirs Lenoir repeatedly expressed his frustration at his inability to convict those protected by a prince or a government minister, "who easily found a way to keep justice from being done." Laws against gambling were ineffective, he believed, because everyone at court gambled. Efforts to clean up the streets were hindered by "many people of rank, of condition, [who] believed themselves exempt . . . the commissaires and police inspectors did not dare to name personages of high and superior standing to be fined." But things were changing slowly. In 1766 even the prince de Condé, a member of the royal family, lost the dinner his servant was bringing him when a zealous police employee confiscated it for infringing the rules on Lenten fasting. Needless to say, this sort of professionalism did not endear the police to the nobility. But it prefigures the "rule of law" that was to be proclaimed after 1789.[55]

The lieutenants general played on their subordinates' desire for respect and status: "I am endeavoring to make your work even more honorable," Lenoir told the inspectors in 1782. Gradually his efforts bore fruit and his subordinates increasingly aspired (as the commissaires put it) "to be useful to society and to merit the good opinion of the public." By the 1780s the growing volume and detail of police reports testify to the increasing attention they were giving their work. Although he was frequently critical of their zeal, Lieutenant General Lenoir later wrote of the commissaires that "forty-eight individuals of equal worth will not be found again."[56]

Other branches of the police moved in the same direction. Record keeping became more centralized and more systematic. The number of employees in the central police offices grew from eight in 1730 to thirty-five in 1788 and their procedures became more bureaucratic. By the 1780s they were keeping central registers so that stolen property or the criminal record of those arrested could easily be traced. Before this no effort was made to recover stolen goods, and the system of branding with hot irons—a V on the shoulder for "vagabond," a G for someone sentenced to the galleys—was the only way to identify those who had been in serious trouble before.[57]

These innovations reflect a new sense of mission. The police were now setting out to *solve* crimes. For much of the century it was extremely rare for them to do any investigation: it was up to the victims to bring an accusation. Until about 1750 petty theft was treated as a civil matter: the victims had to prosecute the offenders themselves and even had to pay to report the theft to the police. But Lieutenant General Berryer, the same man who was chased from his house by the enraged crowd in 1750, obliged the commissaires to accept reports of theft gratis and required the inspectors to follow them up. As this became known, the numbers of reports of theft rose dramatically: people began to use the police in a new way. By the 1780s those who had been robbed actually began to stand some chance of getting their property back thanks to police efforts.[58]

The guard too became increasingly professional, turning from an unreliable home guard of retired soldiers and unemployed craftsmen into a semimilitary force containing a significant number of long-serving career guardsmen. Discipline was reinforced and in the 1770s one of their commanding officers began deliberately to train them for crowd control. In the late 1780s the authorities felt confident enough to use them in this way and on more than one occasion they obeyed the order to open fire. Hardly surprisingly, they became increasingly unpopular![59]

The dramatic extension of police activity into every area of daily life reflects a boundless desire to improve the physical and moral environment of the city. In the past, street sweeping had been the task of each shopkeeper or ground-floor resident, and lighting the candles in the dim street lamps had also been a local responsibility. But these jobs were often not done regularly, and in 1734 the police assumed responsibility for both lighting and cleaning. They employed subcontractors and levied a special tax to pay for the work. To improve safety in the streets at night they sponsored experiments with different types of lamps, using mirrors and different types of candles. Not only did the number of lights more than double across the century but their brightness was greatly improved. By 1789 oil lamps had begun to replace the old candles and Paris literally had become, by the standards of the time, a city of light.[60]

Another "service" that was extended greatly in the early 1750s was that of lettres de cachet: imprisonment by royal order, without trial, most often of women whose husbands accused them of infidelity or of sons and daughters whose behavior their parents could not control. "At that time," Lenoir wrote later, "people felt that an individual's dishonor rebounded on the family, so the government and the police came to the assistance of parents who had a legitimate reason to fear that they would be dishonored." The police saw this as a public service, and the number of families from all social groups who asked for their black sheep to be locked up shows that it was meeting a demand within Parisian society. Though it was perhaps a demand the police had themselves created. They were taking over the regulatory role of families, clergy, and local communities.[61]

The lieutenants general of police—generally with the support of other city authorities—also took an active interest in broader areas of public welfare. They tried to combat the pollution of the river by designating places where the water carriers could fill their buckets away from the sewer outlets. They regulated the disposal of human waste and checked the quality of food. They were primarily responsible for the creation of a fire brigade: since Paris houses were built mainly of wood, one against the next, and along streets often so narrow that the roofs nearly touched, a fire could easily destroy an entire quarter. In 1724 alone the infant Paris fire service was called to one hundred fires, most of them small, but all with the potential to destroy large areas of the city. In the course of the century the central hospital burned down twice, the opera twice, the Palais de Justice once. In 1718 the houses on one of the bridges were all destroyed after a bereaved mother set a candle afloat on the river, praying to Saint Anthony of Padua to guide it to her drowned son's body. The whole city center was endangered.[62]

The police, in alliance with other city authorities, tackled the fire hazard on a number of fronts. They banned exposed wooden beams and thatched roofs. Fires and fireworks in the streets were prohibited. Citizens were enjoined to have their chimneys cleaned regularly. The fire service was expanded and experiments were carried out with new, more efficient pumps.[63]

Another domain of police action in the second half of the century was the regulation of wet-nursing. Many Parisian babies were sent, at one or two days old, to be wet-nursed in the villages surrounding the capital until they were one or two years of age. As Lieutenant General Lenoir explained, "the wives of workers and domestics, being themselves for the most part workers and servants, calculate that if they breast-fed their children themselves they would have to renounce the greater income that they derive from their service or daily work."

Only too often this income was indispensable to the family's survival. But better-off families also used wet-nurses, partly because they believed that the country was a far healthier place for children—even though one in three of the babies did not return. We can only speculate on the psychological consequences of wet-nursing for generations of young Parisians.[64]

The police were given responsibility for wet-nursing in 1715 and immediately set about reorganizing it. They created four central *bureaux* to put nurses and parents in touch and supervised the record keeping. Following growing criticism of mortality rates among nurslings, in 1762 they provided free medical examinations for the nurses and babies. In the late 1760s there was a serious shortage of wet-nurses, apparently because many Parisians did not pay regularly. So Lieutenant General of Police de Sartine set up a new agency to recruit wet-nurses and guarantee the regular monthly payments. When the nurses arrived to collect the babies they were given food and lodging and underwent a medical examination. All of this was funded by a modest commission paid by the parents, and the new agency proved a remarkable success. It brought the cost down to 8 or 9 livres per month, an amount that all but the poor could afford.[65]

This example demonstrates that the police were more than "cultural missionaries," imposing the values of the educated classes on the mass of the population. Rousseau's novel *Emile,* and an increasing number of doctors in the 1760s, stressed the dangers of wet-nursing and urged mothers to breast-feed their babies themselves. Lieutenant General Lenoir was persuaded and sponsored a pamphlet encouraging maternal nursing. Yet he continued to support the wet-nursing agency, which was intended for working-class families.[66]

Lenoir was active in other domains too. He placed a tax on licensed gambling houses and used it to fund a free hospital for the treatment of venereal disease and a spinning workshop for poor women. The same tax paid for the establishment in 1777 of the Mont-de-Piété, a state-run pawnbroker. Until then anyone wanting to borrow a small amount of money had to pay extortionate rates of interest to a moneylender or at one of the innumerable pawnshops. In 1752, for example, Etienne Viallet borrowed 60 livres from a moneylender near the Porte St-Martin, providing as surety a silver box and a cap that together were worth 200 livres. He was charged 10 percent for the first month's interest—deducted in advance from the 60 livres he received—and 5 percent for each following month.[67] The Mont-de-Piété, on the other hand, lent money on items of all sorts at a fixed 10 percent per annum. Within a few years it was making large profits, some of which were used to make up the funding shortfall of the Hôpital général—the lieutenant general of police was a key member of the hospital board.[68]

These examples of police action, well beyond immediate concerns of law and order, testify to the penetration of Enlightenment thought into the Old Regime bureaucracy. The whole approach to policing had been transformed. It was now proactive, trying to anticipate problems. It was often humanitarian and undoubtedly improved the lives of Parisians. It was also bureaucratic: the lieutenants general of police were sticklers for procedures, which they saw as the best way of making their subordinates accountable and of preventing them from building individual networks of patronage inimical to the public good (the very notion that such networks were a form of corruption was itself new). Yet in the final analysis the police chiefs were firm believers—as was Voltaire—in "enlightened absolutism," in the key role of state power in reforming society according to principles of utility, rationality, and humanity. There was never any doubt in their minds that "the people" needed to be treated like eighteenth-century children: guided by enlightened mentors, chastened and encouraged, but never consulted. Yet the civilizing process also extended to the great nobles, who must be forced—in the common good—to respect the law. Society could be improved, the police believed, but only through the paternalistic foresight of enlightened administrators. And while expressions such as "the public good" were forever on the lips of the police chiefs, the master they served was a state that was growing more distant from its subjects.

PERCEPTIONS OF DESPOTISM

The cumulative effect of much of this activity, even when motivated by humanitarian concern, was to make people feel that the government of Paris (and by extension of the entire country) had become increasingly despotic. Ironically the police themselves, as Lenoir explained in his memoirs, "encouraged the belief that nothing that happened in Paris was unknown to the lieutenant of police," giving him a reputation for omniscience designed to make him feared and obeyed. For the same reason the police cultivated the idea that their spies were everywhere, although the real number was quite small.[69]

As a result, the reciprocal relationships that both the commissaires and the guard formerly had with the people of their quarter were undermined. By the 1770s and 1780s popular attitudes to all branches of the police were more negative. In return, the police had learned to fear the people's anger. Back in 1725 the commissaire Labbé had marched fearlessly into the midst of a rioting crowd, confident that his office and his long black robes would protect him. And he was right, for although he was threatened no hand was laid upon him and nor—unlike the unfortunate soldiers he brought with him—did he have stones thrown at him. But by the last years of the Old Regime the commissaires were afraid to behave in this way. During widespread bread riots in Paris in 1775 all but one of them remained firmly inside their hôtels. In August 1787 the commissaire Ninnin, based in the plebeian quarter at the foot of the rue St-Denis, wrote to his superiors with a note of panic, "of a risk that we are running; that is, that after handing over to the guard . . . some individual who must be taken to prison, our houses remain unguarded, and may be assailed and plundered by the crazed populace, while we ourselves are in the very greatest danger."[70]

His fear was well founded. At moments of crisis even those elements of the police who in 1750 had been respected were now coming under attack. The guard too had become unpopular. In 1780 Lieutenant General Lenoir instructed his subordinates that "it is dangerous for the guard to spend [too long] escorting a delinquent through the streets. . . . The people, who always follow, can get angry [and] riot." Shortly after, Mercier wrote of the guard's "blind brutality" and commented that "the common people are always on the point of conflict [with them], never having been spared by them." Relations worsened at the end of August 1788, after the guard forcibly cleared demonstrators from the Place Dauphine. In retaliation, over the following weeks, eight guard posts—wooden shelters with a fireplace to keep the guardsmen warm in winter—were burned or pulled down. The house of their commanding officer was besieged by an angry crowd. Guardsmen were attacked in the streets, to the point that in mid-September one patrol refused to go out, saying "that since they had become odious to the people . . . there was hardly a day passed that someone did not use some new stratagem to draw them from their post so as to attack them more easily."[71]

But it was not just the relationship between the police and the working people that had deteriorated. Many bourgeois too now distrusted the police as never before and saw in them the quintessence of despotism. Again Mercier spoke for an important element of Paris public opinion when he complained about spies and about imprisonment without trial.

> In practice the secretary of the Lieutenant of Police alone decides on imprisonment and on its duration. . . . Accusations are usually brought by members of the guard; and it is most surprising that a single man should thus dispose of the liberty of such a large number of individuals. . . .

> They may have enemies among this horde of officers, spies and their creatures, who are believed without question.[72]

The widespread distrust of the police among the middle classes became clear in July 1789 when the local district committees assumed control of the city. The position of lieutenant general was immediately abolished and the police bureaucracy disbanded, while the inspectors vanished from the scene and the guard was replaced by a citizen militia. Only the commissaires were retained (until 1791)—testimony to the vital role they fulfilled and to the respect they still enjoyed among the middle classes. Yet even they were not entirely trusted. Their decisions were now taken in the presence of two citizens appointed by the district, to avoid any abuse of power. For the local bourgeois the police had become a necessary evil but a potential threat to liberty.

ROME OR BABYLON?

As Paris became, in the literary imagination of the later eighteenth century, a new Babylon, so reform was pursued with ever-increasing urgency. But the attempts to transform the urban environment cannot be separated from changes in Parisian society. Underlying the late-eighteenth-century chorus of complaint about traffic, urban nuisances, and the state of the streets were not simply growing problems of urban congestion or disease, but new ideologies and social practices. Inherent in many reform proposals was a new social philosophy that was very different from those that prevailed in customary Paris. It set "rational," utilitarian, and economic principles above older religious, paternalistic, and communitarian ones.

This reordering of priorities was already clear in the cemetery controversy, which set those persuaded by "enlightened" medical arguments against what they saw as a "superstitious" attachment to the parish graveyards. A similar division is evident in changing attitudes to poor relief. In the early eighteenth century fear of sturdy beggars and hostility to the unknown poor had been accompanied by a lingering belief that the poor were particularly dear to God and that charity was a Christian obligation. For the well-to-do, according to the abbé de St-Pierre in 1740, good works were "the only foundation for hopes of Paradise."[73] But confidence in the redemptive qualities of charity was waning. It was being replaced by a belief that the obligation to assist depended on the personal qualities of the poor: on whether they were worthy individuals rather than whether they belonged to the community or the parish. Numerous authors now began to suggest that while many of the poor were victims of their birth in an unequal society, many more were poor because they were lazy or morally deficient. "These are the false needy," wrote a clergyman in the mid-1770s. The problem was, he went on, that

> Christian morality . . . has so often preached charity . . . that Christians have gone beyond the limits imposed by reason. They have . . . created free handouts to all who ask, in bread, in soup, in money. These institutions, together with a host of small alms badly allocated, have produced an infinity of paupers. For if a man can live without working, it cannot be hoped that any law will make him work.[74]

According to this logic, the poor needed to be reformed rather than given handouts, and should be forced to contribute to the national economy.

This new attitude had a serious impact on poor relief funds, both in the parishes and in the monasteries and hospitals.[75] There was growing distrust among the educated classes of large institutions like the Grand Bureau des pauvres and the central hospital, which did not discriminate between the worthy and the unworthy poor. For the nuns at the Hôtel-Dieu "all the charitable duties of hospitality must have for their end and principal purpose not at all the person of the sick man but the sacred Person of Jesus."[76] In practice this meant that some of those admitted were old or homeless rather than ill, and that some who were well enough to leave were allowed to stay longer because they had nowhere to go—though only, no doubt, if they were suitably pious. But under the 1787 decree the nuns' control of the hospital was removed and the doctors were placed in charge. Henceforth only the clinically ill were to be accepted, and the atmosphere changed markedly: the nuns accused the doctors of treating the sick "like prisoners" and they attacked "the businessmen of the administration" for their hard-hearted devotion to economy and efficiency.[77]

But growing support for the new approach is reflected in falling donations to the Grand Bureau des pauvres and the Hôtel-Dieu. Philanthropic money now went to new secular charities, like the Société philanthropique founded in 1780, which more strictly targeted widows, orphans, the blind, the old, and the infirm.[78] The final two decades of the Old Regime also witnessed the proliferation of new private or parish hospices where the benefactors had more control. That at St-Merri was established primarily by the head of the municipality and the aldermen; the one at St-Jacques-du-Haut-Pas by its enlightened curé, Cochin; that in the faubourg St-Honoré by the financier Beaujon; and the most famous, at St-Sulpice, by Madame Necker and her husband. "No one gets in without being recommended by some rich and powerful parishioner," wrote a critic. "The discipline established in this hospice," responded a defender, "keeps away from it that mass of vagabonds and do-nothings who have yet to be removed from the Hôtel-Dieu."[79]

In their attempts to transform Babylon, the reformers held the upper hand. They included many powerful people and had ready access to the press. And the social and political evolution of Paris operated in their favor. They were able to deploy the full arsenal of Enlightenment rhetoric: the forces of medicine, of reason, and of progress confronted irrationality, superstition, and disease. The reformers firmly believed that the changes they sought would create a better environment for all Parisians, and in certain respects they were right: better street cleaning and the removal of nuisances certainly improved public health in the long run. But urban reform, especially the clearing of the streets for traffic, involved a cost that was borne primarily by the common people. They were the ones expelled from the houses that were demolished. The street lay at the heart of the local community, a place where working women set their chairs and artisans took their work; where tradesmen and stallkeepers gossiped; where the young of all ages played skittles, quoits, and ball games. But the increase in traffic and the clearing of the streets forced all these activities into the houses and courtyards and in doing so changed the character of neighborhood relations. While in the faubourgs and in quiet side alleys a lively street life subsisted, sometimes right through the nineteenth century, it could not survive in the busy streets of the city center.

Had all the projects of the reformers been executed, the changes would have been far more brutal. The free circulation of goods and labor, for all the benefits it promised, had far more to offer merchants and wealthy consumers than wage earners or the poor. In an eighteenth-century context free markets meant more expensive bread, and greater competition generally led to lower wages or higher unemployment. The more far-reaching urban reform proposals would have involved mass evictions, as later happened under Haussmann. The closure of the central hospital, which would have taken place but for the Revolution, would have meant the loss of an institution located close to where the majority of the working population still lived. As it was, the reorganization after 1787 did mean that many of the poor and desperate could no longer gain admission. In short, the new Rome held more benefits for the wealthy and the middling sort than for the vast majority of the population.

Yet the reformers did not agree among themselves—or not on everything. While most applauded the humanitarian measures taken by the Paris police and by other branches of government, they were simultaneously critical of the methods used. There was growing criticism of the arbitrariness and "despotism" of the Paris police and therefore, indirectly, of the monarchy. It was a recurrent theme of Mercier's best-selling *Tableau de Paris*. Arbitrary arrest was the principal target of the widely distributed work *Des lettres de cachet et des prisons d'état* (1782) by Honoré-Gabriel Riqueti, comte de Mirabeau, and of the more sensational *Mémoires de la Bastille* (1783) by the well-known lawyer Simon Linguet. Even the reform of the hospitals could provoke similar charges, when it suited particular political purposes: in the reorganization of the Quinze-Vingts hospital for the blind, the Parlement itself argued, "Charity had given way to despotism."[80]

One of the great ironies of the reign of Louis XVI was that the government in fact became less arbitrary, more humanitarian, and more devoted to the well-being of the people. By the 1780s the goals of the police, summed up by Lieutenant General Lenoir, were nothing less than "public order, the safety of individuals, and the good of humanity."[81] Police officers became more accountable to their superiors and more responsive to pressure from educated Parisians for better services, a healthier, more pleasing environment, and for a more efficient and "rational" city government.[82] Their work did make Paris a safer and healthier place to live. Yet in pursuing the goal of urban reform the police and other agencies became more intrusive, more bureaucratic, and less flexible. They were less in tune with the people whose lives they ruled ever more closely, at precisely the moment when many of those people were aspiring to become citizens with a voice in their own government.

CHAPTER TEN

THE INTEGRATION OF THE CITY

In June 1779 men with ladders and brushes invaded the faubourg St-Germain and began painting numbers above or beside each door. Behind them people watched with unconcealed hostility: this was some new classification system that would undoubtedly be followed by a new tax. But the painters took no notice. When they came to the residence of Guillaume-François-Louis Joly de Fleury, one of the principal magistrates of the Paris Parlement, the porter—no doubt alerted in advance by the neighbors—came out and warned them off. But they pushed him aside and painted the number next to the gate. When Joly de Fleury learned of it he sent an angry letter to Lieutenant General of Police Lenoir. Within hours the work had stopped, and Joly de Fleury's number was removed.[1]

This was the first serious attempt to number the houses of Paris and most people did not see the need for it. In their own neighborhoods they knew the houses and had no use for numbers. When they gave directions they referred to local landmarks: taverns, churches, statues, fountains, shop signs, distinctive houses, or simply the names of local people. When they ventured further afield they asked the way. Almanacs gave a person's name and the street, and where necessary additional information such as "near St-Magloire" or "on the corner of the rue du Mouton." Letters were addressed the same way: "To M. Aubert, merchant sword-cutler, rue Bourg-l'abbé, at the sign of Alexander the Great."[2] This system worked perfectly adequately.

Yet by 1789 nearly every house in the city had a number. Joly de

Fleury's residence was redone in 1785. Nor was Paris the only place where this was happening. In fact the French capital was behind many provincial towns and ten to fifteen years behind London.[3]

House numbering was not, as one might at first think, a response to the growth of the city. After all, even with nearly half a million people in 1700 Paris had managed without it (and until the 1730s even without street names on the corners). Even after the houses had numbers they were often not used. An almanac of 1787, for example, indicated the address of "Mademoiselle Joséphine, Porte S-M. [St-Martin], opposite the door under the second streetlight, at a wine merchant's house, next to the cul-de-sac de l'Egout."[4] Even the semiofficial *Almanach royal,* which listed government officials, magistrates, lawyers and notaries, doctors, stockbrokers, and many others, still did not use the numbers in 1788. The numbering was partly a reflection of an official desire to classify, to make urban space more uniform. But it was also a response to new ways of moving round the city.

Right across the early modern period a process of integration was taking place in Paris. City government was becoming more centralized and uniform, its economy more interconnected. There was growing interdependence between quarters, so that the city was functioning more as an organic whole. Nor was this phenomenon solely administrative and economic: social and cultural practices were also becoming more citywide, more "metropolitan."

House numbers were part of this process, not only because they served to classify and control the city, but because they made it easier for people to move around areas they did not know and to find places quickly. This was something that most Parisians, hitherto, had not had to do. But in the later eighteenth century people were moving more, and some of them began to avoid the social rituals involved in asking the way.

NEW SOURCES OF INFORMATION

One way of observing this process is to examine the almanacs, trade directories, and guidebooks that, along with the house numbers, helped people find what they were looking for. It was no coincidence that the man behind the house numbering, Marin Kreenfelt, owned the new *Almanach de Paris,* a directory "containing the abode, the name and quality of persons of rank in the city and suburbs of Paris." The work of painting the numbers began immediately after he obtained a monopoly for his almanac on 2 June 1779. He no doubt hoped it would put him a step ahead of his competitors, the annual *Guide parisien ou Almanach des rues de Paris* and especially the *Almanach Dauphin*.[5]

The new almanacs and directories were directed to several sorts of clients. The needs of wealthy consumers were addressed by what was probably the earliest guide, Nicolas de Blegny's *Adresses de la ville de Paris* of 1691, which included information about transport, schools, and shops. It went through several editions in the early eighteenth century. There seems to have been nothing quite the same until the 1750s, although it is difficult to be certain because almanacs went out of date quickly and copies often do not survive. But from then on at least three guides of this sort appeared every year.

Alongside shoppers' guides were calendars of events. At first publications like the *Almanach de Paris* and the *Agenda du voyageur* focused on civil and religious ceremonies but later titles specialized in theater, concerts, balls, cafés, and other leisure facilities.[6] The *Almanach historique et chronologique de tous les spectacles* was published annually from 1752 to 1794 and sold at the modest price (for a book) of 1 livre 4 sols—a day's wages for a laborer. The *Parties de plaisir de la bourgeoisie* of 1753 explicitly targeted the prosperous middle classes and provided not only a calendar of "the pleasures of each month" but also songs, the names of different types of dances, and a list of the best products of Paris and where to find them.[7] Similar titles were constantly on the market throughout the second half of the eighteenth century and their success reflects the emergence of a middle-class consumer market. The approximate number of guides to Paris, by decades, typifies the phenomenon:[8]

APPROXIMATE NUMBERS
OF GUIDES TO PARIS, BY DECADE

1700–1709	9
1710–19	10
1720–29	13
1730–39	25
1740–49	20
1750–59	51
1760–69	56
1770–79	61
1780–89	63

SOURCE: John Grand-Carteret, *Les almanachs français* (Paris, 1896)

Another type of guide was the commercial handbook, though it was usually not confined to Paris. The *Esprit du commerce,* appearing annually from 1729 to 1760, included rules for bookkeeping, a list of foreign exchange markets, and details of reductions in interest rates on government bonds. Like de Blégny's guide it named the principal shops and manufactories of Paris, though more from a merchant's than a consumer's perspective. Other handbooks gave the addresses of offices and administrators, of lawyers, investment agencies, postal services, and transport companies. Foremost among them was the hugely popular *Almanach royal,* published annually from 1702 on. Already in 1705 it had an enormous print run (for the time) of 3,000 copies.[9]

Sales of Paris guides were boosted by the ever increasing numbers of visitors to the city. English aristocrats on their grand tour were the first "tourists," and they were followed by educated Europeans of all sorts. Growing numbers came on business, both from abroad and from the French provinces, and they seized the opportunity to see the sights. When Thomas Bentley, the associate of Josiah Wedgwood, went to Paris in 1776 looking for markets for English porcelain, he visited the Palais-Royal and the boulevards, all the principal churches, the Tuileries and Luxembourg gardens, Versailles and Montmartre, the opera, and the main theaters.[10]

For people like Bentley—but also for Paris residents—there was a wide choice of helpful titles. Whereas older city descriptions had listed only churches, convents, and palaces, the *Etat ou tableau de la ville de Paris* of 1760 was divided into sections headed "the essential, the useful, the agreeable, and the administration." For only 12 sols a visitor's guide, the *Almanach pour l'étranger qui séjourne à Paris* of 1777, included public gardens, newspapers, lotteries, manufactories, the locations of cabs for hire, and the price of chairs in public promenades. And for local consumers and tourists alike, at least 132 maps of the city were produced in the eighteenth century, fifty-one of them between 1770 and 1790.[11]

There were also periodic attempts to set up city information offices. A couple had existed briefly in the seventeenth century and one office next to the Pont Neuf lasted at least from 1703 to 1707. It proposed to be of use to business people buying, selling, or seeking an employee or an associate. "Strangers, who know no one in Paris" were welcome. Later, in the early 1740s, the office of the chevalier de Mouchy in the rue St-Honoré functioned in a similar way, and in 1763 a similar agency was set up in the same area—by then the business center of the city. In 1766 there were three, which the government closed down in order to establish a new official one, granting it a monopoly in return for a substantial payment. Another unauthorized office in the faubourg St-Honoré was closed down in 1778.[12]

The appearance in 1751 of the weekly *Affiches de Paris,* which carried advertisements and local news (including theatrical performances and funerals), as well as editorials and international items, gave the city a permanent information service. After 1777 it encountered a formidable competitor in the *Journal de Paris.* An equally important innovation, in 1759, was the creation of an internal postal service, the *petite poste,* which probably did more to encourage communication and movement within the city than any other institution.[13]

ECONOMIC INTEGRATION

One of the key forces pulling the city together, encouraging Parisians to use urban space in new ways, was the transformation of the Parisian economy in the eighteenth century. One indicator of commercial integration was the development of the financial quarter in the faubourg St-Honoré and of key institutions like the Bourse (stock exchange). Initially created in 1720, it was at first not open to the public. But during the 1770s and 1780s modern forms of speculation on shares became commonplace. It became possible to cash bonds easily, and the sums traded became enormous by the standards of the day. Other financial institutions grew in importance as commercial companies began to proliferate in the second half of the century and as larger numbers of Parisians began to invest in government bonds. Even better-off wage earners began to buy them: the proportion of their estates containing bonds more than doubled across the century.[14]

The demand for financial information grew correspondingly. News of foreign exchanges and markets was vital for the growing numbers of businesses that dealt internationally. The engravers Gabriel Huquier, Jacques Chéreau, and Pierre-François Basan all had networks as far-flung as Stockholm, Warsaw, Amsterdam and London.[15] For people like them the twice-weekly *Affiches, annonces et avis divers* and later the daily *Journal de Paris* provided information on the major money markets: in 1781 the latter listed the share prices for eight institutions. There is no way of measuring the traffic of stockbrokers or of other agents between the financial centers and other parts of the city, but it certainly increased steadily. By 1786 the office of stockbroker—a monopoly supported by the government—was worth 100,000 livres, and two years later it had almost doubled in price, a clear indication of the money these men were making.[16]

The growth of cross-city commercial networks was assisted by an increase in the numbers of large businesses. Réveillon's wallpaper manufactory is always mentioned, with 300 or more workers. So is Oberkampf's mill just south of Paris, one of the largest enterprises in France. The publisher Charles-Joseph Panckoucke had 800 employees in 1788. But there were others less well known: the embroiderer Walbecq employed some 200 women, and the printer Firmin Didot had over 100 employees in 1791. The mercer Jean-François Barbier, specializing in silk, had stock worth over 1 million livres and dealt with more than 80 suppliers in Lyon. Manufacturers of cotton and silk lace had anywhere up to 800 workers each, many of them outside Paris. It is true that enterprises of this size had existed in some sectors for a long time, in blanket manufacturing for instance. But now there were many more of them and in a wider range of industries. Their financial needs were greater, and while most capital was still raised through family networks, the private credit market in Paris grew steadily from 1765 until the crisis of the late 1780s.[17]

In some industries this growth was accompanied by concentration in the hands of the large producers. The number of tanners fell from forty in midcentury to about twenty in the 1770s and the major tanneries were several times larger. The brewers went from fifty or sixty to sixteen. In printing the government deliberately reduced the number of authorized shops, yet whereas only two of those in operation in 1701 employed more than twenty workers, by 1787 twenty-five did so and six provided work for over forty men. Similar concentration occurred in the small silk industry.[18] This too was a form of integration, a move away from dispersed and small-scale production toward capitalist concentration.

Not all businesses grew in the same way. In the rapidly growing furnishing and textile sectors they expanded more through subcontracting rather than by increasing workshop size. Michael Sonenscher has demonstrated the extraordinary complexity of the decorative arts businesses built up by two generations of the Martin family. They extended their range from furniture and coaches to snuffboxes, screens, papier-mâché products and trinkets of every kind. Each of the five original brothers ran his own enterprise but formed strategic alliances with the others. Much of the work was farmed out to regular subcontractors: gilders, cabinetmakers, wood carvers, marble cutters and sculptors, painters, farriers, harness makers and others. One of the brothers added decorative plants and fruit trees to his activities. It was an enormous but diffuse commercial empire spread across all the northern districts of Paris.[19]

Extensive networks were also created by some of the mercers and upholsterers, who became the kings of consumer production in furnishings. These entrepreneurs were not simply retailers but subcontracted different artisans to work—for example—on a single chest of drawers. Some had huge lists of clients, and we can imagine their shops forming the nodes of commercial webs reaching in every direction. These complex networks of production and distribution reinforced the bonds between quarters.[20]

Such connections were complemented by an increase in commuting to and from work, although here the change was slower: most people still lived close to their place of work and at the end of the century 85 percent of servants and a significant proportion of journeymen continued to be lodged in their employer's house. Yet it was getting harder to find accommodation in Paris, and the doubling of rents during the century drove workers to the cheaper areas on the periphery. At the fall of day, observed Louis-Sébastien Mercier around 1781, "the crowd of laborers, carpenters, stonecutters regain in dense mobs the faubourgs where they live."[21] Typical of them were the 350 employed by lace and gauze makers Bellanger and Dumas-Descombes in northcentral Paris, of whom some 230 lived in the distant faubourgs St-Antoine and St-Marcel. They had up to an hour's walk to work each day and the same distance home. So did many stall keepers and hawkers. Of twenty-five women given permission to sell oranges on the Pont Neuf in December 1784 only half a dozen lived locally: one came from the faubourg St-Antoine and twelve from the faubourg St-Marcel. Even clerks and office workers, whose numbers were growing during the latter part of the century, were increasingly obliged to travel short distances to work in order to find suitable lodgings.[22]

In industries where artisans commonly worked in their homes, the commute took a different form: outworkers would deliver finished products and collect more raw materials every few days. This happened particularly in textiles and accessories, where women were employed to spin thread, make buttons, do embroidery, and make lace. Much of the work was done in the faubourgs and even in the villages around Paris. One study of the northcentral area—along the rue St-Denis—reveals that there were over 200 large employers of outworkers in this quarter alone. The rug and mirror manufacturer Félix employed thirty people, of whom twenty worked in their homes in the faubourg St-Antoine. This structure was also customary in the fine cloth industry.[23] Workers, like investors and employers, were increasingly obliged to move around the city.

NEW CULTURAL PRACTICES

The multiplication of sources of information after midcentury, aimed primarily at these social groups, testifies to the growth of another sort of mobility: the quest for pleasure. Whereas in the early eighteenth century most leisure activity had taken place in the streets, squares, and wineshops or along the river, the later 1700s witnessed the development of new, specialized commercial leisure venues. Yet it was not simply a replacement of one form of leisure with another. There were still sideshows and marionettes on the quais, and some of the annual fairs remained, attracting large audiences. Indeed, the St-Laurent and St-Germain fairs both enjoyed renewed success in the 1750s when the Opéra-Comique was one of their attractions. It provided audiences with the mix of farce, wit, and music but without the vulgarity of the older fairground theaters so that "respectable" people would also attend. It introduced new forms like the Italian *opera buffa,* provoking stormy debates in the press and in drawing rooms all over Paris on the relative merits of French opera and Italian arias.[24]

But by the 1770s and 1780s the annual fairs could not compete with the permanent attractions on the northern boulevards. There were fashionable cafés, like the Café Turc, famous for its ice cream. There were restaurants, street performers, automatons, marionettes and shadow puppets, animal displays, scientific exhibits, acrobats, and—observed the normally sober English visitor Arthur Young—"*filles* without end." Curtius's waxworks were famous. And every Parisian knew the theaters run by Jean-Baptiste Nicolet and Nicolas-Médard Audinot, specializing in pantomime and charging such modest prices that almost everyone could afford them. By the 1780s there were several other theaters, too, as well as indoor establishments like the summer Waux-Hall with mixed entertainments: fireworks, dancing, pantomime, gardens, cafés, and various sideshows. Even for those without money there were ample free entertainments, and on a fine day (as Figure 31 suggests) the spectacle of the crowds themselves, the parade of jostling, laughing humanity.[25]

The Palais-Royal, after its renovation in the early 1780s, became another permanent center of entertainment and a mecca for Parisians and visitors alike. It too offered marionettes, freaks, acrobats, and magic lanterns, and Curtius soon moved his waxworks there. There were shops, restaurants and cafés, billiard rooms, and a natural history display. The Palais-Royal had the advantage of having long been a fashionable garden, and the opera had been there since 1770. Like the boulevards, it at-

Figure 31. The boulevards. Augustin de Saint-Aubin, *La promenade des remparts,* engraved by Pierre-François Courtois (1780s). Musée Carnavalet, © Photothèque des musées de la ville de Paris, photo Jean-Yves Trocaz.

tracted people of all ranks, becoming—according to the baron de Frénilly, who regretted the disappearance of its more exclusive past—"a bazaar."[26]

Another innovation of the late eighteenth century was public baths on boats in the Seine, at least seven of them by the mid-1780s—men and women carefully segregated. Longer established, but increasing in number and popularity as the tax on wine entering the city rose progressively, were the suburban taverns: the *guinguettes.* They guaranteed the prosperity of the villages on the outskirts of Paris—Charonne, Belleville, Vaugirard—and of new suburbs at La Courtille, Les Porcherons, and Nouvelle France. Working people went there on holidays, and the stroll through the city and out the toll gates, sometimes even a promenade in the fields beyond, was a favorite group activity. Although these taverns had existed since the late seventeenth century, it was in the second half of the eighteenth that they became renowned as a Parisian institution, celebrated in poetry and plays, and a destination for visitors to the city.[27]

Other long-established Paris recreations were also attracting expanded audiences. The growing popularity of theater is reflected in the increase in the number of seats available, from around 4,000 in 1700 to nearly 13,000 in 1789.[28] The runaway success of the century was Beaumarchais's *Mariage de Figaro.* In 1784 it played to packed houses for sixty-eight performances in a row, attracting close to 100,000 spectators. This reflects the growing appeal of elite culture to a wider social range, yet the nature of theater was changing to cater to the tastes of a wider audience.[29]

The same phenomenon—the democratization and modification of elite culture—is visible with the institution of the biennial art salons, held at the Louvre. They began in 1737 and attracted ever larger crowds, around 15,000 in 1759 and over 30,000 by 1781. Observers were astonished, amused, or irritated at the numbers and variety of people who flocked to the Louvre, not only the educated and discerning but "a swarm of would-be connoisseurs," "people of every sort," "countless young clerks, merchants, and shop assistants."[30] Here was another aspect of the development of a new "public sphere," taking place not just in the political domain but in the cultural one too.

The new leisure patterns fostered further mobility around Paris. Of course people had long been coming from all over the city to the annual fairs, to see fireworks displays or executions in the Place de Grève, to watch street players on the Pont Neuf. But fairs and public festivities were held only occasionally, and other street entertainments were to be found in places where people lived or worked. In the second half of the eighteenth century more and more people went looking for entertainment and left their everyday haunts in search of it. For the nobility and the very rich this was nothing new: they had always gone to the opera and the theater, to balls and promenades, to and from their country estates. But now the growing disposable incomes of the middling ranks and even of some of "the people" enabled them too to pursue fashionable forms of entertainment.

The growth in the numbers and range of people frequenting public leisure venues was accompanied by other cultural trends that followed a similar pattern, but in more private settings. In his memoirs, Charles-Alexis Alexandre recalls that in the early 1780s, when he was approaching thirty and making his career as a legal clerk, he attended a "society" run by Madame Moreau, a mistress seamstress near the church of St-Sulpice. "She enjoyed," he noted, "a kind of affluence." Her husband was a painter. She intended her son to pursue a career in the Church and eventually married her daughter to another young guest at her weekly Sunday afternoon gatherings. Three other female relatives were invited, together with a variety of young men. The purpose of the society was "literary culture, and that of the arts and sciences." "Each person who claimed the title of author brought along his production, read it to the assembly, and received an impartial and polite critique." But in addition there were occasional "metaphysical conversations." And Madame Moreau had a small stage constructed in her apartment where the company enacted various plays, including Beaumarchais's *Eugénie,* Marivaux's *Fausses confidences,* and Philippe Destouches's *Philosophe marié.*[31]

Alexandre could almost be describing one of the Enlightenment salons. They too were regular gatherings of invited guests who met for an early afternoon meal, then discussed literature, philosophy, the arts and sciences, listened to readings of one another's work or of correspondence, and offered a critique. They too were hosted and structured by a woman, who enforced—by her planning, intervention, and in certain respects her very presence—the rules of polite conversation. The famous literary salons run by Madame Geoffrin and Madame du Deffand did not go in for acting, but others did: Madame de Montesson had a theatrical salon that Voltaire attended on two occasions in 1778.[32] In other respects, though, the literary society run by Alexandre's Madame Moreau differed significantly from the salons of the "high Enlightenment." It was run by a seamstress, not a noblewoman or even a rich bourgeoise. It was frequented not by nobles and philosophes, but by law clerks: hence the need to hold it on Sunday afternoons, not working days. Yet they too were "living the Enlightenment."[33]

Some of the elite societies have been much studied, like Julie de Lespinasse's brilliant salon where the young Condorcet met most of the key Enlightenment figures of his day. Others are less well known. Mercier and the equally prolific writer Restif de la Bretonne attended the salon run by the countess de Beauharnais, where they met, among others, the former colonial official-turned-writer Jacques Cazotte and the future revolutionary Anarcharsis Cloots.[34] Less solemn was the salon that Louise Vigée-Le Brun ran after her marriage to the rich art dealer Jean-Baptiste Pierre Le Brun: the court nobles on her guest list sang the latest *ariettes,* played in amateur theatricals, but also played parlor games. More serious and bourgeois was the regular Thursday musical gathering hosted by Madame de La Perrière, which her cousin, the lawyer Louis Paulmier, remembered as the place where he had learned "the tone of urbanity and *politesse* so necessary to a man in society (*homme du monde*), that one learns only through frequenting virtuous people, and especially women."[35] Yet there were also extraordinary numbers of far humbler gatherings taking place all over Paris. Manon Phlipon, the daughter of an engraver, attended the weekly meetings of a middle-class musical society and there encountered her first suitor, a young man named Claude-Mammès Pahin de La Blancherie. He later asked her to write for a journal he proposed to found. In 1788 a surgeon's young understudy was an enthusiastic participant in a *société bourgeoise,* "a society of young men of modest means [who] perform plays." A couple of years earlier another *société bourgeoise* employed a professional painter to prepare the decor for their latest theatrical production.[36]

These were, in terms of membership, means, education, and no doubt quality of performance, very different groups. Yet they were all part of the same cultural form, a development of the mid eighteenth century. Its common features are best summed up in Daniel Gordon's outline of the ideal types of the new concept of "sociability." All of these societies, whatever the rank of those who attended, were based on sociable exchange. They were not hierarchical or were a lot less so than was normal in interaction between people of different ranks or occupations. They acted as a kind of finishing school, introducing literature and new ideas to people with limited educational possibilities (whether women like Madame Geoffrin and the seamstress Madame Moreau, or "young men of modest means"); while for others, who thirsted for distinction, they offered training in polite behavior. They created "sanctuaries of secure interaction" in a city for people uncertain about or unhappy with their place in the everyday hierarchies of Old Regime society. And finally, they offered a sphere outside the control of the absolutist state, where individuals could discuss issues in private.[37]

There were other new forms of social interaction, too, which although they did not necessarily share all these features also belonged among the new cultural practices of the period. The many learned academies—at their peak the Académie française and the Académie des sciences—were for men only, but included both noble and non-noble intellectuals and artists. They were important above all in disseminating new scientific and social thinking and in creating networks of like-minded men within Paris, nationally, and through their correspondence outside France with the entire Enlightenment world, from Saint Petersburg to Philadelphia.[38] But the most popular and open of the new forms was freemasonry, which first appeared in France in the 1720s, introduced by Jacobite refugees from Scotland and possibly by British merchants. After being condemned by the pope in 1738 it was persecuted by the Paris police for some years. But gradually it became respectable, particularly after 1743 when the comte de Clermont, a member of the royal family, became grand master of the Grande Loge de France. In the 1770s and 1780s there were over two hundred lodges founded in Paris, affiliated either with the Grande Loge or with the rival Grand Orient. Together they had perhaps 16,000 members: nobles, priests, administrators and officeholders, merchants and master artisans.[39] There were also unaffiliated lodges, of which no records usually remain. Despite the overall social diversity of freemasonry, each individual lodge tended to group people of similar rank and outlook, since new members had to be nominated and accepted by the existing ones.[40]

The lodges were different from other societies in some obvious ways. They had their own vocabulary and rites and belonged to a larger organization rather than being self-governing. Most did not include women. Yet many Paris lodges did not conform strictly to the rules of the Grand Orient or the Grande Loge, and according to Mercier were regarded by strict adherents elsewhere as not being true masons at all. Many allowed women to attend, presumably because they agreed with Paulmier that women were indispensable to "urbanity and *politesse*."[41] Furthermore, like other new forms of sociability the lodges were regular gatherings that took place in private venues. Like them, freemasonry was participatory and egalitarian, in that it placed its members on an equal footing (though within limits: hierarchy was to some degree observed in their ceremonics, and some upper-class lodges had "serving brothers"!) It provided its members with practice in polite and educated intercourse. Meetings were followed by a convivial meal, and much emphasis was placed on "brotherly" interaction and virtuous behavior. According to Mercier, himself a lodge member, "the freemasons eat, drink together, make music, read verse or prose." They also engaged in philanthropic good works, taking up collections for the poor. "Men who need and desire sociable gatherings worry little what sign they assemble under," Mercier added, indicating the link in his own mind between freemasonry and other contemporary forms of association.[42] He might have added that the lodges, like the salons, were exclusive, by-invitation bodies open only to the "enlightened." In fact, eighteenth-century freemasons prided themselves on their "enlightenment," and referred to nonmembers as "the vulgar."

There is a long-standing myth that freemasonry was anti-religious. This is not true of eighteenth-century freemasonry, but it did embody a broadly deist and Newtonian spirit, combining religious symbolism and readings from Scripture with secular imagery. Masonic ritual celebrated the Supreme Being, the Architect of the Universe, who as deists pointed out was no longer required after the masterpiece was constructed and the laws of Nature set in motion. Freemasonry was thus linked to the general movement of religious ideas. It was also very much outside the state and provided—if not necessarily a republican education—at least a civic one. It stressed equality, tolerance, and free debate, civic values. It was therefore, in its form, subversive of the absolutist state.[43] The same can be said for many of the other manifestations of sociability.

Alongside these associations that can be categorized—salons, theatrical or musical societies, freemasonry—the late eighteenth century witnessed an extraordinary proliferation of other groups. There were semimasonic gatherings of a bewildering variety. Next to regular salons—of which there were many—were innumerable theatrical societies: almost every noble house had its own stage, and the number of private theaters in Paris has been estimated at 160.[44] There were dining clubs like the Société du mercredi, which met every week for meals and conversation, but also made philanthropic donations. The Mesmerist Society of Universal Harmony, including among its aims the pursuit of education, justice, humanity, and generosity, thrived in the 1780s. So did the *musées,* devoted to education but usually excluding women.[45] While each organizational form had a specific content that distinguished it from the others, what unites them is their common commitment to "sociability."

It has often been suggested that the salons contributed to bringing nobles and bourgeois together. Some did, though most were socially uniform and exclusive.[46] Yet whatever the combination of status groups, the various societies brought together people who previously had had little to do with one another: sometimes nobles and commoners, different components of the city elites, but increasingly the different ranks of the "middling sort"—lawyers, officeholders, merchants, and better-off artisans and their family members. In the past these people had been divided between different quarters, parishes, and occupational organizations. In sixteenth- and seventeenth-century Paris, the legal and commercial middle classes had been quite rigidly divided.[47] But now they were coming together, and the effect was far-reaching. As the *Nouvelles ecclésiastiques* observed of the Jansenist-leaning bourgeois who in the 1740s began coming to the Hôtel-Dieu to visit the sick poor, "gathering from nearly every quarter of the city, they did not know each other; but, as they met frequently, the spirit of charity soon formed between them a special connection."[48] This "special connection" across the boundaries of parish and quarter was one of the features that distinguished the new forms of sociability from older ones such as parish confraternities—less through a "spirit of charity" (though philanthropy remained an important element of many of the new societies) than through shared literary and musical tastes and a common culture of *politesse.*

The extent of this social and geographical mixing is best documented in the case of the freemasons. The Lodge of St-Jean-de-la-Fidélité included men with addresses on both banks of the river and spread fairly evenly from St-Germain-l'Auxerrois in the west to the rue St-Antoine in the east. The Réunion des amis intimes drew its members from right across the Left Bank and included a *négociant* (businessman), a priest, an apothecary, a surgeon, an architect, a clockmaker, a clerk, two minor legal officials, a goldsmith, a minor noble, and a medical student.[49] Almost all of the new cultural forms drew their devotees from different parts of the city, and their regular meetings created connections and loyalties across Paris, bonding not only the city elites but also bringing together the professional, merchant, office-holding, and artisanal classes. The new forms of association thus contributed not only to the social integration of Paris, but to the dramatic increase in mobility within the city.

EFFECTS OF GROWING MOBILITY

The growth in movement may be glimpsed if we compare the addresses of the "clients" of the commissaire Langlois in 1709 with those of people who appeared before his successor Picard Desmaret in 1788 (see Maps 3 and 4). The subjects that brought them were very similar: disputes with neighbors, fellow workers, drinking partners, or shopkeepers; traffic accidents; complaints of theft. Most came voluntarily, though some were brought in by the guard. They represent a comparable sample, eighty years apart, of the people who were in the streets of the quarter. The wider distribution in 1788 reflects the increase in daily movement from all parts of the city into and through the center.

These maps, nevertheless, primarily reflect pedestrian movement and underestimate the carriage traffic. But the growth in the numbers of carriages and cabs for hire also testifies to increasing movement around the city, as well as to the extension of carriage use to new social groups. At the start of the 1700s carriages were reserved—the *Encyclopédie* tells us—for "*les grands* and the rich." During the eighteenth century inventories of deceased estates show carriage ownership gradually spreading through the ranks of officeholders and wealthy professionals, even including the occasional rich merchant. The new and cheaper vehicles introduced from the 1750s on—cabriolets drawn by a single horse and the

Map 3. Movement around the city, 1709: the "clients" of the commissaire Langlois. The map points to two major divisions within early-eighteenth-century Paris: the Seine, since only four p appearing before the commissaire came from the Left Bank and none from the islands; and the St-Martin, the principal north-south axis of the city—again, despite Langlois's proximity to the St-Martin, only four people came from the other side. Number of cases = 62. *Source:* Archives nationales, Paris, Y15418. Map drawn by Gary Swinton, Monash University.

two-wheeled *chaises de poste*—were available to a wider range of people.[50] No one would now walk if they could afford a carriage—not, at any rate, if they wanted to actually go somewhere: there was a short period in the early 1780s when fashionable people adopted the advice of the doctor Tronchin and took morning walks in the open air.[51]

Increasing use of carriages by people who would once have walked was partly ostentation, for "this vehicle, apart from its great convenience, distinguishes people from the common herd."[52] In itself a vehicle promoted new ways of using urban space. Well-to-do Parisians in the thousands took the air along the newly fashionable northern boulevards. A provincial visitor was amazed, in June 1782, to see "the boulevards covered with more than 2,000 carriages . . . in two rows. The outer one is stationary, while the inner one drives continually; when one wishes to observe the passers-by one remains in the outer one, and all the women parade there, who have come to watch one another pass."[53] This sort of

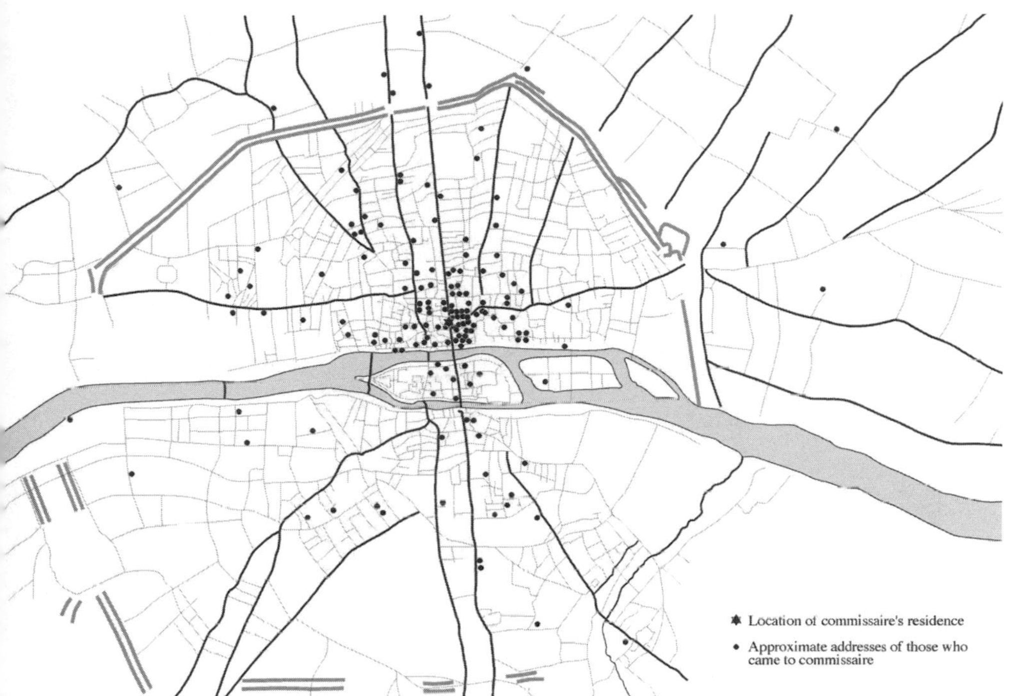

4. Movement around the city, 1788: the "clients" of the commissaire Picard Desmaret. Neither ver nor the rue St-Martin was by then a barrier. Number of cases = 155. *Source:* Archives nales, Paris, Y15099 and Y15100. Map drawn by Gary Swinton, Monash University.

display was by no means new, but it now involved a larger number and greater range of people and was undertaken all along the tree-lined perimeter of the city.

At the same time, hired cabs were much more widely used. In 1711 there were around 1100 cabs, by the late 1780s over 1650. By then there were fifty-six public cab stations, and an astonished visitor could remark that "men and women here, except for the common people, seem to have lost or never known the use of their legs."[54] Yet even the common people, on occasion, used cabs. In May 1788 several journeymen bakers and a worker from the laundry of the Bicêtre prison, on a drinking spree, hired a vehicle to go from the Louvre to a suburban tavern. In March of the same year an unemployed servant girl and a laundrywoman were accused of deliberately leaning out of their hired cab and knocking a basket of plates off a porter's head.[55] But it was overwhelmingly the middle classes who now hired cabs with growing frequency, moving around the city in pursuit of leisure and good company.

Along with new patterns of leisure, another factor increasing mobility among the middling ranks was the wider family alliances discussed

Figure 32. A light carriage, the phaeton. One of a number of fast vehicles adapted for urban use. Anonymous drawing, late eighteenth century, Musée Carnavalet, Suite Le Campion, © Photothèque des musées de la ville de Paris, photo Habouzit.

in chapter 8. Whereas in the early eighteenth century the sons and daughters of many bourgeois families had married locally, in the course of the eighteenth this pattern changed. The Paulmier family exemplifies the new family patterns typical of the conservative upper ranks of the bourgeoisie in the 1780s. Two of the Paulmier brothers were notaries, a third a procureur (thus a minor legal officeholder) in the Châtelet courts, married to the sister of another notary. Two more brothers were merchants, one in the provinces and one in Paris. Through their mother they were linked with a number of other wealthy Paris merchants. The elder brother lived near the Place Maubert on the Left Bank, the second notary in the faubourg St-Honoré on the far side of the city, and the procureur in the Marais, some distance from both of them. Other relatives, whom they saw frequently, lived in still other parts of the city. One was near St-Germain-des-Prés but often invited family and friends to his country house just outside the city at Auteuil. Another, a merchant, lived near the Innocents cemetery but in summer he too entertained lavishly at his country house at Chaillot. Other friends included the family of the fermier général Lavoisier, who lived near the Bastille.[56] Those with whom the Paulmier family socialized were drawn from a range of occupational groups, though all of comparable status. They kept in close touch but were scattered right across the city, so every visit involved taking a carriage. Changing family behavior, like other new cultural practices, promoted new uses of urban space and accelerated the social integration of the city, crisscrossing it with networks of kinship, acquaintanceship, and loyalty.

CENTRALIZATION AND BUREAUCRATIZATION

Other forms of integration were just as important. Accompanying the decline of the quarter as a social and economic unit was a reduction in its importance as an administrative and political entity. Until the late seventeenth century most aspects of day-to-day administration were handled locally, either by prominent local citizens or by the various seigneurial authorities scattered across Paris. As we have seen, by the eighteenth century the monarchy had substantially reduced both the number and the powers of the seigneurial institutions. By then only the Temple, with 4,000 inhabitants, remained of significant size. The jurisdiction of the royal courts had been extended, and in ecclesiastical matters the archbishop of Paris was given far wider powers. The police took over the prosecution of criminal offences and the enforcement of bylaws, including health measures and the inspection of weights and measures.[57]

The powers of the local notables underwent a similar erosion. By the early eighteenth century public health, fire prevention, street maintenance, law and order, and taxation had all been transferred to the police or to other authorities. The citizen militia and its officers were replaced by paid soldiers. Nor, by then, did the local notables have any real say in municipal elections: but it had long been public knowledge, as the head of the municipality admitted publicly in 1777, that "they are given the names of those they must elect."[58]

Only the churchwardens retained a significant local administrative role, but positions in the churches were less prized in the final decades of the Old Regime. The abolition of five parishes on the Ile-de-la-Cité does not seem to have provoked much public comment and at least two other parishes had the number of churchwardens reduced. Parish politics lost its vitality as attention shifted away from religious issues.[59]

In every domain the monarchy had displaced the notables who had once run the city. Its intention was not necessarily to increase its own control: centralization often arose from a desire for greater efficiency, or else for financial reasons. Some of the trades corporations pointed out frankly in 1775, in their struggle against abolition, that "the financial avidity [of the Crown] has for two centuries made the corporations into sponges, with which it has mopped up the wealth of the people."[60] By transferring functions to newly created offices, the government was able to raise money by selling these new offices to the highest bidder.

In the second half of the eighteenth century the Crown found a new source of income in semiautonomous bodies called *régies,* which were placed in charge of a particular industry. One was created to regulate tanning, another to oversee brewing, each one paying an annual sum to the government and recouping its costs (sometimes with a profit) through charges levied on producers or consumers. Both of these provoked bitter complaints. A similar regulator took over the production of saltpeter, used in making gunpowder and hence a government monopoly. Another built and ran the new veal market, and yet another was responsible for public carriages. In 1786 the creation of a new one to establish a parcel post within Paris provoked violent protest by largely Auvergnat errand boys. In 1780, Finance Minister Necker partially dismantled the Ferme générale, whose directors made a fortune from collecting indirect taxes on behalf of the government. Instead he confided some tax collection to regulators whose officials had fixed salaries.[61]

Whatever the motive, the net effect of government action was both a centralization and a bureaucratization of administration. All the *régies* employed inspectors and office workers of different sorts, most either doing new jobs or taking over those formerly done by elected officials in the corporations. The royal lottery, created in 1776, institutionalized a game of chance that was popular in Paris and provided permanent work for 250 people. The postal service, which competed with the city's errand boys, had a hierarchy of *intendants, contrôleurs,* and *chefs de bureaux.* The *Almanach royal* for 1788 lists thirty-three administrators and does not include either the mail sorters or the 200 postmen who made deliveries several times each day.[62]

The Ferme générale, although created much earlier (in 1726), underwent a similar bureaucratization in the late 1750s. Instead of each fermier général having his own staff who worked in his private residence, the offices were centralized in a single secretariat in the Hôtel des fermes. The number of employees increased dramatically, reaching 685 in 1774, not including the inspectors at the gates of Paris. At the same time a more rigorous selection process was introduced, and more of a career structure, with long-serving employees granted a retirement scheme to which they contributed half and the Ferme half. Regular office hours were introduced: nine to one and three to seven. I have already noted the similar process of bureaucratization within the Paris police: the administrative staff grew nearly six-fold, while procedures were streamlined and guided by written rules.[63] The same was true of the various government ministries, shared between Paris and Versailles. The number of inspectors, "subinspectors," clerks, and secretaries grew steadily. The jobs of all these functionaries became increasingly specialized, as we can see from the creation in 1746 of an apprenticeship system for the inspectors of manufactures, recognition that they need particular knowledge and training.[64]

Along with growing bureaucratization and professionalization went the new concept of "public service." In 1752 the Finance Ministry could refer to "the good of the state and the King's service," treating the two terms as synonymous. But by 1780 Lieutenant General of Police Lenoir was telling his subordinates to devote themselves "to the service of the public, which is the most necessary and the most elevated of your functions."[65] No longer was this foremost servant of the Crown talking about the service of the king.

THE CONSEQUENCES OF INTEGRATION

The growing centralization and integration of every aspect of the city's life—administration, finance, economy, leisure, and family ties—had enormous social and political consequences. The development of a "public sphere," at least in Paris itself, was one of them. All the key factors that historians have suggested to explain its emergence had a strongly urban character: the appearance of new forms of sociability, the growth of the press and of pamphlet literature, the increasingly frequent appeals to "public opinion," the experience of political involvement through the midcentury religious disputes, even the transmogrification of the administration into a "public service." Cities were also the motors of the expansion in trade, of the merchant capitalism, and of the growing national economies that Jürgen Habermas, who developed the concept of the "public sphere," saw as central to its appearance.[66]

The very concepts of a "public" and of "public opinion" implied unity and consensus. The experience of people who met in the salons, lodges, and other societies was one of a common urbanity, of agreement on many matters of taste and on ways to discuss and resolve difference. These forms of sociability enabled them to believe, like the revolutionaries in the early 1790s, that a "general will" was achievable.

But there were other political consequences as well. The centralization of power, and its shift from local bourgeois and trades corporations to government bureaucrats, gave the word "state" a real meaning. It was both an abstract term and—in the shape of officials and administrative buildings—a physical reality. It was far harder to influence than were elected officials and local notables, its acts and motivation far more mysterious. State power had long affected Parisians, of course, yet it had long been mediated through or kept at a distance by local authorities.

By the eve of the Revolution Parisians were simultaneously more politically aware than in the past, and more helpless in the face of governmental action. The local elites—including merchants and lawyers—had lost the influence they had once exerted through local administration, through the parishes, and through the trades corporations that were greatly reduced in number and power after 1776. Power and influence now passed increasingly through central institutions. Admittedly, officeholders and government employees were overwhelmingly drawn from those same educated elites and they now exerted influence through expressions of public opinion. Yet that influence was diffuse. The main recourse most people had to challenge government decisions was through the courts, as corporations often did. But the erosion of corporations' power in the trades and other areas of city life now contributed to a sense, justified or not, of helplessness and of growing "despotism." When the Revolution came, one of the first things that the Paris middle classes did was to move into the vacuum left by the collapse of the state and create sovereign local institutions of their own—the districts and their committees.

The social consequences of urban integration, on a day-to-day level, were also far-reaching. Urban space was becoming more uniform and easier to navigate. Growing movement around the city, and its greater speed, were slowly transforming the character of social interaction. Larger numbers of strangers were passing along the main roads and through the city center. What better evidence than the attempt in the 1780s to set up a *dépôt* for lost children![67] In busy areas people often did not know those they were dealing with. Nobles in their carriages or the very poor in their rags were easy to pick out, but finer social gradations were becoming harder to detect. The old "hierarchy of appearances"—to use Daniel Roche's term—was breaking down. Parisians responded by treating all strangers in a similar way: without deference but with cautious politeness. There was a gradual accentuation of what we still think of as "urban" forms of interaction.

The multiplication of cross-city ties of all kinds did not necessarily conflict with local ones. But they weakened commitment to the locality.

And the undermining of local patronage systems severed many of the paternalistic ties and mutual dependence that formerly bound "the people" and the city elites. New forms of government, more bureaucratic, had taken their place.

In a variety of ways these changes made the city more of a single unit. We can see the beginnings of a citywide bourgeoisie in late-eighteenth-century Paris, formed of ties between individuals and families of similar status and culture. But plebeian networks expanded as well. As workers commuted between quarters they too formed ties further afield. They took with them news from other parts of the city, reinforcing the informal information networks otherwise provided by hawkers and porters, or by servants and journeymen looking for work. Strong links formed between the workers of the northcentral districts and the faubourgs, in particular the faubourg St-Antoine. Such bonds were to become enormously important during the Revolution when these areas repeatedly formed the core of popular mobilization.[68] Although the integration of the city was a long-term process, beginning well before the eighteenth century and continuing across the nineteenth, by the 1780s and 1790s the magnitude of its consequences was becoming clear.

CHAPTER ELEVEN

PLEBEIAN CULTURE, METROPOLITAN CULTURE

In late April 1789, the bookseller Siméon-Prosper Hardy recorded a dramatic event, almost unprecedented in scale:

> During the afternoon the people of Paris were much frightened . . . by a sort of popular Insurrection that spread from the Faubourg St-Antoine to the Quarter of Notre-Dame. It involved a large number of Workers, claiming to be from this Faubourg and aroused by Brigands against a Man named Réveillon, a very rich Manufacturer of printed paper for furnishings, and another fairly opulent Man named Henriot, a Saltpeter Maker, the two of them Friends and living in the said Faubourg.[1]

These so-called Réveillon riots are often presented as a curtain-raiser to the French Revolution and an early example of class conflict between the working classes and wealthy manufacturers. There were certainly hints of this, but it was not a class conflict in the nineteenth-century sense. In many respects the 1789 incident bore more resemblance to the periodic attacks on Paris bakers. The crowd was attempting, as in the classic bread riot, to reimpose community values by punishing two individuals who had infringed them. In this case it was the principle of a fair wage that Réveillon and Henriot had reportedly attacked: Réveillon was supposed to have said that the workers could live on 15 sous a day, and this at a time of unusually high bread prices. The local women had played much the same role as in the 1725 riots and "provoked everyone to riot by saying that they were cowards not to break into Réveillon's house to pillage and steal his things."[2]

Rather than a conflict of classes, it was two cultures that collided here. One was the customary culture that was strongest in the neighborhood communities of the city and in the trades corporations. The other was a "metropolitan" culture, citywide, consumer-oriented, and outward-looking, embodying new social and gender ideologies.

THE EVOLUTION OF CUSTOMARY CULTURE

Until around the middle of the eighteenth century, for most Parisians—regardless of their social station—the proper way to behave in almost every context was defined by custom and precedent. It applied to wages and working conditions, to the way merchants treated their customers, to death rituals and the order of processions, to local and citywide celebrations. Even the obligations of governments and the relationship between rich and poor were dictated, in most people's minds, by long-established patterns, with deeply entrenched beliefs in moral community and natural justice.

But custom was constantly evolving, adapting to new circumstances as people used it to defend rights and values. Already in the seventeenth century, Robert Descimon has suggested, many corporate festivals which had formerly served to unify the city and to tie it to the monarchy had fragmented, becoming more likely to foster loyalty to the trade, the parish, or the neighborhood.[3] New customs were appearing and old ones being reinvented. The election of a carnival queen in the laundry boats appears to date from just before the Revolution, though it may be older. There also are hints that the *compagnonnages* and their rites were reappearing in Paris in the late 1780s. Other customs were disappearing, like the procession of the dragon of St-Marcel, which had been associated with the springtime Rogations festival at Notre-Dame. It had apparently been abandoned early in the century.[4] Gradually changing beliefs led to the decline of baroque elements in religious festivities, and by the 1780s religious customs associated with the cemeteries were no longer being vigorously defended.

But the most important transformation in eighteenth-century customary culture in Paris was produced by the growing alienation of the urban elites and their adoption of new social and economic practices. In the seventeenth or early eighteenth century they had generally respected custom and had used it for their own ends. The annual burning in effigy of a Swiss soldier who had attacked a statue of Our Lady had remained perfectly acceptable to the Parisian elite. As a ritual expurgation of the blasphemy it was consistent with the public atonements that Church and state inflicted on blasphemers, heretics, and sorcerers. And the hostility of the population to Protestantism could only increase respect for the "perfect Catholic magistrate," the model on which members of the Paris Parlement based their behavior in the late sixteenth and early seventeenth century. But to the newly tolerant late-eighteenth-century elites, this rite appeared symptomatic of the "superstition" of the masses and was condemned on all sides. The midsummer festivities of the St-Jean, with their bonfires and popular celebrations, were no better—they were suppressed in 1768.[5]

The attitude to a customary festival like Carnival had undergone a similar evolution. Each year just before the fasting and atonement of Lent there was a Rabelaisian explosion of feasting and rejoicing. Masks appeared in the streets and people indulged in behavior normally not permitted. Women and men cross-dressed, fishwives wore the clothes of princesses and young noblemen those of market porters. "The mask renders [people] equal in appearance, even though they are of very different rank," observed a hostile police ordinance of 1719. Carnival was an affirmation of the fundamental unity of the urban community, a moment when the normal spatial, social, and sexual barriers came down. In the mid seventeenth century, on the eve of Ash Wednesday, musicians could "enter into any chamber and speak with any lady or person."[6] But the annual "world upside down" was also a reaffirmation of the normal hierarchy: its very abnormality helped make the breaking of social taboos unthinkable at other times. The opportunities it presented for insult and mockery allowed the expression of social tensions but limited the duration of reprisals and confined them to a period of general good humor. On *mardi gras* (Shrove Tuesday) the ritual burning of a carnival figure symbolized the end of the festival and the return to sober normality.[7]

Some people had no doubt always disliked certain practices of Carnival but by the late eighteenth century there was a torrent of disapproval. For the austere, college-educated, and Jansenist-leaning bookseller Hardy they "have no appeal for reasonable people." The writer-lawyer Mercier condemned the "grotesque" and "indecent" costumes of some of the masks. The printer-turned-writer Restif de la Bretonne attacked the way that "children, and errand boys on the street corners, spoil women's dresses with dirty substances." The clergy, added Mercier, "display the Host in the churches, because they consider a profanation what the government allows [during Carnival]." The police were convinced that masks facilitated thefts and assaults. And they tried to stamp out practices such as "the liberty that the common people and even young men of good family take during the festival of giving passers-by what they call 'rats' or of insulting them."[8]

Those who disliked Carnival tried to channel it into acceptable forms. Respectable people ran their own masked balls by subscription, not open to all. And in 1790 the very bourgeois and prudish Paris Commune banned masks and dances altogether, ostensibly as a measure against counterrevolutionary aristocrats who might profit from the anonymity of masks but also "to restrain popular license and prevent passers-by from being insulted." Only when bread and circuses returned under Napoleon did Carnival rise again from the dead.[9]

What was happening in all these areas was a gradual abandonment of customary culture by the local elites of Paris. To put it another way, customary culture was becoming plebeian culture. This change had several sources. Changes in the religious beliefs of the educated classes were one. For them religion was becoming more of an individual matter and was less tied to collective observance. They no longer believed that the sins of the few would bring retribution down on the whole community or that collective repentance could prevent it. For these people community rituals of cleansing, atonement, and celebration were losing their force. They threw their weight behind campaigns for urban reform that challenged popular commitment to the cult of the dead, to miracles, to Carnival, and other customary rituals.

The political and social integration of Paris was another powerful force for change. As city government was centralized, attempts to improve traffic flow targeted the street life on which the health of the neighborhood communities depended. And as the local notables lost their former role in the administration of the city, they gradually also lost their sense of responsibility for the people formerly under their leadership. The same thing was happening in the parishes, which middle-class Parisians were beginning to abandon as their families spread across the city and they sought their pleasures further afield.

Yet another factor was the adoption by the educated elite, beginning with lawyers and magistrates, of an entirely different philosophy of social regulation: the rule of law. The alternative to sanctions preserved in the memory and practice of the community was the rules enshrined in written law codes, laws made by rulers and enforced by administrators and courts. The absolute monarchy used laws to impose its will on unruly subjects, the great nobles foremost among them. Already by the mid seventeenth century, the Parlement and the royal council had constructed a legal definition of nobility—requiring documentation of descent and of a family's right to titles. It superseded an earlier customary definition based on land and on way of life ("living nobly"), and the new definition in effect made access to noble status dependent on royal favor.[10]

Another application of the rule of law was the imposition of the same rules on everyone, regardless of rank. Paris had been progressively disarmed as the state affirmed its monopoly on force. By the late eighteenth century the nobility and their lackeys were under control: the pitched battles between rival political factions or against the police, which in the seventeenth century had left many dead and wounded, were now unimaginable.[11] Now nobles might even find themselves in court for assaulting a social inferior. In 1782 the comte de Moreton-Chabrillant, captain of the guard of the king's brother, was successfully sued by a minor legal official in the Parlement, despite attempts by his family to influence the judges in his favor. Twenty lawyers refused, one after the other, to defend him. The case was unusual enough to be reported by a chronicler of the time, but it was a sign that the rule of law was being imposed even on the military nobility. This was clearly in the interests not only of the Crown and of the Parlement, but also of other elements of the Paris population, particularly the middle ranks who suffered most from aristocratic disdain. The applause of the huge audience at the trial verdict was "as loud as it was long, so satisfied was it to be avenged against the excesses of an irresponsible nobleman."[12]

The same appeal to law could also be used to evade the customary obligations of trades corporations and neighborhood. A good example is the fate of *charivaris*—rowdy ridiculing and even manhandling of cuckolded husbands, of the partners in second marriages or "mismatches," of wife-beaters and other misbehavers. Such sanctions disappeared early from Paris, probably by the late 1750s, although they remained common in the countryside well into the nineteenth century. Like other collective sanctions, these rituals became ineffective once a significant number of people refused to accept the norms of the community, particularly in a city where the offended parties could call on the police.[13] Thus the new culture and interests of the educated classes threatened the survival of many customary practices.

In another way though, the transformation of customary culture into a plebeian culture gave it new life. In areas like the faubourg St-Antoine, neighborhood solidarity was to become one of the sources of nineteenth-century working-class identity. Yet its more plebeian character eventually also helped this new working-class culture to transcend the locality by making working people right across the city more aware of their common interests.[14] Already the Réveillon riots of early 1789 demonstrated the growing permeability of local boundaries. Whereas in the bread riots of 1725 both the targets and the attackers were all locals, in the assault on Réveillon's house there was significant representation from other parts of the city, particularly from the ports and from the distant faubourg St-Marcel. Only half of those wounded or arrested were from the faubourg St-Antoine, a smaller number still from the immediate vicinity. Before the riot bands of men ranged across the entire city mustering support: on the Left Bank, in the Temple quarter, and on the Pont Neuf. All of this points to the beginnings of an identification, by working people, across the boundaries of individual quarters. In the context of 1789, with elections to the Estates General under way, it also facilitated the linking of local issues with wider political ones.[15]

METROPOLITAN CULTURE

As customary culture was becoming more plebeian, the social groups who were increasingly rejecting it were evolving their own culture. Nicholas Green's term "metropolitan" describes this developing culture well, because it appeared first in the cities of Europe and the urban environment was integral to its development.[16] The new forms of "sociability" that the upper and middle classes of Paris were now adopting were part of the growing integration of the city. Relationships within the various societies and lodges were not based on neighborhood familiarity or on corporate obligation but on voluntary participation and on *politesse,* a form of behavior that was both urban and urbane.

The activities of these types of association, furthermore, encouraged a new worldview that was cosmopolitan and outward looking. Central to the literary societies was reading, which extended people's awareness of distant places and other times, broadened their horizons, and often led them to question received certainties. The culture of the new reading public of the Enlightenment was increasingly "scientific" and prided itself on being "rational." People knew something of Newton and Buffon, even if that knowledge came mainly from novels and conversation. They had become scornful of miracles and other "superstitions" and were adopting more private and socially exclusive forms of religious devotion and of recreation.

Metropolitan culture also implied new uses of urban space and new attitudes to the city environment itself. The new forms of sociability involved unprecedented movement around Paris. But they were also inseparable from the developing social and gender ideologies of the late eighteenth century. These were in turn linked—like many changes in the city—to medicine. For it was during the late eighteenth century that the educated discovered dirt and smells and began to associate them with disease. "One might think," commented one writer in 1782, "hearing the complaints that are mounting daily, that the roads were always clean in the past. However, the truth is that people did not even think of complaining in earlier times."[17] Now, educated Parisians objected to the smells from the Innocents cemetery. They were becoming more sensitive to the excrement and dirt in their environment and viewed the public streets with increasing distaste. A new street trade appeared, that of *décrotteur* (literally "dirt-remover"). Reformers pondered how to get rid of "that stinking mud" for which Paris was notorious. Mercier railed against the state of the streets. In this respect as in so many others he spoke for middle-class Parisians, those less able to avoid the streets than the nobility and more worried about dirt than the working classes were.[18]

The concern with cleanliness gradually began to extend to bodies themselves. Medical opinion, reflecting on the excretory functions of the skin and on chemical experiments with fermentation in closed containers, began to recommend more frequent washing: dirt, the experts now suggested, clogged up the pores and prevented the skin from breathing. It thus turned the body into an airtight vat, within which unpleasant humors could accumulate and fester, causing illness. By the mid eighteenth century the wealthier classes were possibly washing more often but were certainly paying more attention to cleaning excrement off their bodies. Bidets appeared in noble homes and even some of the middle classes began to use disposable toilet paper instead of rags. Babies were less often swaddled because the close-fitting bands of cloth prevented air from getting in and allowed excrement to accumulate.[19] The new sanitary concerns sharply distinguished educated Parisians from the workers, who could hardly afford to be squeamish about dirt and smells and found the difficulty of getting clean water in itself a disincentive to washing.[20] Indeed excrement was very much part of popular humor and often afforded the stuff—sometimes literally—of practical jokes. One of the regular carnival characters who appeared, with other masks, around the time of *mardi gras* each year was the *chienlit* (literally "bed-shitter"), described by Louis-Sébastien Mercier: "A mask parades around the *beaux quartiers,* beneath the windows of ladies young and old, appearing to be in a shirt with no trousers; the back of the shirt is covered in mustard; other masks, following behind, hurry up to this walking mustard pot with pieces of sausage, and the common people shriek appreciatively at this disgusting humor."[21] Mercier's distaste underlines the cultural gap that had opened up between the "common people" and affluent, educated Parisians. It is no coincidence that the *chienlits* chose the *beaux quartiers.*

Concerns about the risk to health were particularly acute when combined with new gender ideologies that stressed the physical and the moral vulnerability of women. While there was a lively debate over the intellectual ability of females, most authors agreed that they were physically more delicate. Women's bodies were softer and more sensitive. Doctors asserted with growing stridency in the final decades of the eighteenth century that the womb and the ovaries made the female body excessively vulnerable. Even Germaine de Staël, a formidable writer but a devoted admirer of Jean-Jacques Rousseau, accepted (at least publicly) his argument that women's "feeble organs" made literary genius a male rather than a female characteristic.[22] Women's greater "sensibility" was not only physical but also emotional. In the 1750s the *Encyclopédie* observed that "nature has set on one side strength, majesty, courage, and reason; on the other, grace and beauty, finesse and feeling."[23]

An extraordinary emphasis on motherhood accompanied the medical preoccupation with reproductive functions, and the art and literature of the period abundantly reflect this emphasis, from the wildly emotional paintings of Greuze to Rousseau's *Nouvelle Héloïse* and Bernardin de Saint-Pierre's *Paul et Virginie.*[24] Women, these and other works insisted, were destined by Nature to be mothers (and therefore also wives). This meant, asserted Rousseau, that "the female . . . needs a soft sedentary life to suckle her babies."[25] Her place was at home, creating a comfortable nest for her children and a cozy retreat for her husband.

All of these commonplaces about sexual difference led to the same conclusion: women were naturally suited to a life removed from the rough masculine world of the streets. The idea that women's domain was maternal and domestic rather than public was not new, but the medical arguments were. And in Paris the image of ladies as delicate and sensitive by nature combined with growing fears about the corruption—physical and moral—that lurked in the city streets. After about 1760, few of the heroines in the increasing numbers of urban novels managed to escape Paris with their "virtue" intact. The city, with its anonymity, its social promiscuity, its very atmosphere, had become—in the educated imagination—a permanent threat to women. When Parisian ladies went out, they were now felt to need protection: for their clothes, their bodies, and their morals. Mercier again made the connection clear when he wrote about obscene graffiti on the walls: "It is not enough for the street sweepers to clean the city; nor should the eyes of our wives and daughters, when they leave their homes, alight on such images." Pierre-Thomas Hurtaut and P-N. Magny, in their historical dictionary of Paris, extended this concern to encompass popular celebrations, suggesting that the burning of the mannequin on 3 July should be banned because pregnant women might be alarmed by the "gigantic and ridiculous figure" promenaded by the crowd.[26] It did not matter that these ideas of female nature were totally at odds with the evidence in the streets of Paris, where women worked as porters and laborers and coped with every aspect of city life. The theorists hardly regarded such creatures as women at all and had in mind a virginal ideal of middle-class womanhood.

For their own protection, therefore, ladies should take a cab when they ventured out. They should also be selective about where they alighted. Part of the appeal of the new boulevards was that—except after heavy rain—they offered relatively clean, open spaces where ladies could show off their finery away from the dirt and bustle of the ordinary streets. There was also a growing vogue, from the 1770s on, for pedestrian passageways lined with shops, forerunners of the early-nineteenth-century arcades, which made it possible to shop without having to loiter in the streets.[27] These were ideal spaces both for noblewomen and for the wives and daughters of the professional middle classes, who by the end of the century were wearing more white and light-colored clothes that showed the dirt.[28] And as shopping began to become a fashionable activity, even for nobles who in the past always had tradespeople call on them, expensive shops were increasingly designed with ladies in mind. They became less open to the street, with glass and curtains in the windows to keep out the elements and protect the customers inside from public view. The furnishings were reminiscent of an affluent apartment, adorned with gilded mirrors, bright lighting, carved and painted panels, all of which created a domestic setting in which ladies could feel at home. The reception area of the famous *marchande de modes* Rose Bertin was referred to as "her *salon*." The famous furnishing and novelty-goods shop Le Petit Dunkerque, which was visited by many society ladies in the 1780s, was heated by a stove and employed a guard to prevent too many people coming in at once: no doubt because it contained so many valuable goods, but also to ensure that only suitable people were admitted. A lady could be sure she would not be jostled, dirtied, or accosted.[29]

Concern about dirt and about moral danger therefore combined to widen the gap between the city elites—particularly the middle classes—and the mass of the population. Needless to say, models of feminine delicacy held little relevance for working women, though sometimes the wives and daughters of shopkeepers tried to live up to them. (The wife of an upholsterer, for example, fell in a faint after the blind owner of the house where she lived waved his cane at her and called her a slut and a strumpet.) Models of delicacy also had a certain attraction for domestic servants, whom Daniel Roche has described as "cultural intermediaries" mimicking the ways of their employers and helping to spread them among the population.[30]

Some nobles accepted the new gender ideologies, but the separation between domestic and public domains made less sense for them. While noblewomen could not hold public office, they were (and were expected to be) public figures. They received supplicants and exercised their influence openly. Nor were they called upon to display any particular modesty: great ladies at court sometimes took baths quite publicly. The comtesse de Menthon said bitchily of Madame de Warens, whose lineage was nevertheless impeccable, that she "covered her bust like a bourgeoise." Nor were noblewomen, unlike middle-class women, expected to occupy themselves with children or to spend most of their time at home.[31] Despite Norbert Elias's model of the "civilizing process" operating from the court outward to the rest of society, it was initially the prosperous middle classes who adopted the ideology of domesticity: lawyers, doctors, officeholders, rentiers, and growing numbers of merchants and prosperous shopkeepers. "It is only ever among the bourgeoisie, and especially in commerce, that one finds examples of domestic virtue," confirmed the financier Grimod de La Reynière in 1783. In increasing numbers such people could afford the female leisure that marked them off from the popular classes.[32]

The new gender ideologies dictated new uses of space not only outside the home but also inside it. If the domestic ideal was to be realized, it required the privacy of a comfortable apartment where women and children were protected from the crass outside world. This was precisely the kind of space to which many of the Paris middle classes now aspired. This period saw the appearance of apartment buildings designed for the middle-class rental market, like the Montholon building (see Figure 33). Where older accommodation generally contained interconnecting rooms rented singly or in pairs, it contained planned apartments, each with a

Figure 33. Immeuble Montholon, carrefour de Buci (author photo).

kitchen, living room, and bedrooms.[33] Being broadly the same on each floor, such buildings were more socially homogeneous than most Paris housing, and for some people that too was an attraction.

Very few families could hope to find this kind of accommodation, but as the evidence of inventories shows, many did their best to create their own domestic haven. It was hardly surprising that middle-class women, who were passing more of their time confined to home, should try to do so. Their spending helped fuel the consumer boom of the late eighteenth century, and in fact women increasingly came to be associated both with luxury and with consumerism.[34] In this sense too, Réveillon and Henriot (the targets of the 1789 riots) exemplify the difference between the affluent middle classes and the mass of the population. They, and their wives, padded their lives with the symbols of wealth and savoir-vivre: fashionable furnishings, paintings, mirrors, tapestries, and rich clothes. They owned clocks—no doubt of the latest style. Madame Henriot, although the wife of a saltpeter manufacturer, had (according to the list given to the police) twelve full dresses made either of silk or of muslin, with matching skirts; eighteen additional skirts and four cloaks; no fewer than 120 shirts; over a hundred bonnets and large quantities of lace. Réveillon owned considerably more: he claimed to have lost over 75,000 livres' worth of furnishings alone.[35] For many of those who attacked his house this sum was the equivalent of about 250 years' income. The luxury they found inside must have seemed unbelievable: evidence of the huge gap between his world and theirs.

Réveillon had exceptional wealth, yet it was consistent with the growing affluence of the Parisian middle classes. In the late eighteenth century the spending power of everyone with income from investments or trade rose significantly, and this included most of the Paris middle classes and even many artisan families, perhaps a third of the city's population. At the same time the price of many consumer items fell thanks to improvements in transport and the expansion of overseas and European trade.[36] Much of the surplus was spent on consumer goods, prompting a boom in industry and trade that further increased their wealth and reduced the cost of luxury items. Again, Réveillon epitomizes the material culture of the late eighteenth century, since his money came from wallpaper, in which he was one of the great names of the period. It was a new industry in France. Although light papers had been available for a long time, only in the 1750s did the heavier flock papers produced in England begin to be imitated in Paris. Their appearance reflects the growth of new markets, for although wallpaper was a luxury product it was within the means of people who could not afford tapestries, silk hangings, or fine wooden paneling. In fact, the early wallpapers often imitated tapestry.[37]

Wallpaper also incarnated the more outward-looking, scientific, and classical culture of the educated classes. There were Pompeian-style panels and classical friezes, or birds and flowers reminiscent of botanical sketches. Admirers of Rousseau might enjoy pastoral scenes with little Emiles playing in happy communion with nature. For more exotic tastes Réveillon offered Chinese, Indian, and Japanese designs or South Sea island scenes. Wallpaper was a cultural and social statement, distinguishing its owners as men and women of culture and taste.[38]

Yet it was only one of the luxury items for which wider markets began to appear in mid-eighteenth-century Paris. Porcelain was another, also decorated with classical, botanical, or exotic patterns. Plates, cups, and bowls proliferated, along with soup tureens, jugs, cruet stands, vases, tea and coffee sets, pitchers, spittoons, and many other novelty products. Ways of serving and eating food were transformed by the diversification of tableware: knife- and fork-rests, jugs, coffee pots and teapots, centerpieces.[39]

Other accessories began to be churned out by Paris workshops: umbrellas; boxes for snuff or jewelry; fans; game boards; glass- and silverware. Rich apartments became crowded with chairs and small tables, clocks, mirrors, paintings, bronzes, lamps, rugs, and screens. Wardrobes and chests of drawers slowly replaced wooden chests. Musical instruments, thermometers, and barometers appeared in the homes of lawyers and doctors, somewhat later in those of merchants, shopkeepers, and artisans. To keep fashion-conscious customers informed a new periodical specializing in clothes and decor, *Le Cabinet des modes,* flagship of a growing fashion press, was launched in 1785.[40]

By then, nearly all social groups in Paris were beginning to be affected by the new consumer culture. In 1794 a starch maker and his wife, according to the inventory drawn up after her death, squeezed into their cramped three-room apartment a double and a single bed, four chests of drawers (two of them marble-topped with brass trim), four wardrobes, a sideboard and a dresser, two small tables and another one large enough to seat twelve people, twelve wooden chairs, four armchairs, and a chest for clothes. The rooms were hung either with tapestry or painted cloth, and on the walls were a total of 70 framed prints, three large mirrors, two barometers, and five paintings, plus a smaller canvas above each doorway. In the dresser they had 140 pieces of porcelain, including serving dishes, plates, soup tureens, and salad bowls. On one of the mantelpieces was a clock on a marquetry base, made in Paris by Lenoir, and three wax figurines in a glass case. There were candlesnuffers with their own holders, two silk umbrellas, a small collection of books, and a white marble sundial. In the kitchen, along with the usual cauldrons and pots, were such refinements as a coffee grinder and coffeemaker, eggcups, and one of the still fairly new cast-iron stoves.[41]

By this date, too, watches were no longer confined to the rich but were owned by most Parisian shopkeepers, artisans, even some laborers. A century earlier stockings had been an aristocratic item, but now nearly everyone wore them. And whereas in the 1720s Paris masters and journeymen owned only two or three pairs, by the end of the century most had a dozen or more. Even the range of colors of clothing, drapery, and upholstery expanded, the predominant black, gray, and brown of the early eighteenth century making way for brighter colors and for stripes and checks.[42]

The value of clothes, furnishings, and other everyday items in the estates of officeholders and professionals increased 250 percent across the century, while those of better-off artisans and shopkeepers went up by 70 percent. By the late eighteenth century the wealthy middle classes were obeying changes in fashion, buying wallpapers from Réveillon and porcelain from Petit, just as nobles did.[43]

Yet the norms of middle-class respectability—and the austere Jansenist principles of many Paris merchants and lawyers—forbade ostentation. Accompanying the bourgeois stress on domesticity was a critique of luxury and of a "decadent" nobility, a critique given legitimacy by writers such as Jean-Jacques Rousseau. "One must concur," wrote the architect of the duc d'Orléans, "that the children of great men have degenerated greatly and become quite debased. Their happiness consists only in women and gambling."[44] This stereotype provided the moral basis for a developing middle-class identity as the numbers, wealth, and the self-assurance of professionals, merchants, shopkeepers, and master artisans grew during the eighteenth century. All of these groups, the liberal professions above all, were adopting a new culture of professionalism that stressed education, personal dignity, and social utility—qualities that these people saw as peculiarly bourgeois. "Be always useful," wrote a Paris procureur in 1782, addressing the younger generation of his family. "Exercise your talents, abandon futile occupations and, fleeing the ruinous brilliance of empty names, do not seek any misplaced alliance with ostentatious nobles."[45] According to the *bourgeoise* Madame de Maraise, "It is important to keep away from our children's eyes all ex-

Figure 34. A bourgeois family at home, 1772: (*from left to right*) Jacques Le Roy, merchant mercer in the rue Mouffetard; Geneviève Barré, his wife; servant; the widow Claude Barré; a messenger. The deliberate informality of the scene reflects adherence to domesticity, also reflected in the prominence of the two cats. The decor is bourgeois, relatively simple but comfortable, but the clothing reflects the family's wealth. Marius-Pierre Le Mazurier, *Réunion de la famille Barré dans son intérieur, 1772*. Musée Carnavalet, © Photothèque des musées de la ville de Paris, photo Lifermann.

amples of luxury, and everything which can excite the passions and above all the desire for outward appearance which always impresses the undiscerning and the young more than the requirements that etiquette and the decency of one's station impose."[46] Moderate consumption—what Denis Diderot called *luxe de commodité*—was necessary for respectability but the excessive luxury (*luxe d'ostentation*) of *les grands* was a sign of moral deterioration.[47]

Similar strictures help explain the intense distaste for foppish *petits maîtres*—middle-class men who mimicked the fashions of the court nobility—that Mercier and other authors expressed in the later years of the eighteenth century. With their red-heeled shoes and plumed hats, their beribboned coats with gold and silver buttonholes, swords or hunting knives by their sides, these men threatened the image of the sober, decorous male that was becoming central to male bourgeois identity. Furthermore, because the social critique of the day now linked love of luxury with women, men who succumbed to its seductions were doubly condemned: "they too are changed into idle women," asserted Rousseau.[48]

Threading through every aspect of the developing metropolitan culture, therefore, were issues both of gender and of class. Just as the middling sort were drawing closer to the upper classes—in terms of education and the culture of sociability—the ideology of domesticity emerged, to valorize a modest and respectable way of life that was neither decadent (like the court nobility) nor dirty and vulgar (like the common sort). It developed at the precise moment when more people could afford comfortable apartments and female leisure. Exclusive shops, separate leisure facilities, and the growing use of cabs enabled these people (but especially women) to avoid unwanted contact with the vulgar sort. So too, in a small way, did the increasingly common guidebooks, maps, and house numbers.

CONSUMERISM AND POLITICAL ECONOMY

With the new products came changes in the values of the Parisian elites that were also part of the new metropolitan culture. It is a feature of a consumer mentality that novelty and innovation are desirable. By the 1780s merchants were appealing to potential customers by advertising "the Newest and most Fashionable Fantasy Products."[49] This was a very recent development. A book on commerce published in 1757 was being controversial when it argued that "fantasy is the sole purpose, the single goal of trade, and can only be attained through variety and change." Still in 1771 it was necessary to defend the belief that "luxury is not only a useful but also an indispensable and necessary source of prosperity for states."[50]

Advertising and overt competition in business were slowly becoming acceptable. They too reflect a very recent change. As late as 1761 the police had banned Paris merchants from advertising cheaper goods than their competitors because of "the fraud that self-interest and cupidity can inspire."[51] But this attitude was being undermined by the new market conditions. Merchants increasingly employed new techniques of marketing, initially in the discreet form of elaborate shop signs, wrapping paper, and trade cards, later more blatantly in the form of notices in the *Journal de Paris* and the *Affiches*.

Réveillon was a master of the art. His purchase of the ostentatious Folie Titon in the faubourg St-Antoine was inspired marketing, since the building was well known. He opened it to the public and it became one of the standard attractions for visitors to Paris. In 1783 it was the site for the trial of the Montgolfier brothers' hot-air balloon—made from Réveillon paper. A short time later their first successful balloon, a gold and blue creation launched at Versailles before a crowd of 100,000 people, was actually called "le Réveillon." Soon after this Réveillon obtained—after much petitioning of government ministers—the right to affix the title of "royal manufactory" to both his paper factory and his printing works. Two years later, in 1786, he won the Necker gold medal for industry. These publicity coups were essential to his success.[52]

Réveillon did much to create his own markets. So did the printed cotton manufacturer Christophe-Philippe Oberkampf, the fashion clothes producer Rose Bertin, and the Paris mercers. All were constantly attentive to shifts in taste, responding quickly when in the 1780s Antoine-Augustin Parmentier's campaign to plant potatoes made potato flowers—for a season—a favorite motif on cloth and in fashion clothes. Success in the new consumer industries required not only technical expertise but an eye for innovation and for what would sell. It also demanded constant self-promotion, not just to attract public attention but to find patrons at court. Oberkampf was not good at networking but his partners were, particularly Sarrasin de Maraise and his wife, whose friends included the future finance minister Jacques Necker and other influential people. Through contacts like these a shrewd operator could win tax exemptions or monopoly distribution rights. Like Réveillon, Oberkampf and twenty or thirty others obtained the title of "royal manufactory," which accorded exemption from ordinary trade rules and provided a formidable advertising tool. Just as good was the coup achieved by the snuff merchant Civette, whose shop was ostentatiously visited by the duchesse de Chartres. After that there was always a crowd of customers waiting in line.[53]

Some of these individuals also brought to their business an entirely new approach to production. Réveillon and Oberkampf used a highly developed division of labor in their factories, and they and others like them demanded new rhythms from their workers. In 1775 the supervisor of a Paris cotton factory followed his employees to a wineshop on a Sunday evening "in order to stop them from amusing themselves." The issue here was undoubtedly "Saint Monday," a prime target for reformers. A great many workers, having celebrated on Sunday, took all or part of the next day off. "It is for them an old and ineradicable custom," according to Mercier, who saw it as a major cause of poverty.[54]

Saint Monday was part of a work rhythm in which there was no rush unless a particular job needed to be completed urgently. Most journeymen worked hard for extremely long hours—sixteen hour days were not unusual—but they saw it as their right to take time off for meals, celebrations, or between jobs, according to the custom of the trade. The idea of endlessly increasing productivity or of accumulating wealth by continuous work was foreign to them, except where a person had a particular goal—putting together a dowry or saving to obtain a master's ticket. And for good reason: in most industries, whether they were paid by the piece or by the hour or day, finishing the job more quickly simply meant being out of work longer. Journeymen quickly learned not to work faster or longer than their mates because there was only a certain amount of work to go round. They would be robbing the others and would be punished for it. Underemployment was chronic, because when things got slack employers—who themselves usually had few reserves—immediately put off excess workers. And being out of work meant both loss of income and isolation from the companionship of the workshop. It might mean not being on hand when the next job came in.[55]

The new breed of political economists and entrepreneurs did not see things this way. They were typically in expanding areas, creating their own markets, and for them production needed to be continuous, the faster the better. The physiocratic Simon Clicquot de Blervache, writing in the 1760s, believed that wages should be determined not by custom but by individual productivity. He had no respect for Saint Monday or other rituals of the workplace. The new supervisor of the Royal Printery agreed: he was accused by Restif de la Bretonne of making the place into "a jail where all the workers are locked up, let out like vile animals at mealtimes. . . . In my time we were free." The entrepreneurs of the tripe factory set up on the urban fringe in 1764 imposed fines on lazy workers and encouraged competition between employees, foreshadowing nineteenth-century work discipline.[56]

The appearance of new markets, of new techniques and work practices, and of entrepreneurs willing to exploit them to the hilt, had profound commercial, social, and theological implications. The quest for endless expansion was, for a minority, displacing the desire for an "honest and happy mediocrity" (as a conservative theologian put it in 1783). A new set of values had begun to take root, stressing the creation of wealth and assessing wages and prices in terms of the market and not according to what was customary. This entrepreneurial spirit was neither new nor universal in the late eighteenth century, but it was coming to be more widely accepted and even praised for its contribution to national prosperity. Merchants, once viewed by theologians as morally suspect, had become "necessary to the state," according to Charles Duclos, a member of the French Academy. They "enrich themselves by increasing a general abundance, encouraging honest industry, and [their] wealth is the proof of their services."[57]

These ideas challenged the whole existing structure of trade. In the first half of the century success in business depended partly on trade skills but also on family connections. But in the new markets an individual with ideas and the ability to sell them was often able to succeed spectacularly without family networks. The hour of the entrepreneur was ticking closer and many of the most successful were self-made. Few of them were women, because of the greater obstacles they had to overcome, but Rose Bertin was an extraordinary exception, rising from humble provincial origins to make a fortune as supplier of fashion clothes to Marie Antoinette. Oberkampf was a German immigrant who arrived in Paris in 1758 with no capital except his knowledge of dyeing: he was to build his cotton-printing workshop into one of the largest businesses in the country. There were many others like him: over half of the cotton manufacturers in France had come from relatively humble social origins. The Paris porcelain manufacturer Christophe Dihl was also German-born, began with very little, and worked his way to fame and riches as an artist and an inventor. Even in the book trade, long inaccessible to anyone without connections with the trade dynasties, new faces appeared. François Morin, son of a tapestry dealer from Strasbourg and married to the daughter of a perfume maker from Verdun, became a Paris bookseller in 1787.[58]

Both the victims of the April 1789 riot were self-made men. Henriot's father was an innkeeper in a village near Paris, comfortably off but far from rich. Réveillon was exaggerating when he claimed that "I began by making a living from the work of my hands" and that when he left his first employer he had no more than 18 livres to his name. He was the son of a comfortable, though not wealthy *bourgeois de Paris*.[59] His claim nevertheless shows that social promotion through the acquisition of wealth, as opposed to royal service, had become respectable, a source even of boast.

It also reflects a growing spirit of individualism that was encouraged by the social climate of late-eighteenth-century Paris. Increasing geographical mobility often obliged young men (less often young women) to make their own lives independently from their families. The decline in birthrates among the urban elites meant that most grew up, in the mid eighteenth century, with just one brother or sister. They were less likely to learn collective values either from siblings or from joining a band of neighborhood children. Their notions of the world came from books, school, and individual instruction by a parent, servant, or tutor. The growth of individualism was reflected in a hesitant but definite shift away from a society in which people had rights and privileges as members of an order or a corporation, to one composed of citizens with individual rights.[60]

It would be misleading to press this argument too far. Most late-eighteenth-century women and men, whatever their background, remained firmly communitarian in much of their thinking: "fraternity" contained far more real meaning for them than it does for us. Extended family ties were still of tremendous importance for all ranks. It is also true that the profit motive and the merchant practices that I have described can be traced back a long way. Yet late-eighteenth-century debates do demonstrate a noticeable shift in the ethos and the moral codes of many educated Parisians.

Those new ideas were fundamentally at variance with the customary culture of the Paris trades. In 1776, trying to prevent the abolition of their organization, the shoemakers insisted on the danger of letting in "newcomers" with no commitment to quality: "sure of not being watched, . . . they would no longer listen to any voice except that of personal interest." Free trade would mean "the general interest sacrificed to individual interest." "A rich individual," wrote the fruiterers, could easily gain a monopoly and hold the city to ransom.[61]

This was not rhetorical armor donned for one particular battle. The trades were using similar language throughout the century. But they might have been describing Réveillon, who was repeatedly in conflict with the corporations: with the papermakers when he began experimenting with paper; with the painters' corporation when he employed painters to work on his models; with the printers, engravers, and decorators who claimed he was infringing their monopoly.[62]

Understandably, he complained bitterly of the "jealous vexations" and "despotism" of the corporations. The publishing entrepreneur Panckoucke later condemned the bodies governing the book trade as "petty aristocratic, despotic groups." He was using the new revolutionary language, yet denunciations of political and economic "despotism" and the corresponding exaltation of "liberty" had become increasingly strident in Paris since at least 1771. "Liberty is the great springboard, the most powerful vehicle of commerce, of the talents produced by genius and the arts," wrote Marie-Catherine Renée Darcel, wife of Oberkampf's partner Sarrasin de Maraise (herself an outsider, having gone from cloth buyer in Rouen to business manager of the largest cotton manufactory in France).[63]

Her "liberty" was not quite that of the Physiocrats, the liberal economists of late-eighteenth-century France. Paris merchants had little to gain from the total abolition of tariffs. Nor did they agree with the Physiocrats that agriculture was more important for national wealth than manufacturing and trade, or that all monopolies and privileges should be abolished. After all, many of them had put a lot of effort into obtaining government protection for their businesses. But a great many did support—as did the Paris *cahiers* of 1789—the removal of barriers to trade within the kingdom.[64]

They certainly agreed with the Physiocrats and most of the philosophes on the virtues of work and self-help. "The government should frighten the lazy," Diderot had once suggested. Having, in many cases, overcome formidable obstacles through their own energy, ambition, and skill, the new men and women saw no reason why others should not do the same. Réveillon boasted that "every one of my workers is certain of his advancement, in proportion to his intelligence and his zeal."[65] In the new world of eighteenth-century consumerism limitless growth was possible; even if this was not the experience of the vast majority of Parisians.

The rioters of April 1789 may have been mistaken in believing that Réveillon had said workers could manage on 15 sous a day. But in a more general sense they were not mistaken. He, and people like him, had little sympathy for those unable or unwilling to compete. The riot was an attempt to enforce community morality, and a rejection of a worldview that by 1789 was becoming ever more influential.

Yet although the culture and philosophy of people like Réveillon was at odds with an established way of thinking, it did not automatically produce conflict. Even if they did not share the customary and communitarian ethos of the neighborhood or the trades, the entrepreneurs might respect it in order to avoid disruption. In 1766 the highly entrepreneurial Etienne-Simon Martin may or may not have shared the feelings of his workers, but he sided with them when they came into conflict with other masters over wages, paid the rate they were claiming as customary, and allowed the usual two hours for lunch. For his mainly aristocratic customers price was not an issue but prompt delivery was, so he could not afford to have his journeymen go on strike. But by the 1780s many entrepreneurs were targeting wider markets, and production costs and work practices were now therefore key concerns. The future revolutionary leader Antoine-Joseph Santerre refused to accord his workers the used hops from his brewery, as was customary. Instead he dried it for sale as fuel. He monitored each detail of expenditure, wringing every possible profit out of his business, though he was generous with sick workers. Réveillon used the same combination of paternalism and force, vigorously crushing a strike at his paper factory outside Paris and imposing new work methods firmly, while paying relatively high wages.[66]

Réveillon was not typical of the thousands of Paris employers in the late eighteenth century. Professional and officeholding families were usually the ones who most decisively turned from customary to metropolitan culture, although even among their ranks many conservatives clung to an older vision of the world. But among the merchant classes most men and women could still move with ease between the two cultures, even if they engaged in the new forms of elite sociability, bought consumer items, and aspired to the domestic ideal. Perhaps women in these social groups were less likely to cross the boundary: the ideology of domesticity made them a symbol of gentility and imposed new forms of behavior on them more strictly than on men. The domestic servants of affluent families also had a foot in both worlds, their work often obliging them to adopt and perhaps internalize their employers' modes of behavior. Yet many servants, when out of work or having taken up different sorts of jobs, slipped easily back into the habits of neighborhood interaction.

Nor was there a straightforward division between those who were members of corporations and those who were not. Wealthy mercers defended their organization in 1776 and were indignant in 1789 when they were not allowed to elect their own deputies to the Estates General. Yet many of them made their living in the metropolitan world of consumption and competition. The trades were not synonymous with customary culture, even if they remained one of its strongholds. There were also key differences between occupations. A poor bookseller was closer to the enlightened reading public and its values than a rich builder. A mercer specializing in silk was more a part of the elite consumer culture than a wineshop keeper, though both belonged to trades corporations.

It would therefore be a gross oversimplification to identify metropolitan and customary cultures with different social classes, even though metropolitan culture was more accessible to the affluent, while customary culture was increasingly condemned by educated people. The two cultures were always potentially in conflict but—as with other sources of tension within Paris society—their interests set them against each other only in certain situations. One such situation arose in the riots of early 1789. Nevertheless, the appearance of the two cultures was an early step toward a class society in Paris.

It is also misleading to think of metropolitan and customary cultures as "modern" and "traditional." Intentionally or not, these value-laden labels may serve to denigrate the culture labeled "traditional." They are also inaccurate, since those forms of behavior often described as "traditional"—social deference, custom, community—have not disappeared from the "modern" world. No longer the dominant forms of social organization in the West, they have nevertheless evolved to fulfil new functions in our society and they remain very powerful in some non-Western societies.

In order to make sense of what was happening in Paris across the eighteenth century I have used a series of oppositions: customary and metropolitan; local and central; elites and working people; early and late. But there is nothing fixed about such categories and oppositions. It is we who impose them, with hindsight. For our own purposes we divide the past into periods, ascribing particular attributes to each one. The people of late-eighteenth-century Paris had no such sense of living between two social systems. There was just the city, with its traffic, its rhythms and rituals, its companionship or loneliness; and for most, the long working day, the daily struggle to make ends meet, the hopes and fears for the future.

CHAPTER TWELVE

THE CITY AND THE REVOLUTION

The Paris of 1789 was a very different city from the Paris of 1700. It was three times larger in official surface area and its population had almost certainly increased substantially. Its economy had expanded and it was a far more mobile society. Immigration had probably accelerated, and movement to and from the city had grown along with the industries it housed. Visitors came for business and for pleasure, and as transport improved they came more often and from further afield. By 1777 the stagecoach made it possible to leave Angers or Le Havre for Paris on Monday morning, conduct one's business, and be back home by Sunday evening.[1]

Young Parisians were increasingly likely to go to other places, too. Growing numbers of merchants and bankers visited other European centers on business. More people even crossed the Atlantic, especially after 1776. In the international commercial dynasties that were multiplying during the century, sons were increasingly likely to serve an apprenticeship with a relative or a partner in another city.[2]

Inside Paris itself the traffic was just as bad as in the late seventeenth century but the congestion was spread over a wider area. Faster vehicles competed with the wagons and with pedestrians. Almost all the streets were now paved and they were easier to navigate at night: the sputtering old tallow candles had been replaced first with brighter twin-candled lamps and most recently with new oil lamps. The first sidewalks were laid in the 1780s. While every quarter remained residential, the city had more differentiated areas specializing in business and commerce, manufacturing, administration, or leisure. As a result there was increasing internal movement. Growing numbers of workers—though still a minority—commuted between quarters and more people sought leisure outside their neighborhood.

Along with real movement went the imaginary mobility created by travel literature, novels, and even by new products from distant lands. Perhaps there were few people who paused in drinking their coffee to consider where the sugar and coffee beans had come from, but when they saw bright piles of oranges and tomatoes in the market even the least educated knew that these were exotic products from distant lands. Faraway places had a taste and a perfume that increasing numbers of Parisians could appreciate.

With European expansion overseas, people from very different backgrounds appeared in the city streets. Since 1774 Guillaume Delorme, a black man from Haiti, had worked as a carriage maker in the faubourg St-Antoine. The American Revolution focused French attention on the New World and the French hero of that war, Marie-Joseph-Gilbert Motier, marquis de La Fayette, brought America back with him—literally when he had two young Indians sent to Paris, where they went to school. The much-fêted ambassadors Benjamin Franklin and Thomas Jefferson gave the infant American republic a cultured and popular face. The expanding press brought news of faraway places, canvassed new ideas, encouraged public debate. In a host of ways, as Helvétius exclaimed, "the horizon of our ideas is expanding from day to day."[3]

Movement became not only more convenient but increasingly desirable, and the faster and farther the better. Distance, remarked Jacques-Henri Bernardin de Saint-Pierre in the mid-1780s, "gives such charm to objects on the horizon."[4] Literary tastes aside, as shorter traveling times produced a significant reduction in the prices of luxury goods, time became money in a very concrete way. Even in the police and other branches of administration, senior figures stressed speed as well as efficiency. The duc de Polignac, director of the national postal service, denounced wagoners who—conforming to an older, unhurried rhythm—caused "a delay prejudicial to the speed of a service that deserves every protection." The emphasis that political economists placed on *la circulation* encouraged them to value speed as well. It is no coincidence that it was Finance Minister Turgot, a key proponent of free trade, who introduced faster vehicles soon dubbed *turgotines*.[5]

Unhindered mobility in all its forms came to be seen as a positive thing.

The economists pushed for free circulation of goods and money; urban reformers for easy and rapid movement around the city, both for vehicles and for air to blow away disease-causing miasmas. There was growing demand for up-to-date information, hence the success of the new daily paper the *Journal de Paris*. Liberal-minded intellectuals argued for the free movement of ideas. Even social mobility became more acceptable, despite the snobbery of the elites. The many examples of self-made men and women testify to a new openness in Parisian society.

Growing movement had profound implications for urban life. It facilitated anonymity, enabling people to escape from the constraints of their village or even of their Paris neighborhood. It is true that there had long been a margin of maneuver in Paris that was absent in smaller places. The two-thirds of the city's population who came from other parts of France could escape the intimate knowledge of their background and family that surrounded them in their place of birth. An unmarried woman who was pregnant could invent a husband, dead or in the army: "I announced myself as a young widow," recounted Nanette in Restif de la Bretonne's novel *Monsieur Nicolas*.[6] But with increasing geographical and social mobility this potential anonymity became even easier. As a result the capacity of the local community to regulate behavior was diminishing. Illegitimacy rates rose and church attendance dropped. People were able to dress and behave in ways once considered inconsistent with their rank. Even the expression of political and religious dissent became easier, and by 1789 Paris was far more secular than most other European cities.

A growing distance between the elites and the common people accelerated the relaxation of older forms of social control. For many newly arrived immigrants, the contrast between the structures of deference in Paris and those in the smaller places they came from must have been striking. Everything conspired to distance members of the middle and upper ranks from other sections of the population: their business interests, their recreations, their reading. At least as an ideal, home became what in 1782 the mother of a lawyer called "l'île enchantée" (enchanted island), a place of respite and delight cut off from the outside world.[7] Middle-class people met their neighbors less often in the street; less often at church. Their children did not go to the same schools. Manon Phlipon's parish priest was pleased when she went to the catechism class run by her uncle, because he thought this example "capable of persuading individuals, who were not among those one called 'the people,' to also send their children there."[8]

He was fighting a losing battle, because the forces of urban change were stretching the ties that bound the local elites to the working population: the new cultural practices and uses of urban space, growing sensitivity to dirt and social promiscuity, shifting gender ideologies, more private religious practices. So was the impact of the state, which relieved merchants and officeholders of their administrative role in their quarter, making them less likely to be known to the local people and less able to influence the thinking and behavior of their neighbors.

The French capital was a far more fluid and less hierarchical place in 1789 than it had been in 1700. People continued to be acutely conscious of fine gradations of wealth and status, yet it was harder to tell who was who. "Paris was a city where people judged by appearances," recalled Giovanni Casanova in his memoirs, and yet "there was no place in the world where it was easier to deceive." Those with the right talents and sufficient bravado could pass themselves off as gentlemen or ladies. It was just as easy to move in the other direction: one day the future Madame Roland, Manon Phlipon, borrowed clothes from her servant and ventured out alone, "running like a real peasant girl, pushing everyone who got in my way, walking through the gutters and at full stretch through the mud, getting pushed by people who would have made way for me if they had seen me in my fine clothes." Appearances were all that distinguished the elite from the masses: hence the growing importance of fashion as a social signifier.[9]

Appearances, together with the cash economy and the greater disposable incomes of a large minority of the population, contributed to what contemporaries described as a "confusion of ranks." In Paris most things could be bought and sold and there were few controls on who could buy what. The last sumptuary law—restricting certain forms of dress—dated from 1665 and was no longer enforced.[10] "The wife of a clerk, or of the corner grocer, can dress like a duchess," Mercier observed disapprovingly. An English visitor recorded meeting her milkman one evening, "dressed in a fashionable suit, with an embroidered waistcoat, silk knee-breeches and lace cuffs."[11] A journeyman could purchase a sword and dress like a young man of good family. The police tried to catch mischievous poseurs, but they faced the same difficulties as everyone else: how could they tell who was who? It was even possible for men and women to cross-dress and get away with it. Paris had an active homosexual scene that the police were aware of but could do little about.[12]

What a novelist termed "this contagious air of liberty that one seems to breathe [in Paris]" was more than a literary trope.[13] When people fell out with their employer or landlord—or even a noble patron—they could give notice and go somewhere else: in a purely commercial relationship, debts and obligations were easily liquidated. Artisans were proud of owning their own tools and boasted of their "liberty." They demonstrated what the elites referred to in horror as "a spirit of independence." As several bakers told a surgeon's wife, "We'll put our racks in front of the doors of greater lords and ladies than you!"[14] Even unskilled laborers sometimes refused conventional deference to their social superiors. A lawyer complained in 1780 that he could not get local errand boys to carry a letter for him. Having refused to employ the first one who came because the fellow did not understand the instructions, the lawyer sent for a second. Another fellow came but said "that he supported his comrades," "that none of them would go and that I could run my errands myself . . . he used the kind of language customary among these sorts of people." The lawyer was outraged: "They form among themselves an insolent little republic."[15] A "republic" was of course quite the opposite of a monarchy and in eighteenth-century French parlance a synonym for anarchy. The expression is significant though. The lack of deference that this witness was condemning was a product of the way the city had developed, and it did threaten the monarchical hierarchy of the old social order.

The same process was under way at all levels of society. I have already mentioned the lawsuit brought in 1782 against a nobleman who had tried to expel a minor legal official from his seat at the theater. The plaintiff's lawyer "emphasized the general interest of the public, in defending an individual whose status as a citizen should in itself have protected him from any insult, in a place where money alone put nobility and commoners on the same level, according them equal rights."[16] There were more and more such places in the new public sphere.

Maintaining deference was made still more difficult by the growing access to information that Parisians enjoyed. Literacy rates were unusually high by eighteenth-century French standards: 90 percent of men and 80 percent of women who made wills were able to sign them, compared with 71 percent and 44 percent in northern France as a whole. The Paris town criers no longer read out a ruling of the Parlement but simply cried "Arrêt du Parlement" and pasted it up for people to read for themselves.[17] Journeymen could consult the statutes of their corporation and the rulings of the Parlement. The elites had no monopoly on written culture.

The high literacy rates also gave women ready access to information and a means of further education. By the late 1760s the literary commentator Friedrich von Grimm quite expected shop girls to be reading

Figure 35. The messenger boy. Note the ragged clothing but slightly insolent air: he has not removed his hat to deliver the letter. On his arm, a stool for cleaning shoes. Engraving by Augustin de Saint-Aubin, in *Mes gens, ou les commissionnaires ultramontains* (Paris, n.d.). Bibliothèque historique de la ville de Paris, photo Jean-Christophe Doerr.

the novels of Baculard d'Arnault (of which he had a low opinion). Manon Phlipon was undoubtedly unusual among artisans' daughters in enjoying Plutarch and teaching herself Italian, but she was a product of a city that, while it placed many constraints on women and denied them equality with men, nevertheless allowed them a degree of freedom that was unusual in late-eighteenth-century Europe.[18]

The evolution of government itself inadvertently undermined traditional social hierarchies. Across the century the growing bureaucracy slowly developed a professional ethos and a concept of public service in the general interest that required equal treatment of all citizens. The nobility still got special handling, but there were some surprising incidents. Nobles were rarely stopped at the Paris customs posts, but in 1758 Madame de Sénac was made to get out of her carriage so the customs employees could search it for undeclared goods. "They paid no attention to my name and quality. . . . They replied in so many words . . . that it made no difference to them." This was the new bureaucratic spirit. The police too were periodically at odds with people of high rank who claimed exemptions from rules that were meant to apply to everyone.[19] Each instance set two opposing concepts of the social order face to face. Well before 1789 ideas of equality before the law and of the rule of law were gaining currency, under the aegis of the monarchy itself.

All of these changes helped create a public that was independent, educated, and politically aware. In this process the widespread Jansenism of the first half century was also an important factor, encouraging an independence of mind and a determination to resist oppression that—thanks to the monarchy's stance in religious affairs—left their stamp on secular politics. At the very least, Jansenism fostered the belief that a merchant or a domestic servant could be more virtuous and express the truth more readily than a priest or a nobleman. Dale Van Kley has even suggested that there was a direct link between the midcentury Jansenist-Gallican coalition and the emerging "patriot party" of the 1770s and 1780s, and there were certainly many who followed this itinerary.[20] At any rate, by then many ordinary Parisians believed that they could legitimately hold a view on political matters, and even the monarchy had begun to accede to this claim.

We might expect nobles to have been particularly hostile to the undermining of traditional hierarchies, and some were. Yet they too appreciated the freedom of the city, if the comte de Mirabeau is to be believed: "It is well known that all the nobles in France have been drawn to the capital by ambition, by the quest for pleasure, by the ease with which income can be had in cash."[21] Furthermore, noble culture was itself changing, becoming more urban, and in the process moving closer to that of other wealthy groups in Paris society. Blue-blooded boys now received as good an education in the classics as in swordplay and blood sports, and the cult of sensibility embraced even the aristocratic faubourg St-Germain. Birth slowly ceased to be the sole basis of civility, and even aristocratic military writers sometimes suggested that true courage drew not on blood lines but on "reflection, knowledge, philosophy, misfortune, and above all the voice of a pure conscience."[22] Nobles and commoners mixed in some of the same societies, though there is debate about the extent of this association. Both certainly joined the Société philanthropique, which boasted "a perfect equality between all its members, whatever their rank and condition."[23] The abandonment of baroque ostentation made the differences between great nobles and lesser ones, even between courtiers and fashionable financiers, more subtle and harder for the uninitiated to pick. "The magistrate, the bishop, the military officer, the financier, the courtier seem to have borrowed something each from the next," observed Mercier. "There are only nuances between them." No longer did great noble households employ literally hundreds of servants as a sign of their wealth and power. Instead they made do with twenty or thirty![24]

Now, too, the sons and daughters of nobles and of wealthy bourgeois could boast similar accomplishments, even if their sense of themselves remained light years apart. Better-off Paris merchants were sending their children not to local establishments but to more exclusive boarding schools where they mixed with young people from a range of affluent backgrounds from all over the city. Already in 1743 "the sons [of merchants] are raised with the same education as people a rank above them," according to the lawyer-diarist Barbier, and the trend was to accelerate. In 1778 Sophie Girard, the daughter of a wood merchant, was a boarder at the Picpus convent on the edge of the faubourg St-Antoine. Her sister Dorothée was at the prestigious convent of Notre-Dame-de-Longchamp—either for schooling or (as one of their mother's letters hints) to keep her out of mischief—for which the family were paying 1,453 livres per year, plus expenses of 1,477 livres. The Picpus fees of 500 livres a year were slightly above average for girls' boarding schools in Paris, while those of Longchamp were at the very top of the price range. As there was a close correlation between the fee scale and the rank of the youngsters attending, the Girard girls were almost certainly mixing with the daughters of higher-ranking families. Their two older sisters, who presumably had a similar education, had married army officers, both minor nobles.[25] This was another form of convergence of ranks.

We must keep all these changes in perspective. In 1789 Paris remained a city of churches, with a large clerical population and, by modern standards, a high rate of religious observance. Bonds of social obligation continued to link most employers and employees, and neighborhood interaction remained strong even between people of very different rank in most parts of the city. Ties of dependence and clientage operated at all levels of society, and deference was still an important part of daily life. The capital's egalitarianism was only relative. Nor did the independence of mind, the decline of religious observance, or the loss of respect for the clergy among part of the population pose any threat to law and order or in normal circumstances to the stability of the regime.

The ideology of monarchy remained a very powerful tool, enabling the enforcement of laws with very limited recourse to force. It was deliberately exploited by the authorities, who each time there was a royal birth or wedding, or a military victory, knew just what sorts of displays would appeal to the crowd. Every year there were processions on New Year's Day and on the principal holy days. Special celebrations always included a procession and usually involved the officials of the municipality, the magistrates, and the leading clergy of the city, symbolizing an ideal and unified hierarchy. Yet changes in religious belief and practice, along with new attitudes to authority, had begun to undermine the power of these rituals, and the "confusion of ranks" in everyday life gradually emptied the ceremonial hierarchy of much of its meaning.

In the last years of Louis XV's reign and under Louis XVI there was growing condemnation of "despotism," even though the government was more responsive to "public opinion" than ever before. The liberalization of the grain trade and subsequent sharp rises in the price of bread revived the belief that the government was profiteering on grain and did immense damage to the authority of royal officials, even if they did not directly touch Louis XVI himself. Within Paris the growing intervention and greater efficiency of the police and other agencies contributed to the feeling that ministerial despotism was increasing. And the impersonal character of the semiautonomous *régies* that mushroomed in the second half of the century, perhaps combined with the mounting exclusion of the middle classes from local administration, fueled criticism of "arbitrary" government. All of this assisted in persuading Parisians that it was not simply individual ministers who needed to be changed, but the system of government itself.

The fragility of authority—rather than its strength—showed up in the state's use of the army against rioters. By the late eighteenth century the authority of the commissaires and of other local notables had waned, and recourse to armed force demonstrated both a fear of the mob and the demise of the paternalistic relationship between the city's rulers and the Paris populace. The military had been employed before, but never so frequently. Soldiers put an end to three days of rioting in 1775 and were used again in April 1789. The newly militarized guard violently dispersed crowds several times from 1787 to early 1789. In July of that year troops were again mobilized. But by then public opinion, including that of the middle classes, had turned decisively against a government the people deemed to be in the hands of a corrupt court, the soldiers refused to obey, and the Parisian Revolution was under way.

PARISIAN SOCIETY AND REVOLUTION

Changes in social relations and government had made a revolution possible. Across the 1790s the character and dynamism of Parisian society continued to shape it. Only a city of some size could have provided the extraordinary human energy that the events of 1789 unleashed. For most of the decade Paris led and powered the Revolution. Many thousands of its citizens turned out to protest and to act in July 1789 and again in October. Up to 30,000 protested after the attempted flight of the royal family in July 1791. Close to 15,000 militants were active in the sections in late 1793 and rather more across the whole period of the Revolution. The members of committees gave up hundreds of hours of leisure and sleeping time to keep the city running and the wheels of revolution turning. Thousands served each week (not all of them willingly, it must be said) in the Garde nationale. The National Guard had over 116,000 members in early 1793—around two out of every three adult males in the city. The revolutionary armies recruited 7,000 volunteers who sometimes spent lengthy periods away from their jobs and families scouring the provinces for grain and for counterrevolutionaries. There were around 10,000 voters in the 1791 legislative elections; 14,000 for the election of the mayor in 1790, and slightly more in 1793. Given people's unfamiliarity with the process and the long and complex voting system, the fact that 15 to 20 percent of the electorate voted in any one election is not bad. (It could take several hours for the electoral officers to be chosen, the credentials of the voters checked, and the candidates voted on, one at a time.)[26]

But numbers were not the only factor. High levels of literacy and well-developed news networks were vital for political participation. So was the decay of the old patronage networks and the capital's relative openness to newcomers and to innovation. Neither the nobility nor the clergy ruled Paris. Nor, any longer, did the magistrates, officeholders, and wealthy merchants who had once been so powerful: even the once-dominant Parlement faded into obscurity overnight. The old power bases, founded on militia rank, local administration and patronage, guild government and family networks, had all crumbled.

The new political landscape was already visible in April 1789, when for the first time significant numbers of Parisians—those paying taxes to the value of 3 livres, about three days' wages for a laborer—got to elect their representatives. The men they chose were often new figures, with no power base in their quarters and no history of public office. The extent of the turnover is reflected in the small numbers of former churchwardens elected in 1789 and after: in the entire faubourg St-Antoine, which after 1790 was divided into three sections, only 6 former churchwardens were among nearly 200 men elected to section committees up to mid-1794.[27]

Some of the new men were schoolteachers, wine merchants, butchers; their occupations had been poorly represented among the old local elites. Even lawyers, who had made up less than 10 percent of the notables chosen to participate in elections at the Hôtel de Ville between 1775 and 1789, now formed over 40 percent of the Third Estate electors. An increasing number of the revolutionary leaders were migrants or sons of migrants whose energy and drive had enabled them to make successful careers in the big city: one was Antoine-Pierre Damoye, an entrepreneurial carriage maker who had diversified into carriage renting, haulage, and real estate.[28]

As the Revolution went on, the numbers of men drawn from outside the old political elite increased. Whereas during the Old Regime the officials of the trades and the parish churchwardens were almost all Paris-born or had been in the city for many years, in 1794 half of the members of the civil committee of the faubourg Montmartre section had been in Paris for less than eight years. And while seniority had been an important prerequisite for an Old Regime notable, now younger men began to play an active role, men like Nicolas-François Bellart, a twenty-two-year-old lawyer who was elected in April 1789 and subsequently became secretary of the Petit-St-Antoine district. He was exceptional, but across the city growing numbers of men in their thirties were elected to public office in the early 1790s.[29]

These newcomers were chosen on the basis less of rank, age, or family background (which was often unknown to many of the voters), but according to their reputation, words, and deeds. The idea that individual worth rather than birth should be the basis for public office was already widespread in the late Enlightenment and was now being put into action. It produced some unlikely leaders. Guillaume Bouland was one, a former servant who became a radical voice in the Observatoire section before winning office in the Finistère section, and who subsequently became a judge in the Paris courts. Just as unexpected was the appearance in a section committee of Guillaume Carrel, a former dancer at the opera; or the career of the former postal clerk Jean Varlet, aged twenty-seven when he came to prominence in the radical Cordeliers Club.[30]

The Parisian Revolution was also precociously egalitarian. Very early, many of the districts displayed an extraordinary spirit of inclusion. "It is right for all citizens in turn to participate in the administration of the commune," felt the St-Marcel district committee, and that of St-Roch threatened to fine notables who did not attend meetings. In recruitment to the new citizen militia—what was to become the National Guard—many districts welcomed volunteers of all ranks and at least two districts stressed the need for simple uniforms that all could afford.[31] These were attitudes rooted in the social and political environment of prerevolutionary Paris, where many artisans were well aware of events and felt they should have a say.

This fertile soil provided the seedbed for other ideas that took root in the course of the Revolution. Republicanism was inconceivable in 1789, and so was universal male suffrage. Yet the precocious appearance of such demands and the widespread support they attracted in Paris as early as 1791 are easier to comprehend if we recognize that the prerevolutionary city already provided a climate in which ordinary people felt themselves ready and able to be citizens. The same was true of the extraordinary outburst of patriotism that accompanied the initial outbreak of revolution in Paris, quickly developing into an unprecedented popular nationalism. The development of a national spirit has been very little studied, but responses to the Seven Years' War of 1756–63 and the appearance of the "patriot party" in the 1770s suggest that it had deep roots, particularly in Paris. The patriotism of these years was a secular mixture of Gallicanism and Jansenism. From the Jansenist belief that Church doctrine should be determined by the community of all true believers, not solely by the pope, the bishops, or the clergy, it was only a step to the conviction that the political sovereignty lay with the people, not with the king and his ministers.[32] Patriotism was inseparable from the growing sense that Parisians had of themselves as citizens of France, not simply subjects of the French king. The political experience of the refusals of sacraments, the Maupeou catastrophe, and distrust of the reforming efforts of the Paris police and other agencies led many people in the city to identify patriotism with hostility to despotism. In July 1789 despotism was symbolized by the king's dismissal of the ever-popular minister Necker and by the well-publicized machinations of the comte d'Artois, Madame de Polignac, and their supporters in what came to be called "the court party" or even "the aristocracy." "The nation asked for Necker to be retained," cried Camille Desmoulins in a famous speech in the Palais-Royal on 12 July 1789. "Could you be more insolently defied?" he asked, now identifying "the nation" with his Parisian audience. "After this coup they will stop at nothing, and they may perhaps be planning a Saint Bartholomew's massacre of patriots."[33]

But perhaps the clearest example of the influence of the urban environment on political events is the way many ordinary Parisian women responded to revolution. The march to Versailles on 5 October 1789 was largely the work of working women from the central market district and from the faubourg St-Antoine—areas linked by numerous work ties. Suspicious of the court and its supporters and firmly believing that the political opponents of the Third Estate were trying to prevent reform by driving up bread prices in Paris, these women gathered thousands of others around them and laid siege to the Hôtel de Ville. They expressed exasperation with the paper shufflers of the municipality, and one group tried to set fire to papers stored in the building, saying "that it was all that had been done since the Revolution began." They were equally scathing about their own menfolk: "these women repeated that the men were not strong enough to avenge themselves and that they would show themselves to be better than the men." "The men are holding back," said others, "the men are cowards . . . we will take over."[34] They did, marching 12 miles through the rain to the royal palace. They returned with promises of lower bread prices and of reform and brought the royal family with them as a guarantee.

This was the most dramatic women's action of the Revolution. But already, in September 1789, members of a deputation to the Hôtel de Ville seeking action on bread shortages and high prices were heard to say that "men did not understand anything about the matter and . . .

they wanted to play a role in affairs."[35] Later the market women were prominent in attacks on nuns whom they perceived to be counterrevolutionary, and in 1793 on radical women whose politics they equally condemned.

Other women were active in around a third of the popular societies and in many sectional assemblies, where they sometimes forced issues onto the agenda. In 1793 there were demands for female suffrage. Women of all ranks attended sittings of the National Assembly and maintained a noisy commentary on debates. The flexible and mobile nature of much female work enabled them to drop in as they were passing, and to listen while knitting or sewing. We know that women were among the most enthusiastic supporters of Robespierre and other key Jacobins, and of radicals like Jacques Hébert, Jacques Roux, Jean Varlet, and other lesser figures who fought to have ceilings placed on food prices. Women were active in most of the insurrectionary movements and finally revolted against the Jacobin leadership. Without their participation the Parisian Revolution would have been a very different affair. But without the independence that the social and economic environment of Paris gave women, and plebeian women in particular, it is hard to imagine them taking, from the very beginning and in large numbers, such independent action. Mary Wollstonecraft firmly believed, having visited Paris in 1794, that "from the enjoyment of more freedom than the women of other parts of the world, those of France have acquired more independence of spirit than any others."[36]

The nature of urban work and social relationships helped shape the distinctive political culture of revolutionary Paris. And revolutionary events helped activate the city's latent hostilities. Mistrust of merchants, and of bakers in particular, is well documented and erupted each time prices rose or shortages were experienced. It was exacerbated by breaches of communitarian ethics by the growing numbers of entrepreneurs for whom profit and consumer clienteles were more important than collective obligations to trade or neighborhood—and the turbulent 1790s provided ample opportunities for speculating of this sort. The Revolution gave older attitudes a new political dimension by making profiteering on necessities not only immoral but also unpatriotic. This outlook was not confined to Paris.

Popular anticlericalism too was not unique to Paris, but its vigor there was unusual. Here the continuities are not so clear, yet once again the character of the city was crucial. Clergy in Old Regime Paris, perhaps more than anywhere else, had to earn the respect of their congregation.

A village priest might have a local monopoly, but in Paris dissatisfied parishioners could attend monastery churches, go to other parishes, and even not go to church at all. The Jansenist inheritance was again important. Going right back to the 1720s and 1730s, Parisians were accustomed to judging their clergy: there were "good" priests and "bad" ones (whether they belonged to the Jansenist opposition or to the "devout" anti-Jansenist party). Although there was no obvious continuity between Jansenist parishes and those where most of the clergy supported the Revolution, the distinction between "good" and "bad" priests reemerged in 1791, when roughly half the curés and just over a third of the ordinary parish clergy took the oath of loyalty to the constitution.[37]

Patriots found more bad apples among the religious orders, where only 42 percent took the oath. This confirmed an already widespread prejudice against the regular clergy, who were increasingly condemned in novels, philosophical literature, and popular story as corrupt, decadent, or at best a waste of potentially productive (and reproductive) citizens. Sentiments in Paris were mixed. Some of the religious orders worked closely with the local people: the Frères de la charité were well regarded by the printing workers for their care of the poor, and so were the Saint Vincent de Paul's Soeurs de la charité. Some, like the Franciscans, were strong supporters of the Revolution. At the same time, grocers and the fruit and butter merchants protested at unfair competition from religious houses. One Paris tanner was possibly putting a common view among the educated classes when he argued in his personal *cahier* in 1789 that monks should be made to do useful work teaching the city's children. A brewer suggested using the income of a number of abbeys to help the poor.[38]

These sentiments, openly expressed, may have strengthened the strand of anticlericalism that existed in prerevolutionary Paris. The very conservative stance of many of the clerical deputies to the Estates General did not help. In August 1789 a number of drunk people called out "A bas la calotte" (down with the priests) during a procession on the Ile-de-la-Cité, and there was outspoken public criticism of the archbishop's politics. In October, when thousands of Parisian women marched to Versailles, some of them invaded the benches of the National Assembly and shouted insults at the bishops, again to cries of "A bas la calotte!" Subsequently the pope's condemnation of the Revolution and the refusal of many clergy to take the oath of allegiance confirmed anticlericals in their prejudices.[39]

Just as significant in determining the fate of the Paris clergy, though, may have been indifference. Across the eighteenth century the role of the

Church in Paris was declining. By the 1780s probably less than half the city's adult population took communion.[40] The Church's role in poor relief was diminishing as secular institutions intruded, and its capacity to provide assistance was lessening along with bequests, donations, and the contents of poor boxes and collection plates. The number of clergy was not keeping up with the growth in population and some Parisians had little contact with the Church.

In the climate of the 1790s, growing indifference or latent hostility to established religion allowed active anticlericalism to emerge and spread. Anticlericalism acquired legitimacy—even "patriotic" credentials—in declarations by public figures like Marat. Well before official persecution of "refractory" clergy began—late in 1791—there were attacks on nonjuror religious in Paris. In April groups of women broke into four convents and took whips to nuns hostile to the Revolution. The following year many priests were imprisoned as "suspects." The most horrific incidents took place in early September 1792 when a band of men went from prison to prison, apparently with the approval of members of the Commune, and battered to death between 1,100 and 1,400 people, including 220 clergy.[41] Most observers were horrified but afraid to intervene, and some public figures were prepared to excuse the violence. As political intimidation grew, the many who believed in freedom of religion were afraid to speak out. The active hostility many religious displayed toward the Revolution also made the defense of patriotic clergy increasingly difficult.

Nevertheless, dechristianization and anticlericalism were only ever minority movements in Paris. There were quite a number of priests like Jean-Jacques Poupart, the well-known curé of St-Eustache, who remained in the city without being bothered.[42] Some of the two thousand nuns driven out of the convents adopted secular clothes but continued community life of a kind, and those who worked with the poor were sometimes defended by their sections.[43] As the political climate changed, in 1795, the churches were reopened, generally by lay people. The restorers of religion were not counterrevolutionaries though, since the churches they reestablished were mostly modeled on the revolutionary Constitutional Church of 1791. They often had a democratic structure, with priests elected by the parish council or in some cases by the entire congregation: as some Jansenists had suggested years before.

Revolutionary anticlericalism, therefore, was a product of the encounter between a long-lived strand of hostility to the Church, widespread indifference, and the particular crises of the 1790s. It illustrates once again the way that prerevolutionary social relations made possible and influenced the Parisian Revolution, yet without predetermining its course.

Sentiment against the nobility probably operated in a similar way. The pretensions of minor nobles were resented by much of the Paris "public," as the 1782 Moreton-Chabrillant incident demonstrated. A long-standing hostility in Paris to the court at Versailles grew acute in the late 1780s, holding the gilded courtesans and self-serving ministers responsible for the woes of Paris and providing a base for revolutionary antipathy to all nobles. There were already isolated threats against Parisian nobles in the middle of 1789. Once the court moved to Paris at the end of 1789, evidence of the numerous counterrevolutionaries within the king's entourage was right under the noses of Parisians. The king's bodyguard were the most unpopular and they clashed frequently with National Guardsmen on duty at the Tuileries palace. In February 1791 quite a number of noblemen at the Tuileries were disarmed by the National Guard following a rumor that they had been about to assassinate the king—further evidence of the population's distrust.[11]

As in the case of the clergy, growing feeling against nobles was probably assisted by widespread indifference. Of all the Parisian elites, nobles had least contact with the ordinary people. Only a handful played any role in the parish churches, and then mainly in an honorific capacity. With the possible exception of the duc d'Orléans, who seems to have attempted to build a power base in the city in 1789, there is little evidence that noble families had more than commercial contacts with the Paris middle classes. People had no reason to disbelieve reports of noble plots against the Revolution, and the fate of the haughty Parisian nobility was a matter of indifference to most of the population.

THE INTEGRATION OF THE CITY AND THE REVOLUTION

Across the late eighteenth century the integration of Paris and changes in the role of the local middle classes were undermining the quarter and the parish as political units and making them less inclusive social entities. The importance of the broader outlook that resulted became clear very early, when the districts quickly formed a central assembly of electors to coordinate their activity. The section representatives formed societies like the Club de l'Evêché and the Club de la Ste-Chapelle to coordinate their activity. Later the Jacobin and Cordeliers Clubs served the same function. Especially after the beginning of 1790, frequent deputations went from district to district and subsequently between the sections. The local leaders were well aware of the way their counterparts elsewhere in the city were thinking and were very conscious of the need to act in unison.[45]

Crowd action too repeatedly transcended local interests and boundaries, displaying a new, citywide approach to politics. Already in April 1789 the Réveillon affair, with its appeals by the population of the faubourg St-Antoine to workers elsewhere in the city, had shown the potential for united action. In mid-July 1789 the same interplay of local and citywide action occurred. The Hôtel de Ville, where the Assembly of Electors was meeting, was the focal point to which the crowds from all over the city returned repeatedly on 12, 13, and 14 July. The takers of the Bastille were primarily people from the faubourg St-Antoine and the neighborhoods immediately adjoining the fortress but included a significant number from other parts of the city, once again particularly from the faubourg St-Marcel. Again on 20 June 1792 citizens from all over the city gathered—with little central organization—to force the king to reinstate the popular ministers he had just dismissed.[46]

These acts had no direct prerevolutionary precedents but were prepared by the city's growing integration and the sense of interdependence that it created. By the 1780s changing uses of urban space were breaking down the psychological and social boundaries between quarters and preparing the way for the citizens' coordinated action.

At the same time, the remarkable local commitment displayed by many of these same people suggests the incompleteness of the city's integration. In July 1789 the defense of the city against possible military attack was conducted on a local basis. While the notables of the district committees organized citizen militia units groups of neighbors spontaneously prepared to repel the expected assault. "The women and children took up the paving stones in the courtyards to attack these traitors to the *patrie* from the windows," wrote a café owner near St-André-des-Arts.[47]

In the following weeks and months lawyers, priests, and merchants, many of them active participants in the new metropolitan culture, reassumed responsibility for food supply, law and order, streetlighting and maintenance, public health, and later poor relief. The boundaries of districts and subsequently of sections took on an administrative and political significance that local divisions of the city had not had for over a century. And even after the initial emergency was over, the local leaders fought to retain their role, onerous as it was. One of the characteristics of both the districts and the sections was their jealous defense of local sovereignty, which repeatedly brought them into conflict with the municipality, the National Assembly, and with one another.[48]

At times they almost literally drew the wagons into a circle around their own enclave. On 25 June 1792, at a time of high tension following renewed rumors of a planned coup by the court, the St-Marcel battalion of the National Guard was summoned by the tocsin to its parade ground in the old cloister. Scouts were sent out into the streets leading toward the city center and returned with news that the area was surrounded by troops loyal to the court. The battalion spent the entire day under arms, its cannon loaded and covering the cloister's entrances.[49] There was in fact no such plot and no army units preparing to attack. Even if there had been, they would hardly have been likely to pay much attention to the outlying faubourg St-Marcel. But the incident illustrates a strong sense that the areas beyond the narrow boundaries of their quarter were potentially hostile.

The popular movement also kept the customary mentality characteristic of the neighborhood communities of the city, often placing collective rights above individual ones within a local context. It remained bitterly opposed to the principles of economic liberalization that dominated successive National Assemblies. The "grocery riots" of 1792, when crowds seized sugar and coffee from warehouses in many parts of the city and sold it at a "just" price, are often passed over as "traditional" forms of protest somehow inconsistent with the "modern" revolutionary political culture. But they were perfectly at one with the aims of social justice that were central to the popular movement. The short-lived victory of that movement in 1793 marked the temporary triumph of this same mentality, particularly with the introduction of a ceiling on the prices of a surprisingly wide range of "necessities." This "maximum" was a measure that militants had sought repeatedly, using all the new techniques of revolutionary action.

Thus the Parisian Revolution was shaped in numerous ways by the long-term evolution of the city. Yet while continuities of all sorts were present, I am not suggesting that its course was predetermined, or wishing to downplay the remarkable changes it wrought. The springs of revolutionary thought and action lay in the past, but the Revolution operated an extraordinary transformation, opening up possibilities previously glimpsed only in dreams. There was little in the prior lives of individual Parisians to indicate what choices each would make when faced with a more dramatic upheaval than most human beings ever have to confront.

Some forms of revolutionary action went far beyond anything the eighteenth-century history of the city would lead us to expect. In October 1789 the women's march to Versailles, though rooted in the community of the central markets, gathered women from all over the city and far exceeded in size, aims, and consequences anything that had happened in the eighteenth century. The republican petition of the Champ de Mars, which five thousand people signed in 1791 to demand the dismissal of the king, was likewise startlingly new, transcended local boundaries, and foreshadowed the techniques of nineteenth- and twentieth-century political movements. On 10 August 1792 the military attack on the royal palace that overthrew the monarchy was an example of coordination and united political purpose worthy of twentieth-century revolutions. In these revolutionary actions we can detect elements of a new political consciousness, of an emerging sense of class, in some instances of modern feminism and of nineteenth-century popular nationalism. These were above all products of the revolutionary context, scarcely detectable within the prerevolutionary population.

Late-eighteenth-century Paris was moving out of a world structured by deference and hierarchy into one governed overwhelmingly by money and appearances. The collective sanctions, limited horizons, and customary culture of small communities were being complemented and modified by wider sources of identity and legitimacy—class and nation. Personal monarchy was giving way to an abstract state. Collective rights were being superseded by individual rights. In all of these areas Parisian society was precocious, because of its dynamic market economy, its relatively large population, and its function as capital. It was only in such a place, already a locus of social, economic, and political experimentation, a city unlike any other in Europe, that revolution could have taken place in the form it did. And the Revolution took this extraordinary city and transformed it still further.

EPILOGUE

The New Paris

To someone who knew Paris in the 1780s, the city of 1800 would have appeared physically quite different. The Bastille was gone, opening up a huge area that no one knew quite what to do with. The Châtelet prison had been demolished. But the most conspicuous physical change, affecting almost every quarter, was the disappearance of churches. The number of parishes had been cut from over fifty to thirty-three, and more than two hundred religious houses had been closed. New streets were being cut through what had once been Church property, continuing the march of new buildings into the green spaces both in and around the city. With the sale and subdivision of convent gardens, whole new quarters appeared.

In the streets the multiform costumes of the clergy had mostly disappeared—hats and veils, the brown habits of the Franciscans, the gray of the Soeurs de la charité. About 400 priests were active in 1796 and many more by the early nineteenth century, but in the 1760s there had been over 3,000 secular clergy, 2,000 male religious, and 2,100 nuns.[1] The change was even more marked on major feast days, when in the past religious processions crisscrossed the city, their route colored by flowers and tapestries, the clergy richly dressed in bright vestments. Even the sounds and smells of the city were affected, as incense, the odor of candles, and the chanting of the clergy disappeared from so many churches. Most of the bells had been melted down for guns, and while some were later replaced there was never again the same profusion.

The urban environment had undergone a wholesale secularization. Now many religious institutions, among the principal landmarks by which people navigated, were gone, along with the statues on street corners and many of the saints' names on house and shop signs. The confraternities, already dwindling before the Revolution, had been swept away, their property confiscated. Many new ones were founded in the nineteenth century but they never recovered their former appeal. The religious idioms that had been an everyday part of prerevolutionary Paris were slowly disappearing: even leases no longer required people to pay their rent for the St-Martin term or the St-Rémy term, but on the first of the month—(a change already noticeable by the late 1780s).

The postrevolutionary state took over functions of poor relief that the churches had once struggled to provide. In the hospitals, where nuns and doctors had battled for control before 1789, medics and bureaucrats now reigned unchallenged. There was a partial secularization of education, although religious schools were quickly reestablished and soon became more numerous than state ones. But the institutions of higher learning—before the Revolution entirely run by clergy—were now all secular. The great Paris schools that would shape the French elite throughout the nineteenth century and well into the twentieth were established in 1794 and 1795: the Ecole normale, the Ecole polytechnique, the "central schools" designed to train future civil servants, along with the Museum of Natural History with its twelve professors in various branches of science.[2]

The effect of the Revolution on religious belief is much harder to measure than its physical consequences. Revolutionary anticlericalism was the work of a minority. Until late 1793 religious services were well attended by the working population, and there was widespread popular enthusiasm for the reopening of churches after 1795. But anticlericals did succeed in imposing bans on public ceremonies, closed the churches for nearly two years, inaugurated attacks on priests and nuns, and no thunderbolts had obliterated them. Anticlericalism had been given legitimacy by the Revolution and was even equated with patriotism for some Parisians. And the Church had been challenged in many other ways, too. There had been over 10,000 Parisian divorces between 1793 and 1800. Jews and Protestants could now practice freely. Births, deaths, and marriages were now primarily the business of the state rather than of the church. The ideology of domesticity that emerged reinforced from the Revolution encouraged a sense that family matters were private and probably facilitated the adoption of contraception: birthrates steadily declined from the 1790s on. And religion had once again become a divisive political issue. The overall result was on the one hand an increase in the fervor of the religious, on the other almost certainly a big increase in the numbers of unbelievers, of anticlericals, and of the indifferent. The nineteenth-century Church, without the assistance of a state that needed legitimation from Catholic faith, was never able to enforce religious practice even to the extent of the 1780s.[3]

In secularizing the city the revolutionary years, for all their drama, were continuing and accelerating trends already under way well before 1789. The same thing happened in a whole range of other areas: in the huge increase in social mobility, for instance. The events of the 1790s hit the old city elites very hard, but unevenly. The great noble families were in the long run less affected financially than many others, since after the Revolution many were indemnified for about 60 percent of what they had lost. But the abolition of venal offices cost thousands of Parisian families a large part of their fortune. The principal magistrates of the Parlement lost hundreds of thousands of livres, the ordinary magistrates tens of thousands. This represented anywhere from 10 to 60 percent of their entire wealth.[4]

Many people from much humbler origins also lost heavily when their offices were abolished—compensation was promised but little was ever paid. Public notaries' offices were selling for nearly 300,000 livres in 1789. Stockbrokers, receivers of taxes, inspectors of factories and of weights and measures all had huge losses. So did some 5,000 judicial functionaries of different sorts, for whom office formed a significant part of their wealth. The abolition of venal offices affected not just individuals but whole families, because like other types of property offices could be passed on to the next generation. Few offices lost value during the eighteenth century, so they were an important type of investment.[5]

Many of the same families were hit very hard by the devaluation of government bonds, worth only a fraction of their face value by the end of the 1790s. Most magistrates, for example, had at least 200,000 or 300,000 livres invested in this way in the 1750s, and some had several million. The fermiers généraux had similar holdings. The banker Jacques Denis Cochin lost some 358,000 livres. A family that had invested heavily in both bonds and offices was unlikely to recover its former position. As a result many great bourgeois dynasties like the Metra, the Quatremère, or the Brochant families, who for generations had been elected to the Paris city council and who had dominated the prestigious guilds, now found themselves in the second rank. In 1815 only a small percentage of these families retained their former prominence.[6]

Many other groups suffered too. The employees of the now-defunct *régies,* of the disbanded trades corporations, of the fermiers généraux, and of the Paris police all lost their jobs. Masters and mistresses in the trades corporations lost their investment in the mastership and—equally important—the status it brought. A very wide range of ordinary Parisians had also invested heavily in government bonds: for better-off servants and wage earners there had been few other places to put their savings.[7]

As the Revolution continued, huge numbers of merchants were crippled by the collapse of the luxury trades. After 1790 nobles left Paris in large numbers and those who did not go were officially expelled in April 1794. Given that up to 200 enormously wealthy noble families spent in Paris most of the huge income that they drew from the struggling peasantry on estates all over France, their disappearance had a drastic effect on the city's economy. The local markets for carriages and luxury furnishings collapsed. There was no way that someone like Rose Bertin, supplier of fashion clothes to the court, could survive: she emigrated some time in 1792. Goldsmiths and expensive mercers went bankrupt.[8]

Many quite ordinary tradesmen were grievously affected by the disappearance of rich customers. In the mid-1780s the baker Gilles Pasquier was owed well over 1,000 livres by four princely households, and the Revolution brought huge losses for him. Nor was it just nobles who left. The closing of convents and monasteries meant the loss of many more clients, some of them very wealthy. And as the Revolution went on, even the bourgeois began to depart in large numbers. Some left for political reasons, like the former lawyer Antoine Joseph Thorillon, a moderate and one of the Paris deputies to the Legislative Assembly in 1791, who retreated to the north of France some time in 1793. Others moved for economic reasons, among them Jacques-Louis Ménétra's wife, who stayed with friends in the provinces, "finding that she could not live on the ounce and a half of bread that was allotted to each individual."[9]

As if this were not enough, almost continuous war after 1792 cut off foreign markets and reduced imports of consumer goods and raw materials. If merchants and manufacturers did not find new outlets, they lost everything. And thanks to the opening of Paris industries to all comers with the abolition of the guilds, there was now far more competition. There had been ten porcelain factories before the Revolution: nineteen new ones appeared when royal monopolies were abolished. Not surprisingly, most did not survive long.[10]

When the new economic conditions affected employers, their workforce suffered as well. "The embroiderers are going bankrupt; the fashion merchants are closing down; the dressmakers are sacking three quarters of their workers, and women of quality soon will no longer have chambermaids," complained a pamphlet of 1790. Hordes of domestic servants found themselves out of work, and few had skills to fit them for other jobs.[11] For many the hopes of 1789 were soon dashed.

Fortunately other changes brought by the Revolution partially compensated for these disasters. Revolutionary institutions provided a huge stimulus to the Parisian economy. The installation of the National Assembly and of the court in Paris in October 1789 brought nearly 1,000 deputies and their servants to the city, putting pressure on housing in the faubourg St-Honoré. The assembly provided new jobs for lawyers, and journalism flourished as observers jostled to send news of the revolutionary changes all over France. As the Revolution tried to transform France from the center, the numbers of employees in the various ministries grew from approximately 670 in the 1780s to over 13,000 by 1795, and despite later cutbacks never returned to the former modest level. And government employees were one of the few groups whose salaries were increased almost in line with the cost of living.[12]

The abolition of the trades corporations, while it disadvantaged some, allowed journeymen and provincials to move into hitherto inaccessible Paris trades. Though most probably did not survive in business long, some were able to seize an unprecedented opportunity. Artisans from the faubourg St-Antoine and other formerly "privileged" areas could now compete on equal terms with masters in the city. It now became legal to cross trade boundaries, as the Salleron brothers did: they were masters in one branch of the leather industry who now were able to take control of the whole production process.[13]

Certain sectors flourished in the new conditions. The status of doctors, scientists, and schoolteachers rose further, elevated by the prominent role that men in these occupations played in the revolutionary assemblies and by their participation in newly established institutions of higher learning, which stressed science, medicine, engineering, and education.[14] The publishing and printing industry, which the monarchy had deliberately restricted, expanded with almost frightening speed. Nearly 200 newspapers appeared in 1789 alone. The 36 established print shops had 11 more rivals in 1789 and by 1799 the city had 223 printing works. Anyone who has dipped into the revolutionary archives has witnessed at first hand the explosion of paper. Every one of the 34 committees of the National Assembly, the 144 committees of the Paris sections, those of the municipality, and of the Paris department, recorded their deliberations. So did the 48 assemblies of the sections and most of the clubs. The National Assembly passed thousands of new laws and had copies printed for widespread distribution. The 48 sections maintained an extensive correspondence, wrote reports, and often published extracts from their deliberations. The work of the ministries, the local police officials, and the justices of the peace added to the demand for paper, producing a general shortage of paper. This was one sector of the Paris economy that boomed, providing work for the rag collectors, papermakers, printers, publishers, binders, booksellers, ink manufacturers, and hawkers.[15]

Paris also benefited from the revolutionary centralization of the economy—an important step in the creation of national markets. As port cities like Bordeaux, Marseille, and Nantes declined, largely because of the wars, the funds once invested there moved to Paris. Some were invested in nationalized property, but the middle-class consumer market began to expand again after 1795 and manufacturing of watches, glass, jewelry, porcelain, and many other artifacts took off.[16]

Above all, after 1792, there was the military. Hundreds of thousands of new soldiers joined the French armies. Every one needed equipment, and the sudden demand for uniforms, blankets, guns, powder, and ammunition turned former monasteries into factories and gave seamstresses, tailors, swordsmiths, and foundries abundant work. The apothecary Michel-Jean Dizé, ruined by the loss of his wealthy clients, found a new position as apothecary major in the army—and there were many like him in a whole range of occupations. More than 7,000 people were directly employed in the Paris armaments industry in 1794. There was a boom in tanning, to provide boots, saddles, and harnesses. Any merchant or manufacturer who could land a good army contract was on the path to riches, though many fortunes were also made by middlemen who promised to find—usually on advance payment—the necessary supplies.[17]

The other great source of new wealth was property confiscated from émigrés and the Church. In the northern part of the city over a quarter of the total land area was nationalized in this way, and the largest share sold to lawyers and other professionals, smaller amounts to wealthy merchants and local manufacturers. The speculators who bought the land formerly belonging to the Filles du Calvaire convent on the edge of the Marais made 100 percent profit on their investment. Many affluent Parisians also bought estates outside Paris, paying less than the full value of the land. Antoine-Pierre Damoye, in a nice twist of fate, bought a château near the village his father had left as a poor emigrant bound for Paris a generation earlier. Anyone who could pay off debts or buy property using *assignats,* the revolutionary bonds that depreciated with amazing speed, was well on the way to fortune. In 1806 a government report stated that the leading figures in each quarter were "individuals whose existence does not go back further than the *assignats.*"[18]

Many historians have seen the Revolution as the victory of the bourgeoisie, as the moment of their arrival in power. This conclusion was valid, insofar as the Revolution prepared the way for the bourgeois society of the mid nineteenth century. Yet like most such generalizations, this is an oversimplification. The Revolution's economic and social effects on Paris were far more complex and nuanced. It provided enormous opportunities for some and ruin for others. It benefited certain sectors and those who backed the right horse did far better than they could have dreamed. Others lost everything. The overall result was unprecedented social mobility, a dramatic reshaping of the old social hierarchy and a redistribution of individuals and families within it. In a sense the Revolution consummated, with breathtaking speed, the destruction of oligarchy and the opening up of new sectors that had begun, very tentatively, in the preceding decades.

On balance, ordinary Parisians were probably materially worse off in 1800 than in 1789. Yet the greatest deterioration took place not during the revolutionary turmoil itself, but in the second half of the decade. In fact, in certain sectors real wages had at first risen. But at the end of 1794 the Maximum, which had placed a ceiling on the prices of many necessities, was abandoned. Both direct and indirect taxes were substantially increased, making everything more expensive and leading landlords to increase rents. The winters of 1794–95 and 1795–96 were long and bitterly cold. Food prices soared, plunging the poor into destitution and pushing the nearly poor over the edge. The good harvests of the following three years were little compensation. Nor did they help the 10 percent or more of the population who were unemployed in 1798. Across the whole city the number of poor receiving assistance increased from nearly 73,000 in 1794—already a high figure—to over 111,000 in 1801. The lost Church charity was probably not made up for by the new institutions, except for a brief moment when the Jacobin government provided bread, meat, and even cash payments to a great many of the city's poor.[19]

As a result of all this turmoil and hardship, the city's population declined for the first time in a century. The first reliable census, in 1801, produced a figure of 547,756. Marcel Reinhard estimated on the basis of bread ration cards that the population was around 660,000 in 1795.[20]

Yet most historians now put the population at over 700,000 at the end of the Old Regime.

Many of the social changes during the Revolution took startling and unforeseeable directions. The extraordinary militarization of Parisian society was one of the most dramatic. It is not that uniforms were new in Paris: under the Old Regime at least one man in twenty served in the army, there were barracks in the faubourgs, and throughout the 1780s troops patrolled the city at night. But the number of soldiers and the army's impact on society now increased. Military industries were vastly more important in the city economy. The visibility of soldiers was greater (see Figure 36). If the number of professional soldiers stationed in Paris remained much the same in 1793 as in the 1780s—about 8,000—there were now an extra 116,000 National Guardsmen in their new royal-blue uniforms. As war took its toll the city took in unprecedented numbers of crippled veterans, not all of whom had originally come from Paris, and of widows and orphans. Used army buttons and braid found their way into the much-mended clothing of the poor.[21] During the revolutionary wars the soldier became the symbol of Liberty and of the Nation. The young Joseph Bara and other boy-soldiers were held up as examples to every patriotic lad, and the song that came to symbolize the Revolution, the Marseillaise, was a military march with amazingly bloodthirsty words.[22]

The army became one of the principal agencies of social mobility, allowing men with luck and talent to rise to undreamed-of heights. Napoleon Bonaparte's rise was the most spectacular, but less dramatic careers were common. Charles-Alexis Alexandre, the artisan's son turned stockbroker, became a general and even (very briefly) minister of war in the revolutionary government. No longer were nobles the only men who could become officers and win glory on the battlefield. Officer rank became one of the high roads to political power, even within Paris, where widely known figures like La Fayette, Antoine-Joseph Santerre, André Acloque, Claude Lazowsky, and others prominent in the sections had their power base in the National Guard. Under the Directory, after 1795, the regular army became a player in national politics.[23] The needs of a nation at war had set the "soldier-patriot" on a pedestal and the conditions were ripe for military rule.

The militarization of Parisian society across the revolutionary decade helped redefine representations of masculinity. Certainly, military "virtues" had never been absent from ideals of manhood, either for the nobility or for working men like Jacques-Louis Ménétra, whose artisan code

Figure 36. Street traders on the Pont-au-Change, ca. 1800. Note the soldiers, including a national guardsman with a pike in the center background. Anonymous drawing, *Marchands ambulants sur le Pont-au-Change*. Musée Carnavalet, © Photothèque des musées de la ville de Paris, photo Andreani.

of honor included dueling. But the Enlightenment had begun to displace those images of manhood, offering the "man of sensibility" as an alternative model. Even the idea of a "philosopher-soldier" was becoming acceptable to military officers in the second half of the eighteenth century. Royal propaganda represented Louis XVI not as a military conqueror but as a benevolent father, and in late-eighteenth-century painting and sculpture domestic authority had eclipsed military virtue as the basis of patriarchal power. Even the Roman generals beloved of history painting in the 1770s and 1780s were hardly victorious figures: Belisarius, unjustly condemned and reduced to begging, was a favorite. The neoclassicism that flourished during the Revolution and under Napoleon, when Roman emperors regained favor, accompanied a revival of military images of manhood.[24]

In turn, neoclassical models had profound consequences for the position of women. It is not so much that revolutionary or Napoleonic legislation patterned family relationships on military ones, although there was a reinforcement of the authority of fathers and husbands from 1795 on. It is rather that military service became one of the key components of citizenship and therefore a key argument deployed to exclude women from political participation during the Revolution.[25]

The early 1790s had brought a whisper of female emancipation, growing out of the supposedly "universal" principles of liberty and equality. The divorce law provided thousands of Parisian women with a means to escape unhappy relationships. Radicals voiced far-reaching demands for political participation, better educational opportunities, and legal reform. The early years of the Revolution made it possible, in an unprecedented way, for women to participate politically. They had access to newspapers and pamphlets. For some—irrespective of class—the liberating experience of revolution provoked a feminist consciousness of sorts, encouraging them to apply political understandings to their personal lives. Before her divorce, wrote *citoyenne* Gavot, "groaning under the grip of a despotic husband, liberty was for her a meaningless word." Now, she rejoiced, she could become a true republican.[26] Yet by 1794 the Jacobin government had introduced oppressive legislation designed to force women out of politics and to subordinate them firmly to their husbands and fathers. It explicitly excluded women from public office and from the key institutions of higher education. But divorce remained until 1816.

The Revolution made only small changes to the property rights of Parisian women. Even before 1789 they could inherit equally and, if single and over twenty-five, had control over their own property, as did widows. One significant change was the reduction in the age of majority to twenty-one, which remained throughout the nineteenth century. But the brief period of legal equality between husband and wife, from late 1793 to 1796, was followed by legislation reaffirming a husband's control over his wife's body and property. Under the Old Regime there had been a significant loophole: membership of the women's and mixed corporations had given several thousand mistresses, married or not, equal legal and civil rights with men. The abolition of the guilds removed those rights and may also—since many of the Paris mistresses were single or widowed—have deprived numerous women of an economically viable alternative to marriage. The new family law of the late 1790s introduced a new loophole, though one probably of lesser value: married women could still enjoy full property rights if the rights were specified in their marriage contract.[27]

The Revolution did not affect all women in the same ways, though. In the longer term, it reinforced the trend to confine middle- and upper-class women to the home, away from the newly emerging "public" domain. Both those who looked on the Revolution as a disaster and supporters who felt it had been betrayed often blamed women. Confirmed Jacobins complained of female support for counterrevolutionary priests. In noble families returning from exile in the early 1800s, many men and women believed that the interference of court ladies in politics and the lax morals of the prerevolutionary nobility—of the women in particular—had contributed greatly to the disaster that had befallen them. Many high-ranking women deliberately turned their back on public affairs and devoted themselves to their families.[28]

Among the Parisian elites, the Revolution thus changed the position of women. Even where something of the revolutionary egalitarianism survived, it could turn to their disadvantage. The Old Regime had allowed a few privileged women access to education and influence, but the new one treated them equally, subjecting all to a more repressive norm. Perhaps, even so, the emphasis placed on mothers as the educators of their children gave some women a new sort of influence and improved the educational opportunities for wealthy women and their daughters.[29]

But for the majority of Parisian women such changes had little effect. For those whose husbands went away with the army or took on long hours of administration and committee work, the Revolution brought a heavier load and new responsibilities. They were often left in a more precarious economic situation. For many, the absence of husbands meant taking over a business, a challenge which might be either onerous or liberating. Nearly all Parisian women, though, suffered from the economic consequences of the Revolution. The job of feeding a family was made far more difficult by the inflation and food shortages. Women were far more likely than men to be abandoned by their partners, and to face the responsibility of bringing up children on grossly inadequate wages.[30]

Both sexes, in slightly different ways, were affected by one of the most important social changes of the 1790s: the dramatic increase in geographical mobility. As many as 80,000 or 100,000 Parisian men left to serve in the army between 1792 and 1796. They were moved all over France and even across its borders, most traveling further than they ever had before. Meanwhile, provincial men were moving toward Paris, leaving small towns or poverty-stricken villages or farms to try their luck in the capital. In the Place des Fédérés section in the Marais the percentage of men from the provinces rose from 60 percent in 1791—about average for the city at any time in the second half of the century—to 73 percent. Right across the city there was a very steep rise in arrivals of immigrants in 1793.[31] Other movement was of shorter duration, but still involved large numbers. Fifty thousand provincial National Guardsmen arrived for the Festival of Federation in 1790, a smaller number the following year. Most had never been to the capital before and many came from well beyond the traditional Paris catchment area. This physical movement, as much as political propaganda, was a key factor in the creation of national identity both in Paris and the provinces.

Geographical mobility affected the wealthier classes even more. Deputies from all over the country converged on Paris in 1789, with new contingents arriving after each election. Some departed again on missions to different parts of France. Emigrés fled toward the borders and political retirees to the provinces: André Aclocque spent the radical phase of the Revolution in Sens, while his wife and son ran the family brewery to keep it safe from confiscation.[32] By the time he came back after the Terror, his former political opponents were looking for quiet places to retire. This movement, some temporary and some permanent, continued a prerevolutionary trend but reached unprecedented levels.

But the movement was not just into and out of Paris. Revolutionary events increased mobility within the city too and in small ways modified people's use of urban space. There was probably some redistribution of population, at least temporarily, though the fragmentary evidence points to big differences between quarters. In 1793 half the men in the Place des Fédérés section (in the Marais) had been living there since 1789, and most of the newcomers had come from the immediate surrounding areas. In this relative backwater there were no huge upheavals. But the faubourg St-Germain was reported to be "quite depopulated" by the emigration of the nobility. Many nobles and bourgeois also left the faubourg St-Honoré, but it experienced an influx of deputies and administrators. Other people escaped the more expensive areas of the city center for the faubourgs, where rents were lower. In April 1795 the administrators of the Finistère section in the faubourg St-Marcel claimed that its population had risen from 11,364 to around 12,000 over the previous few months. And in the Popincourt section, part of the faubourg St-Antoine, about 40 percent of the male population in late 1793 had been there for less than a year.[33]

The increase in day-to-day movement is not quantifiable, but it was very visible. On 3 August 1789 the wineshop keeper's boy Alexis Pailla, serving as sergeant in the National Guard of the St-André-des-Arts district on the Left Bank, arrested a man in the village of Vaugirard on the southeastern fringe of the city and took him to the Hôtel de Ville on the other side of the river, before returning to his own district to report.[34] This was typical of the movement created by service in the National Guard, which took men all over Paris. In the first half of the 1790s, too, deputations flew between the districts, from section to section, between political clubs, to and from the Commune and the National Assembly. Men and women from all over the city attended sessions of the National Assembly and of the Jacobin Club. There was constant coming and going between central government authorities and the committees of all the different sections.

The economic upheavals of the decade also contributed to short-term movement, as people went from one site to another in search of work. The large manufactories producing military supplies attracted workers, while the workshops set up in 1793 to provide work for poor women "are located in such a manner that we spend as long going to get or deliver the work as to do it," the women complained. At any one time, from 1790 to 1795, around 3,000 were employed in these two spinning workshops.[35] All of this movement—both residential mobility and day-to-day travel around the city—further speeded the integration of the city.

In one respect, as the last chapter observed, the Revolution gave renewed life to the sense of locality. Many working-class Parisians identified closely with their section. Even members of the middle classes who in the preceding decades had tended to withdraw from local life now became deeply involved in local politics and administration and through these responsibilities got to know a large number of local people. Yet in the longer term the most important ties created by this participation were with others of similar status and interests. Within each district and section, and after 1795 in each of the new *arrondissements*, administrative responsibilities created new and denser networks of educated Parisians that complemented existing bonds. For the men chosen to represent their sections as electors—nearly a thousand every year across the city—there were even more opportunities to form wider ties. "The electors affiliated with major societies, with clubs, have a striking advantage," explained the Club de la Ste-Chapelle in 1791 to justify its establishment. "From the first moment [they are] among their friends and their acquaintances."[36]

Through all these activities and organizations the Revolution furthered the mixing of the Paris middle classes across professional boundaries and between different quarters. It also hastened the development of a bourgeois identity in other ways. Ideas of male equality, of the rule of law, and of social distinctions based on merit and education rather than birth were taking hold at the very end of the Old Regime, but the Revolution made these the basic principles of society. By 1795 it had added the conviction that the "middle way" of the "middle class"—between reaction and revolution—was the right one. And it provided the foundation myth of the nineteenth-century bourgeoisie, expressed in 1824 by François Mignet: "The constitution of 1791 . . . was the work of the middle class, then the strongest." Even though by the late 1790s the role of the local middle classes had again been eroded by central government power, their newfound confidence remained.[37]

The abolition of all the corporate bodies that had been central to the Old Regime's social order gave class consciousness in Paris a further boost. These bodies had been under attack before 1789 but the Revolution destroyed them all, and with them the title and the special identity that had given each group and each member their standing in society. The titles of "master" and "mistress" disappeared, and so did the hierarchy of guild officials. Distinctions within and between trades were blurred by the removal of the corporations that had defined their separate identities, and by the opening of all trades to all comers. Neither masters nor journeymen, as a group, could now take cases to the courts in defense of their collective rights because those rights no longer existed. The new legal system treated them as employers or as workers more than as members of a trade that had its own rules. All workers now had to carry the *livret,* a record of employment that had to be signed by their employer before they could legally change jobs. This was a system used in some trades before 1789, but it was now universal.[38]

In the new regime that emerged from the Revolution a person's rights were based on individual characteristics, especially gender, wealth, and public office. Men had more rights than women, and employers more than employees. In order to vote, adult males had to be public officials or to pay a certain amount of tax each year, and a higher figure applied for those wanting to stand for election. The same criteria also underlay the honorific system of early-nineteenth-century France. To become a "notable" one had to pay a certain level of tax, and only "notables" could become mayors or hold other influential offices. The new system of status was compatible with a class society, whereas the corporate social hierarchy of the Old Regime was not.

Class divisions within Paris were reinforced by the revolutionary identification of particular parts of the city with particular political and social attitudes. The faubourgs St-Antoine and St-Marcel developed a reputation for radicalism that made successive regimes fear them. This owed something to political reality, in that they often did take a radical stand during the Revolution. The eastern sections, particularly in the faubourg St-Honoré, tended to be more conservative, even royalist. But Parisians now increasingly linked these political differences with the social character of east and west. The faubourgs St-Antoine and St-Marcel were plebeian areas far removed from the new centers of elite leisure and from the eastern faubourgs St-Germain and St-Honoré where many rich families lived. Identification with particular areas of the city helped encourage both working-class and bourgeois consciousness.

The Revolution also attempted to complete the Enlightenment program of rational space and orderly streets. It streamlined city government, completing the removal of seigneurial jurisdictions and privileged areas that the monarchy had begun. Exactly the same administration and bylaws now extended to the entire city. In 1800 the Prefecture of Police was created, and it gradually extended its reach to include virtually the same responsibilities as the old police, but with far fewer obstacles to its authority. Within the city the various administrative units—the sections, the new parishes created in 1791, and the later *arrondissements*—were more uniform in size and population than any of the old city divisions. House numbers became the official way to indicate addresses.

Dreams of an entirely new, reformed city underlay many of the revolutionary festivals. Processions no longer went through the crowded central streets, preferring the wide tree-lined boulevards and the quais along the Seine. Ceremonies were rarely held in Notre-Dame—a symbol of the gothic city condemned by many eighteenth-century writers—or in other churches, but instead in places where the air could circulate, especially on the Champ de Mars where the Eiffel Tower now stands. Thus the Revolution could be identified (explicitly) with nature and (implicitly) with good health. Large semicircular spaces like the one created in front of the new Panthéon appealed to the classical taste of reformers.[39]

Only after 1796 did the dreams of a reformed city begin to take shape on paper and in stone. Plans were drawn up for the new Paris, beginning—in proper Enlightenment fashion—with a classification (never completed) of all the streets. Widening major roads to facilitate circulation of air and traffic was a high priority, and the confiscation of extensive church properties allowed whole quarters to be reshaped. The demolition of the Châtelet prison (also the old police headquarters) was originally ordered for political reasons as much as urbanizing ones, but in 1798 the work was completed to facilitate the north-south flow of traffic on one of the major city axes and to prepare the way for a wide east-west thoroughfare.[40]

The clearing of the streets also went ahead. The revolutionary authorities clamped down on street games, especially games of chance that, as the commissaire de police of the Arcis section put it in 1791, "maintain workers in idleness and enable them to find ways of dictating to their employers." The notables who ran the sections for most of the 1790s objected to such activities both on moral grounds and as an intolerable hindrance to traffic.[41] They also objected to popular celebrations, customary and spontaneous ones alike. In 1791 the municipality banned the annual burning of a mannequin at the corner of the rue aux Ours, the very same commemoration of a Protestant attack on a statue of Our Lady that Lieutenant of Police Lenoir had wanted to suppress some years earlier. The revolutionary authorities also prohibited Carnival's "disorderly" celebrations that were very much part of the street life of the Paris neighborhoods. And even in official revolutionary festivals the authorities tried to prevent the crowd from joining in.[42]

In 1799 Louis-Sébastien Mercier—author of the best-selling *Tableau de Paris*—published a major new work, *Le nouveau Paris*. It was greeted with almost complete silence. Mercier was a man of the eighteenth century, of the past. The new Paris was another world. As much had changed in the city since 1789 as in the whole of the preceding century. In some ways the Revolution had interrupted the course of eighteenth-century developments, cutting deep new channels into which the energy and thinking of Parisians were diverted. Yet in other ways it had hastened underlying trends, centralizing, speeding social and geographical mobility and the emergence of a class society.

The new Paris was in some ways a harsher world, one in which the collective instincts and solidarities of the past offered less protection against more individualistic and utilitarian ideologies backed by a more powerful state. In the new Paris wealth was flaunted, and almost everything had a price. Social divisions were sharper, not only in response to the Revolution but because the city contained greater numbers of affluent people and more who had nothing. Yet the principles of equality before the law and of promotion on merit were now entrenched (even if not always observed in practice). The city was far more secular and far less deferential, less regulated by deeply internalized habits of obedience. The new ideologies of nationalism, of progress, and of liberalism were forces for change, not stability. For the postrevolutionary generation the notion that the future would reproduce the past, characteristic of customary Paris, was gone for ever. For all these reasons the new Paris was more turbulent, more rebellious, its social tensions deeper and the potential for violence far greater than in the eighteenth century, the tumultuous events of the 1790s notwithstanding.

NOTES

ABBREVIATIONS

All manuscript references that are not preceded by one of the following abbreviations or by the name of another library or archive are to the collections of the Archives nationales, Paris.

AP	Archives de Paris
APP	Archives de la préfecture de Police
Bastille	Bibliothèque de l'Arsenal, Bastille manuscripts
BHVP	Bibliothèque historique de la ville de Paris
BM	Bibliothèque municipale
BN	Bibliothèque nationale
JF	Joly de Fleury collection, Bibliothèque nationale
MC	Minutier central des notaires, Archives nationales

NOTE ON SOURCES

Because this book is aimed at a general rather than a specialized readership, I have refrained from multiplying examples, either in the text or in the notes, but have occasionally referred the reader to major studies that provide fuller details. For the same reason, wherever there was a choice I have referred to English translations and to English-language works rather than French ones, and to published rather than manuscript sources. Where some piece of information is widely documented, I have not given a reference for it in the notes.

INTRODUCTION

1. Louis-Sébastien Mercier, *Tableau de Paris* (Amsterdam, 1782–88), 1:34.

2. Jean-Aimar Piganiol de la Force, *Description historique de la ville de Paris et de ses environs* (Paris, 1765), 1:31–32.

3. Daniel Roche, *The People of Paris: An Essay in Popular Culture in the Eighteenth Century,* trans. Marie Evans and Gwynne Lewis (Leamington Spa, 1987), 19–20.

4. Jean-Jacques Rousseau, *La nouvelle Héloïse,* in *Oeuvres complètes* (Paris, 1961), 2: 232 (letter 14).

5. Contant d'Orville, *Sophie* (1779), quoted in Simon Davies, "L'idée de Paris dans le roman du dix-huitième siècle," in *La ville au XVIIIe siècle* (Aix-en-Provence, 1975), 13; see discussion 11–17.

6. *Letters on the French Nation by a Sicilian Gentleman* (1749), quoted in Jeffry Kaplow, *The Names of Kings: The Parisian Laboring Poor in the Eighteenth Century* (New York, 1972), 27; Christian de Mannlich, quoted in Pierre Gaxotte, *Paris au XVIIIe siècle* (Paris, 1968), 24; Fougeret de Monbron, *La capitale des gaules, ou la nouvelle Babylone* (Paris, 1759). On these literary images see Peter Preston and Paul Simpson Housley, eds., *Writing the City: Eden, Babylon and the New Jerusalem* (London, 1994).

7. Daniel Roche, *France in the Enlightenment,* trans. Arthur Goldhammer (Cambridge, Mass., 1998), 558.

8. Peter Campbell, *Power and Politics in Old Regime France* (London, 1996), 315.

9. Robert Darnton, *The Forbidden Best-Sellers of Pre-Revolutionary France* (New York, 1995); idem, *The Great Cat Massacre and Other Episodes in French Cultural History* (London, 1984); idem, *The Literary Underground of the Old Regime* (Cambridge, Mass., 1982). See also Jack Censer and Jeremy Popkin, eds, *Press and Politics in Prerevolutionary France* (Berkeley, 1987).

10. An excellent recent study is Rochelle Ziskin, *The Place Vendôme: Architecture and Social Mobility in Eighteenth-Century Paris* (New York, 1999).

11. L. W. B. Brockliss, *French Higher Education in the Seventeenth and Eighteenth Centuries: A Cultural History* (Oxford, 1987); L. W. B. Brockliss and Colin Jones, *The Medical World of Early Modern France* (Oxford, 1997).

12. Among recent work, see especially Julian Swann, *Politics and the Parlement of Paris under Louis XV, 1754–1776* (Cambridge, 1994); and Sarah Maza, *Private Lives and Public Affairs: The Causes Célèbres of Prerevolutionary France* (Berkeley, 1993).

13. See particularly Richard Mowery Andrews, *Law, Magistracy and Crime in Old Regime Paris, 1735–1789,* vol. 1, *The System of Criminal Justice* (Cambridge, 1994); François Bluche, *Les magistrats du Parlement de Paris au XVIIIe siècle,* 2d ed. (Paris, 1986); David A. Bell, *Lawyers and Citizens: The Making of a Political Elite in Old Regime France* (Oxford, 1994); Michael P. Fitzsimmons, *The Parisian Order of Barristers and the French Revolution* (Cambridge, Mass., 1987); Bailey Stone, *The Parlement of Paris, 1774–1789* (Chapel Hill, 1981).

14. Michael Sonenscher, *Work and Wages: Natural Law, Politics and the Eighteenth-Century French Trades* (New York, 1989). The key works of Steven L. Kaplan are *The Bakers of Paris and the Bread Question, 1700–1775* (Durham,

N.C., 1996); *Provisioning Paris: Merchants and Millers in the Grain and Flour Trade During the Eighteenth Century* (Ithaca, 1984); *La Fin des corporations* (Paris, 2001); and among many articles, "Social Classification and Representation in the Corporate World of Eighteenth-Century France: Turgot's 'Carnival,'" in *Work in France: Representations, Meaning, Organization and Practice,* ed. Steven L. Kaplan and Cynthia J. Koepp (Ithaca, 1986), 176–228.

15. Arlette Farge, *Fragile Lives: Violence, Power, and Solidarity in Eighteenth-Century Paris,* trans. Carol Shelton (Cambridge, Mass., 1993); David Garrioch, *Neighbourhood and Community in Paris, 1740–1790* (Cambridge, 1986); and idem, *The Formation of the Parisian Bourgeoisie, 1690–1830* (Cambridge, Mass., 1996). A good anecdotal survey is Evelyn Farr, *Before the Deluge: Parisian Society in the Reign of Louis XVI* (London, 1994). Clare Crowston, *Fabricating Women: The Seamstresses of Old Regime France, 1675–1791* (Durham, N.C., 2001).

16. On Jews see P. Hildenfinger, ed., *Documents sur les juifs à Paris au XVIIIe siècle* (Paris, 1913); and Léon Kahn, *Les juifs à Paris pendant la Révolution* (Paris, 1899). On Protestants, Janine Driancourt-Girod, *L'insolite histoire des luthériens de Paris* (Paris, 1992) and *Ainsi priaient les luthériens: la vie religieuse, la pratique et la foi des luthériens de Paris au XVIIIe siècle* (Paris, 1992). On homosexuals, Michel Rey, "Police and Sodomy in Eighteenth-Century Paris: From Sin to Disorder," in *The Pursuit of Sodomy: Male Homosexuality in Renaissance and Enlightenment Europe,* ed. Kent Gerard and Gert Hekma (New York, 1989), 129–46. On prostitutes, Erica-Marie Benabou, *La prostitution et la police des moeurs au XVIIIe siècle* (Paris, 1987).

17. Quoted in Jacques Revel, "Les corps et communautés," in *The French Revolution and the Creation of Modern Political Culture,* vol. 1, *The Political Culture of the Old Regime,* ed. Keith M. Baker (Oxford, 1987), 225.

18. The term "metropolitan" is taken from Nicholas Green, *The Spectacle of Nature: Landscape and Bourgeois Culture in Nineteenth-Century France* (New York, 1990).

19. Catherine Duprat, *Le temps des philanthropes: la philanthropie parisienne des lumières à la monarchie de juillet* (Paris, 1993), 101; Jurgen Habermas, *The Structural Transformation of the Public Sphere: An Inquiry into a Category of Bourgeois Society,* trans. Thomas Burger and Frederick Lawrence (Cambridge, Mass., 1989), 27.

CHAPTER 1. THE PATTERNS OF URBAN LIFE

1. Mémoire sur les cimetières, presenté par MM les curé et marguilliers de la paroisse de St-Germain-l'Auxerrois, 9 août 1763, JF ms 1207, fol. 131.

2. Françoise Boudon, "La salubrité du grenier de l'abondance à la fin du siècle," *Dix-huitième siècle* 9 (1977): 174.

3. Mercier, *Tableau de Paris,* 1:123.

4. Ibid., 7:229–30.

5. On smells in Paris, the best source is Mercier, *Tableau de Paris.* On the history of perceptions of smell see Alain Corbin, *The Foul and the Fragrant: Odor and the French Social Imagination* (Cambridge, Mass., 1986). For a survey of the Paris quarters in the late eighteenth century see Kaplow, *Names of Kings,* ch. 1.

6. LL690, fol. 74; Louis-Sébastien Mercier, *Le nouveau Paris,* ed. Jean-Claude Bonnet (Paris, 1994), 1308.

7. Nicolas-Edme Restif de la Bretonne, *Les contemporaines du commun* (1782–83), quoted in Pierre Testup, "La ville dans les Contemporaines du commun," in *Rétif de la Bretonne et la ville* (Strasbourg, 1993), 188–89.

8. Daniel Roche, *A History of Everyday Things: The Birth of Consumption in France, 1600–1800,* trans. Brian Pearce (Cambridge, 2000), 161.

9. P. Scarron, *La foire Saint-Germain* (1692), quoted in Robert M. Isherwood, *Farce and Fantasy: Popular Entertainment in Eighteenth-Century Paris* (New York, 1986), 6.

10. Isherwood, *Farce and Fantasy,* 18; Colin Jones, "Pulling Teeth in Eighteenth-Century Paris," *Past and Present* 166 (May 2000): 100–106.

11. William Cole, *A Journal of My Journey to Paris in the Year 1765,* ed. Francis Griffin Stokes (London, 1931), 212.

12. Thomas Bentley, *Journal of a Visit to Paris, 1776,* ed. Peter France (Brighton, 1977), 31.

13. Steven L. Kaplan, "Religion, Subsistence, and Social Control: The Uses of Saint Genevieve," *Eighteenth-Century Studies* 13 (1979–80): 142–68.

14. On the university see Robert R. Palmer, *The School of the French Revolution* (Princeton, 1975), 16–31.

15. Mercier, *Tableau de Paris,* 5:14 and 4:164; Y11265bisB.

16. Siméon-Prosper Hardy, "Mes loisirs, ou journal d'événemens tels qu'ils parviennent à ma connoissance," BN ms fr. 6682, fol. 23 (28 January 1775). Hardy's diary fills 8 manuscript volumes in the Bibliothèque nationale: ms fr. 6680–87. Most of the entries covering 1764 to 1773 are published as "*Mes loisirs,*" *par S.-P. Hardy: journal d'événements tels qu'ils parviennent à ma connaissance,* ed. Maurice Tourneux and Maurice Vitrac (Paris, 1912).

17. Hardy, "Mes loisirs," BN ms fr. 6686, fol. 451 (19 May 1788).

18. On "reading" ceremonies, see Michèle Fogel, *Les cérémonies de l'information dans la France du XVIe au milieu du XVIIIe siècle* (Paris, 1989); Robert Descimon, "Le corps de ville et les élections échevinales à Paris aux XVIe et XVIIe siècles,"*Histoire, économie et société* 13 (1994):507–30; and idem, "Le corps de ville et le système cérémonial parisien au début de l'âge moderne" in *Individual, Corporate and Judicial Status in European Cities,* ed. Marc Boone and Maarten Prak (Louvain, 1996), 73–128; Sarah Hanley, *The Lit de Justice of the Kings of France: Constitutional Ideology in Legend, Ritual, and Discourse* (Princeton, 1983); see also Robert Darnton, "A Bourgeois Puts His World in Order: The City as a Text," in *The Great Cat Massacre and Other Episodes in French Cultural History* (London, 1984), 107–43; Edmond Jean François Barbier, *Journal historique et anecdotique du règne de Louis XV,* ed. A. de La Villegille, 4 vols. (1847–56; reprint, New York, 1966).

19. Andrews, *System of Criminal Justice,* 91.

20. Stephen Rombouts, "Art as Propaganda in Eighteenth-Century France: The Paradox of Edme Bouchardon's 'Louis XV,'" *Eighteenth-Century Studies* 27 (1993–94): 270.

21. Y15099, 10 January 1788.

22. Garrioch, *Neighbourhood and Community,* ch. 1.

23. Jacques-Louis Ménétra, *Journal of My Life,* ed. Daniel Roche, trans. Arthur Goldhammer (New York, 1986), 169.

24. Y15765, 3 March 1722.

25. Y15747, 2 November, 24 September 1700.

26. Y15756, 27 June 1709.

27. Y14078, 10 November 1752.

28. Y13751, 19 October 1746.

29. Y15747, 24 September 1700.

30. Arlette Farge, "The Honor and Secrecy of Families" in *A History of Private Life,* ed. Philippe Ariès and Georges Duby, vol. 3, *Passions of the Renaissance,* ed. Roger Chartier (Cambridge, Mass., 1989), 571–607.

31. Y11239, 1 November 1752; Y15350, 21 July 1752.

32. Y15350, 20 July, 19 June 1752.

33. MC XVII 481, 30 April 1702.

34. On joiners, François de Salverte, *Les ébénistes du XVIIIe siècle* (Paris, 1962); on grain merchants, Kaplan, *Provisioning Paris,* 131–35; Schulz and Kraus, *Beschreibung und Abbildung der Poissarden in Paris* (1789), quoted in Kaplow, *Names of Kings,* 46.

35. Garrioch, *Parisian Bourgeoisie,* ch. 3; Annik Pardailhé-Galabrun, *Naissance de l'intime* (Paris, 1988), 120, 185; available in an abridged English translation as *The Birth of Intimacy: Privacy and Domestic Life in Early Modern Paris,* trans. Jocelyn Phelps (Cambridge, 1991); Giles Barber, "The Parisian Fine Binding Trade in the Last Century of the *Ancien Régime*" in *Luxury Trades and Consumerism in Ancien Régime Paris: Studies in the History of the Skilled Workforce,* ed. Robert Fox and Anthony Turner (Aldershot, 1998), 46; Kaplan, *Bakers of Paris,* 303–5.

36. Roche, *People of Paris,* 75.

37. Alfred Franklin, *Dictionnaire historique des arts, métiers et professions exercés dans Paris depuis le treizième siècle* (Paris, 1908), 329–330. On tanners, Haim Burstin, *Le faubourg Saint-Marcel à l'époque révolutionnaire* (Paris, 1983), 204.

38 Sonenscher, *Work and Wages,* 224–25. On use of credit see Kaplan, *Bakers of Paris,* 137–51.

39. Steven L. Kaplan, "Les corporations, les 'faux ouvriers' et le faubourg St-Antoine au XVIIIe siècle," *Annales: économies, sociétés, civilisations* 43 (1988): 353–78.

40. Jacques Wilhelm, *La vie quotidienne des parisiens au temps du Roi-Soleil, 1660–1715* (Paris, 1977), 67; Franklin, *Dictionnaire,* 127–29; *Pierre Prion, scribe: mémoires d'un écrivain de campagne au XVIIIe siècle,* ed. Emmanuel Le Roy Ladurie and Orest Ranum (Paris, 1985), 128.

41. Barbier, *Journal historique,* 1:xv–xxi; Pierre Chaunu, *La mort à Paris* (Paris, 1978), 227, 436–37, 442.

42. Roche, *People of Paris,* 22–31.

43. Mathieu Marraud, *La noblesse de Paris au XVIIIe siècle* (Paris, 2000), 31.

44. Albert Soboul, *Les sans-culottes parisiens en l'an II: mouvement populaire et gouvernement révolutionnaire, 1793–1794,* abridged ed. (Paris, 1968), 22.

45. Marc Botlan, "Domesticité et domestiques à Paris dans la crise (1770–1790)" (thesis, Ecole nationale de Chartes, 1976), 10–16, 27–29, 151; Cissie Fairchilds, *Domestic Enemies: Servants and Their Masters in Old Regime France* (Baltimore, 1984), see esp. 31–46, 54–99.

46. Farge, *Fragile Lives,* 28–29, 98–99; Garrioch, *Neighbourhood and Community,* 127–39.

47. Ménétra, *Journal of My Life,* 151, 180.

48. Y15756, 6 October 1709.

49. Angela Groppi, "Le travail des femmes à Paris à l'époque de la Révolution française," *Bulletin d'histoire économique et sociale de la Révolution française* (1979): 27–49; Arlette Farge, "Les artisans malades de leur travail," *Annales: économies, sociétés, civilisations* 32 (1977): 993–1006, esp. 997.

50. Olwen Hufton, "Women and the Family Economy in Eighteenth-Century France," *French Historical Studies* 9 (1975): 8; Fairchilds, *Domestic Enemies,* 86–88, 181–83.

51. Y11706, 26 August 1775.

52. Y12596, 1 June 1752.

53. Sabine Juratic and Nicole Pellegrin, "Femmes, villes et travail en France dans la deuxième moitié du XVIIIe siècle: quelques questions," *Histoire, économie et société* 13 (1994): 489.

54. Ménétra, *Journal of My Life,* 25.

55. Y10994, 30 September 1752.

56. Y11239, 8 and 18 September 1752; Ménétra, *Journal of My Life,* 209–10, 216–17, 235–36.

57. Jonathan D. Spence, *The Question of Hu* (New York, 1989), 62, 84; *Pierre Prion,* 160.

58. Kaplan, *Bakers of Paris,* 11.

59. Y15973, 21 July 1773; Y10994, 16 April 1752.

60. Michael Sonenscher, *The Hatters of Eighteenth-Century France* (Berkeley, 1987), 18; and idem, *Work and Wages,* 174–209; Katie Scott, *The Rococo Interior: Decoration and Social Spaces in Early-Eighteenth-Century Paris* (New Haven, 1995), 63; Y11239, 11 February, 12 October 1752.

61. *Offices propres de la paroisse de St-Martin* (Paris, 1774); Y9525, ribbon makers, 1763.

62. BN Fm 23954, mémoire signifié, pour les Sieurs curé et marguilliers de l'église paroissiale et archipresbytériale de St-Séverin (1764), 17; JF ms 345, fol. 133.

63. *Nouveau coutumier général, ou Corps des Coutumes générales et particulières de France* (Paris, 1724). Quotation from *Etrennes financières* (Paris, 1789), 231.

64. [Père de Colonia], *Dictionnaire des livres jansénistes, ou qui favorisent le jansénisme* (Anvers, 1752), 1:ix.

65. Dale Van Kley, "From the Lessons of French History to Truths for All Times and All Peoples: The Historical Origins of an Anti-Historical Declaration," in *The French Idea of Freedom: The Old Regime and the Declaration of Rights of 1789,* ed. Dale Van Kley (Stanford, 1994), 72–113.

66. Nicolas Edme Restif de la Bretonne, *Monsieur Nicolas* (Paris, 1959),

1:393; Natalie Z. Davis, "Ghosts, Kin and Progeny: Some Features of Family Life in Early Modern France," *Daedalus* 106 (1977): 87–114, esp. 93–94; Roche, *France in the Enlightenment,* 75–108.

67. Edward P. Thompson, "The Moral Economy of the English Crowd," reprinted in his *Customs in Common* (Harmondsworth, 1993), 188.

68. Thompson, "Moral Economy"; George Rudé, "La taxation populaire de mai 1775 à Paris et dans la région parisienne," *Annales historiques de la Révolution française* 28 (1956), 139–79.

69. Garrioch, *Neighbourhood and Community* , ch. 1; Cynthia M. Truant, "Independent and Insolent: Journeymen and their 'Rites' in the Old Regime Workplace," in *Work in France: Representations, Meaning, Organization and Practice,* ed. Steven L. Kaplan and Cynthia J. Koepp (Ithaca, 1986), 132–33.

70. Hardy, "Mes loisirs," BN ms fr. 6684, fol. 322 (19 June 1783).

71. Thompson, *Customs in Common,* 1–15.

72. Sonenscher, *Work and Wages,* 23, 78; Philippe Minard, *Les typographes des lumières* (Seyssel, 1989), 102–3.

73. Bastille 10200, police report, 15 February 1742.

74. Steven L. Kaplan, "Luxury Guilds in Paris in the Eighteenth Century," *Francia* 9 (1981): 262–63;Franklin, *Dictionnaire,* 80, 192.

75. Y11239, 28 October 1752.

CHAPTER 2. THE POOR YOU HAVE WITH YOU ALWAYS

1. Nicolas-Edme Restif de la Bretonne, *Vie de mon père* (1779) (Paris, 1949), 29; Marcel Lachiver, *Les années de misère: la famine au temps du Grand Roi* (Paris,1991), 268–316.

2. Lachiver, *Années de misère,* 319–30.

3. Wilhelm, *Vie quotidienne,* 263; Lachiver, *Années de misère,* 351.

4. Daniel Roche, "A Pauper Capital: Some Reflections on the Parisian Poor in the Seventeenth and Eighteenth Centuries," *French History* 1 (1987): 191–92; Lachiver, *Années de misère,* 365; Y15496, registre des enfants trouvés.

5. Lachiver, *Années de misère,* 352, 377; Chaunu, *La mort à Paris,* 186.

6. *Pierre Prion,* 129.

7. Georges Dethan, *Paris au temps de Louis XIV* (Paris, 1990), 151; Chaunu, *La mort à Paris,* 186. Kaplow, *Names of Kings,* 86–87. One of the best surveys of disease and mortality in eighteenth-century France is John McManners, *Death and the Enlightenment* (Oxford, 1981), ch. 1.

8. Bastille 10201, mémoire concernant l'état de la paroisse St-Médard (1743); Leon Bernard, *The Emerging City: Paris in the Age of Louis XIV* (Durham, N.C., 1970), 137.

9. Kaplow, *Names of Kings,* 32.

10. Roche, "Pauper Capital," 189–90; Daniel Roche, *The Culture of Clothing: Dress and Fashion in the 'ancien régime,'* trans. Jean Birrel (Cambridge, 1994), 78–82.

11. Ernest Labrousse, *Esquisse du mouvement des prix et des revenues en France au XVIIIe siècle* (Paris,1984), 2:598–99; Roche, *People of Paris,* 84, 107–10; Johan Söderberg, "Real Wage Trends in Urban Europe, 1730–1850:

Stockholm in a Comparative Perspective," *Social History* 12 (1987): 155–76 ; Roche, "Pauper Capital," 190.

12. Olwen Hufton, *The Poor of Eighteenth-Century France, 1750–1789* (Oxford, 1974), 22.

13. Y10993A, 26 January 1750.

14. Y12557, 24 April 1709.

15. Anne-Amable Augier du Fot, mémoire to intendant of Soissons (1773), quoted in Jacques Gélis, *History of Childbirth: Fertility, Pregnancy, and Birth in Early Modern Europe,* trans. Rosemary Morris (Boston, 1991), 232.

16. Lachiver, *Années de misère,* 41–42; and Marcel Lachiver, *Vins, vignes et vignerons: histoire du vignoble français* (Paris, 1988), 340.

17. Y11239, 6 March 1752; Ménétra, *Journal of My Life,* 26; Y15418, 14 September 1709; sentence de police, 20 April 1725, in Edme la Poix de Fréminville, *Dictionnaire ou traité de la police générale des villes, bourgs, paroisses et seigneuries de la campagne* (Paris, 1771), 222–24; Nicolas Delamare, *Traité de la police* (Paris, 1705–38), 1:204; Y15350, 11 January 1752.

18. Christian Romon, "Le monde des pauvres à Paris au XVIIIe siècle," *Annales: économies, sociétés, civilisations* 37 (1982): 750.

19. Kaplow, *Names of Kings,* 88; Farge, "Artisans malades"; Hufton, *The Poor,* 67.

20. Roche, *Culture of Clothing,* 95.

21. Benabou, *La prostitution,* 311–12; Hufton, *The Poor,* 115–17.

22. Romon, "Monde des pauvres," 735, 737.

23. McManners, *Death and the Enlightenment,* 18. Contemporary estimates of consumption varied greatly: Kaplan, *Bakers of Paris,* 447–48.

24. Labrousse, *Esquisse,* 2:591, gives the figure of 200 working days a year. Jean-Pierre Bardet suggests 270 in *Rouen aux XVIIe et XVIIIe siècles: les mutations d'un espace social* (Paris, 1983), 260; Roche, *People of Paris,* 109; and idem, *Everyday Things,* 58, 64–67.

25. Guy Antonetti, "La crise économique de 1729–1731 à Paris d'après les règlements de faillites," in *Etudes et documents: comité pour l'histoire économique et financière de la France* (Paris, 1989–), 2:35–181; AD I 23 B, ordinance of 23 June 1716, renewed 8 October 1730; Maurice Garden, *Lyon et les lyonnais au XVIIIe siècle* (Paris, 1975), 230; Barbier, *Journal historique,* 3:13 (March 1747)

26. F7 4774 (93).

27. Y35, fol. 104, 8 July, 1693.

28. E. M. Desbois de Rochefort, *Mémoire sur les calamités de l'hiver, 1788–1789* (Paris, 1789), 7.

29. Y12571, 26 June 1725.

30. Arrêt du Parlement, 7 August 1764, in JF1570, fol. 86.

31. BN 4° Fm 23890, mémoire pour Remy Chapeau, curé de . . . St-Germain-l'Auxerrois, 1761. LL690, fol. 8v°.

32. Mercier, *Tableau de Paris,* 6:20; Marie-José Michel, "Clergé et pastorale jansénistes à Paris (1669–1730)," *Revue d'histoire moderne et contemporaine* 27 (1979): 188.

33. [D. Jousse], *Traité du gouvernement spirituel et temporel des paroisses* (Paris,1769), 402.

34. Bastille 10171, collection of requests addressed to "Mesdames de l'assemblée de la paroisse de St-Séverin" in 1734–36.

35. Règlement de l'assemblée de Charité, établie en la paroisse de St-Laurent (ca. 1709), quoted in Louis Brochard, *Histoire de la paroisse et de l'église St-Laurent à Paris* (Paris, 1923), 367–77.

36. JF 1590, fol. 175.

37. JF 1587, fol. 27, règlement pour la compagnie de Charité de St-Jean-en-Grève (1674). See Roche, "Pauper Capital," 196.

38. LL 836, 27 September 1763. See also Kaplow, *Names of Kings*, 193 n.28.

39. L685, nos. 52–56. H5* 3824, Ste-Marguerite; Bastille 10200, curé to lieutenant général, 27 October 1742; Bastille 10200, mémoire concernant le commissaire des pauvres de St-Médard (1742); Bastille 10201, mémoire concernant le commissaire des pauvres (1743).

40. On the Grand Bureau see François Furet, "Structures sociales parisiennes au XVIIIe siècle: l'apport d'une série fiscale," *Annales: économies, sociétés, civilisations* 16 (1961): 939–58; Kaplow, *Names of Kings*, 93, 98–99; Bernard, *Emerging City*, 140.

41. Jean Imbert, ed., *Histoire des hôpitaux en France* (Toulouse, 1982), 215–16; Romon, "Monde des pauvres," 752–53; Jean Chagniot, *Nouvelle histoire de Paris: Paris au XVIIIe siècle* (Paris, 1988), 401.

42. JF 1588, will of Jean Michelin, 2 May 1785; Bastille 10200, undated and unsigned petition (1741).

43. Curé to [Cardinal Fleury], 2 October (1732); curé to lieutenant general, 1 April 1736; Y13290, 8 November 1788.

44. Jean-Pierre Gutton, "L'enfermement à l'âge classique," in *Histoire des hôpitaux en France*, ed. Jean Imbert (Toulouse, 1982), 182; Kaplow, *Names of Kings*, 63, 162; Roche, "Pauper Capital," 191; Robert Schwartz, *Policing the Poor in Eighteenth-Century France* (Chapel Hill, 1988), 43–44.

45. Romon, "Monde des pauvres," 740–41, 753; Wilhelm, *Vie quotidienne*, 117, 121.

46. Hufton, *The Poor*, 159.

47. Hufton, *The Poor*, 155–57; Lachiver, *Années de misère*, 85–88; Schwartz, *Policing the Poor*, chs. 1, 2; Gutton, "Enfermement à l'âge classique."

48. On changing ideas of poverty see Philippe Sassier, *Du bon usage des pauvres: histoire d'un thème politique (XVIe–XXe siècles)* (Paris, 1990).

49. Hufton, *The Poor*, chs. 3 and 4; Y12596, 24 January 1752.

50. Y12596, 21 April 1752; Y12596, 18 April 1752, witness 1; Y14078, 27 March 1752; Y10994, 8 July 1752.

51. Y11239, 7 March 1752; Arlette Farge, *Délinquance et criminalité: le vol d'aliments à Paris au XVIIIe siècle* (Paris, 1974), 123.

52. Lachiver, *Vins, vignes et vignerons*, 350; Y13290, 5 February 1788.

53. Hufton, *The Poor*, 213–14. Farge, *Délinquance*, 162; Y14078, 27 August 1752.

54. Benabou, *La prostitution*, esp. 187–209, 267–329.

55. Jacques Dupâquier, "Croissance démographique régionale dans le bassin parisien au XVIIIe siècle," in *Hommage à Marcel Reinhard: sur la population française aux XVIIIe et XIXe siècles* (Paris, 1973), 230–50.

56. Roche, *People of Paris,* 75–79.

57. Mercier, *Tableau de Paris,* 3:214.

CHAPTER 3. NOT SERVANTS BUT WORKERS

1. David Garrioch and Michael Sonenscher, "Compagnonnages, Confraternities and Associations of Journeymen in Eighteenth-Century Paris," *European History Quarterly* 16 (1986): 25–45. What follows is taken from this and from Y14391 and Y13751.

2. Lachiver, *Vins, vignes et vignerons,* 351–52; Thomas Brennan, "Beyond the Barriers: Popular Culture and Parisian *Guinguettes,*" *Eighteenth-Century Studies* 18 (1984–85): 154.

3. Kaplan, *Bakers of Paris,* 61–80, 355–56. Sonenscher, *Work and Wages,* 16–17, 378–88.

4. Minard, *Typographes,* 26–27, 97–106, 162–64.

5. Sonenscher, *Work and Wages,* 273–78.

6. Jacques Savary des Bruslons, "Communauté," in *Dictionnaire universel de commerce* (Paris, 1723 ed.); Franklin, *Dictionnaire,* 208, 295.

7. Savary, "Mercier," in *Dictionnaire universel* (1741 ed.).

8. See the illustration in Carolyn Sargentson, *Merchants and Luxury Markets: The Marchands Merciers of Eighteenth-Century Paris* (London, 1996), 14, who also quotes the description.

9. Y11239, 12, 18, 30 October, 23 November 1752; Franklin, *Dictionnaire,* 202; Kaplan, *Fin des corporations,* 241–50.

10. Sargentson, *Merchants and Luxury Markets,* 8, 11; Juratic and Pellegrin, "Femmes, villes et travail," 484; Roche, *Culture of Clothing,* 278, 280; Franklin, *Dictionnaire,* 98, 437, 627, 685; Marcel Reinhard, *Nouvelle histoire de Paris: la Révolution, 1789–1799* (Paris, 1971), 409.

11. Franklin, *Dictionnaire,* 525; Geraldine Sheridan, "Women in the Book Trade in Eighteenth-Century France," *British Journal for Eighteenth-Century Studies* 15 (1992): 57; Kaplan, "Luxury Guilds," 286 and passim; MC XVII 670, 20 January 1732.

12. Steven L. Kaplan, "L'apprentissage à Paris au XVIIIe siècle," *Revue d'histoire moderne et contemporaine* 40 (1993): 449–51.

13. Joseph Di Corcia, "Bourgeois, Bourgeoisie, Bourgeois de Paris from the Eleventh to the Eighteenth Century," *Journal of Modern History* 50 (1978): 207–33; Ménétra, *Journal of My Life,* 208.

14. Fabrice Piwnica, "Les résistances à l'introduction du libéralisme en France: le témoignage des mémoires des corporations en 1776," *Revue d'histoire moderne et contemporaine* 40 (1993): 43; Cynthia Maria Truant, "Parisian Guildswomen and the (Sexual) Politics of Privilege: Defending Their Patrimonies in Print," in *Going Public: Women and Publishing in Early Modern France,* ed. Elizabeth C. Goldsmith and Dena Goodman (Ithaca, 1995), 50; Guyot, *Répertoire universel et raisonné de jurisprudence civile, criminelle, canonique et*

bénéficiale, 2d ed. (Paris, 1776), vol. 24, article "Femme"; *Nouvelle coutume de Paris,* art. 234, in *Nouveau coutumier général,* 3:46.

15. Z1E 307, tax lists of 1738, 1757, 1764. Sabine Juratic, "Les femmes dans la librairie parisienne au XVIIIe siècle," in *L'Europe et le livre: réseaux et pratiques du négoce de librairie, XVIe–XIXe siècles,* ed. Frédéric Barbier et al. (n.p., 1996), 252. "Avis de l'éditeur," *Almanach royal* (1788), ii; Franklin, *Dictionnaire,* 368, 437, 727–28; Savary, *Dictionnaire universel* gives the rules for most trades corporations.

16. Piwnica, "Résistances," 43.

17. Judith Coffin, *The Politics of Women's Work: The Paris Garment Trades, 1750–1915* (Princeton, 1996), 34–35. Kaplan, "Apprentissage," 440; and idem, "Social Classification," 193.

18. Y10994, 16 April 1752; Y15350, 1 May 1752; Kaplan, *Bakers of Paris,* 212, 238, 321; Daniel Roche, "Work, Fellowship, and Some Economic Realities of Eighteenth-Century France," in *Work in France: Representations, Meaning, Organization and Practice,* ed. Steven L. Kaplan and Cynthia J. Koepp (Ithaca, 1986), 73; Mercier, *Tableau de Paris,* 9:173–75.

19. Franklin, *Dictionnaire,* 194–96, 456.

20. Kaplan, "Social Classification"; Gail Bossenga, "Protecting Merchants: Guilds and Commercial Capitalism in Eighteenth Century France," *French Historical Studies* 15, no. 4 (Fall 1988): 693–703; Cissie Fairchilds, "Three Views on the Guilds," *French Historical Studies* 15, no. 4 (Fall 1988): 688–92; Liliane Perez, "Invention, politique, et société en France dans le deuxième moitié du dix-huitième siècle," *Revue d'histoire moderne et contemporaine* 37 (1990): 36–63.

21. Leora Auslander, *Taste and Power: Furnishing Modern France* (Berkeley, 1996), 45, 67–89, 120–21; Cissie Fairchilds, "The Production and Marketing of Populuxe Goods in Eighteenth-Century Paris," in *Consumption and the World of Goods,* ed. John Brewer and Roy Porter (London, 1993), 228–48; Roche, *Everyday Things,* 44–45, 178–81; Sonenscher, *Work and Wages,* 200.

22. Sonenscher, *Work and Wages,* 25, 200; Ménétra, *Journal of My Life,* 239; Piwnica, "Résistances," 43; Fairchilds, "Populuxe Goods," 238.

23. Kaplan, "Corporations"; Alain Thillay, "Le faubourg St-Antoine et la liberté du travail sous l'ancien régime," *Histoire, économie et société* 11 (1992): 217–36; Fairchilds, "Populuxe Goods," 237.

24. Serge Chassagne, *Oberkampf: un entrepreneur capitaliste au siècle des lumières* (Paris, 1980), 10–17; Sonenscher, *Work and Wages,* 216; Kaplan, *Bakers of Paris,* 176–77; Kaplan, *Fin des corporations,* 228–30.

25. Sonenscher, *Work and Wages,* 107; Kaplan, *Bakers of Paris,* 280; Roche, *Culture of Clothing,* 316–17; Clare Crowston, "Engendering the Guilds: Seamstresses, Tailors, and the Clash of Corporate Identities in Old Regime France," *French Historical Studies* 23 (2000): 353; and for other trades, Kaplan, *Fin des corporations,* 215–22.

26. Kaplan, "Corporations."

27. Kaplan, "Luxury Guilds," 274. Fairchilds, "Populuxe Goods," 236, 241.

28. Sonenscher, *Work and Wages,* 208–9, 256–59, 264.

29. Steven L. Kaplan, "La lutte pour le contrôle du marché du travail à Paris

au XVIIIe siècle," *Revue d'histoire moderne et contemporaine* 36 (1989): 363, 387–409.

30. Sonenscher, *Work and Wages,* 138 n.35, 179–82; Daniel Roche, "Jacques-Louis Ménétra, an Eighteenth-Century Way of Life" in *Journal of My Life,* ed. Daniel Roche, trans. Arthur Goldhammer (New York, 1986), 285.

31. Y15099, 6 May, 26 March 1788. Y15117, 29 December 1788; Garrioch and Sonenscher, "Compagnonnages," 29. See also Steven L. Kaplan, "Réflexions sur la police du monde de travail, 1700–1815," *Revue historique* 261 (1979): 65–66.

32. Kaplan, "Contrôle du marché," 363.

33. Ibid., 365, 367; Garrioch and Sonenscher, "Compagnonnages," 26.

34. Sonenscher, *Work and Wages,* 70–98; Kaplan, *Fin des corporations,* 299–303.

35. Audigier, *La maison réglée* (1700), quoted in Kaplan, "Apprentissage," 446. More generally, see 437–48.

36. Ibid., 446; Minard, *Typographes,* 77–81, 101, 147–57; Roche, "Ménétra," 293–94. See also Auslander, *Taste and Power,* 122–29.

37. Garrioch and Sonenscher, "Compagnonnages," 28–29; Cynthia M. Truant, *The Rites of Labor: Brotherhoods of Compagnonnage in Old and New Regime France* (Ithaca, 1994), 110; Kaplan, "Réflexions," 59.

38. Garrioch, *Parisian Bourgeoisie,* 97.

39. Groppi, "Travail des femmes"; Farge, "Artisans malades," 997; Dominique Godineau, *Citoyennes tricoteuses: les femmes du peuple à Paris pendant la Révolution française* (Aix-en-Provence, 1988), 71–78; Y12596, 7 April 1752; Y12597, 15 November 1752.

40. Bastille 10321.

41. Sonenscher, *Work and Wages,* 97.

42. See Truant, "Independent and Insolent."

43. Hans-Ulrich Thamer, " 'L'art du menuisier': Work Practices of French Joiners and Cabinet-makers in the Eighteenth Century," *Mélanges de l'école française de Rome* 99 (1987): 1045.

44. Sonenscher, *Work and Wages,* 97.

45. Ibid., 332. See also Kaplan, "Contrôle du marché," 381.

46. Sonenscher, *Work and Wages,* 35, 87.

47. Y15364, 17 September 1741; Sonenscher, *Work and Wages,* 90; Kaplan, "Luxury Guilds," 289.

48. Sonenscher, *Hatters,* 44; Kaplan, "Luxury Guilds," 258; Nicolas Contat, *Anecdotes typographiques, où l'on voit la description des coutumes, moeurs et usages singuliers des compagnons imprimeurs* (1762), ed. Giles Barber (Oxford, 1980).

49. Ménétra, *Journal of My Life,* 213; Bastille 12202, 21 December 1764; Sonenscher, *Work and Wages,* 142, 179.

50. Y14560, 13 September 1755.

51. Savary, "Cordonniers," in *Dictionnaire universel* (1723 ed.); Kaplan, "Luxury Guilds," 258; Sonenscher, *Work and Wages,* 26.

52. Malesherbes, *Mémoires sur la librairie* (1759), quoted in Jean-Marc Chatelain, "Famille et librairie dans la France du XVIIIe siècle" in *L'Europe et*

le livre: réseaux pratiques du négoce de librairie, XVIe–XIXe siècles, ed. Frédéric Barbier et al. (n.p., 1996), 230.

53. Minard, *Typographes,* 172. In 1749 half the masters who married had fathers living in Paris but only about one-eighth of the journeymen who married did: François Furet and Adeline Daumard, *Structures et relations sociales à Paris au milieu du XVIIIe siècle* (Paris, 1961), 63.

54. Garrioch and Sonenscher, "Compagnonnages," 37.

55. See, for example, Y14436, 6 February 1788.

56. Di Corcia, "Bourgeois, Bourgeoisie, Bourgeois de Paris," 230.

57. Kaplan, *Bakers of Paris,* 190–91.

CHAPTER 4. EACH ACCORDING TO HIS STATION

1. This account is taken from René Pomeau, *D'Arouet à Voltaire, 1694–1734* (Oxford, 1985), 203–7.

2. *Journal et mémoires du marquis d'Argenson, publiés pour la première fois d'après les manuscrits de la Bibliothèque du Louvre pour la Société de l'Histoire de France,* ed. E. J. B. Rathery (1859–67; New York, 1968), 1:55.

3. Reinhard, *Nouvelle histoire de Paris,* 32; Chagniot, *Paris au XVIIIe siècle,* 330; Roland Mousnier, *Les institutions de la France sous la monarchie absolue: 1598–1789* (Paris, 1974), 1:125; Roche, *Culture of Clothing,* 77; Marraud, *Noblesse de Paris,* 31–32.

4. François Bluche, *La noblesse française au XVIIIe siècle,* 2d ed. (Paris, 1995), 34; Frédéric Grendel, *Beaumarchais: The Man Who Was Figaro* (New York, 1977), 22.

5. Yves Durand, *Les fermiers généraux au XVIIIe siècle* (Paris, 1996), 316–17. For the legal definitions and rights of nobles see Marcel Marion, "Noblesse," in *Dictionnaire des institutions de la France aux XVIIe et XVIIIe siècles* (Paris, 1923); and Mousnier, *Institutions de la France,* 1:94–187.

6. *Saint-Simon at Versailles,* ed. and trans. Lucy Norton (1958; Harmondsworth, 1985).

7. Franklin L. Ford, *Robe and Sword: The Regrouping of the French Aristocracy after Louis XIV* (New York, 1965); Robert Forster, *The House of Saulx-Tavanes: Versailles and Burgundy, 1700–1830* (Baltimore, 1971); Guy Chaussinand-Nogaret, *La noblesse au XVIIIe siècle* (Brussels, 1984); Bluche, *Magistrats du Parlement,* 43–50, 233–50; Durand, *Fermiers généraux,* 197–250, 551–74. For the view that magistrates were an entirely separate group, see Andrews, *System of Criminal Justice.*

8. Charles Philippe d'Albert, duc de Luynes, *Mémoires du duc de Luynes sur la cour de Louis XV (1735–1758),* ed. J. Dussieux and E. Soulié (Paris, 1860–65), 9:429; Jean Nagle, *Luxe et charité: le faubourg St-Germain et l'argent* (Paris, 1984), 109.

9. Chaussinand-Nogaret, *Noblesse,* 77.

10. Bluche, *Magistrats du Parlement,* 108–9.

11. Nagle, *Luxe et charité,* 108; Bluche, *Noblesse française,* 17–18; Chaussinand-Nogaret, *Noblesse,* 77–87. For the gap between noble wealth and merchant wealth see Furet and Daumard, *Structures et relations sociales.*

12. Harold A. Ellis, *Boulainvilliers and the French Monarchy: Aristocratic Politics in Early-Eighteenth-Century France* (Ithaca, 1988), 20; for a fuller explanation of this idea of race, see Smith, *Culture of Merit,* ch. 2.

13. Chassepot de Beaumont (n.d.), quoted in Bluche, *Magistrats du Parlement,* 202.

14. Chaussinand-Nogaret, *Noblesse,* 53; Bluche, *Noblesse française,* 24–26; Smith, *Culture of Merit,* chs. 1, 2; Jean-François Labourdette, ed., "Conseils à un duc de la Trémoille à son entrée dans le monde," *Enquêtes et documents* (Centre de recherches sur l'histoire de la France Atlantique, Université de Nantes) 2 (1972): 167; Thomas M. Kavanagh, *Enlightenment and the Shadows of Chance: The Novel and the Culture of Gambling in Eighteenth-Century France* (Baltimore, 1993), 41–42. See also Ellis, *Boulainvilliers,* 19–30.

15. Chaussinand-Nogaret, *Noblesse,* 98–102; Bluche, *Magistrats du Parlement,* 188–90. Mark Motley, *Becoming a French Aristocrat: The Education of the Court Nobility 1580–1715* (Princeton, 1990), 98–122; Micheline Cuénin, *Le duel sous l'Ancien Régime* (Paris, 1982), 256.

16. La Rochefoucauld, quoted in Nagle, *Luxe et charité,* 103; Bluche, *Noblesse française,* 43.

17. Chaussinand-Nogaret, *Noblesse,* 96–97. See the example of the duchesse de La Trémoille: Labourdette, "Conseils à un duc de la Trémoille," esp. 93–99.

18. On women courtiers, Bonnie S. Anderson and Judith P. Zinsser, *A History of Their Own: Women in Europe from Prehistory to the Present,* rev. ed. (New York, 2000), 2:12–14; Bluche, *Magistrats du Parlement,* 261.

19. Marraud, *Noblesse de Paris,* 456.

20. Quoted in Bluche, *Noblesse française,* 47.

21. Charles Duclos, *Considérations sur les moeurs de ce siècle,* 7th ed. (1751; Paris, 1780), 136.

22. Sarah Maza, *Servants and Masters in Eighteenth-Century France: The Uses of Loyalty* (Princeton, 1983), 205, 208–11; Daniel Roche, "Recherches sur la noblesse parisienne au milieu du XVIIIe siècle: la noblesse du Marais," *Actes du 86e congrès national des sociétés savantes, Montpellier, 1961* (Paris 1962), 565; Jacqueline Sabattier, *Figaro et son maître: maîtres et domestiques à Paris au XVIIIe siècle* (Paris, 1984), 29. On noble consumption in general, Natacha Coquery, *L'hôtel aristocratique: le marché du luxe à Paris au XVIIIe siècle* (Paris, 1998).

23. Roche, *Culture of Clothing,* 130.

24. Ibid., 95–96.

25. Ibid., 59, 130–31; Bluche, *Magistrats du Parlement,* 284.

26. Pardailhé-Galabrun, *Birth of Intimacy,* 141–42, 149–50, 301. Cf. Durand, *Fermiers généraux,* 498–527.

27. Françoise Boudon, André Chastel, Hélène Couzy, Françoise Hamon, *Système de l'architecture urbain: le quartier des Halles à Paris* (Paris, 1977), 1:229–34; vol. 2, plate 25.

28. Forster, *House of Saulx-Tavanes,* 118.

29. Nagle, *Luxe et charité,* 38; Andrews, *System of Criminal Justice,* 102; Chaussinand-Nogaret, *Noblesse,* ch. 5; Kavanagh, *Enlightenment and the Shadows of Chance,* 49–50.

30. Forster, *House of Saulx-Tavanes,* 204–5; Marraud, *Noblesse de Paris,* 84–97; on Helvétius, Jean de Viguerie, *Histoire et dictionnaire du temps des lumières* (Paris, 1995), 1032.

31. Ibid., 40; Robert Darnton, "Peasants Tell Tales," in *The Great Cat Massacre and Other Episodes in French Cultural History* (London, 1984), 11, 62–63.

32. Bluche, *Magistrats du Parlement,* 155–58; Sabattier, *Figaro et son maître,* 108–10.

33. Nagle, *Luxe et charité,* 46.

34. Chagniot, *Paris au XVIIIe siècle,* 321; Coquery, *Hôtel aristocratique,* 217–27.

35. Daniel Roche, "Recherches sur la noblesse parisienne," 555; Bluche, *Magistrats du Parlement,* 130, 304–6.

36. Marc Chassaigne, *La lieutenance générale de police de Paris* (Paris, 1906), 53–77; Andrews, *System of Criminal Justice,* 92, 148–49; Alan Williams, *The Police of Paris 1718–1789* (Baton Rouge, 1979).

37. *Almanach royal.*

38. Anne Muratori-Philip, *Parmentier* (Paris, 1994), 48.

39. Maarten Ultee, *The Abbey of Saint-Germain-des-Prés in the Seventeenth Century* (New Haven, 1981), 176–80; Brochard, *St-Laurent,* 101 n.1; JF 1570, fol. 107.

40. Chagniot, *Paris au XVIIIe siècle,* 38; Chassagne, *Oberkampf,* 14.

41. *Correspondance complète de Jean Jacques Rousseau,* ed. R. A. Leigh (Oxford, 1965–91), vol. 28, letters 4903–7; Chagniot, *Paris au XVIIIe siècle,* 38.

42. Kaplan, "Corporations," 356–57; Alain Thillay,"L'économie du bas au faubourg St-Antoine (1656–1776)," *Histoire, économie et société* 17 (1998): 683–84; H. M. Delsart, *La dernière abbesse de Montmartre: Marie-Louise de Montmorency-Laval, 1723–1794* (Paris, 1921), 24.

43. Bernard Plongeron et al., *Le diocèse de Paris,* vol. 1, *Des origines à la Révolution* (Paris, 1987), 334–35.

44. LL690, register of St-André-des-Arts; LL932, register of St-Séverin.

45. LL794, register of St-Jacques-du-Haut-Pas, fol. 375; on Maboul, Daniel Roche, "Censorship and the Publishing Industry," in *Revolution in Print: The Press in France, 1775–1800,* ed. Robert Darnton and Daniel Roche (Berkeley, 1989), 7.

46. LL863, deliberations of St-Nicolas-des-Champs, 1682–1746, fols. 77v, 95v, 109v, 134, 253.

47. *Mémoires de Madame Roland,* ed. Cl. Perroud (Paris, 1905), 2:1 n. 1; Jean-Dominique Augarde, "Noël Gérard (1685–1736) et le Magasin général à l'hôtel Jabach," in *Luxury Trades and Consumerism in Ancien Régime Paris: Studies in the History of the Skilled Workforce,* ed. Robert Fox and Anthony Turner (Aldershot, 1998), 72; l'abbé Baloche, *Eglise St-Merry de Paris: histoire de la paroisse et de la collégiale* (Paris, 1911), 1:427.

48. Coquery, *L'hôtel aristocratique,* 32; Bluche, *Magistrats du Parlement,* 262–63.

49. Viguerie, *Histoire et dictionnaire,* 1083. Natacha Coquery, "Les hôtels parisiens du XVIIIe siècle" *Revue d'histoire moderne et contemporaine* 38 (1991): 215–16.

50. Quoted in Francis Steegmuller, *A Woman, a Man, and Two Kingdoms: The Story of Madame d'Epinay and the Abbé Galiani* (Princeton, 1991), 70.

51. Viguerie, *Histoire et dictionnaire,* 142, 1216; Barbara G. Mittman, "Women and the Theatre Arts," in *French Women and the Age of Enlightenment,* ed. Samia I. Spencer (Bloomington, 1984), 157.

52. Paolo Piasenza, *Polizia e città: strategie d'ordine, conflitti e rivolte a Parigi tra Sei e Settecento* (Bologna, 1990), 45, 67.

53. Ibid., 84–85.

54. Daniel Roche, "Les lectures de la noblesse dans la France du XVIIIe siècle," in *Les républicains des lettres: gens de culture et lumières au XVIIIe siècle* (Paris, 1988), 85, 90, 92–93, 96–97; Roger Chartier, *The Cultural Uses of Print in Early Modern France,* trans. Lydia G. Cochrane (Princeton, 1987), 192–94, 201, 204–5.

55. Chaussinand-Nogaret, *Noblesse,* 103–5.

56. Maza, *Servants and Masters,* chs. 6, 7, esp. 264–65, 317; Fairchilds, *Domestic Enemies,* 153–59.

57. Forster, *House of Saulx-Tavanes,* 130; Coquery, *Hôtel aristocratique,* 173.

58. Nougaret, *La paysanne pervertie* (1777), quoted in Simon Davies, *Paris and the Provinces in Prose Fiction,* Studies on Voltaire and the Eighteenth Century (Oxford, 1982), 214:37; D. Campan, *Le mot et la chose* (1752), quoted in ibid., 19; Durand, *Fermiers généraux,* 551–52; Chagniot, *Paris au XVIIIe siècle,* 372–74.

59. Roche, *Everyday Things,* 113–14.

60. Chagniot, *Paris au XVIIIe siècle,* 14, 406–15.

61. Isherwood, *Farce and Fantasy,* esp. ch. 8.

62. Maza, *Servants and Masters,* 214–15.

63. Elie Barnavi and Robert Descimon, *La Sainte-Ligue, le juge et la potence: l'assassinat du président Brisson, 15 novembre 1591* (Paris, 1985), 15.

64. Marraud, *Noblesse de Paris,* 106–18; S7493, dossier St-Gervais.

65. Duclos, *Considérations sur les moeurs,* 130.

66. Bibliothèque Thiers, ms Masson 211, fol. 157.

67. Joseph di Corcia, "*Bourg, Bourgeois, Bourgeois de Paris* from the Eleventh to the Eighteenth Century," *Journal of Modern History* 50 (1978): 207–33. See also Robert Descimon, " 'Bourgeois de Paris': les migrations sociales d'un privilège," in *Histoire globale: histoire sociale: actes du colloque des 27–28 janvier 1989,* ed. Christophe Charle (Paris, 1993).

68. Jean Buvat, *Journal de la Régence (1715–1723),* ed. Emile Campardon (Paris, 1865), 2:78.

69. See the discussion of the term in Piasenza, *Polizia e città,* 59–61.

70. Reinhard, *Nouvelle histoire de Paris,* 41.

71. Jean-Jacques Expilly, *Dictionnaire géographique, historique et politique des Gaules et de la France* (Amsterdam, 1762–70), 5:450–61, 560; Philippe Minard, *La fortune du Colbertisme: état et industrie dans la France des lumières* (Paris, 1998), 30; Brockliss, *French Higher Education,* 18.

72. Toby Gelfand, *Professionalizing Modern Medicine: Paris Surgeons and Medical Science and Institutions in the Eighteenth Century* (Westport, Conn., 1980), 55.

73. Daumard and Furet, *Structures et relations sociales,* 30–31; Pardailhé-Galabrun, *Naissance de l'intime,* 199, 242, 464.

74. Roche, *Culture of Clothing,* 102–6, 124, 131–32.

75. Y13622, Register of elections for street lighting, Faubourg St-Germain; Y11963, election of syndic on Quai de Gesvres, 6 July 1775. On the Bièvre administration, Z1E 307–8. For the fairs, *Mémoires des intendants sur l'état des généralités,* vol. 1, *Mémoire de la généralité de Paris* (Paris, 1881), 673 n.1; BN f° Fm 15067 for the "syndics des propriétaires des grandes halles, loges, boutiques et préau de la foire St-Germain-des-Prés" against the abbot of St-Germain, 1694; JF 1869, fol.78, *Mémoire pour les syndics en charge, anciens syndics et adjoints des propriétaires de la foire St-Germain . . . contre . . . les administrateurs de l'hôpital des Cent Filles* (Paris, 1766).

76. Bell, *Lawyers and Citizens,* 120.

77. Y13377, petition from Jeanne Ménage, n.d. (1752); Bastille 11040, doss. Catherine and Marie Anne Bouillerot, 1729.

78. JF 1487, fol. 244; Y12424, 15 November 1753.

79. Garrioch, *Parisian Bourgeoisie,* 45; Michel, "Clergé et pastorale jansénistes."

80. JF 1570, fols. 86–87.

81. René Taveneaux, *La vie quotidienne des jansénistes* (Paris,1973), 131; Louis Brochard, *St Gervais: histoire de la paroisse* (Paris, [1950]), 296. On St-André, LL690, fol. 9 (2 February 1742) and JF1567, fol. 2; Laurence H. Winnie, *Family Dynasty, Revolutionary Society: The Cochins of Paris, 1750–1922* (Westport, Conn., 2002), 83; see also Roche, "Pauper Capital," 196.

82. Bell, *Lawyers and Citizens,* 28–29.

83. Catherine Junges, "Les échevins de Paris au XVIIIe siècle," in *Positions des thèses de l'Ecole des Chartes, 1996* (Paris, 1996), 165.

84. Pardailhé-Galabrun, *Naissance de l'intime,* 465. Very similar figures are given by Camille Pascal for the St-Martin quarter: "Politique immobilière et esprit de quartier: l'exemple de St-Martin-des-Champs au XVIIIe siècle," *Les quartiers de Paris du moyen âge au début du XXe siècle, Cahiers du CREPIF,* no. 38 (March 1992): 83–84.

85. S*1637, fol. 561bis and S*1668, fol. 551. S*1637, fol. 571 and S*1641, rue Censier no. 16

86. Junges, "Echevins," 169.

87. JF 1568, fol. 262, mémoire pour Louis Charton (ca. 1728).

88. Chassepot de Beaumont, n.d. (before 1724), quoted in Bluche, *Magistrats du Parlement,* 213.

89. Miscellaneous notes in the back of a manuscript entitled "Réglemens et usages de la maison," 1782, fol. 865. Bibliothèque de Port-Royal.

90. Roche, *Culture of Clothing,* 106–7, 120–34.

91. Pierre-Thomas Hurtaut and P. N. Magny, "Luxe," in *Dictionnaire historique de la ville de Paris et de ses environs* (Paris, 1779).

92. Roche, *Culture of Clothing,* 133–34.

93. Chaussinand-Nogaret, *Noblesse,* 41–57.

94. The classic study is Edgar Faure, *La banqueroute de Law: 17 juillet 1720* (Paris, 1977); see also Roche, *France in the Enlightenment,* 459–60.

95. Gelfand, *Professionalizing Modern Medicine,* esp. 57–93.

96. Brockliss and Jones, *Medical World,* ch. 9; Bell, *Lawyers and Citizens,* esp. 51–66; Roger Chartier, Dominique Julia, and Marie-Madeleine Compère, *L'éducation en France du XVIe au XVIIIe siècles* (Paris, 1976), 278; Antoine Picon, *French Architects and Engineers in the Age of Enlightenment,* trans. Michael Thom (Cambridge, 1992), 31–34; Bénédicte Dehillerin and Jean-Pierre Goubert, "A la conquête du monopole pharmaceutique: le collège de Pharmacie de Paris (1777–1796)," *Historical Reflections/Réflexions historiques* (special number *La médicalisation de la société française, 1770–1830,* ed. Jean-Pierre Goubert) 9 (1982): 233–48; Colin Jones, "Pulling Teeth in Eighteenth-Century Paris," *Past and Present* 166 (May 2000): 136.

97. Albert Babeau, *Paris en 1789* (Paris, 1889), 218; Didier Masseau, *L'invention de l'intellectuel dans l'Europe du XVIIIe siècle* (Paris, 1994), 87–111; William Doyle, *Venality: The Sale of Offices in Eighteenth-Century France* (Oxford, 1996), 223–27.

CHAPTER 5. BREAD, POLICE, AND PROTEST

1. The source for this and what follows is the testimonies in Y12571 and Y10033; and Steven L Kaplan, "The Paris Bread Riot of 1725," *French Historical Studies* 14 (1985): 23–56.

2. Kaplan, "Paris Bread Riot," 32.

3. Ibid., 50.

4. Steven L. Kaplan, "The Famine Plot Persuasion in Eighteenth-Century France," *Transactions of the American Philosophical Society* 72 (1982): 5–7.

5. *Pierre Prion,* 128. A *muid* was approximately 270 litres. In about 1700, according to Lachiver, Paris consumed roughly 220,000 *muids* of wine each year: *Vins, vignes et vignerons,* 287.

6. Roche, *France in the Enlightenment,* 624–26; Mercier, *Tableau de Paris,* 2:303, 305; Y 11239, 20 May, 24 June 1752; Ultee, *St. Germain des Prés,* 16–120; Martin Lister, *A Journey to Paris in the Year 1698,* ed. R. Stearns (Urbana, 1967), 152–55.

7. Barbara Wheaton, *Savoring the Past: The French Kitchen and Table from 1300 to 1789* (Philadelphia, 1983), 80.

8. Roche, *France in the Enlightenment,* 625; Wheaton, *Savoring the Past,* 78–79.

9. Lachiver, *Vins, vignes et vignerons,* 322–23, 351.

10. Alexandra Michell, "The Paris Food Industry in the Eighteenth Century" (Ph.D. thesis, Monash University, 1999); Roche, *France in the Enlightenment,* 627–28.

11. Kaplan, *Bakers of Paris,* 24–45; Jean-Marc Moriceau, *Les fermiers de l'Ile-de-France: l'ascension d'un patronat agricole, XVe–XVIIIe siècles* (Paris, 1994), 464; Kaplan, *Provisioning Paris,* 88–91; Bernard, *Emerging City,* 237–38.

12. Richard Cobb, *Les armeés revolutionnaires: instrument de la Terreur dans les départements, avril 1793–floréal an II* (Paris, 1961–63), 2:370–81.

13. Kaplan, *Provisioning Paris,* 222, 232, 299, 339–41; Delamare, *Traité de la police,* 2:627.

14. Kaplan, *Provisioning Paris,* 66–79; Y11239, 17 July 1752; Boudon, "Salubrité," 177.

15. Mercier, *Tableau,* 7:146–47.

16. Steven L. Kaplan, *Bread, Politics and Political Economy in the Reign of Louis XV* (The Hague, 1976), 1:56 (my translation here).

17. Ibid., ch. 2.

18. Kaplan, "Famine Plot Persuasion," 14; Fréminville, *Dictionnaire,* 104–5.

19. Savary, "Cordonniers," in *Dictionnaire universel* (1723 ed.); Y11239, 18 and 30 October, 23 and 29 November 1752.

20. Kaplan, *Bakers of Paris,* 472.

21. This and what follows is taken from Kaplan, "Famine Plot Persuasion."

22. Williams, *Police of Paris,* 165, 175–85; Steven L. Kaplan, "Lean Years, Fat Years: The 'Community' Granary System and the Search for Abundance in Eighteenth-Century Paris," *French Historical Studies* 10 (1977–78): 197–230.

23. *Almanach royal,* 1725, 1730.

24. Paul Bairoch, *Cities and Economic Development: From the Dawn of History to the Present* (Chicago, 1988), 141; Jacques Dupâquier, ed., *Histoire de la population française* (Paris, 1988), 2:94.

25. Z1F 946

26. Roche, *People of Paris,* 15.

27. Mousnier, *Institutions de la France,* 1:451, 454–55; K996, elections of municipality. On the older history of this system see Barbara B. Diefendorf, *Paris City Councilors in the Sixteenth Century: The Politics of Patrimony* (Princeton, 1983), esp. ch. 1.

28. Vincent Milliot, "La surveillance des migrants et des lieux d'accueil à Paris du XVIe siècle aux années 1830," in *La ville promise: mobilités et accueil à Paris (fin XVIIe–début XIXe siècles),* ed. Daniel Roche (Paris, 2000), 32.

29. Mousnier, *Institutions de la France,* 1:451; Robert Descimon, "Milice bourgeoise et identité citadine à Paris au temps de la Ligue," *Annales: économies, sociétés, civilisations* 48 (1993): 885–906.

30. Piasenza, *Polizia e città,* 56.

31. Georges Picot, "Recherches sur les quartiniers, cinquanteniers et dixainiers de la ville de Paris," *Mémoires de la société de l'histoire de Paris et de l'Ile-de-France* 1 (1875): 132–66; Piasenza, *Polizia e città,* 169; Descimon, "Milice bourgeoise"; and Robert Descimon, "Paris on the Eve of Saint Bartholomew: Taxation, Privilege and Social Geography," in *Cities and Social Change in Early Modern France,* ed. Philip Benedict (London, 1989), 69–104.

32. Williams, *Police of Paris,* 25–28; Bernard, *Emerging City;* and esp. Chassaigne, *Lieutenance générale,* 35–45.

33. Yves-Noël Genty, *Le domaine de la ville de Paris au XVIIIe siècle* (Paris, 1986), 24–25; Isabelle Backouche, *La trace du fleuve: la Seine et Paris (1750–1850)* (Paris, 2000).

34. Buvat, *Journal de la Régence,* 2:208 (February 1721); Babeau, *Paris en 1789,* 293–94; Alfred Franklin, *La vie privée d'autrefois: arts et métiers, modes,*

moeurs, usages des parisiens du XIIe au XVIIIe siècle, 2d series: *La vie de Paris sous Louis XV: devant les tribunaux* (Paris, 1899), 23.

35. Descimon, "Corps de ville et les élections," 521; Roche, *People of Paris,* 83; Babeau, *Paris en 1789,* 286–95.

36. K996, no. 25 (5 August 1777).

37. Babeau, *Paris en 1789,* 290–92. See also Barbier, *Journal historique* 3:94–98 (August 1749), 3:160–61 (August 1750).

38. K996, K997.

39. BN ms fr. 11356, 22 August 1737; Y11741, 5 August 1744.

40. Bernard, *Emerging City,* 156–62; Chagniot, *Paris au XVIIIe siècle,* 422.

41. Piasenza, *Polizia e città,* 101–17, 157–68; and Paolo Piasenza, "Opinion publique, identité des institutions, 'absolutisme': le problème de la légalité à Paris entre le XVIIe et XVIIIe siècles," *Revue historique* 290 (1993): 97–142, see 116.

42. Chassaigne, *Lieutenance générale,* 210–31; Williams, *Police of Paris,* 94–104; Francis Freundlich, *Le monde du jeu à Paris: 1715–1800* (Paris, 1995), 57–62; Piasenza, "Opinion publique," 120–33.

43. Piasenza, "Opinion publique," esp. 121–22; and Paolo Piasenza, "Juges, lieutenants de police et bourgeois à Paris au XVIIe et XVIIIe siècles," *Annales: économies, sociétés, civilisations* 45 (1990): 1189–1215; Williams, *Police of Paris,* 94–95.

44. Auguste-Philippe Herlaut, *Le recrutement de la milice à Paris en 1743* (Coulommiers, 1921), 27.

45. Ménétra, *Journal of My Life,* 21–22.

46. The commissaire's account is in Y13756, 23 May 1750; Arlette Farge and Jacques Revel, *The Rules of Rebellion: Child Abductions in Paris in 1750,* trans. Claudia Miéville (Cambridge, 1991); Piasenza, *Polizia e città,* 7–41.

47. Piasenza, *Polizia e città,* 29–30.

48. Ibid, 28.

49. Plongeron et al., *Diocèse de Paris,* 257; Chaunu, *La mort à Paris,* 209.

50. JF 1570, fol. 98; Mercier, *Tableau de Paris,* 7:131.

51. Y10852, 25 January 1742; Kaplan, *Bakers of Paris,* 625 n.70; Y15418, 14 September 1709; Martine Sonnet, *L'éducation des filles au temps des lumières* (Paris, 1987), 82.

52. Quoted in Sonnet, *Education des filles,* 267.

53. Mercier, *Tableau de Paris,* 3:143; Garrioch, *Neighbourhood and Community,* 60–61.

54. Garrioch, *Neighbourhood and Community,* 59.

55. Kaplan, "L'apprentissage," 440, 454–55; Roche, *Culture of Clothing,* 316.

56. Roche, *France in the Enlightenment,* 61.

57. APP, Fonds Lamoignon, ordonnance du bureau de la Ville, 7 July 1749; Ménétra, *Journal of My Life,* 22–26.

58. Piasenza, *Polizia e città,* 34; Garrioch, *Neighbourhood and Community,* 62.

59. See Jean Chagniot, "Le guet et la garde de Paris à la fin de l'Ancien Régime," *Revue d'histoire moderne et contemporaine* 20 (1973): 58–71; and idem, *Paris et l'armée au XVIIIe siècle: étude politique et sociale* (Paris, 1985), 135–44; David Garrioch, "The People of Paris and Their Police in the Eighteenth Century: Reflec-

tions on the Introduction of a 'Modern' Police Force," *European History Quarterly* 24 (1994): 511–35.

60. Piasenza, *Polizia e città,* 21.

61. AD I 23 B, 9 August 1698; Y15350, 18 January 1752.

62. Y15350, 18 January 1752

63. Y10994, 1 June 1752.

64. Steven L. Kaplan, "Note sur les commissaires de police de Paris au XVIIIe siècle," *Revue d'histoire moderne et contemporaine* 28 (1981): 669–86; Arlette Farge, *Vivre dans la rue à Paris au XVIIIe siècle* (Paris, 1979); Garrioch, "The People of Paris and Their Police."

65. Kaplan, *Bakers of Paris,* 11–13.

CHAPTER 6. WOLVES IN SHEEP'S CLOTHING

1. On Pâris see B. Robert Kreiser, *Miracles, Convulsions, and Ecclesiastical Politics in Early-Eighteenth-Century Paris* (Princeton, 1978), 82–91.

2. Arsenal ms 10196; JF 1566, fols. 1–7; Kreiser, *Miracles,* 91–100, 149.

3. Kreiser, *Miracles,* 78.

4. The best general introduction is Dale Van Kley, *The Religious Origins of the French Revolution* (New Haven, 1996), 58–74. On seventeenth-century Jansenism see Robin Briggs, *Early Modern France* (Oxford, 1977), and for more detail Alexander Sedgwick, *Jansenism in Seventeenth-Century France: Voices from the Wilderness* (Charlottesville, 1977).

5. Michel, "Clergé et pastorale jansénistes," 196; also Monique Cottret, "Aux origines du républicanisme janséniste: le mythe de l'église primitive et le primitivisme des lumières," *Revue d'histoire moderne et contemporaine* 31 (1984): 107–9.

6. John McManners, "Jansenism and Politics in the Eighteenth Century," in *Church, Society and Politics: Papers Read at the Thirteenth Summer Meeting and the Fourteenth Winter Meeting of the Ecclesiastical History Society,* ed. D. Baker (Oxford, 1975), 259; Catherine-Laurence Maire, *Les convulsionnaires de St-Médard: miracles, convulsions et prophéties à Paris au XVIIIe siècle* (Paris, 1985), 36–37, 42; Elisabeth Labrousse and Robert Sauzet, "Au temps du Roi Soleil" in *Histoire de la France religieuse,* ed. Jacques Le Goff and René Rémond, vol. 2, *Du christianisme flamboyant à l'aube des lumières,* ed. François Lebrun (Paris, 1988), 531.

7. On this and what follows see, in English, Van Kley, *Religious Origins,* 85–100; Kreiser, *Miracles,* chs. 1–5; and Jeffrey Merrick, *The Desacralization of the French Monarchy in the Eighteenth Century* (Baton Rouge, 1990), 49–69; Catherine [-Laurence] Maire, *De la cause de Dieu à la cause de la nation* (Paris, 1998).

8. Campbell, *Power and Politics,* 222–74.

9. Andrews, *System of Criminal Justice,* 28, 29; Sonenscher, *Work and Wages,* 88–89.

10. Bluche, *Magistrats du Parlement,* 101–11.

11. Bluche, *Magistrats du Parlement,* 210; Y13728, letter of 9 February 1764.

12. Bluche, *Magistrats du Parlement,* 207–8, 213.

13. Bastille 10201, mémoire on events at St-Médard after 1732 (ca. 1740).

14. Maza, *Private Lives,* 45–50, 99–102.

15. Maire, *Convulsionnaires,* 39–40, 42; François de Dainville, "La carte du jansénisme à Paris en 1739 d'après les papiers de la nonciature," *Bulletin de la société de l'histoire de Paris et de l'Ile-de-France* 96 (1969): 113–24.

16. Labrousse and Sauzet, "Au temps du Roi Soleil," 527; Maire, *Convulsionnaires,* 43.

17. Quoted in Bruno Neveu, *Erudition et religion au XVIIe et XVIIIe siècles* (Paris, 1994), 297.

18. Pierre Goubert and Daniel Roche, *Les français et l'Ancien Régime,* 2d ed. (Paris, 1991), 1:367.

19. Bastille 10171, 22 April 1732.

20. On the curés see Garrioch, *Parisian Bourgeoisie,* 89–90.

21. Bastille 10201, letters of 8 November 1743, 27 January and 29 May 1744.

22. Bastille 10196, Pillerault [exempt de robe courte] to [lieutenant général], n.d. (1730). Bastille 10171, Bouettin to [lieutenant général], 20 March 1744.

23. Brochard, *St-Gervais,* 282.

24. JF 1570, fols. 24, 37, 49; Van Kley, *Religious Origins,* 177–78.

25. Maire, *Convulsionnaires,* 33.

26. Barbier, *Journal historique,* 6:49–50, 52, 59.

27. JF 1570, fols. 44–50; Z1O 233, abrégé des faits et discours de Marie Vilmondel (1761).

28. Bastille 10171, curé of St-Etienne-du-Mont to [lieutenant général], 20 March 1744.

29. Bastille 10197, fol. 302, letter of 16 May 1734; Y13751, 29 September 1746, interrogation 2; d'Argenson, *Journal et mémoires,* vii, 270.

30. Dale Van Kley, *The Damiens Affair and the Unraveling of the Ancien Régime, 1750–1770* (Princeton, 1984), 145–47, 185–90; Arsenal ms 11583, fols. 2–12. Bell, *Lawyers and Citizens,* 73–128.

31. JF 1569 and JF 1587.

32. Bastille 10197, fol. 238, déclaration du curé de St-Médard, 15 April 1733; Bastille 10199, Dame Tirman to [lieutenant général], 23 December 1740.

33. S7493 (St-Germain-le-Vieux); Garrioch, *Parisian Bourgeoisie,* 79; Brochard, *St-Laurent,* 69; and idem, *St-Gervais,* 424–34; LL690.

34. Brochard, *St-Laurent,* 85–88.

35. Garrioch, *Parisian Bourgeoisie,* 48–51.

36. Y13751, 29 September 1746, interrogations 1 and 2.

37. Ibid.

38. Garrioch, *Parisian Bourgeoisie,* ch. 2.

39. Bastille 10171, letter to [archbishop], 19 March 1733; Mathieu Marais, *Journal et mémoires de Mathieu Marais sur la Régence et le règne de Louis XV* (Paris, 1863–68), 4:361; JF 1570, fols. 1–118.

40. Bastille 10197, fol. 282.

41. Brochard, *St-Gervais,* 222–48; BN Fm 23949, *Second mémoire pour les marguilliers en charge, comptable et anciens de l'oeuvre et fabrique de l'église de St-Roch* (1786).

42. Maire, *Convulsionnaires,* 140–49; Kreiser, *Miracles;* Kaplow, *Names of Kings,* 122–26.

43. Quoted in Arlette Farge, *Subversive Words: Public Opinion in Eighteenth-Century France,* trans. Rosemary Morris (Cambridge, 1994), 42.

44. JF 1567, fol. 28; JF 1567, fol. 2.

45. JF 1487, fol. 233; JF 126, fol. 296; JF 1567, fol. 228.

46. John Quincy Adams, *The Diary of John Quincy Adams,* ed. David Grayson Allen et al. (Cambridge, Mass., 1981), 1:227 (February 1785).

47. McManners, *Death and the Enlightenment,* 234–38.

48. Jacqueline Thibaut-Payen, *Les morts, l'église et l'état: recherches d'histoire administrative sur la sépulture et les cimetières dans le ressort du parlement de Paris aux XVIIe et XVIIIe siècles* (Paris, 1977), 130–47, 150; Van Kley, *Damiens Affair,* 155–62; BN ms fr. 6680, fol. 92 (11 April 1766); ms fr. 6681, fol. 291 (15 February 1774). On Villemsens, JF 1570, fol. 24. On Cousin, JF 1487, fols. 233–44.

49. For a detailed account see Van Kley, *Damiens Affair,* ch. 3.

50. D'Argenson, *Journal et mémoires,* 8:35 (19 May 1753).

51. JF 1570, fol. 76, archbishop to procureur général, 27 March 1765.

52. Adrien Friedmann, *Paris, ses rues, ses paroisses du moyen âge à la Révolution* (Paris, 1959), 311; Expilly, *Dictionnaire géographique,* 5:481; Bastille 10171, letter of 1 November 1725.

CHAPTER 7. *AFFAIRES DU TEMPS*

1. Z2 3676.

2. Kaplan, "Religion, Subsistence."

3. Michel Antoine, *Louis XV* (Paris, 1989), 839–40.

4. Z2 3676; Roche, *People of Paris,* 74–78.

5. Farge, *Subversive Words,* 22–26; E. R. Briggs, "Le rôle des sentiments religieux dans la formation de l'esprit philosophique et anti-gouvernemental en 1732, d'après les gazetins secrets de la police parisienne et d'autres inédits," *Lias* 6 (1977): 214; Bastille 10197, police report, 28 July 1733. See also Van Kley, *Religious Origins,* 128–33.

6. Barbier, *Journal historique,* 3:63; d'Argenson, *Journal et mémoires,* 5:362; Van Kley, *Damiens Affair,* 47–48.

7. Van Kley, *Damiens Affair,* 36, 39, 43.

8. Van Kley, *Damiens Affair,* 69, 72, 232, 251. Van Kley, *Religious Origins,* 186–87. See also Farge, *Subversive Words,* 165.

9. Faure, *Banqueroute de Law,* esp. 612–20.

10. Police report, mid-November 1729, in Briggs, "Rôle des sentiments religieux," 214.

11. On the Hôpital général affair see Farge, *Subversive Words,* 48–49; *Nouvelles ecclésiastiques,* 16 January 1755, 9; Dominique Julia, "L'affaiblissement de l'église gallicane" in *Histoire de la France religieuse,* ed. Jacques Le Goff and René Rémond, vol. 3, *Du roi Très Chrétien à la laïcité républicaine,* ed. Philippe Joutard (Paris, 1991), 35; Barbier, *Journal historique,* 4:30 (July 1754).

12. Quoted in Merrick, *Desacralization,* 95.

13. Marc Bloch, *The Royal Touch: Sacred Monarchy and Scrofula in England and France,* trans. J. F. Anderson (London, 1973); Mousnier, *Institutions de la France,* 1:506–10; Rombouts, "Art as Propaganda," 267 n.27; Jacques-Bénigne Bossuet, "Sermon pour le dimanche des rameaux" (1699), quoted in Van Kley, *Religious Origins,* 49; Michel Antoine, "La monarchie absolue," in *The Political Culture of the Old Regime,* ed. Keith M. Baker (Oxford, 1987), 5; Merrick, *Desacralization,* 1–26.

14. "Autorité politique," in *Encyclopédie ou dictionnaire raisonné des sciences, des arts, et des métiers,* ed. Denis Diderot and Jean Le Rond d'Alembert, 17 vols. (Paris, 1751–65); Van Kley, *Religious Origins,* 111–14, 129–30, 191–218; Merrick, *Desacralization,* 126–34; Bloch, *Royal Touch,* 217–18, 223–28.

15. Barbier, *Journal historique,* 4:289.

16. Ibid., 2:224 (April 1739); Arsenal 10167, fol. 88.

17. Julia, "L'affaiblissement de l'église gallicane," 36; Farge, *Subversive Words,* 96–102; Durand Echeverria, *The Maupeou Revolution* (Baton Rouge, 1985), 28.

18. Jeffrey Merrick, "Politics on Pedestals: Royal Monuments in Eighteenth-Century France," *French History* 5 (1991): 234–64; H 1862, quoted in Rombouts, "Art as Propaganda," 256–57; Thomas E. Crow, *Painters and Public Life in Eighteenth-Century Paris* (New Haven, 1985), 156–57.

19. Merrick, "Politics on Pedestals," 242, 246–47. Roche, *France in the Enlightenment,* 271–72, 275–76.

20. Roche, *France in the Enlightenment,* 273–76. Van Kley, *Religious Origins,* 306.

21. Jeffrey Merrick, "Fathers and Kings: Patriarchalism and Absolutism in Eighteenth-Century French Politics," *Studies on Voltaire and the Eighteenth Century* 308 (1993): 281–303. On Greuze see Carol Duncan, "Fallen Fathers: Images of Authority in Pre-revolutionary French Art," *Art History* 4 (1981): 190–92. On the good father see Lynn Hunt, *The Family Romance of the French Revolution* (London, 1992), 18–40; and Roche, *France in the Enlightenment,* 527–30.

22. Merrick, *Desacralization,* 57.

23. John Markoff, "Images du roi au début de la Révolution," in *L'image de la Révolution française,* ed. Michel Vovelle, 4 vols. (Paris, 1989).

24. Farge, *Subversive Words,* 177.

25. On the Prince Edward affair, Thomas Kaiser, "The Drama of Charles Edward Stuart, Jacobite Propaganda, and French Political Protest, 1745–1750," *Eighteenth-Century Studies* 30 (1997): 365–81; Bastille 10167, fol. 83, police report of 21–22 April 1740. For a more detailed exploration of all these points see Thomas E. Kaiser, "Louis *le Bien-Aimé* and the Rhetoric of the Royal Body" in *From the Royal to the Republican Body: Incorporating the Political in Seventeenth- and Eighteeenth-Century France,* ed. Sara E. Melzer and Kathryn Norberg (Berkeley, 1998), 131–61; and Robert Darnton, "Poetry and the Police in Eighteenth-Century Paris," *Studies on Voltaire and the Eighteenth Century* 371 (1999): 1–23.

26. Robert Darnton, *The Forbidden Best-Sellers of Pre-Revolutionary France* (New York, 1995), 237.

27. Steven L. Kaplan, *Le complot de famine: histoire d'une rumeur au XVIIIe*

siècle (Paris, 1982), 40 (my translation here). Much of what follows is drawn from this work.

28. Kaplan, "Famine Plot Persuasion," esp. 18, 31, 46–47, 58–61; Ferdinando Galiani, *Dialogues sur le commerce des blés* (1770), quoted in Grenier, "Consommation et marché," 376.

29. Antoine, *Louis XV*, 484–506; Darnton, "Poetry and the Police."

30. Antoine, *Louis XV*, 887–88. Nicolas Ruault, *Gazette d'un parisien sous la Révolution* (Paris, 1976), 402, Ruault to Fritel (28 January 1772).

31. Goubert and Roche, *Français et l'Ancien Régime*, 1:214–15; Chartier, *Cultural Origins*, 111–13; Michel Vovelle, "La représentation populaire de la monarchie," in *The Political Culture of the Old Regime*, ed. Keith M. Baker (Oxford, 1987), 77–78.

32. Hunt, *Family Romance*, 90; Timothy Tackett, *Becoming a Revolutionary: The Deputies of the French National Assembly and the Emergence of a Revolutionary Culture, 1789–1790* (Princeton, 1996), 79–80; Maza, *Private Lives*, ch. 4.

33. Hunt, *Family Romance*, ch. 4; and Lynn Hunt, "The Many Bodies of Marie-Antoinette: Political Pornography and the Problem of the Feminine in the French Revolution," in *Eroticism and the Body Politic*, ed. Lynn Hunt (Baltimore, 1991), 108–30; Jeffrey Merrick, "Sexual Politics and Public Order in Late Eighteenth-Century France: The *Mémoires secrets* and the *Correspondance secrète*," *Journal of the History of Sexuality* 1 (1990): 68–84; Antoine de Baecque, *The Body Politic: Corporeal Metaphor in Revolutionary France, 1770–1800* (1993; Stanford, 1997), 29–75; Darnton, *Forbidden Best-Sellers*, chs. 3, 5, 8, and pt. 4 for samples of this literature; Chartier, *Cultural Origins*, 67–112. On the queen's brief popularity in June 1789, A. Brette, "Documents inédits: relation des événements depuis le 6 mai jusqu'au 15 juillet 1789: bulletins d'un agent secret," *La Révolution française* 23 (1892): 348–68, 443–71, 520–47; 24 (1893): 69–84, 162–78.

34. Van Kley, *Religious Origins*, 95, 193–94. Bell, *Lawyers and Citizens*, 130–55.

35. Edmond Dziembowski, *Un nouveau patriotisme français, 1750–1770: la France face à la puissance anglaise à l'époque de la guerre de Sept Ans* (Oxford, 1998), 355–89, 519–21.

36. Keith M. Baker, *Inventing the French Revolution: Essays on French Political Culture in the Eighteenth Century* (Cambridge, 1990), 170–72, 186–88; Maza, *Private Lives*, 52–55, 314–17; Tackett, *Becoming a Revolutionary*, 80; Chartier, *Cultural Origins*, 27–37; Mona Ozouf, "Public Opinion at the End of the Old Regime," *Journal of Modern History* 60 (1988): supplements S1–S21.

37. Farge, *Subversive Words*, 191–92; Baker, *Inventing the French Revolution*, 169–70; Ozouf, "Public Opinion"; Merrick, *Desacralization*, 12–13.

38. Chartier, *Cultural Origins*, 27–30; Barbier, *Journal historique*, 4:455.

39. Hardy, *Loisirs*, 187 (11 April 1770); 254 (5 April 1771).

40. Jack Censer, *The French Press in the Age of Enlightenment* (London, 1994), 7, 215–17.

41. Maza, *Private Lives;* see also Fitzsimmons, *Parisian Order of Barristers*,

18–19; Jeremy Popkin, "Pamphlet Journalism at the End of the Old Regime," *Eighteenth-Century Studies* 22 (1989): 351–67.

42. F12 1464; F12 2286; F12 2457, *Réflexions sur le mémoire du Régisseur des Cuirs,* n.d. (1775); F7 4670, doss. Derubigny; Haim Burstin, *Le faubourg St-Marcel à l'époque révolutionnaire: structure économique et composition sociale* (Paris, 1983), 211–12.

43. Burstin, *Faubourg St-Marcel,* 213 n.150; Garrioch, *Parisian Bourgeoisie,* 129–30.

44. *Journal de Paris,* 10 April 1780; Colin Jones, "The Great Chain of Buying: Medical Advertisement, the Bourgeois Public Sphere, and the Origins of the French Revolution," *American Historical Review* 103 (1996): 36–37; *Annonces, affiches, et avis divers:* see, for example, no. 19 (8 mai 1754); *Journal économique,* September 1765; Censer, *French Press,* 7, 101, 121–37.

45. Ozouf, "Public Opinion," S9.

46. Jeremy Popkin, *Revolutionary News: The Press in France, 1789–1799* (Durham, 1990), 25–26.

CHAPTER 8. SECULARIZATION

1. Ménétra, *Journal of My Life,* 19; Y10994, 12 and 13 June 1752; Mercier, *Tableau de Paris,* 8:301–3.

2. Ménétra, *Journal de ma vie* (Paris, 1982), 31 (my translation).

3. Chaunu, *La mort à Paris;* Robert Favre, *La mort dans la littérature et la pensée française au siècle des lumières* (Lyon,1978). McManners, *Death and the Enlightenment.* More generally, see Philippe Ariès, *The Hour of Our Death* (New York, 1981), trans. Helen Weaver (Harmondsworth, 1983).

4. For a vivid treatment of this belief system see Jean Delumeau, *Sin and Fear: The Emergence of a Western Guilt Culture, 13th–18th centuries,* trans. Eric Nicholson (New York, 1990), esp. chs. 11–13. McManners, *Death and the Enlightenment,* 134.

5. Chaunu, *La mort à Paris,* 234, 435, 436; Georges Minois, *Histoire des enfers* (Paris, 1991), 298.

6. Daniel Roche, "La mémoire de la mort: les arts de mourir dans la librairie et la lecture en France aux XVIIe et XVIIIe siècles," in *Les républicains des lettres* (Paris, 1988), 111–15.

7. Garrioch, *Parisian Bourgeoisie,* 51–52.

8. JF 1586, fol. 159 (St-Hippolyte), fol. 243 (St-Jean-en-Grève); Brochard, *St-Laurent;* LL847, fols. 100–101 (St-Martin-du-Cloître); Y14911, 8 January 1709 (St-Sauveur).

9. Brochard, *St-Laurent,* 184–205; idem, *St-Gervais,* 251–67; LL836, fol. 8; Garrioch, *Parisian Bourgeoisie,* 144.

10. S7493, St-Jacques-de-la-Boucherie.

11. L635, arrêt de règlement pour les confréries du St-Sacrement établies à Paris, dans les églises paroissiales de St-Etienne-du-Mont, St-Sulpice et St-Roch, 1786.

12. *An Agreeable Criticism* (1706), quoted in Kaplow, *Names,* 111; Mercier, *Tableau de Paris,* 4:160; and Louis-Sébastien Mercier, *Parallèle de Paris et de Lon-*

dres: un inédit de Louis-Sébastien Mercier, ed. Claude Bruneteau and Bernard Cottret (Paris, 1982), 104–5.

13. Chaunu, *La mort à Paris,* 452; Cissie Fairchilds, "Marketing the Counter-Reformation: Religious Objects and Consumerism in Early Modern France," in *Visions and Revisions of Eighteenth-Century France,* ed. Christine Adams, Jack Censer, and Lisa Jane Graham (University Park, Pa., 1997), 31–57 (36); Mercier, *Tableau de Paris,* 4:41; Jean-François Butini, *Traité de luxe* (1774), quoted in Etienne Van de Walle, "Motivations and Technology in the Decline of French Fertility" in *Family and Sexuality in French History,* ed. Robert Wheaton and Tamara K. Hareven (Philadelphia, 1980), 165; Jean-Pierre Bardet, "Acceptation et refus de la vie à Paris au XVIIIe siècle" in *La vie, la mort, la foi, le temps: mélanges offerts à Pierre Chaunu,* ed. Jean-Pierre Bardet and Madeleine Foisil (Paris, 1993); Durand, *Fermiers généraux,* 324; Garrioch, *Parisian Bourgeoisie,* 114–16.

14. François Lebrun, *Etre chrétien en France sous l'Ancien Régime, 1516–1790* (Paris, 1996), 177–78.

15. Alexandre, "Mes souvenirs," Bibliothèque Thiers, ms Masson 211, fols. 88v-89.

16. C. A. Dauban, ed., *Lettres de Madame Roland aux demoiselles Cannet* (Paris, 1867), 2:23 (16 January 1777); Mercier, *Tableau de Paris,* 6:182; Duclos, quoted in McManners, *Death and the Enlightenment,* 262; Barbier, *Journal historique,* 3:394.

17. Alexandre, "Mes souvenirs," ms Masson 211, fol. 89.

18. BHVP ms 678, second part, fol. 59. I am very grateful to Daniel Roche for providing me with a copy of his transcription of these writings.

19. Ménétra, *Journal of My Life,* 193.

20. BHVP ms 678, second part, fols. 62–64.

21. Roche, "Ménétra," 411–13.

22. Alexandre, "Mes souvenirs," ms Masson 211, fol. 88 verso.

23. Ménétra, *Journal of My Life,* 21, 159; Roche, "Ménétra," 338–56. The same mixture may be found in songs from Louis XVI's reign: see Rolf Reichardt and Herbert Schneider, "Chanson et musique populaires devant l'histoire à la fin de l'Ancien Régime," *Dix-huitième siècle* 18 (1986): 129.

24. Lise Andries, "Paris et l'imaginaire de la ville dans les almanachs français du XVIIIe siècle," in *The Secular City: Studies in the Enlightenment Presented to Haydn Mason,* ed. T. D. Hemming, E. Freeman and D. Meakin (Exeter, 1994), 17–19; David Garrioch, "House Names, Shop Signs and Social Organisation in Western European Cities, 1500–1900," *Urban History* 21 (1994): 29.

25. Y15747, 19 July, 9 and 10 September 1700; Y12015, January 1722; Y11705, 3 February 1775.

26. Norman Hampson, *The Enlightenment* (Harmondsworth, 1968), 132.

27. Minois, *Histoire des enfers,* 299.

28. Jeanne Ferté, *La vie religieuse dans les campagnes parisiennes (1622–1695)* (Paris, 1962), 279, 284.

29. Roche, "Ménétra," 353.

30. K996, no. 28 (15 July 1777).

31. BM Orléans ms 1422, fol. 454.

32. Merrick, *Desacralization,* 44. Official thinking had begun to change in

the sixteenth century, with the Counter-Reformation: Descimon, "Corps de ville et le système cérémonial," 109–11.

33. Hurtaut and Magny, *Dictionnaire historique,* 4:417–18.

34. BM Orléans ms 1421, fols. 95, 137.

35. [Clicquot de Blervache], *Le Réformateur,* new enlarged edition (Amsterdam, 1762), 1:63.

36. Edicts of 14 February 1776, art. 14, and 28 August 1776, art. 43; Hippolyte Monin, "Les juifs à Paris à la fin de l'Ancien Régime," *Revue des études juives* 23 (1891): 85–96.

37. Darnton, *Forbidden Best-Sellers,* 60–71.

38. Farge, *Subversive Words,* 39–40. Van Kley, *Religious Origins,* 164.

39. D'Argenson, *Journal et mémoires,* 8:12, 35 (6 and 19 May 1753); Van Kley, *Damiens Affair,* 50–51. Cole, *A Journal,* 95.

40. Dominique Julia, "Jansénisme et 'déchristianisation,'" in *Du roi Très Chrétien à la laïcité républicaine,* ed. Philippe Joutard (Paris, 1991), 254; Charles H. O'Brien, "Jansenists on Civil Toleration in Mid-Eighteenth-Century France," *Theologische Zeitschrift* 37 (1981): 71–93.

41. Brockliss, *French Higher Education,* 362. Hampson, *Enlightenment,* 90.

42. McManners, *Death and the Enlightenment,* 46–49; see also Favre, *La mort,* 221–44; Jones, "Great Chain of Buying," 27–29. For one of Maille's advertisements, *Mercure de France,* February 1753.

43. "Mémoires de J.C.P. Lenoir," Bibliothèque municipale d'Orléans, ms 1421, fol. 605.

44. McManners, *Death and the Enlightenment,* 92–93. Franklin to Joseph Priestley, 8 February 1780, in Lester G. Crocker, ed., *The Age of Enlightenment* (New York, 1969), 294–95; Louis S. Greenbaum, "Nurses and Doctors in Conflict: Piety and Medicine in the Paris Hôtel-Dieu on the Eve of the French Revolution," *Clio Medica* 13 (1979); see also James C. Riley, *The Eighteenth-Century Campaign to Avoid Disease* (London, 1987).

45. D'Holbach, *Common Sense* (1772), in Isaac Kramnick, ed., *Portable Enlightenment Reader* (New York, 1995), 140.

46. Madeleine Foisil, "L'époque moderne" in *Le diocèse de Paris,* vol. 1, *Des origines à la révolution,* ed. Bernard Plongeron et al (Paris, 1987), 367. Figure for Milan based on figures for Porta Comasina, given in Lucia Sebastiani, "La riorganizzazione delle parrocchie milanesi nel periodo giuseppino," *Quaderni storici* 15 (1970): 871.

47. Bastille 10201, mémoire concernant l'état de la paroisse de St-Médard (1743).

48. Julia, "L'affaiblissement de l'église gallicane," 49; Viguerie, *Histoire et dictionnaire,* 1215–16.

49. Olwen Hufton, "The French Church," in *Church and Society in Catholic Europe of the Eighteenth Century,* ed. William J. Callahan and David Higgs (Cambridge, 1979), 20–21; Lebrun, *Etre chrétien,* 178.

50. Andrews, *Letter to a Young Gentleman* (1784), in John Lough, *France on the Eve of Revolution: British Travellers' Observations, 1763–1788* (London, 1987), 151.

51. Greenbaum, "Nurses and Doctors," 261.

52. F. Rousseau-Vigneron, "La section de la place des Fédérés pendant la Révolution," in *Contributions à l'histoire démographique de la Révolution française,* ed. Marcel Reinhard, 3d series (Paris, 1970), 204; Jeffry Kaplow, "Sur la population flottante de Paris à la fin de l'Ancien Régime," *Annales historiques de la Révolution française* 39 (1967):1–14.

53. Y12425, 29 June 1754.

54. Ménétra, *Journal of My Life,* 173; Garrioch, *Neighbourhood and Community,* 158.

55. Arrêt du Parlement, 18 April 1760; Lamennais, *Réflexions sur l'état de l'église en France* (1808; Paris, 1819), 141.

56. Roche, *La France des lumières,* 321–22; Plongeron et al., *Diocèse de Paris,* 353–54.

57. Louis S. Greenbaum, "Jean-Sylvain Bailly, the Baron de Breteuil and the 'Four New Hospitals' of Paris," *Clio Medica* 8 (1973): 263; Duprat, *Temps des philanthropes,* 90.

58. Porphyre Petrovitch, "Recherches sur la criminalité à Paris dans la seconde moitié du XVIIIe siècle," in *Crimes et criminalité en France sous l'Ancien Régime,* ed. A. Abbiateci et al. (Paris, 1971), 215; Chagniot, *Paris et l'armée,* 547.

59. Jeffrey Merrick, "Patterns and Prosecution of Suicide in Eighteenth-Century Paris," *Historical Reflections/Réflexions historiques* 16, no. 1 (1989):26–40, 51–52; McManners, *Death and the Enlightenment,* 409–37.

60. Kaplan, "Religion, Subsistence," 166–67; Annik Pardailhé-Galabrun, "Les déplacements des parisiens dans la ville aux XVIIe et XVIIIe siècles: un essai de problématique," *Histoire, économie, société* 2 (1983): 216.

61. Garrioch, *Neighbourhood and Community,* 155–56; Y12596, 14 June 1752.

62. Charles Manneville, *Une vieille église de Paris: St-Médard* (Paris, 1906), 91 n.2; John McManners, *Church and Society in Eighteenth-Century France* (Oxford, 1998), 1:309.

63. Chaunu, *La mort à Paris,* 436–37, 440, 452.

64. I have reconstructed the family tree from a range of notarial and judicial sources and from property records.

65. Winnie, *Family Dynasty,* 22–23. For further examples see Garrioch, *Parisian Bourgeoisie,* ch. 5.

66. Roche, *People of Paris,* 212–13; and *La France des lumières,* 456–57; Chartier, *Cultural Origins,* 69–70.

67. Darnton, *Forbidden Best-Sellers,* 63; Roche, *Républicains des lettres,* 96–97, 100–101.

68. XXVIII 558, 11 October 1792; XVII 683, 25 May 1734.

69. *Mémoires de Madame Roland,* 1:91. Ménétra, *Journal of My Life,* 130.

70. Y18703, *procès-verbal* of 14 December 1780 and letters of 29 December 1780 and 9 January 1781.

71. AP D5 B6 472.

72. Thouret, *Rapport sur les exhumations du cimetière et de l'église des Sts-Innocents* (1789), quoted in Foisil, "Attitudes devant la mort," 322.

CHAPTER 9. URBANISM OR DESPOTISM?

1. Greenbaum, "Jean-Sylvain Bailly," 265; Dora B. Weiner, *The Citizen-Patient in Revolutionary and Imperial Paris* (Baltimore,1993),30–36, 52–57.

2. Hardy, *Loisirs,* 372–73.

3. Michel Möring, Charles Quentin, and M. Brièle, eds., *Collection de documents pour servir à l'histoire des hôpitaux de Paris* (Paris, 1881–85), 2:22.

4. Ibid.

5. Greenbaum, "Jean-Sylvain Bailly," 265; Möring et al., *Collection de documents,* 2:24–30.

6. Möring et al., *Collection de documents,* 2:28.

7. Louis S. Greenbaum, "Tempest in the Academy: Jean-Baptiste Le Roy, the Paris Academy of Sciences and the Project of a New Hôtel-Dieu," *Archives internationales d'histoire des sciences* 24 (1974): 122–37; Mercier, *Tableau de Paris,* 3:231.

8. Jacques Rustin, "La séquence de l''arrivée à Paris' dans le roman français de la seconde partie du XVIIIe siècle, de *Julie* à *René* (1761–1802), principalement dans l'oeuvre de Rétif de la Bretonne," in *Rétif de la Bretonne et la ville* (Strasbourg, 1993), 7–36. See also Davies, *Paris and the Provinces,* 67–78.

9. *Les confessions d'une courtisane* (1784), quoted in Rustin, "Séquence de l''arrivée,' " 17.

10. Andrews, *System of Criminal Justice,* 42.

11. Louis-Sébastien Mercier, *L'an deux mille quatre cent quarante* (ca. 1770), ed. Raymond Trousson (Paris, 1971), 106–10.

12. Quoted in Richard Sennett, *Flesh and Stone* (New York, 1994), 270.

13. Thomas Chatelus, "Thèmes picturaux dans les appartements de marchands et artisans parisiens au dix-huitième siècle," *Dix-huitième siècle* 6 (1974): 317; Nicole Mounier, "Le quartier des porcherons, 1720–1789: description du processus d'urbanisation d'un faubourg de Paris" (thesis, Ecole nationale des Chartes, 1978), 2:273; Marc-Antoine Laugier, *An Essay on Architecture,* trans. W. and A. Herrmann (Los Angeles, 1977), 128.

14. Laugier, *Essay,* 121; James A. Leith, *Space and Revolution: Projects for Monuments, Squares, and Public Buildings in France, 1789–1799* (Montreal, 1991), 28.

15. On the 1769 plan, Backouche, *Trace du fleuve,* 202–13; Voltaire (François Marie Arouet), "Des embellissements de Paris" (1749) in *Oeuvres complètes* (Paris, 1869), 13:182; Rombouts, "Art as Propaganda," 260.

16. Boudon et al., *Système de l'architecture urbaine,* 1:294; Jean-Louis Harouel, *L'embellissement des villes* (Paris, 1993), 11–12.

17. Jacques-François Blondel, *Cours d'architecture* (Paris, 1771), 2:308.

18. Mercier, *Tableau de Paris,* 1:216.

19. *Mémoire de réclamation à mettre sous les yeux de l'Assemblée, par un citoyen inutile et qui se lasse de l'être* (1789), quoted in Friedmann, *Paris, ses rues*, xxvii n. 2.

20. James C. Riley, *Population Thought in the Age of the Democratic Revolution* (Durham, N.C., 1985), 25, 29–37, 44–56, 83–103.

21. Madeleine Foisil, "Les attitudes devant la mort au XVIIIe siècle: sépul-

tures et suppressions de sépultures dans le cimetière parisien des Sts-Innocents," *Revue historique* 510 (April–June 1974): 306–12; JF1207, fols. 8, 20v, 165, 201; Cole, *A Journal,* 297–99.

22. JF 1207, fol. 7.
23. Thibaut-Payen, *Les morts,* 210–17.
24. Collected in JF 1207.
25. Kaplow, *Names of Kings,* 113
26. JF 1207, fol. 17.
27. Ibid.
28. Chaunu, *La mort à Paris,* 443.
29. McManners, *Death and the Enlightenment,* 316; Y15390, 30 May 1780, dossier on Sts-Innocents.
30. McManners, *Death and the Enlightenment,* 316–17; Thibaut-Payen, *Les morts,* 221.
31. Claude Nicolas Ledoux, *L'architecture considérée sous le rapport de l'art, des moeurs et de la législation* (1804), quoted in Harouel, *Embellissement des villes,* 10.
32. Georges Vigarello, *Concepts of Cleanliness: Changing Attitudes in France since the Middle Ages* (Cambridge, 1988), 147; Louis Petit de Bachaumont, *Mémoires secrets pour servir à l'histoire de la république des lettres en France* (London, 1777–89), 23:74 (19 July 1783).
33. Sennett, *Flesh and Stone,* 261–70.
34. Jean Ducros, "La place de Louis XV," in *Les Gabriel,* ed. Michel Gallet andYves Bottineau (Paris, 1982), 255.
35. Mark K. Deming, *La halle au blé de Paris* (Brussels, 1984), 29–32; Harouel, *Embellissement des villes,* 150.
36. Isherwood, *Farce and Fantasy,* 217–25.
37. Harouel, *Embellissement des villes,* 176–77; Durand, *Fermiers généraux,* 496–97; Pierre Pinon, "Lotissements spéculatifs, formes urbaines et architectes à la fin de l'Ancien Régime," in *Soufflot et l'architecture des lumières* (Paris, 1986), 178–91.
38. Françoise Boudon, "Urbanisme et spéculation à Paris au XVIIIe siècle: le terrain de l'hôtel de Soissons," *Journal of the Society of Architectural Historians* 32(1973): 280.
39. Yves Durand, "Répartition de la noblesse dans les quartiers de Paris," in *Contributions à l'histoire démographique de la Révolution française,* ed. Marcel Reinhard, 2d series (Paris, 1965), 21–23.
40. "Mémoires d'un soldat de l'Ancien Régime" (1719), quoted in Pardailhé-Galabrun, "Déplacements des parisiens," 207.
41. Chagniot, *Paris au XVIIIe siècle,* 285; Pardailhé-Galabrun, "Déplacements des parisiens," 224. Nicholas Papayanis, *Horse-Drawn Cabs and Omnibuses in Paris: The Idea of Circulation and the Business of Public Transit* (Baton Rouge, 1996), 16, gives higher figures; Boudon et al., *Système de l'architecture urbaine,* vol. 2, plates 24, 25.
42. Y15350, 10 January 1752; Y15117, reports of guard, 1 February 1788.
43. Boudon et al., *Système de l'architecture urbaine,* 1:25–26.
44. Harouel, *Embellissement des villes,* 156.

45. Mounier, "Quartier des porcherons," 96, 102.

46. Jean-Aymar Piganiol de la Force, *Description historique de la ville de Paris*, new ed. (Paris, 1765), 3:219; Harouel, *Embellissement des villes*, esp. 24–25, 47–48, 201–12.

47. Y12830, *mémoire* sent to commissaires for discussion, n.d. (ca. 1780).

48. AD I 23 B, ordonnances du bureau des Finances; Y13728, letter of 17 January 1785; Y13163, letters of 1779.

49. AD I 23 B, lettres patentes du roi, May 1784; Jean Chagniot, "La lieutenance générale de police de Paris à la fin de l'Ancien Régime," in *Les institutions parisiennes à la fin de l'Ancien Régime et sous la Révolution française* (Paris, n.d.), 24.

50. Chagniot, *Paris et l'armée*, 151; Y15117, 29 December 1788; Jean Chagniot, "Le guet," 68–70; *Arrêté des soldats de la garde de Paris dits tristes-à-pattes* (1789), BHVP, 605 708.

51. Dussausoy, *Le citoyen désintéressé* (1767), quoted in Mona Ozouf, "Le cortège et la ville: les itinéraires parisiens des fêtes de la Révolution," *Annales: économies, sociétés, civilisations* 26 (1971): 893; Corbin, *The Foul and the Fragrant*, 96–97.

52. Harouel, *Embellissement des villes*, 28–29. S 7493, doss. St-Louis-en-l'Ile.

53. Piasenza, "Opinion publique," 106–8.

54. See the letters in Y13728, Y12830, Y13163.

55. BM Orléans ms 1421, fols. 284, 285, 698; Hardy, *Loisirs*, 34, 19 February 1766).

56. Y12830, 7 September 1782; Y13728, 22 January 1777; Williams, *Police of Paris*, 122.

57. Chassaigne, *Lieutenance générale*, 227–28; Williams, *Police of Paris*, 69, 124–33.

58. Chassaigne, *Lieutenance générale*, 165, 210–31; Williams, *Police of Paris*, 94–104.

59. Chagniot, *Paris et l'armée*, 127–35; and idem, "Le guet," 61–62, 68–70; Williams, *Police of Paris*, 71–84.

60. Y11741, 5 August 1744; Williams, *Police of Paris*, 223–26; Roche, *Everyday Things*, 119–20.

61. Chassaigne, *Lieutenance générale*, 68; Williams, *Police of Paris*, 226–28; Arlette Farge and Michel Foucault, *Le désordre des familles: lettres de cachet des archives de la Bastille au XVIIIe siècle* (Paris, 1982); BM Orléans ms 1422, fols. 21, 78, 1009; Claude Quétel, *De par le Roy: essai sur les lettres de cachet* (Paris, 1981), 137–60.

62. Williams, *Police of Paris*, 260, 267–70; JF1325, fols. 141–150; Arnaud, *Pompiers de Paris* (Paris, 1958), 25–57.

63. Williams, *Police of Paris*, 250–58.

64. BM Orléans ms 1421, 364; George D. Sussman, *Selling Mothers' Milk: The Wet-Nursing Business in France, 1715–1914* (Urbana, 1982), 21, 65.

65. BM Orléans ms 1421, 363; Sussman, *Selling Mothers' Milk*, chs. 2, 3.

66. Sussman, *Selling Mothers' Milk*, 27–32; BM Orléans ms 1421, 364.

67. Y15350, 14 January 1752.

68. BM Orléans ms 1421, 285, 364–46; ms 1422, 682; ms 1423, fols. 357–60;

Williams, *Police of Paris,* 113–15. Robert Bigo, "Aux origines du Mont-de-Piété parisien: bienfaisance et crédit," *Annales d'histoire économique et sociale* 4 (1932): 113–26.

69. BM Orléans ms 1422, fol. 28; Williams, *Police of Paris,* 104–11, esp. 109.

70. Y15114B, Ninnin to syndics, 21 August 1787. For another example see Thomas Manley Luckett, "Hunting for Spies and Whores: A Parisian Riot on the Eve of the French Revolution," *Past and Present* 156 (August 1997): 121.

71. Y12830, Lenoir to commissaires, 27 December 1780. Chagniot, "Le guet," 69; Mercier, *Tableau de Paris,* 10:316; BN ms fr. 6687, fols. 62–63 (29 August 1788), 79 (13 September), 91 (22 September), 98 (25 September), 101 (29 September), 138 (9 November).

72. Mercier, *Tableau de Paris,* 1:203–4.

73. Quoted in Duprat, *Temps des philanthropes,* xix.

74. Joseph-Alphonse de Véri, *Journal* (mid-1770s), reprinted in Arnault de Maurepas and Florent Brayard, eds, *Les français vus par eux-mêmes: le XVIIIe siècle* (Paris, 1996), 545.

75. Chaunu, *La mort à Paris,* 418–19.

76. Greenbaum, "Nurses and Doctors," 254.

77. Ibid., 248–57. See also Dora B. Weiner, "The French Revolution, Napoleon, and the Nursing Profession," *Bulletin of the History of Medicine* 46 (1972): 278–86.

78. Duprat, *Temps des philanthropes,* 3–88.

79. Weiner, *Citizen-Patient,* 36–40; "Mémoires de Lenoir," bibliothèque municipale d'Orléans, ms 1421, fols. 367–68; [J-M. Dufour de Saint-Pathias], *Diogène à Paris* (Paris, 1787), 93; *Journal de médecine, chirurgie, pharmacie* 63, no. 26 (January 1785). On this debate, Roche, "Pauper Capital," 194–95, 197–98; Jean-Pierre Gutton, *La société et les pauvres: l'exemple de la Généralité de Lyon, 1534–1789* (Paris, 1970), 419–37; Duprat, *Temps des philanthropes,* 13–15; Colin Jones, *Charity and Bienfaisance: The Treatment of the Poor in the Montpellier Region, 1740–1815* (Cambridge, 1982), 86–90.

80. Darnton, *Literary Underground,* 139–40, 144; and idem, *Forbidden Best-Sellers,* 63, 75–76; Maza, *Private Lives,* 279–80; Van Kley, *Religious Origins,* 306–7.

81. BM Orléans ms 1422, 701.

82. Quétel, *De par le Roy,* 33, 137.

CHAPTER 10. THE INTEGRATION OF THE CITY

1. Jeanne Pronteau, *Les numérôtages des maisons de Paris du XVe siècle à nos jours* (Paris, 1966), 83–86.

2. Y11994, Aubert papers (1772).

3. Pronteau, *Numérôtages,* 85 and n. 98; Ambrose Heal, *The Signboards of Old London Shops* (London, 1947), 3.

4. *Almanach historique et chronologique de tous les spectacles* (1787), quoted in John Grand-Carteret, *Les almanachs français* (Paris, 1896), 57.

5. Pronteau, *Numérôtages,* 85. Grand-Carteret, *Almanachs français.*

6. *Almanach de Paris ou calendrier historique* (1726); *Agenda du voyageur*

pour l'année 1727, ou Journal instructif de ce qui se passe de curieux à Paris et à la cour (1727).

7. Grand-Carteret, *Almanachs français,* 54, 62.

8. Andries, "Paris et l'imaginaire," 16–18, 20; Grand-Carteret, *Almanachs français,* 36–37, 143, 158.

9. Anne Boyer, "Crédits et faillites: le problème des financements dans la librairie d'Ancien Régime," in *L'Europe et le livre: réseaux pratiques du négoce de librairie, XVIe–XIXe siècles,* ed. Frédéric Barbier et al. (n.p., 1996), 357–69 (360).

10. Bentley, *Journal of a Visit.*

11. Grand-Carteret, *Almanachs français,* 143; Roche, *People of Paris,* 13.

12. Farge, *Subversive Words,* 99; Christopher Todd, "French Advertising in the Eighteenth Century," *Studies on Voltaire and the Eighteenth Century* 266 (1989): 523–25; Henri Sée, "La création d'un bureau de correspondance générale en 1766," *Revue d'histoire moderne* 7 (1927): 51–55; AD I 23 B, arrêt du conseil, 12 juin 1778.

13. Censer, *French Press,* 54–55; Todd, "French Advertising," 526–27.

14. Fernand Braudel, *The Identity of France* (London, 1988–90), 2:616; David D. Bien, "Property in Office under the Ancien Régime: The Case of the Stockbrokers," in *Early Modern Conceptions of Property,* ed. John Brewer and Susan Staves (London, 1995), 487–88; Jean-Paul Poisson, "Constitutions et dissolutions des sociétés commerciales à Paris au XVIIIe siècle, d'après les registres du greffe de la juridiction consulaire," *Bulletin de la société de l'histoire de Paris et de l'Ile-de-France* 101–2 (1974–75): 103–7; Roche, *People of Paris,* 80.

15. Sonenscher, *Work and Wages,* 146.

16. Bien, "Property in Office," 488.

17. Godineau, *Citoyennes tricoteuses,* 74, 78; Roche, *Culture of Clothing,* 313–14; Carla Hesse, *Publishing and Cultural Politics in Revolutionary Paris, 1789–1810* (Berkeley, 1991), 68; Thamer, "L'art du menuisier," 1043; Y14935, 8 December 1724; Sargentson, *Merchants and Luxury Markets,* 27, 30; Philip Hoffman, Gilles Postel-Vinay, and Jean-Laurent Rosenthal, "Economie et politique: les marchés du crédit à Paris, 1750–1840," *Annales: économies, sociétés, civilisations* 49 (1994): 71–72.

18. Garrioch, *Parisian Bourgeoisie,* 129–30; Burstin, *Faubourg St-Marcel,* 172–74, 194–95; Minard, *Typographes,* 26–27.

19. Sonenscher, *Work and Wages,* 218–33.

20. Sargentson, *Merchants and Luxury Markets,* 30–32.

21. Roche, *People of Paris,* 104–5, 108; Mercier, *Tableau de Paris,* 4:149.

22. Richard Mowery Andrews, "Political Elites and Social Conflicts in the Sections of Revolutionary Paris: 1792–Year III" (Ph.D. thesis, Oxford University, 1970), 335 n.78; Godineau, *Citoyennes tricoteuses,* 75; Y12526, list of *marchandes* on Pont Neuf; Pardailhé-Galabrun, "Déplacements des parisiens," 229–31.

23. Piwnica, "Résistances," 43; Godineau, *Citoyennes tricoteuses,* 70–81; Andrews, "Political Elites," 313–22, 335 n.78.

24. Isherwood, *Farce and Fantasy,* ch. 5.

25. Ibid., ch. 7; Arthur Young, *Travels in France during the Years 1787, 1788,*

1789, ed. M. Betham-Edwards (London, 1890), 100; see also Lough, *France on the Eve of Revolution,* ch. 5.

26. Isherwood, *Farce and Fantasy,* 161–207, 217–49; François-Auguste Faveau de Frénilly, *Recollections of Baron Frénilly,* ed. Arthur Chuquet (London, 1909), 18.

27. Isherwood, *Farce and Fantasy,* 212; Brennan, "Beyond the Barriers," 153–69; Roche, *People of Paris,* 250–53.

28. Martine de Rougemont, *La vie théâtrale en France au XVIIIe siècle* (Paris, 1988), 223.

29. Maza, *Private Lives,* 290–95; John Lough, *An Introduction to Eighteenth-Century France* (London, 1960), 273.

30. Udolpho Van de Sandt, "Le salon de l'Académie de 1759 à 1781," in *Diderot et l'art de Boucher à David: les salons, 1759–1781* (Paris, 1984), 79–93 (see 81); Crow, *Painting and Public Life,* 14–16, 19.

31. "Mémoires d'Alexandre," ms Masson 211, fols. 244–46.

32. Dena Goodman, "Enlightenment Salons: The Convergence of Female and Philosophic Ambitions," *Eighteenth-Century Studies* 22 (1989): 329–50; and idem, *The Republic of Letters: A Cultural History of the French Enlightenment* (Ithaca, 1994), chs. 2, 3; Mittman, "Women and the Theatre Arts," 159.

33. The expression is from Margaret C. Jacob, *Living the Enlightenment: Freemasonry and Politics in Eighteenth-Century Europe* (Oxford, 1991).

34. Raymond Trousson, introduction to Mercier, *L'an deux mille quatre cent quarante,* 21–22.

35. Goodden, *Sweetness of Life,* 38–41; Jean-Paul Poisson, "La sociabilité des notaires parisiens à la fin du XVIIIe siècle: l'exemple des fêtes de famille en 1782 chez le notaire Paulmier," in *Notaires et société* (Paris, 1985–90), 2:75, 77.

36. Goodman, *Republic of Letters,* 243; Y15115A, draft complaint (January 1788); O1 1918, 6 May 1785.

37. Daniel Gordon, *Citizens without Sovereignty: Equality and Sociability in French Thought, 1670–1789* (Princeton, 1994), 33–42. Dena Goodman points to essentially the same characteristics in *Republic of Letters,* chs. 1, 2.

38. Roger Hahn, *The Anatomy of a Scientific Institution: The Paris Academy of Sciences, 1666–1803* (Berkeley, 1971); Roche, *France in the Enlightenment,* 340, 438–40.

39. Margaret C. Jacob, *The Radical Enlightenment: Pantheists, Freemasons, and Republicans* (London, 1981), 128; Garrioch, *Neighbourhood and Community,* 173–80; Duprat, *Temps des philanthropes,* 96–100; Alain Le Bihan, *Francs-maçons parisiens du Grand Orient de France* (Paris, 1966), 7; and *Francs-maçons et ateliers parisiens de la Grande Loge de France au XVIIIe siècle* (Paris, 1973), 96–97.

40. In the early 1780s Charles-Alexis Alexandre joined an unaffiliated "private" lodge at the invitation of a legal clerk: "Mes souvenirs," ms Masson 211, fol. 308.

41. Jacob, *Living the Enlightenment,* ch. 5; Mercier, *Tableau de Paris,* 7:228. For an example of a lodge that admitted high-ranking women as full members, see Loge St-Charles, BN Fonds maçonnique, FM3, 162.

42. Mercier, *Tableau de Paris,* 7:227–29.

43. See the detailed report of a meeting in Y13750, 8 June 1745: I am grateful to Michael Sonenscher for this reference. Jacob, *Living the Enlightenment,* 22, 30, 145–46, 152–53.

44. Mittman, "Women and the Theatre Arts," 156.

45. Goodman, *Republic of Letters,* 242–80; Wallace Kirsop, "Cultural Networks in Pre-Revolutionary France: Some Reflections on the Case of Antoine Court de Gébélin," *Australian Journal of French Studies* 18 (1981): 231–47; Hervé Guénot, "Musées et lycées parisiens (1780–1830)," *Dix-huitième siècle* 18 (1986): 248–67.

46. Marraud, *Noblesse de Paris,* 455–76.

47. Descimon, "Paris on the Eve of Saint Bartholomew," 91, 101.

48. *Nouvelles ecclésiastiques,* 10 April 1749, quoted in Farge, *Subversive Words,* 48.

49. BN Fonds maçonnique, FM2 76, fol. 108 (1773); FM2 97, fol. 48 (1783).

50. "Carrosse," in *Encyclopédie;* Pardailhé-Galabrun, *Naissance de l'intime,* 130, 145, 153; Christophe Studeny, *L'invention de la vitesse: France XVIIIe–XIXe siècles* (Paris, 1995), 52, 64, 66–67.

51. Jacques-Hippolyte Ronesse, *Vues sur la propreté des rues de Paris* (1782), 30; on Tronchin, BM Orléans ms 1421, fol. 605.

52. "Carrosse," *Encylopédie.*

53. L. Remacle, ed., *Voyage de Paris en 1782* (1900), quoted in Pardailhé-Galabrun, "Déplacements des parisiens," 243.

54. Pardailhé-Galabrun, "Déplacements des parisiens," 207, 225–26. Papayanis, *Horse-Drawn Cabs,* 16.

55. Y15099, 6 May 1788. Y15117, 2 March 1788.

56. Poisson, "Sociabilité des notaires"; *Almanach royal.*

57. Babeau, *Paris en 1789,* 180–281; Ultee, *Saint-Germain-des-Prés,* 176–80; Bernard, *Emerging City,* 46–47.

58. K996, no. 28.

59. Garrioch, *Parisian Bourgeoisie,* 143–45.

60. Piwnica, "Résistances," 36.

61. Burstin, *Faubourg St-Marcel,* 172–73, 209–10; H. Depors, *Recherches sur l'état de l'industrie des cuirs en France pendant le XVIIIe siècle et le début du XIXe siècle* (Paris, 1932), 49–50; Marion, *Dictionnaire des institutions,* 448; BN 4° Fm 24434, mémoire pour la compagnie des entrepreneurs du nouveau Marché aux Veaux (1773); AD I 23B, 17 July 1787; Marcel Rouff, "Une grève de gagne-deniers en 1786 à Paris," *Revue historique* 105 (1910): 338–40; Y12816, 2 and 4 January 1786; Durand, *Fermiers généraux,* 67.

62. Freundlich, *Monde du jeu,* 40; *Atlas de la Révolution française,* vol. 1, *Routes et communications,* ed. Guy Arbellot, Bernard Lepetit, and Jacques Bertrand (Paris, 1987), 82; Babeau, *Paris en 1789,* 269; Franklin, *Dictionnaire,* 318.

63. Durand, *Fermiers généraux,* 72–75; Williams, *Police of Paris,* 124–33.

64. Minard, *Fortune du Colbertisme,* 120–21.

65. Durand, *Fermiers généraux,* 64; Y12830, Lenoir to commissaires, 27 December 1780.

66. Habermas, *Structural Transformation,* esp. 18–56. See also Craig Calhoun,

ed., *Habermas and the Public Sphere* (Cambridge, Mass., 1992). Habermas's ideas have been developed and applied to France particularly by Joan Landes, *Women and the Public Sphere in the Age of the French Revolution* (Ithaca, 1988); by Chartier, in *Cultural Origins,* esp. 20–37; and by Keith M. Baker in "Defining the Public Sphere in Eighteenth-Century France: Variations on a Theme by Habermas," in *Habermas and the Public Sphere,* ed. Craig Calhoun (Cambridge, Mass., 1992), 181–211; and in his *Inventing the French Revolution.* On the importance of advertising in creating a bourgeois public sphere see Jones, "Great Chain of Buying."

67. Mercier, *Tableau de Paris,* 12:132.

68. Andrews, "Political Elites," 315; David Garrioch, "The Everyday Lives of Women and the October Days of 1789," *Social History* 24 (1999): 247–49.

CHAPTER 11. PLEBEIAN CULTURE, METROPOLITAN CULTURE

1. Hardy, "Mes loisirs," BN ms fr. 6688, fols. 297–98.

2. Y13981, 12 May 1789.

3. Descimon, "Corps de ville et le système cérémonial," 123–24.

4. Alain Faure, *Paris Carême-prenant: du carnival à Paris au XIXe siècle* (Paris, 1978), 136; Garrioch and Sonenscher, "Compagnonnages," 29; Jacques Le Goff, *Pour un autre moyen âge: temps, travail et culture en Occident* (Paris, 1977), 270–71.

5. Colin Kaiser, "Les cours souveraines au XVIe siècle: morale et Contre-Réforme," *Annales: économies, sociétés, civilisations* 37 (1982):15–31. See also Emmanuel Le Roy Ladurie, *The Carnival at Romans,* trans. M. Feeney (New York, 1979), 341–42; Hurtaut and Magny, *Dictionnaire historique,* 4:417–18; Chagniot, *Paris et l'armée,* 81.

6. Faure, *Paris Carême-prenant,* 56, 77; Richard Symonds, *Travel Notes* (1649), quoted in John Lough, *France Observed in the Seventeenth Century by British Travellers* (Boston, 1985), 117.

7. Faure, *Paris Carême-prenant;* Le Roy Ladurie, *Carnival at Romans;* Natalie Zemon Davis, "The Reasons of Misrule: Youth Groups and Charivaris in Sixteenth-Century France," *Past and Present* 50 (February 1971): 66–69.

8. Hardy, "Mes loisirs," BN ms fr. 6686, fol. 364 (3 February 1788) and ms fr. 6687, fols. 244–45 (23 February 1789); Restif de la Bretonne, *Les nuits de Paris* (1788), quoted in Faure, *Paris Carême-prenant,* 28. Mercier, *Tableau de Paris,* 4:166. Y13728, lieutenant general to commissaires, 3 February 1768.

9. Faure, *Paris Carême-prenant,* 46, 55, 93–94.

10. Robert Descimon, "The Birth of the Nobility of the Robe: Dignity versus Privilege in the Parlement of Paris, 1500–1700," in *Changing Identities in Early Modern France,* ed. Michael Wolfe, 2d ed. (Durham, N.C., 1997); Ford, *Robe and Sword,* 22–26.

11. Piasenza, *Polizia e città,* 44–45.

12. Chagniot, *Paris et l'armée,* 62–63; Hardy, "Mes loisirs," BN ms fr. 6684, fols. 140, 144–45, 195, 198, 202–4 (9, 15, and 17 April, 31 July, 7 and 19 August).

13. Craig J. Calhoun, "Community: Toward a Variable Conceptualization for Comparative Research," *Social History* 5 (1980): 105–29; Garrioch, *Neighbourhood and Community,* 218–20; Daniel Fabre, "Families: Privacy versus Custom," in *History of Private Life,* vol. 3, *Passions of the Renaissance,* ed. Roger Chartier (Cambridge, Mass., 1989), 531–69.

14. This is explored by Ronald Aminzade, *Ballots and Barricades: Class Formation and Republican Politics in France, 1830–1871* (Princeton, 1993), esp. 22–24.

15. George Rudé, *The Crowd in the French Revolution* (London, 1967), 52–55; Luckett, "Hunting for Spies and Whores," esp. 134–36.

16. Green, *Spectacle of Nature,* esp. 13.

17. Ronesse, *Vues sur la propreté des rues de Paris* (1782), quoted in Corbin, *The Foul and the Fragrant,* 59–60.

18. Mercier, *Tableau de Paris,* 1:121; Studeny, *Invention de la vitesse,* 36.

19. Sennett, *Flesh and Stone,* 262; Corbin, *The Foul and the Fragrant,* 71–72; Vigarello, *Concepts of Cleanliness,* 93–111; Jacques Gélis, Mireille Laget, and Marie-France Morel, *Entrer dans la vie: naissances et enfances dans la France traditionelle* (Paris, 1978), 117–21.

20. Roche, *Everyday Things,* 157–61; Vigarello, *Concepts of Cleanliness,* 142–63.

21. Mercier, *Tableau de Paris,* 5:242.

22. Yvonne Knibiehler and Catherine Fouquet, *La femme et les médecins* (Paris, 1983), esp. 107–112; Lieselotte Steinbrügge, *The Moral Sex: Women's Nature in the French Enlightenment* (Oxford, 1995); Germaine de Staël, "On the *Letter on Spectacles,*" in *An Extraordinary Woman: Selected Writings of Germaine de Staël,* ed. and trans. Vivian Folkenflik (New York, 1987), 42–43. See also Jean H. Bloch, "Women and the Reform of the Nation," in *Woman and Society in Eighteenth-Century France,* ed. Eva Jacobs et al. (London, 1979), 3–18.

23. "Femme (Morale)," in *Encyclopédie.*

24. Carol Duncan, "Happy Mothers and Other New Ideas in Eighteenth-Century French Art," in *Feminism and Art History: Questioning the Litany,* ed. N. Broude and M. Garrard (London, 1982), 201–19.

25. Jean-Jacques Rousseau, *Emile* (Paris, 1969), book 5, 697. See also Outram, *The Enlightenment,* 80–89.

26. Mercier, *Tableau de Paris,* 1:109–10; Hurtaut and Magny, *Dictionnaire historique,* 4:418.

27. Boudon et al., *Système de l'architecture urbaine,* 1:385.

28. Roche, *Culture of Clothing,* 146 and n. 63.

29. Sargentson, *Merchants and Luxury Markets,* 122–23, 130–33; Oberkirch, *Mémoires,* 1:230.

30. Y14484, 7 March 1789; Roche, *People of Paris,* 66–67.

31. Margaret Darrow, "French Noblewomen and the New Domesticity," *Feminist Studies* 5 (1979): 44–48. The comment about Mme de Warens is in book 5 of Jean-Jacques Rousseau, *Les confessions* (Paris, 1972), 1:296. See also Vigarello, *Concepts of Cleanliness,* 93–95. Cissie Fairchilds nevertheless gives instances of noblewomen who aspired to domesticity: "Women and Family," in

French Women and the Age of Enlightenment, ed. Samia I. Spencer (Bloomington, 1984), 97–110.

32. Norbert Elias, *The Civilizing Process,* vol. 2, *Power and Civility* (1939; New York, 1982); Garrioch, *Neighbourhood and Community,* 72–77; Darrow, "French Noblewomen"; Alexandre-Balthazar Grimod de la Reynière, *Réflexions philosophiques sur le plaisir par un célibataire* (1783), quoted in Robert Mauzi, *L'idee de bonheur dans la littérature et la pensée française au XVIIIe siècle* (Paris, 1967), 274. Cf. Leonore Davidoff and Catherine Hall, *Family Fortunes: Men and Women of the English Middle Classes, 1780–1850* (London, 1987).

33. François Loyer, *Paris, Nineteenth Century: Architecture and Urbanism,* trans. Charles Lynn Clark (New York, 1988), 48–49; Pardailhé-Galabrun, *Naissance de l'intime,* 473–77.

34. Sylvana Tomaselli, "The Enlightenment Debate on Women," *History Workshop Journal* 20 (1985), 101–24; Jennifer Jones, "*Coquettes* and *grisettes:* Women Buying and Selling in Ancien Régime Paris," in *The Sex of Things: Gender and Consumption in Historical Perspective,* ed. Victoria de Grazia, with Ellen Furlough (Berkeley, 1996), 26–27, 35–38.

35. Y13454A, 6 May 1789; JF 1103, fols. 35–40, Jean Baptiste Réveillon, "Exposé justificatif," n.d. (1789).

36. Roche, *People of Paris,* 74–94; Bernard Lepetit, *Les villes dans la France moderne, 1740–1840* (Paris, 1988), 280–82, 300–301.

37. Scott, *Rococco Interior,* 38–40.

38. Françoise Teynac, Pierre Nolot, and Jean-Denis Vivien, *Wallpaper: A History* (London, 1982), 59–75, 86–94, 99; Colin Campbell, "Understanding Traditional and Modern Patterns of Consumption in Eighteenth-Century England: A Character-Action Approach," in *Consumption and the World of Goods,* ed. John Brewer and Roy Porter (London, 1993), 49.

39. Régine de Plinval de Guillebon, *Paris Porcelain, 1770–1850* (London, 1972), 13–83, 160–324.

40. Pardailhé-Galabrun, *Birth of Intimacy,* 366–401; Roche, *Everyday Things,* 180, 186–88; Fairchilds, "Populuxe Goods," 229; Roche, *Culture of Clothing,* 470–82.

41. MC XXVII 531, 16 prairial an II.

42. Roche, *People of Paris,* 153–55; Pardailhé-Galabrun, *Birth of Intimacy,* 147–63, 366–401; Fairchilds, "Populuxe Goods," esp. 230–32; Sargentson, *Merchants and Luxury Markets,* passim. Roche, *Culture of Clothing,* 137.

43. Roche, *Culture of Clothing,* 109; Roche, *Everyday Things,* 207–8.

44. Yolande Zephirin, "Un habitant de la rue Lhomond: Henri Piètre, architecte du duc d'Orléans," *La montagne Ste-Geneviève et ses abords* (Société historique et archéologique du 5e arrondissement), no. 275 (February 1986): 13.

45. Poisson, "Sociabilité des notaires," 85.

46. Serge Chassagne, ed., *Une femme d'affaires au XVIII siècle: la correspondance de Madame de Maraise, collaboratrice d'Oberkampf* (Toulouse, 1981), 136 (16 December 1786).

47. Poisson, "Sociabilité des notaires," 78, 85; "Luxe," in *Encyclopédie.*

48. Jones, "*Coquettes* and *grisettes*," esp. 35–38; Rousseau, *Emile,* book 4, 438.

49. Bill from a shop in the rue de Richelieu (1780s), quoted in Forster, *House of Saulx-Tavanes,* 119.

50. Clicquot de Blervache, *Considérations sur le commerce* (1757), quoted in Piwnica, "Résistances," 35 n.15; *Théorie du luxe* (1771), cited in Sargentson, *Merchants and Luxury Markets,* 6.

51. Franklin, *Dictionnaire,* 80, 192.

52. Teynac et al., *Wallpaper,* 88–90; F12 1477, doss. Réveillon. See also Leonard N. Rosenband, "Jean-Baptiste Réveillon: A Man on the Make in Old Regime France," *French Historical Studies* 20 (1997): 481–510.

53. Chassagne, *Oberkampf,* 21–72, ; Sargentson, *Merchants and Luxury Markets,* 104; Sonenscher, *Work and Wages,* 216. On Rose Bertin, see Emile Liez and Pierre de Nouvion, *Ministre des modes sous Louis XVI: Madame Rose Bertin* (Paris, 1912); Muratori-Philip, *Parmentier,* 133.

54. Y11705, 1 January 1775; Mercier, *Tableau de Paris,* 10:344.

55. John Rule, *The Experience of Labour in Eighteenth-Century Industry* (London, 1981), esp. 195–99; Minard, *Typographes,* 60–64, 135–37; Sonenscher, *Work and Wages,* 174–209. The classic work is E. P. Thompson, "Time, Work Discipline and Industrial Capitalism," *Past and Present* 38 (1967): 56–97.

56. [Clicquot de Blervache], *Le Réformateur,* 1:63; Restif de la Bretonne, *Monsieur Nicolas,* 3:17; Backouche, *Trace du fleuve,* 135.

57. Duclos, *Considérations sur les moeurs,* 206. On the development of "commercial humanism" and its consequences, see Gordon, *Citizens without Sovereignty,* esp. ch. 4.

58. Liez and de Nouvion, *Ministre des modes,* 7–30; Chassagne, *Oberkampf;* and Serge Chassagne, *Le coton et ses patrons: France, 1760–1840* (Paris, 1991), 94–95; Plinval de Guillebon, *Paris Porcelain,* 200–205; Chatelain, "Famille et librairie," 229–30.

59. XXII 67, will of 11 February and inventory of 19 February 1791; VI 872, *partage,* 7 September 1791; JF 1103, "Exposé justificatif," ; Rosenband, "Jean-Baptiste Réveillon," 485.

60. Roche, *France in the Enlightenment,* 519–51; Kaplan, "Social Classification," 210–11.

61. Quoted in Piwnica, "Résistances," 35, 37; JF 462, fol. 113; Kaplan, "Social Classification," 195–97.

62. F12 1477, doss. 6.

63. JF 1103, "Exposé justificatif." Panckoucke, "Sur les chambres syndicales" (23 January 1790), quoted in Suzanne Tucoo-Chala, *Charles-Joseph Panckoucke et la librairie française, 1736–1798* (Paris, 1977), 429; Chassagne, *Oberkampf,* 78.

64. Charles-Louis Chassin, *Les élections et les cahiers de Paris en 1789* (Paris, 1888–89), 2:409–500.

65. "Hôpital," in *Encyclopédie.* JF 1103, "Exposé justificatif."

66. Sonenscher, *Work and Wages,* 236–39; Raymonde Monnier, *Un bourgeois sans-culotte: le général Santerre* (Paris, 1989), 19–21; Teynac et al., *Wallpaper,* 88.

CHAPTER 12. THE CITY AND THE REVOLUTION

1. Studeny, *Invention de la vitesse,* 78, 80.

2. Julie Burbidge (née Barton) is preparing a Monash University thesis on French contacts with America.

3. On Delorme, Raymonde Monnier, *Le faubourg Saint-Antoine, 1789–1815* (Paris, 1981),143–44; on Indians, Burbidge (forthcoming); Helvétius quoted in Studeny, *Invention de la vitesse,* 83.

4. *Etudes de la nature* (1784–87), quoted in Studeny, *Invention de la vitesse,* 83–84.

5. Studeny, *Invention de la vitesse,* 62–87, esp. 80–81.

6. *Monsieur Nicolas,* 5e époque.

7. Poisson, "Sociabilité des notaires," 75.

8. *Mémoires de Madame Roland,* 1:12.

9. Roche, *Culture of Clothing,* 86, 501–19; *Lettres de Madame Roland,* 2:18 (14 January 1777); Roche, *Everyday Things,* 218–20.

10. Nagle, *Luxe et charité,* 84; Roche, *Culture of Clothing,* 49–52, and ch. 3 more generally.

11. Mercier, *Tableau de Paris,* 2:331; Mrs Fanny Cradock (mid-1780s), quoted in Fairchilds, "Populuxe Goods," 228.

12. Michel Rey, "Parisian Homosexuals Create a Lifestyle, 1700–1750: The Police Archives," in *'Tis Nature's Fault: Unauthorised Sexuality during the Enlightenment,* ed. Robert Maccubbin (Cambridge, 1987); Jeffrey Merrick, "Sodomitical Inclinations in Early-Eighteenth-Century Paris," *Eighteenth-Century Studies* 30 (1997): 289–95.

13. Baculard d'Arnaud, "Pauline et Suzette" (1780s), quoted in Rustin, "Séquence de l''arrivée,' " 31 n.54.

14. Y10994, 22 November 1752, witness 2.

15. Y15115A, Niort de Charsat to commissaire Ninnin, 19 May 1780.

16. BN ms 6684, fol.198 (7 August 1782).

17. *Atlas de la Révolution française,* vol. 2, *L'enseignement, 1760–1815,* ed. Dominique Julia, Huguette Bertrand, Serge Bonin, Alexandra Laclau (Paris, 1987), 13; Pierre Chaunu, Madeleine Foisil, Françoise de Noirfontaine, *Le basculement religieux de Paris au XVIIIe siècle* (Paris, 1998), 289.

18. *Correspondance littéraire, philosophique et critique par Grimm, Diderot, Raynal, Meister, etc,* ed. Maurice Tourneux (Paris, 1877–82), 8:479; *Mémoires de Madame Roland,* 1:22–23.

19. Farge, *Subversive Words,* 176.

20. Van Kley, *Religious Origins,* 252–81. Van Kley's argument is rejected by Bell, *Lawyers and Citizens,* 189; and Maire, *De la cause de Dieu,* 515.

21. Mirabeau, quoted in Nagle, *Luxe et charité,* 109.

22. Norbert Elias, *The Civilizing Process,* vol. 1, *The History of Manners,* trans. Edmund Jephcott (Oxford, 1978), ch. 2; marquis de Pezay, quoted in Chagniot, *Paris et l'armée,* 542–43. For the late-eighteenth-century debate on military virtues see David Bien, "The Army in the French Enlightenment: Reform, Reaction, and Revolution," *Past and Present* 85 (1979): 68–98.

23. Duprat, *Temps des philanthropes,* 69.

24. Bluche, *Noblesse française,* 42 (for Mercier quotation), 43–52; Fairchilds, *Domestic Enemies,* 15.

25. Barbier, *Journal historique,* 2:354; Y13149, papers of the widow Girard; Sonnet, *Education des filles,* 44–48, 89–93, 329.

26. Reinhard, *Nouvelle histoire de Paris,* 230, 258–59, 318–19.

27. Robert Barrie Rose, "How to Make a Revolution: The Paris Districts in 1789," *Bulletin of the John Rylands University Library* 59 (1977): 441, 448049; LL836, vestry of Ste-Marguerite, 1759–88; Raymonde Monnier and Albert Soboul, *Répertoire du personnel sectionnaire parisien en l'an II* (Paris, 1985), 271–82, 283–94, 295–310.

28. Maurice Genty, *Paris 1789–1795: l'apprentissage de la citoyenneté* (Paris, 1987), 21; K996–97, elections of municipality, 1776–89; Richard Mowery Andrews, "Paris of the Great Revolution, 1789–1796," in *People and Communities in the Western World,* ed. Gene Brucker (Homewood, Ill., 1979), 73.

29. Richard Mowery Andrews, "Social Structures, Political Elites and Ideology in Revolutionary Paris, 1792–1794: A critical evaluation of Albert Soboul's *Sans-culottes parisiens en l'an II,*" *Journal of Social History* 19 (1985–86): 86; Rose, "How to Make a Revolution," 448–49; Garrioch, *Parisian Bourgeoisie,* 163–64.

30. Georges Garrigues, *Les districts parisiens pendant la Révolution française* (Paris, 1931), 22, 169–71; Garrioch, *Parisian Bourgeoisie,* 157–81; Robert Barrie Rose, *The Enragés: Socialists of the French Revolution* (University Park, Pa., 1968), 10–35.

31. BN Lb40 1621, district de St-Marcel: *Assemblée générale de la Commune dudit District, pour le mardi 1er septembre 1789* (n.p., [1789]); Garrigues, *Districts parisiens,* 22, 169–71.

32. Dziembowski, *Nouveau patriotisme français;* Van Kley, *Religious Origins,* 255–60; McManners, *Church and Society,* 2:672–78.

33. Antoine-Joseph Gorsas, *Le courrier de Versailles à Paris et de Paris à Versailles,* 13 July 1789; Edward Rigby, *Letters from France,* ed. Elizabeth Rigby Eastlake (London, 1880), 12 July 1789; Desmoulins's speech quoted in Jacques Godechot, *The Taking of the Bastille, 14th July 1789,* trans. Jean Stewart (New York, 1970), 187–88.

34. *Procédure criminelle,* witness 81; Olwen Hufton, *Women and the Limits of Citizenship in the French Revolution* (Toronto, 1992), 16; and idem, *The Prospect Before Her,* 473; Darlene Gay Levy and Harriet B. Applewhite, "Women of the Popular Classes in Revolutionary Paris, 1789–1795," in *Women, War and Revolution,* ed. Carol R. Berkin and Clara M. Lovett (New York, 1980), 15.

35. Hardy, "Mes loisirs," BN ms fr. 6687, fol. 469.

36. Godineau, *Citoyennes tricoteuses,* esp. 116–53; Dominique Godineau, "Le rapport masculin-féminin dans l'espace urbain (Paris XVIIIe siècle–Révolution française)" in *Marseillaises: les femmes et la ville,* ed. Yvonne Knibiehler et al. (Paris, 1993), 112–14; Mary Wollstonecraft, *An Historical and Moral View of the Origins and Progress of the French Revolution and the Effect It Has Produced in Europe,* 2d ed. (London ,1795), 425–26.

37. Reinhard, *Nouvelle histoire de Paris,* 196–97.

38. Ibid., 189–91,197; John McManners, *The French Revolution and the Church* (London, 1969), 8–10; Contat, *Anecdotes typographiques,* 78; Chassin, *Elections et les cahiers,* 2:482, 522, 545; Ba 64A, dossier 2, fols. 1–5.

39. BN ms fr. 6687, fols. 435, 436.

40. McManners, *French Revolution and the Church,* 11.

41. Célestin Guittard de Floriban, *Journal de Célestin Guittard de Floriban, bourgeois de Paris sous la Révolution* , ed. Raymond Aubert (Paris, 1974), 41; McManners, *French Revolution and the Church,* 62.

42. Ménétra, *Journal of My Life,* 224 n. 287.

43. Jean Boussoulade, "Les religieuses et les serments," *Annales historiques de la Révolution française* 25 (1953): 127, 133; and idem, "Soeurs de charité et commissaires de bienfaisances des faubourgs Saint-Marcel et Saint-Antoine (septembre 1793–mai 1794)," *Annales historiques de la Révolution française* 200 (1970): 350–74.

44. Reinhard, *Nouvelle histoire de Paris,* 167–68; Guittard de Floriban, *Journal,* 28; Patrice Higonnet, *Class, Ideology and the Rights of Nobles during the French Revolution* (Oxford, 1981), 83–84.

45. *Compte rendu des séances électorales de 1791 et de la division du Corps électoral en deux sociétés, sous les noms de Club de l'Evêché, Club de la Ste-Chapelle* (Paris, 1791); Garrigues, *Districts,* 51.

46. Rudé, *The Crowd in the French Revolution,* 58–59, 100–101.

47. Letter of Joseph Carol, 18 July 1789, in G. Capon, ed., "La prise de la Bastille: lettre inédite," *Intermédiaire des chercheurs et des curieux* 86 (1923): cols. 517–20.

48. Richard Cobb, *The Police and the People* (Oxford, 1970), 122.

49. Jacques Godechot, "Fragments des mémoires de Charles-Alexis Alexandre sur les journées révolutionnaires de 1791 et 1792," *Annales historiques de la Révolution française* 24 (1952): 182.

EPILOGUE. THE NEW PARIS

1. Expilly, *Dictionnaire géographique,* 5:515; Roche, *France in the Enlightenment,* 649.

2. Reinhard, *Nouvelle histoire de Paris,* 382–87, 391, 395.

3. Ibid., 394, 400; Martyn Lyons, *Napoleon Bonaparte and the Legacy of the French Revolution* (New York, 1991), 47–49; Olwen Hufton, "The Reconstruction of a Church, 1796–1801," in *Beyond the Terror: Essays in French Regional and Social History, 1794–1815,* ed. Gwynne Lewis and Colin Lucas (Cambridge, 1983), 21–53; Garrioch, *Parisian Bourgeoisie,* 190–96.

4. Nagle, *Luxe et charité,* 190; Bluche, *Magistrats du Parlement,* 118–23.

5. Isser Woloch, *The New Regime: Transformations of the French Civic Order, 1789–1820* (New York, 1994), 334; Andrews, *System of Criminal Justice,* 28; William Doyle, "The Price of Offices in Pre-revolutionary France," *Historical Journal* 27 (1984): 831–60.

6. Bluche, *Magistrats du Parlement,* 108–13; Andrews, *System of Criminal*

Justice, 28; Durand, *Fermiers généraux,* 647–64; Winnie, *Family Dynasty,* 60–61; Adeline Daumard, *La bourgeoisie parisienne de 1815 à 1848* (Paris, 1963), 291–92.

7. Roche, *People of Paris,* 80.

8. Nicole Pellegrin, *Les vêtements de la liberté* (Paris, 1989), 119.

9. Kaplan, *Bakers of Paris,* 138; Alexandre Tuétey, *Répertoire général des sources manuscrites de l'histoire de Paris pendant la Révolution française* (Paris, 1912), vol. 10, no. 414; Ménétra, *Journal of My Life,* 228.

10. Plinval de Guillebon, *Paris Porcelain,* 85–86.

11. *Motion de la pauvre Javotte* (1790), quoted in Groppi, "Travail des femmes," 35.

12. Clive H. Church, *Revolution and Red Tape: The French Ministerial Bureaucracy, 1770–1830* (Oxford, 1981), 30, 94; William Doyle, *The Oxford History of the French Revolution* (Oxford, 1989), 403.

13. Garrioch, *Parisian Bourgeoisie,* 215–25.

14. Jean Dhombres, "Savants en politique, politique des savants: les expériences de la Révolution française," in *Les savants et la politique à la fin du XVIIIe siècle,* ed. Gisèle Van de Vyver and Jacques Reisse (Brussels, 1991), 23–41; John Frangos, *From Housing the Poor to Healing the Sick: The Changing Institution of Paris Hospitals under the Old Regime and Revolution* (Madison, 1997), esp. 122–43.

15. Hesse, *Publishing and Cultural Politics,* 173; Edna Hindie Lemay and Alison Patrick, *Revolutionaries at Work: The Constituent Assembly, 1789–1791* (Oxford, 1996), 60.

16. Paul Butel, "Revolution and the Urban Economy" in *Reshaping France: Town, Country, and Region during the French Revolution,* ed. Alan Forrest and Peter Jones (Manchester, 1991), 47–49.

17. Groppi, "Travail des femmes," 45–46. Muratori-Philip, *Parmentier,* 180. Reinhard, *Nouvelle histoire de Paris,* 322.

18. Reinhard, *Nouvelle histoire de Paris,* 358–59, 379; Andrews, "Paris of the Great Revolution," 74; Daumard, *Bourgeoisie parisienne,* 292.

19. Reinhard, *Nouvelle histoire de Paris,* 366; Doyle, *Oxford History,* 403; Monnier, *Faubourg Saint-Antoine,* 312.

20. Reinhard, *Nouvelle histoire de Paris,* 347.

21. Ibid., 423; Williams, *Police of Paris,* 92; Alan Forrest, *Soldiers of the French Revolution* (Durham, N.C., 1971), 27, 82, 153; Roche, *Culture of Clothing,* 221–56; Richard Cobb, *Death in Paris, 1795–1801* (Oxford, 1978), 77–80.

22. Hunt, *Family Romance,* 78–80.

23. Godechot, "Mémoires de Charles-Alexis Alexandre"; Garrioch, *Parisian Bourgeoisie,* 168–70.

24. Chagniot, *Paris et l'armée,* 629–33; Dorinda Outram, *The Body and the French Revolution: Sex, Class and Political Culture* (New Haven, 1989), 86–87; Duncan, "Fallen Fathers," 188–96. Cf. George Mosse, *The Image of Man: The Creation of Modern Masculinity* (New York, 1996), 23–24.

25. Hunt, *Family Romance,* 153–71; Garrioch, *Parisian Bourgeoisie,* 209–13; Geneviève Fraisse, *Muse de la raison: la démocratie exclusive et la différence des sexes* (Paris, 1989), 133.

26. Godineau, *Citoyennes tricoteuses,* 53; Jane Abray, "Feminism in the French Revolution," *American Historical Review* 80 (1975): 43–62.

27. Bernard Schnapper, "Liberté, égalité, autorité: la famille devant les assemblés révolutionnaires (1790–1800)," in *L'enfant, la famille et la Révolution française,* ed. Marie-Françoise Lévy (Paris, 1990), 325–30.

28. Hufton, *Women and the Limits of Citizenship,* 136–54; Darrow, "French Noblewomen," 41–43, 53–58.

29. Geneviève Fraisse, "Rupture révolutionnaire et l'histoire des femmes," in *Femmes et pouvoirs sous l'Ancien Regime,* ed. Danielle Haase-Dubosc and Elian Viennot (Paris, 1991), 294–95.

30. Olwen Hufton, "Women in Revolution, 1789–96," *Past and Present* 53 (1971): 90–108.

31. Andrews, "Paris of the Great Revolution," 104; Rousseau-Vigneron, "Place des Fédérés," 187, 193–96; Robert Leguillois, "Etude de la population masculine de Paris en 1793 d'après les cartes de sûreté" in *Paris et la Révolution,* ed. Michel Vovelle (Paris, 1989), 15.

32. Fitzsimmons, *Parisian Order of Barristers,* 108–9; Geneviève Aclocque, *Un défenseur du Roi: André-Arnoult Aclocque* (Paris, 1947), 168, 174–75.

33. Rousseau-Vigneron, "Place des Fédérés," 204–5; Doyle, *Oxford History of the French Revolution,* 402; Reinhard, *Nouvelle histoire de Paris,* 316; archives de l'Assistance publique, nouvelle série 96, 1e liasse, 15 floréal an III; Martine Sévegrand, "La section de Popincourt pendant la Révolution française," in *Contributions à l'histoire démographique de la Révolution française,* ed. Marcel Reinhard, 3d series (Paris, 1970), 63–64.

34. Y11207B, 3 August 1789.

35. Groppi, "Travail des femmes," 46 n.55. Godineau, *Citoyennes tricoteuses,* 89–92.

36. *Compte rendu des séances électorales* (1791).

37. Garrioch, *Parisian Bourgeoisie,* 282–87; Mignet, *History of the French Revolution,* 99.

38. Jean Tulard, *Nouvelle histoire de Paris: le Consulat et l'Empire* (Paris, 1970), 93–94

39. Ozouf, "Cortège"; and Mona Ozouf, "Space and Time in the Festivals of the French Revolution," *Comparative Studies in Society and History* 17 (1975): 372–84.

40. Reinhard, *Nouvelle histoire de Paris,* 370–80.

41. Freundlich, *Monde du jeu,* 102, 190–92.

42. Faure, *Paris Carême-prenant,* 93–94; Ozouf, "Cortège," 908.

SELECTED READING

A full listing even of secondary works on Paris would be longer than this book. This selected list does not include manuscript sources, or all the printed works referred to in the notes, but focuses on further reading in English and a very small selection of the major works in French. Alongside the major sources for the social and cultural history of eighteenth-century Paris, I have included works that readers may find of interest, either because they go into greater depth or deal with areas that I have not covered. I have also listed a number of works that go beyond Paris but that cover important themes. And a number of works that I have listed offer an original approach to the city's history, especially those I consider a "good read."

PRIMARY SOURCES

Chassagne, Serge. *Une femme d'affaires au XVIIIe siècle: la correspondance de Madame de Maraise, collaboratrice d'Oberkampf.* Toulouse: Privat, 1981. Letters of a Paris businesswoman.

Cole, William. *A Journal of My Journey to Paris in the Year 1765.* Edited by Francis Griffin Stokes. London: Constable, 1931.

Lister, Martin. *A Journey to Paris in the Year 1698.* Edited by Raymond Stearns. Urbana: University of Illinois Press, 1967.

Lough, John. *France on the Eve of Revolution: British Travellers' Observations, 1763–1788.* London: Croom Helm, 1987.

Ménétra, Jacques-Louis. *Journal de ma vie.* Paris: Montalba, 1982. Translated by Arthur Goldhammer as *Journal of My Life,* edited by Daniel Roche. New York: Columbia University Press, 1986.

Mercier, Louis-Sébastien. *Tableau de Paris.* 12 vols. Amsterdam, 1782–88. There are various partial English translations, most recently *Panorama of Paris: Se-*

lections from "Le Tableau de Paris," based on the translation by Helen Simpson, with additions, edited by Jeremy D. Popkin. University Park: Pennsylvania State University Press, 1999.

SECONDARY SOURCES

Andrews, Richard Mowery. *Law, Magistracy and Crime in Old Regime Paris, 1735–1789.* Vol. 1, *The System of Criminal Justice.* Cambridge: Cambridge University Press, 1994.

Baker, Keith M., ed. *The French Revolution and the Creation of Modern Political Culture.* Vol. 1, *Political Culture of the Old Regime.* Oxford: Pergamon, 1987.

Bell, David. *Lawyers and Citizens: The Making of a Political Elite in Old Regime France.* Oxford: Oxford University Press, 1994.

Benabou, Erica-Marie. *La prostitution et la police des moeurs au XVIIIe siècle.* Paris: Perrin, 1987.

Bernard, Leon. *The Emerging City: Paris in the Age of Louis XIV.* Durham, N.C.: Duke University Press, 1970.

Bien, David D. "Property in Office under the Ancien Régime: The Case of the Stockbrokers." In *Early Modern Conceptions of Property,* edited by John Brewer and Susan Staves, 481–94. London: Routledge, 1995.

Bluche, François. *Les magistrats du Parlement de Paris au XVIIIe siècle.* 2d ed. Paris: Economica, 1986.

Brennan, Thomas. *Public Drinking and Popular Culture in Eighteenth-Century Paris.* Princeton: Princeton University Press, 1988.

Brockliss, L. W. B. *French Higher Education in the Seventeenth and Eighteenth Centuries: A Cultural History.* Oxford: Oxford University Press, 1987.

Brockliss, L. W. B., and Colin Jones. *The Medical World of Early Modern France.* Oxford: Oxford University Press, 1997.

Censer, Jack. *The French Press in the Age of Enlightenment.* London: Routledge, 1994.

Chagniot, Jean. *Nouvelle histoire de Paris: Paris au XVIIIe siècle.* Paris: Hachette, 1988.

Chartier, Roger. *The Cultural Origins of the French Revolution.* Translated by Lydia G. Cochrane. Durham, N.C.: Duke University Press, 1991.

Chaunu, Pierre. *La mort à Paris.* Paris: Fayard, 1978.

Cobb, Richard. *The Police and the People.* Oxford:Oxford University Press, 1970.

———. *Paris and Its Provinces.* London: Oxford University Press, 1975.

Coquery, Natacha. *L'hôtel aristocratique: le marché du luxe à Paris au XVIIIe siècle.* Paris: Publications de la Sorbonne, 1998.

Corbin, Alain. *The Foul and the Fragrant: Odor and the French Social Imagination.* Cambridge, Mass.: Harvard University Press, 1986.

Cottret, Monique. *Jansénisme et Lumières: pour un autre XVIIIe siècle.* Paris: Albin Michel, 1998.

Crow, Thomas E. *Painters and Public Life in Eighteenth-Century Paris.* New Haven: Yale University Press, 1985.

Darnton, Robert. *Mesmerism and the End of the Enlightenment in France.* Cambridge, Mass.: Harvard University Press, 1968.

———. *The Great Cat Massacre and Other Episodes in French Cultural History.* New York: Basic Books, 1984.

Delasselle, C. "Abandoned Children in Eighteenth-Century Paris." In *Deviants and the Abandoned in French Society*, edited by Robert Forster and Orest Ranum. Baltimore: Johns Hopkins University Press, 1978.

Descimon, Robert. "The Birth of the Nobility of the Robe: Dignity versus Privilege in the Parlement of Paris, 1500–1700." In *Changing Identities in Early Modern France,* edited by Michael Wolfe, 95–123. 2d ed. Durham: University of North Carolina Press, 1997.

Duprat, Catherine *Le temps des philanthropes: la philanthropie parisienne des lumières à la monarchie de juillet.* Paris: Editions du Comité des travaux historiques et scientifiques, 1993.

Durand, Yves. *Les fermiers généraux au XVIIIe siècle.* 2d ed. Paris: Maisonneuve et Larose, 1996.

Echeverria, Durand. *The Maupeou Revolution.* Baton Rouge: Louisiana State University Press, 1985.

Etlin, R. A. *The Architecture of Death: The Transformation of the Cemetery in Eighteenth-Century Paris.* Cambridge, Mass.: Harvard University Press, 1984.

Fairchilds, Cissie. *Domestic Enemies: Servants and Their Masters in Old Regime France.* Baltimore: Johns Hopkins University Press, 1984.

———. "The Production and Marketing of Populuxe Goods in Eighteenth-Century Paris." In *Consumption and the World of Goods,* edited by John Brewer and Roy Porter, 228–48. London: Routledge, 1993.

Farge, Arlette. *Fragile Lives: Violence, Power, and Solidarity in Eighteenth-Century Paris.* Translated by Carol Shelton. Cambridge, Mass.: Harvard University Press, 1993.

———. *Subversive Words: Public Opinion in Eighteenth-Century France.* Translated by Rosemary Morris. Cambridge: Polity, 1994.

Farge, Arlette, and Jacques Revel. *The Rules of Rebellion: Child Abductions in Paris in 1750.* Translated by Claudia Miéville. Cambridge: Polity, 1991.

Fitzsimmons, Michael P. *The Parisian Order of Barristers and the French Revolution.* Cambridge, Mass.: Harvard University Press, 1987.

Frangos, John. *From Housing the Poor to Healing the Sick: The Changing Institution of Paris Hospitals under the Old Regime and Revolution.* Madison: Fairleigh Dickinson University Press, 1997.

Garrioch, David. *Neighbourhood and Community in Paris, 1740–1790.* Cambridge: Cambridge University Press, 1986.

———. "House Names, Shop Signs and Social Organisation in Western European Cities, 1500–1900." *Urban History* 21 (1994): 20–48.

———. *The Formation of the Parisian Bourgeoisie, 1690–1830.* Cambridge, Mass.: Harvard University Press, 1996.

Gelfand, Toby. *Professionalizing Modern Medicine: Paris Surgeons and Medical Science and Institutions in the Eighteenth Century.* Westport, Conn.: Greenwood Press, 1980.

Godechot, Jacques. *The Taking of the Bastille, 14th July 1789*. Translated by Jean Stewart. New York: Scribner, 1970.

Godineau, Dominique. *Citoyennes tricoteuses: les femmes du peuple à Paris pendant la Révolution française.* Aix-en-Provence: Alinéa, 1988. Translated by Katherine Streip as *The Women of Paris and Their French Revolution* (Berkeley: University of California Press, 1998).

Goodman, Dena. *The Republic of Letters: A Cultural History of the French Enlightenment.* Ithaca: Cornell University Press, 1994.

Gordon, Daniel. *Citizens without Sovereignty: Equality and Sociability in French Thought, 1670–1789*. Princeton: Princeton University Press, 1994.

Harouel, Jean-Louis. *L'embellissement des villes*. Paris: Picard, 1993.

Hesse, Carla. *Publishing and Cultural Politics in Revolutionary Paris, 1789–1810.* Berkeley: University of California Press, 1991.

Hufton, Olwen. *The Poor of Eighteenth-Century France, 1750–1789*. Oxford: Oxford University Press, 1974.

Isherwood, Robert. *Farce and Fantasy: Popular Entertainment in Eighteenth-Century Paris*. New York: Oxford University Press, 1986.

Jacob, Margaret C. *Living the Enlightenment: Freemasonry and Politics in Eighteenth-Century Europe*. Oxford: Oxford University Press, 1991.

Jones, Colin. "The Great Chain of Buying: Medical Advertisement, the Bourgeois Public Sphere, and the Origins of the French Revolution." *American Historical Review* 103 (1996): 13–40.

———. "Pulling Teeth in Eighteenth-Century Paris." *Past and Present* 166 (May 2000): 100–145.

Kaplan, Steven L. "Religion, Subsistence, and Social Control: The Uses of Saint Genevieve." *Eighteenth-Century Studies* 13 (1979–80): 142–68.

———. "Luxury Guilds in Paris in the Eighteenth Century." *Francia* 9 (1981): 257–98.

———. *Provisioning Paris: Merchants and Millers in the Grain and Flour Trade During the Eighteenth Century*. Ithaca: Cornell University Press, 1984.

———. *The Bakers of Paris and the Bread Question, 1700–1775*. Durham, N.C.: Duke University Press, 1996.

Kaplan, Steven L., and Cynthia Koepp, eds. *Work in France: Representations, Meaning, Organization and Practice*. Ithaca: Cornell University Press, 1986.

Kaplow, Jeffry. *The Names of Kings: The Parisian Labouring Poor in the Eighteenth Century*. New York: Basic Books, 1972.

Kors, Alan C. *D'Holbach's Coterie; An Enlightenment in Paris*. Princeton: Princeton University Press, 1976.

Kreiser, B. Robert. *Miracles, Convulsions, and Ecclesiastical Politics in Early Eighteenth-Century Paris*. Princeton: Princeton University Press, 1978.

Lough, John. *Paris Theatre Audiences in the Eighteenth Century*. Oxford: Oxford University Press, 1957.

———. *France on the Eve of Revolution: British Travellers' Observations*. London: Croom Helm, 1987.

Maire, Catherine [-Laurence]. *De la cause de Dieu à la cause de la nation*. Paris: Gallimard, 1998.

Marraud, Mathieu. *La noblesse de Paris au XVIIIe siècle*. Paris: Seuil, 2000.

Maza, Sarah. *Servants and Masters in Eighteenth-Century France: The Uses of Loyalty*. Princeton: Princeton University Press, 1983.

———. *Private Lives and Public Affairs: The Causes Célèbres of Prerevolutionary France*. Berkeley: University of California Press, 1993.

McManners, John. *Death and the Enlightenment*. Oxford: Oxford University Press, 1981.

Merrick, Jeffrey. "Patterns and Prosecution of Suicide in Eighteenth-Century Paris." *Historical Reflections/Réflexions historiques* 16, no. 1 (1989): 1–53.

———. "Sodomitical Inclinations in Early Eighteenth-Century Paris." *Eighteenth-Century Studies* 30 (1997): 289–95.

Northeast, Catherine M. *The Parisian Jesuits and the Enlightenment, 1700–1762*. Oxford: Voltaire Foundation, 1991.

Ozouf, Mona. "Space and Time in the Festivals of the French Revolution." *Comparative Studies in Society and History* 17 (1975): 372–84.

———. "Public Opinion at the End of the Old Regime." *Journal of Modern History* 60 (1988): supplements S1–S21.

Pardailhé-Galabrun, Annik. *Naissance de l'intime*. Paris: Presses universitaires de France, 1988. Translated by Jocelyn Phelps as *The Birth of Intimacy: Privacy and Domestic Life in Early Modern Paris* (Cambridge: Polity, 1991).

Reinhard, Marcel. *Nouvelle histoire de Paris: la Révolution, 1789–1799*. Paris: Hachette, 1971.

Roche, Daniel. *The People of Paris: An Essay in Popular Culture in the 18th Century.* Translated by Marie Evans and Gwynne Lewis. Berkeley: University of California Press, 1987.

———. "A Pauper Capital: Some Reflections on the Parisian Poor in the Seventeenth and Eighteenth Centuries." *French History* 1 (1987):182–290.

———. *The Culture of Clothing: Dress and Fashion in the 'ancien régime.'* Translated by Jean Birrel. Cambridge: Past and Present Publications, 1994.

———. *France in the Enlightenment.* Translated by Arthur Goldhammer. Cambridge, Mass.: Harvard University Press, 1998.

———. *A History of Everyday Things: The Birth of Consumption in France, 1600–1800*. Translated by Brian Pearce. Cambridge: Cambridge University Press, 2000.

Root-Bernstein, Michèle. *Boulevard Theatre and Revolution in Eighteenth-Century Paris*. Ann Arbor: UMI Research Press, 1984.

Rosenau, Helen. *Social Purpose in Architecture: Paris and London Compared, 1760–1780*. London: Studio Vista, 1970.

Sargentson, Carolyn. *Merchants and Luxury Markets: The Marchands Merciers of Eighteenth-Century Paris*. London: Victoria and Albert Museum, 1996.

Scott, Katie. *The Rococo Interior: Decoration and Social Spaces in Early-Eighteenth-Century Paris*. New Haven: Yale University Press, 1995.

Sonenscher, Michael. *Work and Wages: Natural Law, Politics and the Eighteenth-Century French Trades*. Cambridge: Cambridge University Press, 1989.

Sonnet, Martine. *L'éducation des filles au temps des lumières*. Paris: Cerf, 1987.

Sussman, George D. *Selling Mothers' Milk: The Wet-Nursing Business in France, 1715–1914*. Urbana: University of Illinois Press, 1982.

Thibaut-Payen, Jacqueline. *Les morts, l'église et l'état: recherches d'histoire ad-*

ministrative sur la sépulture et les cimetières dans le ressort du parlement de Paris aux XVIIe et XVIIIe siècles. Paris: F. Lanore, 1977.

Todd, Christopher. "French Advertising in the Eighteenth Century." *Studies on Voltaire and the Eighteenth Century* 266 (1989): 513–47.

Truant, Cynthia Maria. "Parisian Guildswomen and the (Sexual) Politics of Privilege: Defending Their Patrimonies in Print." In *Going Public: Women and Publishing in Early Modern France,* edited by Elizabeth C. Goldsmith and Dena Goodman, 46–61. Ithaca: Cornell University Press, 1995.

Tulard, Jean. *Nouvelle histoire de Paris: la Révolution.* Paris: Hachette, 1989.

Van Kley, Dale. *The Damiens Affair and the Unraveling of the Ancien Régime, 1750–1770*. Princeton: Princeton University Press, 1984.

Williams, Alan. *The Police of Paris 1718–1789*. Baton Rouge: Louisiana State University Press, 1979.

INDEX

Compositor: Integrated Composition Systems
Text: 10/13 Sabon
Display: Bodoni Book and Akzidenz Grotesk Bold Condensed
Printer and Binder: Sheridan Books, Inc.